Cloud Data Design, Orchestration, and Management Using Microsoft Azure

Master and Design a Solution Leveraging the Azure Data Platform

Francesco Diaz
Roberto Freato

Apress®

Cloud Data Design, Orchestration, and Management Using Microsoft Azure

Francesco Diaz
Peschiera Borromeo, Milano, Italy

Roberto Freato
Milano, Italy

ISBN-13 (pbk): 978-1-4842-3614-7
https://doi.org/10.1007/978-1-4842-3615-4

ISBN-13 (electronic): 978-1-4842-3615-4

Library of Congress Control Number: 2018948124

Managing Director, Apress Media LLC: Welmoed Spahr
Acquisitions Editor: Celestin Suresh John
Development Editor: Laura Berendson
Coordinating Editor: Divya Modi

Cover designed by eStudioCalamar

Distributed to the book trade worldwide by Springer Science+Business Media New York, 233 Spring Street, 6th Floor, New York, NY 10013. Phone 1-800-SPRINGER, fax (201) 348-4505, e-mail orders-ny@springer-sbm.com, or visit www.springeronline.com. Apress Media, LLC is a California LLC and the sole member (owner) is Springer Science + Business Media Finance Inc (SSBM Finance Inc). SSBM Finance Inc is a **Delaware** corporation.

For information on translations, please e-mail rights@apress.com, or visit http://www.apress.com/rights-permissions.

Apress titles may be purchased in bulk for academic, corporate, or promotional use. eBook versions and licenses are also available for most titles. For more information, reference our Print and eBook Bulk Sales web page at http://www.apress.com/bulk-sales.

Any source code or other supplementary material referenced by the author in this book is available to readers on GitHub via the book's product page, located at www.apress.com/978-1-4842-3614-7. For more detailed information, please visit http://www.apress.com/source-code.

Printed on acid-free paper

To my daughter Valentina
—Francesco Diaz

To my amazing wife and loving son
—Roberto Freato

Table of Contents

About the Authors

Francesco Diaz joined Insight in 2015 and is responsible for the cloud solutions & services area for a few countries in the EMEA region. In his previous work experience, Francesco worked at Microsoft for several years, in Services, Partner, and Cloud & Enterprise divisions. He is passionate about data and cloud, and he speaks about these topics at events and conferences.

Roberto Freato works as a freelance consultant for tech companies, helping to kick off IT projects, defining architectures, and prototyping software artifacts. He has been awarded the Microsoft MVP award for eight years in a row and has written books about Microsoft Azure. He loves to participate in local communities and speaks at conferences during the year.

About the Technical Reviewers

Andrea Uggetti works in Microsoft as Senior Partner Consultant, and has a decade of experience in the databases and business intelligences field. He specializes in the Microsoft BI platform and especially Analysis Services and Power BI and recently he is dedicated to the Azure Data & AI services. He regularly collaborates with Partners in proposing architectural or technical insight in Azure Data & AI area. Throughout his career he has collaborated with the Microsoft BI Product Group on several in-depth guides, suggesting product's innovations and creating BI troubleshooting tools.

After getting a Master's in Computer Science at Pisa University, **Igor Pagliai** joined Microsoft in 1998 as Support Engineer working on SQL Server and Microsoft server infrastructure. He covered several technical roles in Microsoft Services organization, working with the largest enterprises in Italy and Europe. In 2013, he moved in Microsoft Corporate HQ as Principal Program Manager in the DX Organization, working on Azure infrastructure and data platform related projects with the largest Global ISVs. He is now Principal Cloud Architect in Commercial Software Engineering (CSE) division, driving Azure projects and cloud adoption for top Microsoft partners around the globe. His main focus and interests are around Azure infrastructure, Data, Big Data and Containers world.

Gianluca Hotz is a consultant, trainer, and speaker and specializes in architecture, database design, high availability, capacity planning, performance tuning, system integration, and migrations for Microsoft SQL Server. He has been working as a consultant in the IT field since 1993 and with SQL Server since 1996 starting with version 4.21 on Windows NT. As a trainer, he was in charge of the SQL Server courses line for one of the largest Italian Microsoft Learning Partner (Mondadori Informatica Education) and still enjoys teaching people through regular class training and on-the-job training. He also supports Microsoft on the field as a speaker and expert at local and international conferences, workshops, and university seminars.

Gianluca joined SolidQ (previously known as Solid Quality Mentors and Solid Quality Learning) as a mentor in 2003, was one of the acquisition editors for The SolidQ Journal between 2010 and 2012, has served in the global board as a voting member between 2012 and 2014 (representing minority shareholders), and as internal advisor between 2014 and 2015.

He was one of the founders of the Italian SolidQ subsidiary where he held the position of ad interim CEO between 2007 and 2014 and director of the Data Platform division between 2015 and 2016.

Being among the original founders of ugiss.org (Italian User Group for SQL Server), and ugidotnet.org (Italian dot NET User Group), he's also a community leader regularly speaking at user group workshops, he served as vice-president for UGISS between 2001 and 2016 where he's currently serving as president. For his contribution to the community, including newsgroup support in the past, he has been a SQL Server MVP (Microsoft Most Valuable Professional) since 1998.

Foreword

In my career I've been fortunate enough to have the chance of experiencing many computing generations: from mini computers when I was still a student, through 8-bit microcontrollers in industrial automation, client-server departmental solutions, the dot. com era that transformed everything, service-oriented computing in the Enterprise and, finally, the cloud revolution. Across the last 25 years and all these transformations, data has always been a constant "center of gravity" in every solution, and moving to public cloud platforms this effect is going to increase significantly due to a number of factors.

First, the economies of scale that large cloud providers can achieve in building huge storage platforms that can store the largest datasets at a fraction of the cost required in traditional infrastructures. Second, the comprehensive offering and flexibility of multiple data storage and processing technologies that let architects and developers to pick up the right tool for the job, without necessarily be constrained by large upfront investments traditionally requires in the on-premises space when selecting a given data platform of choice. Third, as we're entering into the second decade of existence for many of these public cloud providers, the constantly increasing level of maturity that these platforms are offering, closing most of the gaps in functional and non-functional that for some customers were preventing a full migration to the cloud, like security, connectivity, and performance.

In fact, it's becoming very frequent these days, to read on both technical and economical sites and newspapers that the largest corporations on the planet announcing their digital transformation strategies where cloud has a prominent position, from financial services to retail and manufacturing businesses, and for workloads like core trading systems, big data and analytical solutions or product lifecycle management.

By working with many of these customers moving their core solution to Microsoft Azure, I had the chance to experience first-hand the dramatic impact that cloud is providing to existing IT practices and methodologies, and the enormous opportunities that these new capabilities can unleash in designing next-generation solutions and platforms, and to collect a series of learnings that are consistent across multiple scenarios and use cases.

One of the most important, when designing brand new storage layers, is that we're not anymore in a world where a single data technology was the cornerstone satisfying all different requirements characterizing a given end to end solution. Today, from highly transactional and low latency data sets to hugely vast amount of data exhausts produced collecting human behaviors like click streams or systems and application logs, it's critical to pick up the right data technology for the job. Microsoft Azure provides full coverage in this space, from relational database services like Azure SQL Database to multi-modal document, key-value and graph solutions like CosmosDB. From the incredibly flexible and inexpensive Azure Storage to the highest performance and scale characteristics of Azure Data Lake. Not mentioning powerful distributed data processing services in Big Data and Analytics like Azure HDInsight and the newest addition to Azure data platform which is Azure Databricks, making Spark incredibly easy to deploy and use within our solutions.

The consequence of the availability of such a rich data platform is that more and more a single solution will use a combination of multiple stores, where usually you'll find a common backbone or main storage technology surrounded by a number of specialized data stores and data processing technologies to serve sophisticated consumer types within a given organization, as one size rarely fits all requirements and use cases.

At the same time, it is very important to be intimately aware of the intrinsic characteristics of these different data technologies to be able to evaluate which one fits a given area in a complex solution. One of the common mistakes that I've seen is not considering that for most of these technologies, while offering almost infinite capacity in terms of performance and scale, this comes in very well-defined scale units, or building blocks, that usually are assembled by scaling them out horizontally to reach the highest goals.

Yes, data services are powered by an impressive amount of compute and storage capacity, now in the order of millions of physical servers, but while these are becoming more and more powerful generation after generation, they are usually not directly comparable to the more sophisticated hardware configurations that can be assembled in your own datacenter in a limited number of instances. That's why most of these storage engines are heavily relying on partitioning large data sets across a number of these scale units that developers and architects can combine into the most demanding scenarios.

This book from Francesco and Roberto is covering a wide spectrum of data technologies offered by the Microsoft Azure platform, providing many of those details and characteristics that are crucial for you to get the most out of these data services.

It's also offering solid guidance on how to migrate your existing data stores to the cloud completely or maintaining a hybrid approach. With this book you have a great tool to just learn and discover new possibilities offered by the platform, but also to start practicing on what will become, I'm sure, your preferred playground of the future. Happy reading!

Silvano Coriani
Principal Software Engineer
Microsoft Corporation

Introduction

Today's mission in IT is reducing the overall time-to-market and, at the same time, preserving project constraints like quality and control over costs. With the cloud revolution of the last ten years, we started (finally) to understand the benefit of value-added services implemented in most of the PaaS (Platform-as-a-Service) of the cloud ecosystem.

We got how a platform can give us much more control on the entire development process, by freeing resources that now can be focused on the business and the design. In many cases, choosing a PaaS solution is the best choice, especially for born-in-the-cloud projects; in some other cases, using a IaaS approach can be beneficial, either because you are migrating from an existing on-premises solution, or because you need a more granular control on the service itself.

This book is around data, and gives you a wide range of possibilities to implement a data solution on Azure, from hybrid cloud up to PaaS services, where we will focus much more. Implementing a PaaS solution requires to cover in detail several aspects of the implementation, including migrating from existing solutions. The next six chapters try to tell the story of Data Services by presenting the alternatives and the actual scope of each one; 5 out of 6 of the chapters are about PaaS, while one of them, mainly focused on SQL Server features for cloud, is related to hybrid cloud and IaaS functionalities.

In Chapter 1 (*Working with Azure Database Services Platform*) we deeply analyze the SQL Database services, trying to bring to the reader the authors' on-the-field experience of designing and managing it for years. We discuss the various SQL Database most important features, trying to propose approaches and solutions to real-world problems.

In Chapter 2 (*Working with SQL Server on Hybrid Cloud and Azure IaaS*) we "downscale" to IaaS. Except for this, we discuss the huge power of SQL Server on VMs and the various scenarios we can address with it. We see how SQL Server can run in VMs and containers, on Linux and how it can be managed with cross-platform tools. But Chapter 2 is not only around SQL Server on VMs: it is around Hybrid Cloud also, mixed environments and complex scenarios of backup/replication, disaster recovery and high-availability.

In Chapter 3 (*Working with NoSQL alternatives*) we want to turn tables on the typical discussion around NoSQL. We choose to not include Cosmos DB in the chapter, either to postpone the topic to a dedicated book, either to highlight how many NoSQL alternatives we have in Azure outside the classics. We center the discussion around Blobs, that are often under-evaluated, around Tables and Redis to finally approach on Azure Search, one of the most promising managed search services in the cloud ecosystem.

In Chapter 4 (*Orchestrate data with Azure Data Factory*) we discover orchestration of data. We want to emphasize the importance of data activities, in terms of movements, transformation and the modern addressing to the concepts we known as ETL for many years. With Data Factory, you will discover an emerging (and growing up) service to deal with pipelines of data and even complex orchestration scenarios.

In Chapter 5 (*Working with Azure Data Lake Store and Azure Data Lake Analytics*) we start to build foundations for the big data needs. We discover how Data Lake can help with storing, managing and analyzing unstructured data, stored in their native format while they are generated. We will learn this important lesson around big data: since we are generating and storing today the data we are using and analyzing tomorrow, we need a platform service to build intelligence on it with minimal effort.

Finally, Chapter 6 (*Working with In-Transit Data and Analytics*) closes the book with a little introduction about messaging and, generally, the in-transit data, to learn how we can take advantage of ingestion to build run-time logics in addition to the most consolidated ones. Messaging is extremely important for several scenarios: almost every distributed system may use messaging to decouple components and micro-services. Once messaging is understood, we can apply the event-based reasoning to move some parts of the business rules before the data is written to the final, persistent data store. Eventually, we learn how to implement in-transit analytics.

We hope this can be a good cue to address how to approach data service in this promising momentum of cloud and Platform-as-a-Service. We know this book cannot be complete and exhaustive, but we tried to focus on some good points to discuss the various areas of data management we can encounter on a daily basis.

CHAPTER 1

Working with Azure Database Services Platform

To get the most out of the power of cloud services we need to introduce how to deal with relational data using a fully managed RDBMS service, which is, in Microsoft Azure, SQL Database.

SQL Database is the managed representation of Microsoft SQL Server in the cloud. Can be instantiated in seconds/minutes and it runs even large applications without minimal administrative effort.

Understanding the Service

SQL Database can be viewed as a sort of Microsoft SQL Server *as-a-Service*, where those frequently-addressed topics can be entirely skipped during the adoption phase:

- License management planning: SQL Database is a pay-per-use service. There is no upfront fee and migrating between tiers of different pricing is seamless

- Installation and management: SQL Database is ready-to-use. When we create a DB, the hardware/software mix that runs it already exists and we only get the portion of a shared infrastructure we need to work. High-availability is guaranteed and managed by Microsoft and geo-replication is at a couple of clicks away.

© Francesco Diaz, Roberto Freato 2018
F. Diaz and R. Freato, *Cloud Data Design, Orchestration, and Management Using Microsoft Azure*,
https://doi.org/10.1007/978-1-4842-3615-4_1

- Maintenance: SQL Database is a PaaS, so everything is given to us as-a-Service. Updates, patches, security and Disaster Recovery are managed by the vendor. Also, databases are backup continuously to provide end-users with point-in-time restore out-of-the-box.

From the consumer perspective, SQL Database has a minimal feature misalignment with the plain SQL Server and, like every Platform-as-a-Service, those touch points can be inferred by thinking about:

- Filesystem dependencies: we cannot use features that correlates with customization of the underlying operating system, like file placement, sizes and database files which are managed by the platform.

- Domain dependencies: we cannot join a SQL Database "server" to a domain, since there is no server from the user perspective. So, we cannot authenticate with Windows authentication; instead, a growing up support of Azure Active Directory is becoming a good replacement of this missing feature.

- Server-wide commands: we cannot (we would say "fortunately") use commands like SHUTDOWN, since everything we make is made against the *logical* representation of the Database, not to its underlying physical topology.

In addition to the perceptible restrictions, we have some more differences related to which is the direction of the service and the roadmap of advanced features. Since we cannot know **why** some of the features below are not supported, we can imagine they are related to offer a high-level service cutting down the surface area of potential issues of advanced commands/features of the plain SQL Server.

For a complete comparison of supported features between SQL Database and SQL Server, refer to this page: `https://docs.microsoft.com/en-us/azure/sql-database/sql-database-features`

At least, there are service constraints which add the last set of differences, for example:

- Database sizes: at the time of writing, SQL Database supports DB up to 1TB of size (the counterpart is 64TB)

- Performance: despite there are several performance tiers of SQL Database, with the appropriate VM set, SQL in a VM can exceed largely the highest tier of it.

For a good introduction of how to understand the differences between the features supported in both products, refer to this page: `https://docs.microsoft.com/en-us/azure/sql-database/sql-database-paas-vs-sql-server-iaas`.

Connectivity Options

We cannot know the exact SQL Database actual implementation, outside of what Microsoft discloses in public materials. However, when we create an instance, it has the following properties:

- Public URL: in the form [myServer].database.windows.net. Public-faced on the Internet and accessible from everywhere.

Yes, there are some security issues to address with this topology, since there is no way to deploy a SQL Database in a private VNet.

- Connection modes:

  - from outside Azure, by default, each session between us and SQL Database passes through a Proxy, which connects to the actual ring/pool of the desired instance

  - from inside Azure, by default, clients are redirect by the proxy to the actual ring/pool after the handshake, so overhead is reduced. If we are using VMs, we must be sure the outbound port range 11000-11999 is open.

We can change the default behavior of the Proxy by changing this property: `https://msdn.microsoft.com/library/azure/mt604439.aspx`. Note that, while connecting from outside Azure, this means multiple IPs can be configured to outbound firewall rules.

- Authentication:
  - Server login: by default, when we create a Database, we must create a *server* before it. A server is just a logical representation of a container of database, no dedicated physical server is mapped to it. This server has an administrator credential, which have full permission on every DB created in it.
  - Database login: we can create additional credentials tied to specific databases
  - Azure AD login: we can bind Azure AD users/groups to the server instance to provide an integrated authentication experience
  - Active Directory Universal Authentication: only through a proper version of SSMS, clients can connect to SQL Database using a MFA
- Security:
  - Firewall rules: to allow just some IPs to connect to SQL Database, we can specify firewall rules. They are represented by IP ranges.
  - Certificates: by default, an encrypted connection is established. A valid certificate is provided, so it is recommended (to avoid MITM attacks) to set to "false" the option "Trust Server Certificate" while connecting to it.

Given this information above as the minimum set of knowledge to connect to a SQLDB instance, we can connect to it using the same tooling we use for SQL Server. SSMS is supported (few features won't be enabled however), client connectivity through the SQL Client driver is seamless (as it would be a SQL Server instance) and the majority of tools/applications will continue to work by only changing the connection string.

Libraries

In recent years Microsoft has been building an extensive support to non-Microsoft technology. This means that now we have a wide set of options to build our applications, using Azure services, even from outside the MS development stack. Regarding SQL Database, we can now connect to it through official libraries, as follows:

- C#: ADO.NET, Entity Framework (https://docs.microsoft.com/en-us/sql/connect/ado-net/microsoft-ado-net-for-sql-server)

- Java: Microsoft JDBC Driver (https://docs.microsoft.com/it-it/sql/connect/jdbc/microsoft-jdbc-driver-for-sql-server)

- PHP: Microsoft PHP SQL Driver (https://docs.microsoft.com/it-it/sql/connect/php/microsoft-php-driver-for-sql-server)

- Node.js: Node.js Driver (https://docs.microsoft.com/en-us/sql/connect/node-js/node-js-driver-for-sql-server)

- Python: Python SQL Driver (https://docs.microsoft.com/en-us/sql/connect/python/python-driver-for-sql-server)

- Ruby: Rudy Driver (https://docs.microsoft.com/en-us/sql/connect/ruby/ruby-driver-for-sql-server)

- C++: Microsoft ODBC Driver (https://docs.microsoft.com/en-us/sql/connect/odbc/microsoft-odbc-driver-for-sql-server)

This extended support makes SQL Database a great choice for who are adopting a RDBMS, for both new and existing solutions.

Sizing & Tiers

The basic consumption unit of SQL Database is called DTU (Database Transaction Unit), which is defined as a blended measure of CPU, memory and I/O. We cannot "reserve" to our SQLDB instance a fixed size VM. Instead, we choose:

- Service Tier: it defines which features the DB instance has and the range of DTU between we can move it.

- Performance Level: if defines the reserved DTU for the DB instance.

Both for the official recommended approach as for the experience maturated in the field, we strongly encourage to avoid too much complicated in-advance sizing activities to know exactly which tier our application needs, before testing it. We think that an order of magnitude can be of course inferred by in-advance sizing, but a more precise estimation of consumption has to be made after a measured pilot, where we can see how the new/existing application uses the database tier and, consequently, how much the DB instance is stressed by that.

Like in any other service offered in a PaaS fashion, we are subject to throttling, since we reach the limits of the current performance level.

For years consultants tried to explain to clients there is no way to predict exactly which is the actual performance level needed for an application since, by design, each query is different and even the most trivial KPI (i.e., queries-per-second) is useless without the proper benchmark information.

To understand how the benchmark behind the DTU blend is developed, see this article: `https://docs.microsoft.com/en-us/azure/sql-database/sql-database-benchmark-overview`

At the time of writing, SQLDB supports those Service Tiers and Performance Levels (Figure 1-1):

- Basic: it supports only a 5DTU level, with 2GB of max DB size and few simultaneous requests.

- Standard: it supports a range of 10-100DTU levels, with 250GB of max DB size and moderate simultaneous requests.

- Premium: if supports the largest levels (125-4000DTU), with 4TB of max DB size and the highest simultaneous requests.

Unfortunately, service tiers and resource limits are subject to continuous change over time. We can fine updated information here:

https://docs.microsoft.com/en-us/azure/sql-database/
sql-database-service-tiers

https://docs.microsoft.com/en-us/azure/sql-database/
sql-database-resource-limits

In addition, Premium levels offer In-Memory features, which are not available in other tiers.

- Premium RS: it supports the 125-1000DTU levels, with the same constraints of the corresponding Premium level.

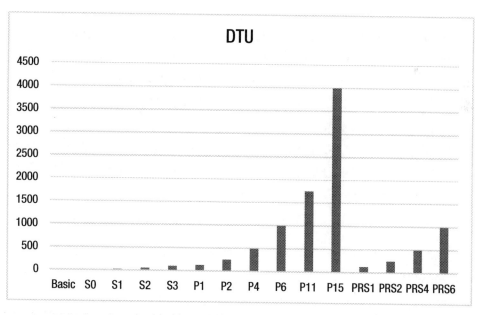

Figure 1-1. *This chart shows clearly the DTU ratio between different Tiers/Levels of SQL Database*

Premium RS is a recent Tier which offers the same features as the Premium counterpart, while guaranteeing a reduced durability, which results in a sensible cost saving and more performance for I/O operations. Unfortunately, the service did not pass the preview phase and it has been scheduled for dismission on January 31, 2019.

Designing SQL Database

SQL Database interface is almost fully compatible with tooling used for SQL Server, so in most cases previous tooling should work with no specific issues. However, since Visual Studio offers the capability to manage the development process of a DB from inside the IDE, it is important to mention it.

Database Projects are Visual Studio artefacts which let DBA to develop every DB object inside Visual Studio, with an interesting feature set to gain productivity:

- Compile-time checks: VS checks the syntax of the written SQL and highlights errors during a pseudo-compilation phase. In addition, it checks references between tables, foreign keys and, more generally, gives consistence to the entire database before publishing it.

- Integrated publishing: VS generates the proper scripts to create (or alter) the database, based on what it finds at the target destination. It means that the target DB can even already exists and Visual Studio will run the proper change script against it without compromise the consistency.

- Data generation: to generate sample data in the database tables

- Pre/Post-deployment scripts: to execute custom logic before/after the deployment

- Source control integration: by using Visual Studio, it is seamless to integrate with Git or TFS to version our DB objects like code files.

Using Database Projects (or other similar tools) to create and manage the development of the database is a recommended approach (Figure 1-2), since it gives a central view of the Database Lifecycle Management. Finally, Visual Studio supports SQL Database as a target Database, so it will highlight potential issues or missing features during the Database development.

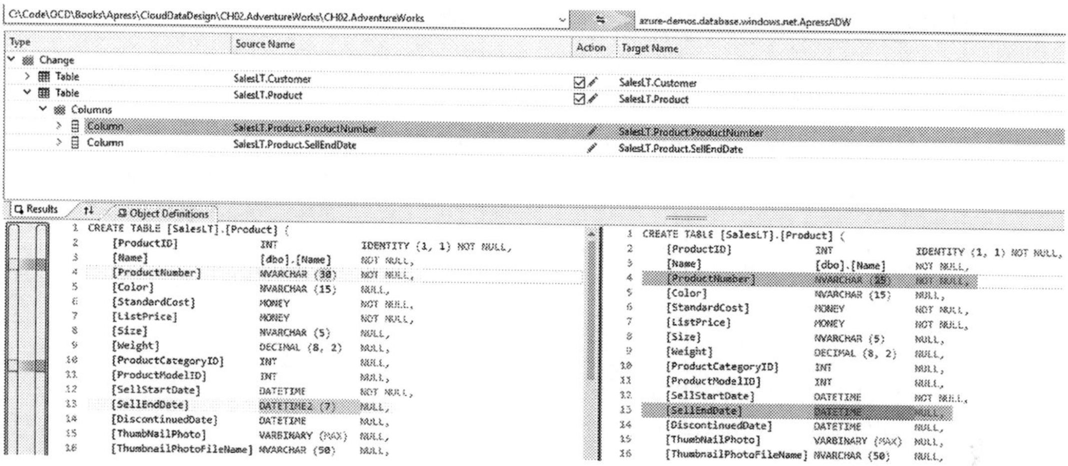

Figure 1-2. *This image show the Schema Compare features of Database Projects, which also targets SQL Database in order to apply changes with a lot of features (data loss prevention, single-change update, backups, etc).*

We can use Database Projects even at a later stage of DB development, using the wizard "Import Database" by right-clicking the project node in Visual Studio. This wizard creates the VS objects by a reverse engineering process on the target Database.

There are other options to design databases. Official documentation follows:

- SSMS design: https://docs.microsoft.com/en-us/azure/sql-database/sql-database-design-first-database

- .NET design: https://docs.microsoft.com/en-us/azure/sql-database/sql-database-design-first-database-csharp

- Code-first design: https://msdn.microsoft.com/en-us/library/jj193542(v=vs.113).aspx

Multi-tenancy

Since many applications should be multi-tenant, where one deployment can address many customers, even the Database tier should follow this approach. This is clearly an architect choice but, since it can have consequences on performance/costs of the SQLDB instance, we analyze the various options.

One Database for Each Tenant

This is the simplest (in terms of design) scenario, where we can also have a single-tenant architecture which we redeploy once for every client we acquire. It is pretty clear that, in case of few clients, can be a solution, while it isn't where clients are hundreds or thousands.

This approach highlights those pros/cons:

- Advantages:

    - We can retain existing database and applications and redeploy them each time we need.

        - Each customer may have a different service level and disaster recovery options

    - An update which is specific to a tenant (i.e., a customization) can be applied to just the database instance affected, leaving others untouched.

    - An optimization, which involves the specific usage of a table, can be applied to that DB only. Think about an INDEX which improves TenantX queries but worsens other tenants.

- Disadvantages:

    - We need to maintain several Databases which, in the best case are just copies with the same schema and structure. In the worst case they can be different, since they proceed in different project forks: but this is another topic, related to business, out of the scope of the chapter.

    - Every DB will need a separate configuration of features on the Azure side. Some of them can be configured at the server side (the logical server) but others are specific.

    - Every DB has a performance level and corresponding costs, which in most cases is not efficient in terms of pooling.

    - In case of Staging/Test/Other development environment, they should be made specifically for each client.

Those are just few of the pros/cons of this solution. To summarize this approach, we would say it is better for legacy applications not designed to be multi-tenant and where new implementations are very hard to achieve.

Single Database with a Single Schema

In this scenario, we are at the opposite side, where we use just ONE database for ALL the clients now or in the future. We would probably create tables which contains a discriminant column like "TenantID" to isolate tenants.

This approach highlights those pros/cons:

- Advantages:

  - A single DB generates a far less effort to maintain and monitor it.

  - A performance tuning which is good for every client, can be applied once

  - A single DB generates just one set of features to configure and a single billing unit

- Disadvantages:

  - An update on the DB potentially affects every deployment and every customer of the solution. This results in harder rolling upgrade of the on top application.

  - If a client consumes more than others, the minor clients can be affected and the performance of each one can vary seriously. In other words, we cannot isolate a single tenant if needed.

  - This is the simplest scenario while dealing with a new solution. During the development phase we have just one database to deal with, one or more copies for other environments (Staging/ UAT/Test) and a single point of monitoring and control when the solution is ready to market. However this can be just the intermediate step between a clean-and-simple solution and an elastic and tailor-made one.

Single Database with Different Schemas

This solution is a mix between the first one and the second, since we have just one database instance, while every table is replicated once for every schema in the database itself, given that every Tenant should be mapped to a specific schema.

This approach has the union of pros/cons of the "One database for each tenant" and "Single Database with single schema" approaches.

In addition, in case we want to isolate a tenant in its own dedicated DB, we can move its schema and data without affecting others.

Multiple Logical Pools with a Single Schema Preference

The latest approach is the one that can achieve the best pros and the less cons, compared to the previous alternatives. In this case, we think about Pools instead of Database, where a Pool can be a DB following the "Single Database with a single schema pattern" which groups a portion of the tenants.

Practically, we implement the DB as we are in the Single Database approach, with a TenantID for every table which needs to be isolated. However, falling in some circumstances, we "split" the DB into another one, keeping just a portion of tenant in the new database. Think about those steps:

1. First the DB is developed once, deployed and in production

2. New clients arrive, new TenantIDs are burned and tables now contains data of different clients (separated by a discriminant).

3. Client X needs a customization or a dedicated performance, a copy of the actual DB is made and the traffic of client X are directed to the appropriate DB instance.

4. Eventually the data of client X in the "old" DB can be cleaned up

Given the pros of that approach, we can mitigate the disadvantages as follows:

- An update on the DB potentially affects every deployment and every customer of the solution. This results in harder rolling upgrade of the on top application.

    - We can migrate one tenant, perform an upgrade on it and then applying the update on every Logical Pool.

- If a client consumes more than others, the minor clients can be affected and the performance of each one can vary seriously. In other words, we cannot isolate a single tenant if needed.

  - We can migrate one or more tenant to a dedicated DB (Logical Pool)

The remaining disadvantage is the effort needed to write the appropriate procedures/tooling to migrate tenants between DBs and create/delete/update different DBs with minimal manual intervention. This is a subset of the effort of the first approach with maximum degree of elasticity.

Index Design

Indexes are standard SQL artefacts which helps to lookup data in a table. Practically speaking, for a table with millions or rows, an index can help *seeking* to the right place where the records are stored, instead of *scanning* the whole table looking for the results. A theoretical approach to index design in out of the scope of the book, so we focus on:

- Index creation

- Index evaluation

- Index management

Index Creation

Let's consider the following table (SalesLT.Customer of the AdventureWorksLT sample Database):

```
CREATE TABLE [SalesLT].[Customer] (
    [CustomerID]    INT                 IDENTITY (1, 1) NOT NULL,
    [NameStyle]     [dbo].[NameStyle] CONSTRAINT [DF_Customer_NameStyle]
    DEFAULT ((0)) NOT NULL,
    [Title]         NVARCHAR (8)        NULL,
    [FirstName]     [dbo].[Name]        NOT NULL,
    [MiddleName]    [dbo].[Name]        NULL,
    [LastName]      [dbo].[Name]        NOT NULL,
    [Suffix]        NVARCHAR (10)       NULL,
    [CompanyName]   NVARCHAR (128)      NULL,
```

```
    [SalesPerson]   NVARCHAR (256)      NULL,
    [EmailAddress] NVARCHAR (50)        NULL,
    [Phone]          [dbo].[Phone]      NULL,
    [PasswordHash] VARCHAR (128)        NOT NULL,
    [PasswordSalt] VARCHAR (10)         NOT NULL,
    [rowguid]        UNIQUEIDENTIFIER  CONSTRAINT [DF_Customer_rowguid]
    DEFAULT (newid()) NOT NULL,
    [ModifiedDate] DATETIME                CONSTRAINT [DF_Customer_ModifiedDate]
    DEFAULT (getdate()) NOT NULL,
    CONSTRAINT [PK_Customer_CustomerID] PRIMARY KEY CLUSTERED ([CustomerID]
    ASC),
    CONSTRAINT [AK_Customer_rowguid] UNIQUE NONCLUSTERED ([rowguid] ASC)
);
```

While creating a SQL Database DB instance, we can even choose between a blank one (the common option) or a preconfigured and populated AdventureWorksLT Database

---

By default the following index is created:

```
CREATE NONCLUSTERED INDEX [IX_Customer_EmailAddress]
    ON [SalesLT].[Customer]([EmailAddress] ASC);
```

However, despite a table definition is about requirements, an index definition is about usage. The index above will produce better performance in queries filtering the EmailAddress field. However, if the application generates the 99% of queries filtering by the CompanyName field, this index is not quite useful and it only worse the write performance (Figure 1-3).

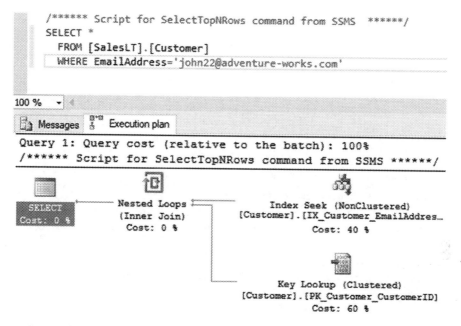

Figure 1-3. *This query uses the index, producing a query cost only on the seek operation (good). In SSMS, to see the query plan, right click the query pane and select "Display Estimated Execution Plan".*

So, indexes are something related to time and usage: today we need an index and tomorrow it can be different, so despite application requirements are the same, indexes can (must) change over time.

Index Evaluation

Which index should we create? First, we can write a Database without any indexes (while some are direct consequences of primary keys). Write performance will be the fastest while some queries will be very slow. An option can be to record each query against the database and analyze them later, by:

- Instrumenting on the application side: every application using the DB should log the actual queries.

- Instrumenting on the SQL side: the application is unaware of tracing, while SQL saves every query passing on the wire

Using the idea above, let's try to edit the query above filtering by CompanyName (Figure 1-4):

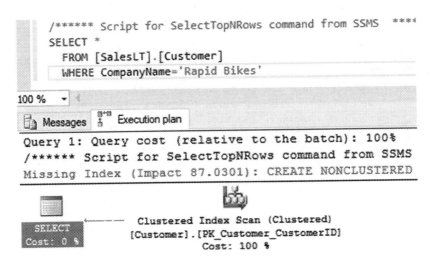

Figure 1-4. *In this case, no seeking is performed. Instead, SSMS suggest us to create an Index, since the 100% of the query cost is on scanning*

For completeness, SSMS suggest us this creation script:

```
/*
USE [AdventureWorksLT]
GO
CREATE NONCLUSTERED INDEX [<Name of Missing Index, sysname,>]
ON [SalesLT].[Customer] ([CompanyName])

GO
*/
```

But SSMS cannot tell us if the **overall** performance impact is positive, since write queries (i.e., a high rate of updates on the CompanyName field) can be slower due to index maintenance.

Index Management

Once an index is created and it is working, it grows and it gets fragmented. Periodically, or even manually but in a planned fashion, we need to maintain indexes by:

- Rebuilding: the index is, as the word suggests, rebuilt, so a fresh index is created. Sometimes rebuilding needs to take a table offline, which is to evaluate carefully in production scenarios.

- Re-organizing: the index is actually defragmented by moving physical pages in order to gain performance. It is the lightest (but often longest) version to maintain an index.

We can use this query to have a look to the current level of fragmentation:

```
SELECT
DB_NAME() AS DBName,
OBJECT_NAME(pstats.object_id) AS DBTableName,
idx.name AS DBIndexName,
ips.index_type_desc as DBIndexType,
ips.avg_fragmentation_in_percent as DBIndexFragmentation
FROM sys.dm_db_partition_stats pstats
INNER JOIN sys.indexes idx
ON pstats.object_id = idx.object_id
AND pstats.index_id = idx.index_id
CROSS APPLY sys.dm_db_index_physical_stats(DB_ID(),
    pstats.object_id, pstats.index_id, null, 'LIMITED') ips
ORDER BY pstats.object_id, pstats.index_id
```

While with this statement we perform Index Rebuild:

```
ALTER INDEX ALL ON [table] REBUILD with (ONLINE=ON)
```

Note   that "with (ONLINE=ON)" forces the runtime to keep table online. In case this is not possible, SQL raises an error which can be caught to notify the hosting process.

Automatic Tuning

SQL Database integrates the Query Store, a feature that keeps tracks of every query executed against the Database to provide useful information about performance and usage patterns. We see Query Store and Query Performance Insight later in chapter but, in the meantime, we talk about Index Tuning.

Since indexes can change over time, SQL Database can use the recent history of database usage to give an advice (Figure 1-5) of which Indexes are needed to boost the overall performance. We say "overall", because the integrated intelligent engine reasons as follows:

1. By analyzing recent activities, comes out that an Index can be created on the table T to increase the performance

2. Using the history data collected up to now, the estimated performance increment would be P% of DTU

3. If we apply the Index proposal, the platform infrastructure takes care of everything: it creates the index in the optimal moment, not when DTU usage is too high or storage consumption is near to its maximum.

4. Then, Azure monitors the index's impacts on performance: not only the positive (estimated) impact, but even the side effects on queries that now can perform worse due to the new Index.

5. If the overall balance is positive, the index is kept, otherwise, it will be reverted.

As a rule, if the index created is good to stay, we can include it in the Database Project, so subsequent updates will not try to remove it as consequence of re-alignment between source code and target database.

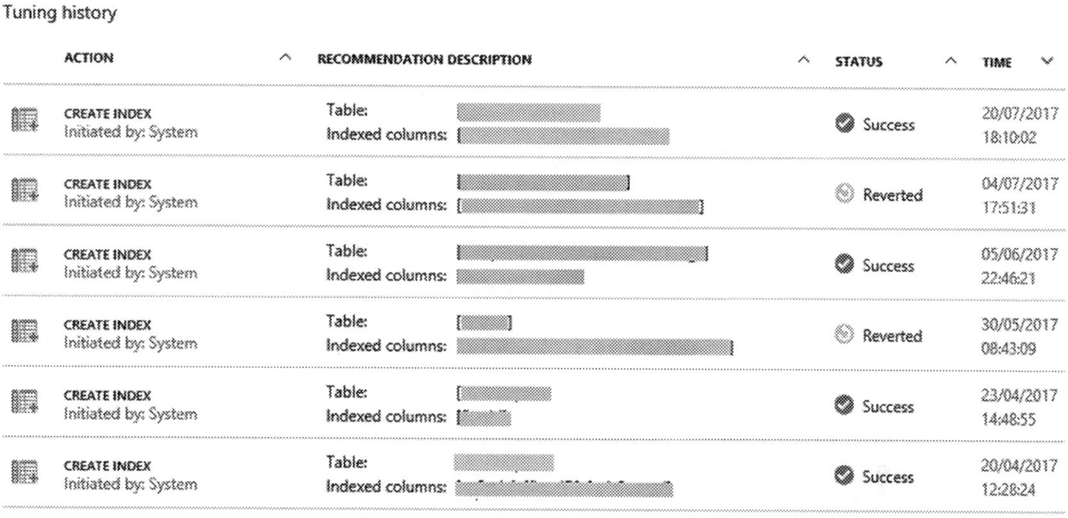

Tuning history

ACTION	RECOMMENDATION DESCRIPTION	STATUS	TIME
CREATE INDEX Initiated by: System	Table: Indexed columns:	✓ Success	20/07/2017 18:10:02
CREATE INDEX Initiated by: System	Table: Indexed columns:	⟳ Reverted	04/07/2017 17:51:31
CREATE INDEX Initiated by: System	Table: Indexed columns:	✓ Success	05/06/2017 22:46:21
CREATE INDEX Initiated by: System	Table: Indexed columns:	⟳ Reverted	30/05/2017 08:43:09
CREATE INDEX Initiated by: System	Table: Indexed columns:	✓ Success	23/04/2017 14:48:55
CREATE INDEX Initiated by: System	Table: Indexed columns:	✓ Success	20/04/2017 12:28:24

Figure 1-5. *Here we have a few recommendations, where someone has been deployed successfully while others have been reverted.*

Note   we should keep Database Project and database aligned to avoid "drifts", which can introduces alterations in the lifecycle of the database. An example of the "classic" drift is the quick-and-dirty update on the production Database, which is lost if not promptly propagated in the Database Projects. Another option could be to define a set of common standard indexes ("factory defaults") and accept that automatic tuning is going to probably be better at adapting to new workload patterns (which doesn't mean the initial effort to define "factory defaults" shouldn't be done at all or that regular review of new indexes shouldn't be done at all).

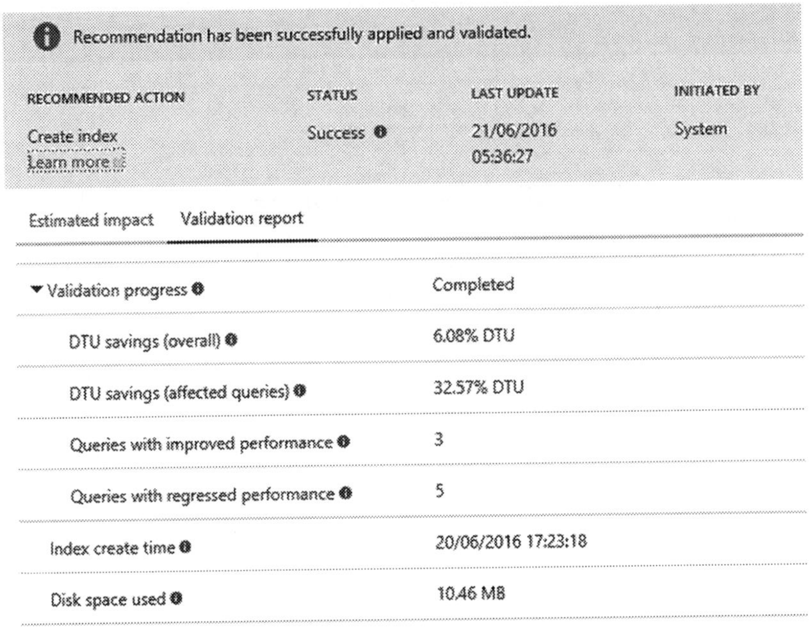

Figure 1-6. This is a detail of the impacts on the performance after an automatic Index has been applied to the Database.

In the image above (Figure 1-6), we see how that Automated Tuning is successfully for this Index. We see a global gain of 6% DTU (which is a huge saving) and, relatively to impacted queries, a 32% DTU savings. Since we are talking about indexes, there's also a connected consumption of storage, which is explicited as about 10MB more.

Migrating an Existing Database

Not every situation permits to start from scratch when we are talking about RDBMS. Actually, the majority of solutions we've seen in the last years moving to Azure, made it by migrate existing solutions. In that scenario, Database migration is a key step to the success of the entire migration.

Preparing the Database

To migrate an existing SQL Server database to Azure SQL Database we must check in advance if there are well-known incompatibilities. For instance, if the on-premises DB makes use of cross-database references, forbidden keywords and deprecated constructs, the migration will probably fail. There is a list of unsupported features (discussed before) which we can check one-by-one or we can rely on an official tool called Data Migration Assistant (`https://www.microsoft.com/en-us/download/details.aspx?id=53595`).

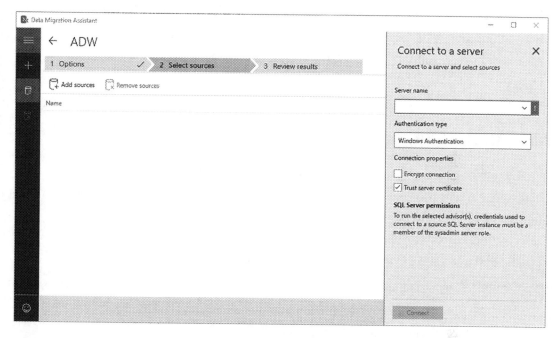

Figure 1-7. *DMA helps to identify in the on-premises database which features are used but not supported on the Azure side.*

During the DMA assessment (Figure 1-7) we are shown with a list of potential incompatibilities we must address in order to export the on-premises Database. Of course, this process affects the existing database so, we suggest this approach:

- Identify all the critical incompatibilities

  - For the ones which can be fixed transparently to the consuming applications, fix them

  - For the other ones, requiring a rework on the applications side, create a new branch where is possible and migrate the existing applications to use the new structures one-by-one

This can be a hard process itself, even before the cloud has been involved. However, we must do this before setting up the migration process, since we must assume that applications' downtime must be minimal.

When the on-premises DB feature set is 100% compatible with Azure SQL Database V12, we can plan the moving phase.

Often, in documentation as well as in the public portal, we see "V12" next to the SQDB definition. V12 has been a way to differentiate two main database server engine versions, supporting different feature sets, in the past but nowadays it's legacy.

Moving the Database

Achieving a Database migration without downtime is certainly one of the most challenging activity among others. Since the Database is stateful by definition and it often acts as a backend tier for various, eterogeneous systems, we cannot replace it transparently with an in-cloud version/backup of it, as it continuously accumulates updates and new data between the backup and the new switch-on. So, there are at least two scenarios:

1. We prepare a checklist of the systems involved into the DB usage and we plan a service interruption

2. We setup a kind of replica in the cloud, to switch transparently to it in a second time

In the first case, the process can be as follows:

- We discard new connections from outside

- We let last transactions closing gracefully. If some transactions are hanging for too long, we should consider killing them

- We ensure no other clients can connect to it except maintenance processes

- We create a copy of the original Database, sure no other clients are changing its data

- We create schema and data in the Database in the cloud

- We change every applications' configuration in order to point to the new database

- We take online them one-by-one

This approach is the cleanest and simplest approach, even if facing with several concurrent applications.

On the other side, if we have NOT direct control over the applications connecting to the database, we must consider to introduce some ad-hoc infrastructure components that denies/throttles the requests coming from sources.

In the second case, the process can be harder (and in some scenarios does not guarantee full uptime):

- On the on-premises side, we setup a SQL Server Replication

- We setup a "New Publication" on the publisher side

- We setup the distributor (it can run on the same server)

- We create a Transactional publication and we select all the objects we would like to replicate

- We add a Subscription publishing to the Azure SQL Database (we need to create an empty one before)

- We run/monitor the Replication process under the SQL Service Agent service account

This approach let us continue to operate during the creation and seeding of the remote SQL Database. When the cloud DB is fully synchronized, we can plan the switch phase.

The switch phase can itself introduce downtime since, in some situations, we prefer to not span writes between the two DBs, since the replication is one way and applications pointing to the old database in the switching window, may work with stale data changed, in the meantime, on the SQL Database side.

Exporting the DB

In the previous Option 1, we generically said "copy the DB" but it can be unclear how to do that. SQL Server standard backups (the ones in .BAK format) cannot be restored into SQL Database on the cloud. So "backup" can be interpreted as follows:

- An option is to create a BACPAC on the on-premises side (Figure 1-8) and restore it on the SQL Database side (with PowerShell, the Portal or SQLPackage)

- Another option is to do it manually, by creating Scripts of the entire DB, execute them on the remote DB and then use tools like BCP to move data.

In both cases, we suggest to perform the migration phase using the most performant tier of SQL Database, to reduce the overall time and, consequently, the downtime. You can always downscale later when the migration is completed.

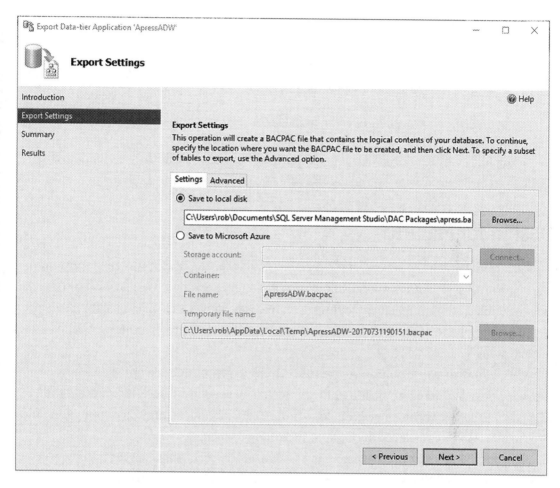

Figure 1-8. *By right-clicking the database in SSMS, we can choose Tasks->Export Data-tier Application, that starts this export wizard to create a self-contained BACPAC file to use later on Azure or on-premises.*

Using SQL Database

In almost every PaaS, performance and reactions are subject to how we use the service itself. If we use it efficiently the same service can serve request better, at the opposite, if we do not follow best practices, it can generate bottlenecks.

The waste of resources in Cloud Computing and, especially, in PaaS services, is perceived of much more impact than in traditional, on-premises infrastructures. This is due to the nature of the billing mechanism, which is often provided as per-consumption. So, in the whole chapter and book, we keep in mind this sentence:

"performance and efficiency are features"

In the following sections we try to setup a set of topics to be addressed while we use SQLDB, to improve efficiency and get the most from the underlying service.

Design for Failures

This is a valid concept for every single piece of code running in distributed system from the beginning of IT. It does not only fit with SQL Database. When we deal with remote dependencies, something can go wrong; in rare cases connectivity can lack for a second or more, often instead the remote service simply cannot execute the request because it is 100% busy.

With cloud-to-cloud solutions, the first is hard to reproduce, except for specific failures in the Azure region hosting our services. The second instead, it related to the bigger topic called Throttling which, to summarize, is about cutting consumer where the producer is too busy to serve the current incoming request.

Throttling is good. The alternative is a congested service which serves badly every request: we prefer a fast service which declines new operations is too much busy.

In ideal world, when a remote dependency is not available anymore, the consumer endpoint should gracefully continue to operate without it. An example can be an autonomous system which tries to write on the SQL Database and, in case of failure, it stores the record locally waiting the next availability window of the DB, to send the it eventually. In real world, this can happen too but, at least, we should write code which reacts to failing events of remote dependencies, even just retrying their operation until success.

Buffering

If we split queries in Read queries and Write queries we easily understand that the first can even fail with few side effects. At the opposite side, a missing write can represent a damage for everyone and if the DB cannot persist the state of the application in a point of time, the application itself have the same responsibility of a DB until service is recovered.

Since this is very hard to achieve (applications which relies on a DB are often stateless and it is desirable they should remain as is), a good approach can be to decouple critical persistence operation between applications and databases, with queues.

Someone can say we are just moving away the problem, since the queue technology must be reliable and available itself. This is why we can use it totally (every write goes to the queue) or partially (only the failed writes go to the queue). In a queue-based solution, the application is the producing actor while another, new component (which takes the items from the queue and writes them in the DB) is the writing actor (Figure 1-9).

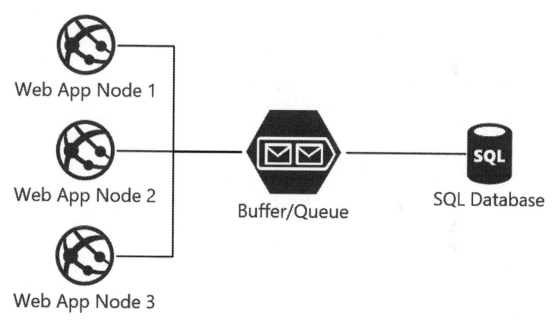

Figure 1-9. *In this scenario we decouple applications from Database access, using a queue to perform operations. This pattern can introduce a new actor (not in the image) which consumes the items from the queue and temporize the queries to the DB to avoid bottlenecks and throttling.*

If we mix this pattern with a robust and reliable distributed queue (as Azure Service Bus Queues or Azure Storage Queues) we can write robust code that is resilient in case of failures.

Retry Policies

The approach above catches all the possible causes of SQL unavailability: either it is for a short timeframe (i.e., for throttling) either it is for a service outage. In the case we cannot or do not want to introduce a new component by modifying the overall topology, we should at least implement, at the client side, a mechanism to retry queries that fail, to mitigate, at least, the short timeframes where the DB is not available or when it is too busy to reply.

A retry policy can be explained with this pseudo-code:

```
using (SqlConnection connection = new SqlConnection(connectionString))
{
    try
    {
        connection.Open();
        command.ExecuteNonQuery();
    }
    catch (TemporaryUnavailabilityException)
    {
        //Retry
    }
    catch (ThrottlingException)
    {
        //Retry
    }
    catch (Exception)
    {
        //Abort
    }
}
```

We should retry the query where the fault can be assigned to transient faults, faults which are by nature (temporary connectivity issues, huge load) transient and that can be restored quickly. In other cases, like failing runtime logic or too many retry attempts (indicating probably a downtime is occurring) should cause an abort of the operation.

Generally, almost each PaaS service in Microsoft Azure defines a specification where, in case of transient faults, special error codes/messages are returned to the client. This, in conjunction with code written to gracefully handle those faults, lets the applications run seamlessly.

By now, many official Microsoft libraries have native support for transient faults: for SQL Database, Entity Framework client has native support, as well as EF Core. For whom using ADO.NET directly, we suggest to investigate the project Polly (http://www.thepollyproject.org/) which is a library that adds some interesting features related to retries, fallback and exception handling.

For a comprehensive list of transient error codes occurring in SQL Database, see this link: https://docs.microsoft.com/en-us/azure/sql-database/sql-database-develop-error-messages.

Split between Read/Write Applications

Catching the in-field experience of some companies we worked with, high-end users of SQL Server are considering, before or later, to split application logic routing request to different DB instances (even in different servers/regions), depending on the type of load and/or operation requested.

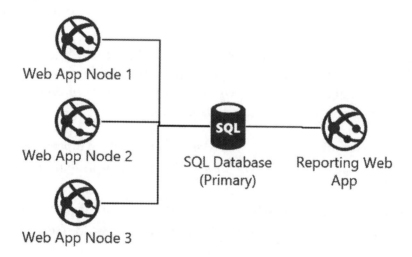

Figure 1-10. *Multiple applications act against the primary DB. If the reporting tool is making an intensive, long-runnig query, Web App nodes can see a degradation of performance.*

In the scenario above (Figure 1-10) out perception is that it is not a great idea to point every process on the same DB instance, because few clients with few complex analytical queries can consume the majority of the available resources, slowing down the entire business processes. Where a Data Warehouse is not an option, we can imagine to split the scenario, at least, as follows:

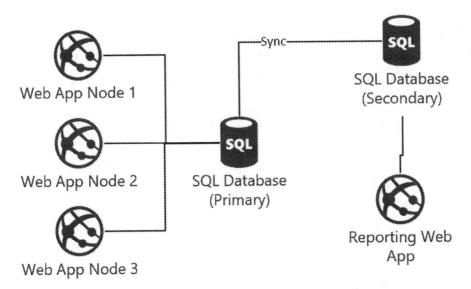

Figure 1-11. *Since a replica relationship has been established between two SQL Databases, making one the secondary read-only replica of the primary, read-only applications (Reporting tools can fit this requirement) can point to the replica, without affecting the performance of the primary node.*

In this second scenario (Figure 1-11) it is clear that analytical processing can, at maximum, consume all the resources of the secondary replica, keeping safe the critical business activities.

This approach can be extended by design in almost every scenario, since the majority of solutions (except ones based on intensive data ingestion) have a high read/write ratio.

Using Geo-Replication

Geo-Replication (Figure 1-12) is a SQL Database feature which permits to setup, with few clicks, a secondary server in the same or different geographical region, with a synchronized (but read-only) copy of the primary DB. This is a killing feature since it can be enabled on every SQL Database DB and with few configuration steps. The time needed to perform the initial seeding (the process where data is completely aligned the secondary) can vary depending on the service tier of both DBs and the quantity of data involved.

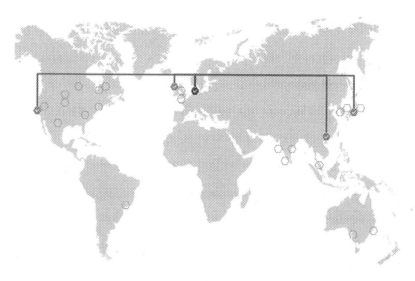

Figure 1-12. *An overview of a Geo-Replication scenario in place. The blue icon is the primary DB and the green ones are the secondary replicas.*

As in the migration process, the suggestion is to upgrade the DB to a large tier before setting up the Geo-Replication, in order to reduce the seeding time. Another suggestion is to have the secondary replica at least at the same performance level of the primary. In case it is weaker, primary can experience delays while propagating updates and notifications.

Despite Geo-Replication is a topic often discussed as a way to improve business continuity and uptime, we suggest to implement that (if budget permits) in almost every scenario, to ensure we always have a copy to be used in several scenarios:

- Read-only APIs/Services

- Read-intensive Web Applications

- Reading production data with no much attention to the optimization of the query (i.e., from SSMS)

- Testing in production (with the guarantee no write will be accepted)

In SQL Database we can have up to 4 secondary copies (read-only) of a primary (read-write) DB (Figure 1-13). We can span the replication across different region or stay in the base region: in this last scenario we achieve a simple replication instead a real Geo-Replication. All of those combinations are valid:

- Primary DB in West Europe, Secondary 1 in North Europe, Secondary 2 in Japan West

- Primary DB in West Europe, Secondary 1 in West Europe

- Primary DB in North Europe, Secondary 1 in North Europe, Secondary 2 in East Asia

- Primary DB in West Europe, Secondary 1 in East Asia, Secondary 2 in UK West, Secondary 3 in Canada Central, Secondary 4 in West India

PRIMARY

✔	West Europe	azure-demos/ApressADW	None	Online

SECONDARIES

✔	East Asia	apress-ea/ApressADW		Readable ...
✔	Japan West	apress-jw/ApressADW		Readable ...
✔	North Europe	apress-ne/ApressADW		Readable ...
✔	West US	apress-wu/ApressADW		Readable ...

Figure 1-13. *In this scenario we have the primary DB in West Europe and 4 additional Readable copies in different regions around the globe.*

Geo-Replication is not only about splitting read/write queries but, mainly, is about Availability. In fact, each secondary database can be promoted to primary by triggering the manual Failover action, in the portal or through the APIs. To be complete, on a secondary DB we can:

1. Stop replication: the secondary DB will stop the replica relationship and becomes a valid read/write DB.

Please note that once the relationship is broken, it cannot be re-established (except by recreating a new secondary DB from scratch).

---

2. Failover: with failover, Azure promotes the secondary to primary and makes the "old-primary" as a read-only secondary replica. In addition, it updates the remaining secondary to synchronize with the new primary.

Figure 1-14. *A Failover action on the Japan West replica. Azure will manage the promotion and the demotion of the respective primary/secondary DBs.*

A common pitfall around Geo-Replication is how to deal with Failover (Figure 1-14), where applications that have connection strings pointing to a primary DB must be updated in order to point to the new primary. If there are multiple applications involved, this can be really hard to achieve (in a small timeframe and without downtime).

Using Failover Groups

By using for a while Geo-Replication comes out that a common pattern is to have just one replica (to separate reads/writes or to increase availability) of a primary DB. Another common requirement is to replicate all the DBs in a server to avoid doing it one-by-one, especially where part of an elastic pool. Finally, companies really don't want to manually switch connection strings in every application during a failover action.

Failover Groups (Figure 1-15) address exactly those requirements. By using the same underlying technology of Geo-Replication, they provide:

- a way to replicate a group of DBs on a source server to a target server (that must be in a different geographical region, however)

- a way to use the same DNS name/endpoint for the primary/ secondary: this ensures that applications can be untouched in case we trigger a failover action

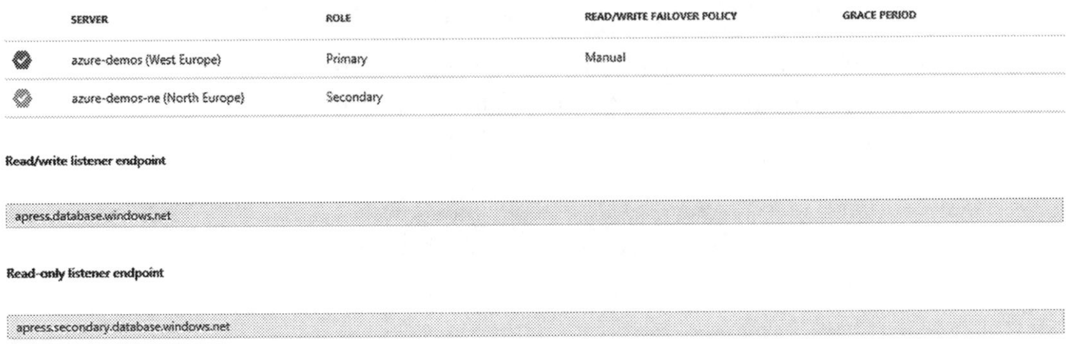

SERVER	ROLE	READ/WRITE FAILOVER POLICY	GRACE PERIOD
⊘ azure-demos (West Europe)	Primary	Manual	
⊘ azure-demos-ne (North Europe)	Secondary		

Read/write listener endpoint

apress.database.windows.net

Read-only listener endpoint

apress.secondary.database.windows.net

Figure 1-15. *In this failover relationship the azure-demos (West Europe) server is Primary and replicates to the azure-demos-ne (North Europe) secondary DBs. To have applications connecting transparently to the Primary/Secondary, we must use the generated DNS names for listeners.*

In both Geo-Replication and Failover Groups solutions, we recommend to use Database-level Logins and Firewall Rules, to be sure they are propagated as database object in the various replica, avoiding potential runtime issues.

Please consider that you can't failover a single DB in the group. When the failover action is triggered, all the DBs in the group will fail to the secondary replica. The only way to failover a single DB is to remove it from the Failover Group. By removing it, it still remains in the replication relationship and can failover individually.

Hot Features

We should avoid to talk directly of specific features of SQL Database, since they are pretty aligned with the latest version of SQL Server (that is, at the time of writing, SQL Server 2016). In fact, almost every enhancement to SQL Server is released to SQL Database on Azure before it is released in GA in the on-premises SQL Server product. This is a great chance to be early adopter of a new technology, since when the features are ready are automatically included in the PaaS with no effort or intervention by the users.

The listing of the hot features of SQL Server and SQL Database is out of the scope of this book, but we mention just a few of them, sure they are relevant to applications and useful to address performance targets.

In-memory

With the Premium Tier of SQL Database (DBs starting with "P", like P1, P2, etc) we have a dedicated storage for in-memory OLTP operations (in the 1GB-32GB range, depending on the performance level).

In-memory technology applies to:

- Tables: with in-memory tables we can address those scenario with a very fast data ingestion rate. Time for transactional processing is reduced dramatically.

- Columnstore Indexes: with Clustered/Non-clustered columnstore indexes we can reduce the index footprint (with great savings on the storage side) and perform analytical queries faster.

Temporal Tables

While dealing with history data, we often see custom development pattern where, before every write, a record is copied to make the history of changes of it. However, this approach binds every touch point to be aware of this logic, where it should be better that the client applications are unaware of this, with the only purpose to write updates to the given table.

Another solution we have seen is the use of triggers. But, triggers are quite cumbersome and they should be placed for every table we would like to historicise.

Temporal tables are tables defined to integrate an history mechanism, where is the SQL Server engine which provides all the necessary stuff to save the old record values before the update occurs. During the creation of the Temporal Tables (or during the migration of an existing non-temporal one) we must specify the name of the underlying backing table which receives every update, including the schema ones. This powerful mechanism ensures that every operation made to the parent table is propagated to the history table.

In case we are altering an existing table, we should add two new fields, to keep track of temporal information, as follows:

```
ALTER TABLE [SalesLT].[Address]
ADD
    ValidFrom datetime2 (0) GENERATED ALWAYS AS ROW START HIDDEN
        constraint MT_ValidFrom DEFAULT DATEADD(SECOND, -1,
        SYSUTCDATETIME())
```

```
, ValidTo datetime2 (0)  GENERATED ALWAYS AS ROW END HIDDEN
    constraint MT_ValidTo DEFAULT '9999.12.31 23:59:59.99'
, PERIOD FOR SYSTEM_TIME (ValidFrom, ValidTo);
```

And next we define the history table:

```
ALTER TABLE [SalesLT].[Address]
SET (SYSTEM_VERSIONING = ON (HISTORY_TABLE = [SalesLT].[Address_History]));
```

If we setup temporal tables while creating them, it is easier:

```
CREATE TABLE MyTable
(
    --... fields ...
  , [ValidFrom] datetime2 (0) GENERATED ALWAYS AS ROW START
  , [ValidTo] datetime2 (0) GENERATED ALWAYS AS ROW END
  , PERIOD FOR SYSTEM_TIME (ValidFrom, ValidTo)
)
WITH (SYSTEM_VERSIONING = ON (HISTORY_TABLE =
[SalesLT].[Address_History]));
```

JSON Support

JSON support extends the language specification of T-SQL by introducing operators and selectors useful to work with JSON data. We can:

Query a SQL table with a JSON field, applying filtering directly on the JSON nodes

Serialize a query result into JSON to let be consumed by others, or to be place into a NoSQL storage

This is a sample query with JSON support:

```
SELECT TOP (2)
      [ProductID] as [ID]
     ,[SalesLT].[Product].[Name]
     ,[Category].[ProductCategoryID] as [ID]
     ,[Category].[Name]
  FROM [SalesLT].[Product] JOIN [SalesLT].[ProductCategory] AS [Category]
  ON [SalesLT].[Product].[ProductCategoryID]= [Category].
[ProductCategoryID]
  FOR JSON AUTO
```

The query above produced a well-formatted JSON document as follows:

```
[{
            "ID": 680,
            "Name": "HL Road Frame - Black, 58",
            "Category": [{
                        "ID": 18,
                        "Name": "Road Frames"
                }
            ]
    }, {
            "ID": 706,
            "Name": "HL Road Frame - Red, 58",
            "Category": [{
                        "ID": 18,
                        "Name": "Road Frames"
                }
            ]
    }
]
```

We can toggle the JSON array definition with the WITHOUT_ARRAY_WRAPPER option.

Development Environments

In almost every context there is a practice to replicate the production environment into few isolated dev/test environments. A common topology can be the following:

- Production: the live environment with hot code and data. Since this chapter is about SQL Database, we see the production environment as the SQL DB instance of production.

- Pre-production: this is usually a pre-roll environment. While the various frontend tiers can be separated from the production environment, the Database can be either separated or the same as production. Often, the preproduction phase is just a last-minute validation of the updates related to the new deployment.

37

- UAT/Staging: this is usually a completely isolated end-to-end lane, with each single block of the application (including database) replicated.

- Dev/Test: those are usually one or more isolated environment where developers can have their own projection of the entire application stack, for development purposes.

With the cloud, especially with Azure, making and maintaining those environment is very easy. There is no more need to even use local development environments, since both the application and the development VM can be in the cloud.

We can also develop locally the code we need but pointing to the remote dependencies (i.e., SQL Database, Storage, Search) if the local-to-cloud connectivity is satisfactory.

Database Copies

In this scenario, we can take advantage of the SQL Database Copy feature, which creates a copy of the source database instance into a fresh instance, on the same or different SQL Server (logical) container.

The copy feature creates a transactionally consistent copy of the source database into a new database and can be triggered, as well as through the Management API (Portal, PowerShell, SDK) even from inside the SQL Server (logical) container, by launching this query on the master database:

```
CREATE DATABASE AdventureWorksLT _staging AS COPY OF AdventureWorksLT;
```

The copy operation (Figure 1-16) will start and it will take some time (depending on the DB size, the performance level and the actual load of the source DB). With a query pane opened on the "master" database, we can query the status of the copy operation as follows:

```
SELECT * FROM sys.dm_database_copies
```

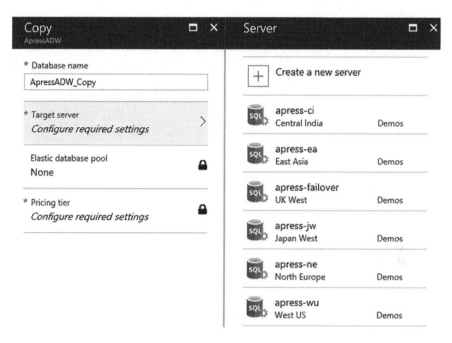

Figure 1-16. *Database can be copied also versus a target server in a different datacenter. This feature is extremely useful in scenarios where regional migrations are required.*

Worst Practices

We can say SQL Database is the cloud version of SQL Server, so almost every attention to be paid to the second, can be applied to the first in order to gain performance. Every T-SQL optimization we have learned in the past, can be reused and this is definitely great.

However, SQL quality is an aspect that can be disattended by several projects, for many reasons:

- The attention paid to the software code is much more than the one paid for the SQL tier

- The skills about SQL are less developed than the ones about software development

- Nobody needs (until now) to invest so much on the DB maintenance/ optimization

Let us show an example of what can happen while migrating an on-premises SQL instance to the cloud. Let's suppose we have a Windows Client intranet application (Figure 1-17), which lets users perform business activities and which relies on SQL Server hosted in a server room in the company's facility. The software is mainly a data-driven, grid-based application, where users consult data and produce reports.

The Database has only 40 tables, no fancy features involved (CLR, file-system dependencies, etc) and, to over-simplify, no stored procedures, views and other database objects than the tables mentioned. In short, let's take as an example a DB 100% compatible with the SQL Database feature surface area, which we migrate with a small amount of IT effort.

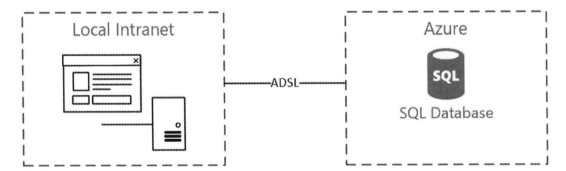

Figure 1-17. *In this scenario we must consider the potential bottleneck of Bandwidth between the company's facility and the cloud.*

Unfortunately, once the connection string of the application has changed, users are hanging on basic operations which before they made in seconds, and now take minutes to run. So, where is the issue? Let's make some hypotheses:

- SQL Database is "slower" than the on-premise version: this can be possible, there are many tiers and performance level to test to know if this is a performance issue. We can scale up and look for improvements, and this can tell us which initial size we should use to get acceptable performance.

- The bandwidth between "us" (the office) and the DB in the cloud is insufficient while queries are executed normally

- The software has something to investigate, since the DB/Bandwidth utilization is low

Some common pitfalls while using SQL in software development follow.

Bad Connection Management

Some of the frameworks discussed below automatically manage all the stuff around connections. it is very common the pattern which, in respond to an object Dispose(), the corresponding underlying DB connection is closed. Anyway, we can fall in several cases where a bad connection management keep resource usage very high and introduces a waste of time and money:

The Driver/Provider to Connect to the DB does not Use Connection Pools

What is a connection pool? When we connect to a DB, basic TCP operations are involved (handshake, authentication, encryption, etc). In case we are connecting from a Web App and, specifically, we have a correlation between user requests/navigation and queries, a high number of concurrent DB connections can be established and consequently, a heavy overhead on both the client machine and the RDBMS server is generated. To avoid this, many frameworks (including ADO.NET) uses Connection Pools. A connection pool is a way to manage DB connections, reusing them between different contexts. The advantage is to avoid to establish fresh connection for each command to execute against the DB; instead, applications using connection pools reuse existing connections (in most cases, transparently).

The Connection Pools are Fragmented

What is the fragmentation of Connection Pools? Looking inside on how ADO.NET, for instance, manages the pools, we see different behaviours. Each connection pointing to a specific database originates a new connection pool, which means that if the Web App is now connecting to Database A and then to the Database B, two connection pools are allocated. In case we were using on-premise SQL Server, with Windows Authentication or Basic Authentication with Integrated Security login (fortunately not available on SQL Database), a connection pool is generated per-user and per-database.

```
//Request coming from User A on DB A
using (var connection = new SqlConnection("Integrated Security=SSPI;Initial
Catalog=DB_A"))
{
    connection.Open();
    //First connection pool for DB A is created
}
```

```
//Request coming from User B on DB A
using (var connection = new SqlConnection("Integrated Security=SSPI;Initial
Catalog=DB_A"))
{
    connection.Open();
    //Second connection pool for DB A is created
}
```

In case we are working on Sharding data, where a master connection can be established to the Shard Map and specific queries are routed to shards, each single DB is mapped to a single Connection pool. A common solution to this second scenario is to use the same connection (for example to the master DB) and then use the USE keyword to switch database inside the query. Unfortunately, even this scenario (the usage of USE statement) is not supported on SQL Database. We will discuss sharding later but keep in mind those limits and operate consequently.

```
//Usage of USE statement, NOT ALLOWED in SQL Database
var command = new SqlCommand();
command.CommandText = "USE MyShard";
using (SqlConnection connection = new SqlConnection(
    connectionString))
{
    connection.Open();
    command.ExecuteNonQuery();
}
```

As many connections lead to more overhead and latency, it is recommended to reduce fragmentation and achieve optimizations, where possible.

The Connections are not Disposed Properly

If we do not follow correctly the recommended actions on existing connections (in ADO. NET this can be done by avoiding to call Dispose() on SqlConnection) the connection cannot be released to the Connection Pool and cannot be reused later. Relying just on garbage collector to dispose them indirectly is not a reliable and efficient solution to the problem. Depending on the framework we are using (ADO.NET directly or Entity Framework or others) we must instruct the framework to free to resources we are not using anymore.

Client-Side Querying

There are frameworks which hide the complexity behind a database request round-trip, which let all the details (i.e., SQL Connection, Commands, Queries and Results) under the hood. Those frameworks/libraries are very useful to speed up the development process. However, if not used appropriately, they can lead to undesired behaviour.

In local-only environment, where the bandwidth is not an issue and, more generally, it isn't a strict constraint, we can fall in the wrong pattern by materializing all the data of a specific dataset to perform the query on the client (and not on the RDBMS server). This can occur with this C# snippet as follows:

```
var ta = new DataSet1TableAdapters.CustomerTableAdapter();
var customers = ta.GetData().Where(p => p.LastName.StartsWith("S"));
```

In the previous example we get ALL THE DATA of the Customer table and we perform the query on the client side. Unfortunately, this worst practice cannot be easily discovered in on-premises scenario, where a very high network bandwidth can give the developers the wrong impression of good performance. In this second case, we make the same mistake using Entity Framework:

```
using (var ctx=new ApressADWEntities())
{
    var customers = ctx.Customer.ToArray().Where(p => p.LastName.
    StartsWith("S"));
}
```

For skilled developers those misusages are clearly wrong, but it worth to remind them in order to make every effort to avoid them in production.

Pay Attention to Entity Framework

We are estimators of Entity Framework for the great capability it had to reduce the gap between developers and SQL specialists.

In ideal world, SQL-related tasks should fall on a specialized database developer and the software part is up to the software developer. In real world, often developers are in charge to write software AND write queries. In this common situation, it can be faster (not better) to teach developers to use a middleware which translates code into the SQL queries, than teach SQL itself.

Let's take the query above:

```
var customers = ctx.Customer.ToArray()
```

Entity Framework translates this expression into the following SQL query:

```
{SELECT
    [Extent1].[CustomerID] AS [CustomerID],
    [Extent1].[NameStyle] AS [NameStyle],
    [Extent1].[Title] AS [Title],
    [Extent1].[FirstName] AS [FirstName],
    [Extent1].[MiddleName] AS [MiddleName],
    [Extent1].[LastName] AS [LastName],
    [Extent1].[Suffix] AS [Suffix],
    [Extent1].[CompanyName] AS [CompanyName],
    [Extent1].[SalesPerson] AS [SalesPerson],
    [Extent1].[EmailAddress] AS [EmailAddress],
    [Extent1].[Phone] AS [Phone],
    [Extent1].[PasswordHash] AS [PasswordHash],
    [Extent1].[PasswordSalt] AS [PasswordSalt],
    [Extent1].[rowguid] AS [rowguid],
    [Extent1].[ModifiedDate] AS [ModifiedDate]
    FROM [SalesLT].[Customer] AS [Extent1]}
```

Which is okay, and it has pros/cons to consider:

As a pro, it considers exactly every table member known at the time of creation of the EF model. This means that if we add new fields without updating the EF mapping, this query continues to work and it fetches only the data we need in the application. In addition, like every query generated by EF, we do not need to use strings to pass queries to the DB, which is definitely one of the best advantages we have by using EF.

As a con, we can obtain the same result by writing the following statement:

```
SELECT * FROM SalesLT.Customer
```

Which reduce the incoming bytes to the SQL instance. However, note that, in case of fields added, they will be fetched also and maybe they are useless for the calling application.

Those examples are trivial, but think about querying complex tables with multiple joins and complex filtering logic. Entity Framework can be the best of allies, but sometimes can even generate a lot of query code which humans can definitely write better (from a performance perspective).

```
var query = ctx.SalesOrderHeader
    .Where(p => p.SalesOrderDetail.Any(q => q.Product.ProductCategory.Name.
    StartsWith("A")))
    .Where(p => p.SubTotal > 10 && p.Address.City == "Milan")
    .Select(p => new
    {
        Order=p,
        Customer=p.Customer,
        Details=p.SalesOrderDetail.Select(q=>new
        {
            Item=q.Product.Name,
            Quantity=q.OrderQty
        })
    });
```

This query hides the complexity of multiple joins, advanced filtering and multiple projection from different tables. It is clear that it can save a lot of time for non-SQL specialist, but keep in mind that the generated SQL query is something like that:

```
{SELECT
    [Project2].[AddressID] AS [AddressID],
    [Project2].[SalesOrderID] AS [SalesOrderID],
    [Project2].[RevisionNumber] AS [RevisionNumber],
    [Project2].[OrderDate] AS [OrderDate],
      ... 30 lines omitted ...
    [Project2].[PasswordHash] AS [PasswordHash],
    [Project2].[PasswordSalt] AS [PasswordSalt],
    [Project2].[rowguid1] AS [rowguid1],
    [Project2].[ModifiedDate1] AS [ModifiedDate1],
    [Project2].[C1] AS [C1],
    [Project2].[ProductID] AS [ProductID],
    [Project2].[Name] AS [Name],
```

```
    [Project2].[OrderQty] AS [OrderQty]
    FROM ( SELECT
        [Extent1].[SalesOrderID] AS [SalesOrderID],
        [Extent1].[RevisionNumber] AS [RevisionNumber],
        [Extent1].[OrderDate] AS [OrderDate],
     ... 30 lines omitted ...
        [Extent3].[Phone] AS [Phone],
        [Extent3].[PasswordHash] AS [PasswordHash],
        [Extent3].[PasswordSalt] AS [PasswordSalt],
        [Extent3].[rowguid] AS [rowguid1],
        [Extent3].[ModifiedDate] AS [ModifiedDate1],
        [Join3].[OrderQty] AS [OrderQty],
        [Join3].[ProductID1] AS [ProductID],
        [Join3].[Name] AS [Name],
        CASE WHEN ([Join3].[OrderQty] IS NULL) THEN CAST(NULL AS int) ELSE
        1 END AS [C1]
        FROM    [SalesLT].[SalesOrderHeader] AS [Extent1]
        INNER JOIN [SalesLT].[Address] AS [Extent2] ON [Extent1].
        [BillToAddressID] = [Extent2].[AddressID]
        INNER JOIN [SalesLT].[Customer] AS [Extent3] ON [Extent1].
        [CustomerID] = [Extent3].[CustomerID]
        LEFT OUTER JOIN  (SELECT [Extent4].[SalesOrderID] AS
        [SalesOrderID], [Extent4].[OrderQty] AS [OrderQty], [Extent4].
        [ProductID] AS [ProductID1], [Extent5].[Name] AS [Name]
            FROM  [SalesLT].[SalesOrderDetail] AS [Extent4]
            INNER JOIN [SalesLT].[Product] AS [Extent5] ON [Extent4].
            [ProductID] = [Extent5].[ProductID] ) AS [Join3] ON [Extent1].
            [SalesOrderID] = [Join3].[SalesOrderID]
        WHERE ( EXISTS (SELECT
            1 AS [C1]
            FROM    [SalesLT].[SalesOrderDetail] AS [Extent6]
            INNER JOIN [SalesLT].[Product] AS [Extent7] ON [Extent6].
            [ProductID] = [Extent7].[ProductID]
            INNER JOIN [SalesLT].[ProductCategory] AS [Extent8] ON
            [Extent7].[ProductCategoryID] = [Extent8].[ProductCategoryID]
```

```
      WHERE ([Extent1].[SalesOrderID] = [Extent6].[SalesOrderID]) AND
      ([Extent8].[Name] LIKE N'A%')
    )) AND ([Extent1].[SubTotal] > cast(10 as decimal(18))) AND
    (N'Milan' = [Extent2].[City])
  ) AS [Project2]
  ORDER BY [Project2].[AddressID] ASC, [Project2].[SalesOrderID] ASC,
  [Project2].[CustomerID1] ASC, [Project2].[C1] ASC}
```

We are not saying it is a wrong query nor a wrong approach; we just need to keep in mind that is just ONE solution to the problem and it may not be the best one.

Batching Operations

An example of abusing Entity Framework can be its usage applied to bulk inserts. Think about this code:

```
using (var ctx = new ApressADWEntities())
{
    for (int i = 0; i < 10000; i++)
    {
        ctx.Customer.Add(new Customer()
        {
            CompanyName = $"Company {i}",
            //Missing other properties assigment
        });
    }
    ctx.SaveChanges();
}
```

On SaveChanges, Entity Framework spans a new INSERT statement for each record we created in the code. This is actually correct, from the EF side, but maybe it's not what we would like to have. Instead, we should focus on some sort of Bulk Insert, using the low-level API of ADO.NET or other commercial frameworks which add performance-related features on top of EF.

Some strategies to batch the operations against SQL Database con be:

- Buffering: when possible, decoupling the data producer from the data writer with a buffer (even a remote Queue) can avoid bottlenecks on the SQL side and it avoids the need of batching at all.

- Transactions: grouping several modify operations in a single transaction, as opposed to executing those same operations as distinct (implicit) transactions, results in optimized transaction-log operations improving performance.

- Table-valued parameters: in case we are grouping a sequence of INSERT operations, we can use user-defined table types as parameters in T-SQL statements. We can send multiple rows as a single table-valued parameter.

For further information about table-valued parameters follow this link: `https://docs.microsoft.com/en-us/sql/relational-databases/tables/use-table-valued-parameters-database-engine`

- SQL Bulk Copy / BCP / Bulk Insert: it is probably the best option for bulk INSERT operations.

Do not think that parallelize operations can always be faster while performing operations against the DB. If we are splitting 1000 operation of a single batch in 4 threads of 250 operations each, it is not guaranteed we notice a save. Indeed, we often observe a degradation of the overall performance, since there are many factors which influences the scenario.

Scaling SQL Database

Scaling a RDBMS is a well-known challenging topic, since few RDBMS can scale horizontally while keeping various limits. Replicas are usually read-only and designed for high-availability and often, the only way to increase the performance of a DB, is to scale up the underlying instance.

Increasing the hardware on the underlying infrastructure is similar to increase the DTU level of the SQLDB: both approaches give to the DB engine more resources to perform queries. In this scenario, options are not on the DB side.

We encourage users to not rely only on changing the Performance Level, since they are fixed in numbers and limited in power (at the time of writing, 4000DTU is the maximum supported). What we should think about is, again, the application architecture.

Let's assuming the following as the evolving path of the DB of a SaaS solution:

1. We develop a single, multi-tenant DB

2. We keep it at Standard S0 (10 DTU) level during the development phase

3. After an hour in production with a single client, we see the DTU is always at 100%, so we increase first at S1 (20 DTU) level.

4. By monitoring the performance, we now see that the DTU is still at 100% but with few moments at 60-70%. We increase the level at S2 (50 DTU).

5. Now the DB is at 60% on average, which can be okay

Now we can realize that DTU consumed are too much for the budget. In that case we can optimize the existing application:

- By using more efficiently the DB resources

- By offload some of the SQL load to other storage types (Polyglot Persistence)

- By introduce layers of caching for frequently accessed data

- By sharding data

If the DTU consumed is aligned with the expectations (or, if not aligned, at least in budget) we can proceed with the evolution:

1. 10 new clients arrive. Since the overload of the DB is a 10% more for each new client, we double the DTU scaling to a S3 (100 DTU) level.

2. Now the DB has reached the maximum level of the Standard Tier, so we need to pay attention to the consequences of a further level increase.

3. A new client, which predicted consumption is of about 45 DTU by itself, subscribed for the service, we have two options:

4. Increase the Standard Tier to Premium. DTU would pass from 100 to 125 (in the Premium P1 plan) but price increases about 3 times.

5. Use the last multi-tenancy technique and create a new S2 (50 DTU) database instance, pointing the new client's application to this DB.

Table 1-1. *We have two database, designed to be multi-tenant individually, with a groups of tenants each*

Database Name	# of clients	Tier	Level	Avg. Consumption
POOL001	11	Standard	S3	60% (60/100 DTU)
POOL002	1	Standard	S2	90% (45/50 DTU)

Now we have implemented the "Multiple Logical Pools with a single schema preference" which results in the best tradeoff between elasticity and governance (just one schema is applied to both DBs) but some drawbacks:

- More management effort:

  - while applying changes to the DBs

  - during backup/restore operations

  - on the entire monitoring process

- Different costs per-client to control and summarize

Please note that some of the drawbacks are have also positive impact to other aspect of the Service Management. Let's suppose you have a client who unintentionally deletes its data from the database. If that client is in a dedicated DB, a simple backup restore can help to get the whole DB at the previous state.

Now think about the same situation in a shared DB: how can we get just the data of the given client without restoring the whole DB? In fact, the restore operation would affect even other tenants, so manual work (or scripted procedures) are needed to perform it at best.

Many SaaS providers offer different price tags for services. Can happen that the underlying infrastructure affects the price and "premium" services are often used to provide clients with dedicated resources and value-added services. One example can be the capability to restore the whole database at any given time.

Managing Elasticity at Runtime

In the ideal scenario, an application would span a query between several DBs to boost performance and distribute the load. However, doing this in real world is quite hard and involves a series of hot topics, related to sharding data.

Let's assume we are working on a multi-tenant solution where each tenant has, in each table, its own unique identifier (i.e., TenantID field). We would need, at least:

- A shard map: a dictionary where, given the key of the query (i.e., TenantID) we know which actual database to point to

- A movement tool: a middleware to organize and move (split and merge) data between sharded databases

- A query tool/library: an artifact which hides the complexity of the shards to the applications, performing the routing of the queries and, in case of queries against multiple DBs, which performs the individual queries and merge results. In this category falls optionally a transaction manager which runs the transactions to multiple DBs

As we can imagine, this can be made 99% by custom software and custom tooling, while Microsoft provides its own support with the Elastic Database Tools.

Elastic Database Tools

Microsoft realized that it is not easy for every developer/ISV to implement by their own a fully-featured set of tools/libraries to deal with sharding. At the same time, it has been proven that sharding is the most efficient way to implement scale out on relational DBs. This spun out a set of technologies which help us to manage even complex sharding scenarios with hundreds of database involved.

The Elastic Database Tools are composed of the following:

- Elastic Database Client Library: a library which helps creating the shard map manager (a dedicated DB as the index of our shards) and the various individual shards databases.

An example of how to use this library is available here: `https://code.msdn.microsoft.com/windowsapps/Elastic-Scale-with-Azure-a80d8dc6`

While an overview of the library is here: `https://docs.microsoft.com/en-us/azure/sql-database/sql-database-elastic-scale-introduction`

- Elastic Database split/merge tool: a pre-configured Cloud Service with a Web Role and a Worker Role which presents a GUI and the routines to perform split/merge activities on the shards. We must notice that Cloud Services are actually not implemented in ARM (Azure Resource Manager) and we do not cover them in this book.

- Elastic Database Jobs: a pre-configured set of services (Cloud Service, SQL Database, Service Bus and Storage) with the necessary running software needed to run jobs against multiple databases.

- Elastic Database Query: a specific feature (in preview) of SQL Database which permits to connect/query to make cross-database queries.

- Elastic Transactions: a library which helps creating a client-coordinated transaction between different SQL Databases. At the time being, there is no server-side transaction support.

Keep in mind that tools above are just provided as individual tools and they are not full PaaS as SQLDB itself. Except the Elastic Database Query, which is a feature of SQLDB, implement the Split/Merge tool, for instance, means to take the ownership of new cloud resources, to provision, monitor and manage.

Pooling Different DBs Under the Same Price Cap

I would suggest to design applications like mentioned in the previous section, to be elastic and resilient by design. However, let's suppose that moving tenants is too hard or too expensive and the best solution is to have "One Database for each tenant". In that case, we can easily grow up to hundreds of DBs as far as clients arrive.

Think about the situation in the table below:

Database Name	# of clients	Tier	Level	Cost	DTU	Peak DTU	Avg. Usage
DB001	1	Standard	S0	~ 15$/m	10	8	40%
DB002	1	Standard	S1	~ 30$/m	20	11	25%
DB003	1	Standard	S1	~ 30$/m	20	13	40%
DB004	1	Standard	S2	~ 75$/m	50	30	20%
DB005	1	Standard	S3	~ 150$/m	100	65	10%
DB006	1	Standard	S3	~ 150$/m	100	70	10%
DB007	1	Standard	S0	~ 15$/m	10	5	20%
DB008	1	Standard	S1	~ 30$/m	20	13	40%

We see that, with 8 clients, we have 8 DBs each one with its own Performance Level, calibrated on the peak DTU usage we need. The monthly cost will be around 495$/month.

Unfortunately, it is a waste of resources: at one side, we need to size the DB based on the Peak we expect. At the other side, we see that average usage (especially for the most expensive DBs) is very low.

From the numbers above we can infer an average global DTU usage of about 57 DTU. In the optimal (and unrealistic) case tenants have peaks during different timeframes, we can even use a single DB of 100 DTU (Standard S3) containing every tenant (but this is against the requirements pointed at the beginning of the "Scaling SQL Database" section).

SQL Database Elastic Pools

For the emerging requirement shown above, Azure has SQLDB Elastic Pools
(Figure 1-18). An Elastic Pool is a logical container of a subset of the DBs of a server
(which is the logical container of our DBs). We can create a Pool by specifying:

- Server: DB pools only apply to a subset of DBs of the same logical
  server. We cannot span between different servers.

- Pricing Tier: each DB pool has its own price, as for the standalone
  DBs

- Configuration: we can set how many DTU has the pool, how much
  capacity (in terms of GBs) and min/max DTU for each database
  contained

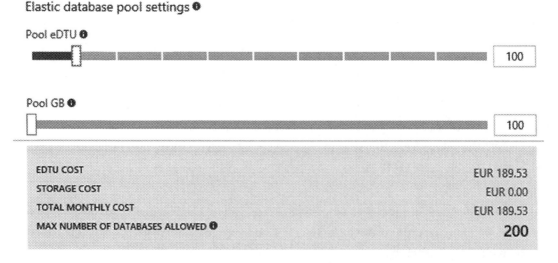

*Figure 1-18.   In this configuration we have a pool with a total of 100 DTU and
100GB for the whole set of contained DBs. The cost is approximately ~224$/month,
which is far less compared to the previous option.*

We can notice, however that only 100 DTU for DBs having peaks of 65-70 DTU can be
too small. At any given time, we can increase the cap of the entire pool without touching
the individual DBs.

Scaling Up

We left intentionally this option as the last of the entire section because we think it is the last resort. Don't misunderstand, scale up is good and it is part of the process, but since we cannot scale up indefinitely, we should start thinking about performance issues in time.

At the same time, we don't recommend to over-engineer a simple solution by adding shards, pools, caching layers, etc. We must know them in advance and, possibly, develop our code accordingly. Crafting the software with those ideas will reduce consumption of the resources from the beginning and solutions consuming 1000 DTU can easily be reduced to a 100 DTU impact.

Anyway, scaling up is the shortest path to gain power immediately, for example if we want to manage an unpredictable peak, or in case of planned increase of load. This is the table of most of the current levels of Tiers/DTU, they can change in time, but we strongly recommend to not design a solution which relies on the top tier, since there is no way to scale more!

Tier	Level	DTUs	Tier	Level	DTUs
Basic	B	5	Premium	P1	125
Standard	S0	10		P2	250
	S1	20		P4	500
	S2	50		P6	1000
	S3	100		P11	1750
Premium RS	PRS1	125		P15	4000
	PRS2	250			
	PRS4	500			
	PRS6	1000			

Offloading the reading operations there is a good alternative to scale up where the scenario permits it. By using the Geo-Replication feature, which creates a read-only copy (always synchronized) of the primary database in an alternative location. Applications can discriminate between reading operations and "everything else", routing the reading operations to the secondary read-only node, keeping the primary just for the core updates. Considered that, at the time of writing, we can have up to 4 copies of a primary database, this can be very useful to distribute the read traffic between replicas, keeping the primary free from the majority (where applicable) of load.

Governing SQL Database

Before letting it run in production, there are few basic actions to be performed onto a SQL Database instance. First, we should define the security boundaries and, more important, we should identify security hot spots. Second, we need to prepare the monitoring activity before the service goes live, otherwise there is a serious risk of loss of control. Third, we should plan every action related to disaster recovery and backup.

Security Options

When a SQL Database has been created, it resides inside the logical and security boundary of the SQL Server (logical) container. Every SQLDB runs inside that container and a single container can contain several DBs.

There is a maximum number of DBs we can put inside a SQL Server (logical) container but, since this number can change over time, think differently. A SQL Server (logical) container, when created, shows a maximum number of DTUs which can be placed inside this. This should be a better indicator of how many DBs (depending on their size) can be placed.

Apart the security features which SQL Database inherits from T-SQL and SQL Server, there are some specific, value-added services of SQL Database itself.

Authentication

When we create a new SQL Database, we must place it into a new or existing SQL Server (logical) container. If a new container is created, we must set the administrative credentials of the entire container. Username and Password specified here will grant a full-control permission set to the entire server and the database contained in it.

So, it is not recommended to use those credentials while connecting to individual DBs. Instead, the best practice is to create specifics users at the database-level (they are called "Contained Users"). This approach makes the database even more portable, since in case of a copy, the copy operation keeps all the database objects (including logins) that otherwise will be lost if defined at the server-level.

```
CREATE USER containedUser WITH PASSWORD = 'myPassword';
```

This method is known as SQL Authentication, which is very similar to the SQL Server counterpart.

However, SQL Database supports also the Azure AD Authentication (Figure 1-19), which binds Azure Active Directory to the SQL Server (logical) instance. To enable this method, we should set first the Active Directory admin on the server blade:

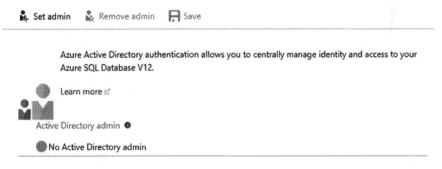

Figure 1-19. *The page where we can setup the Azure Active Directory admin for a given SQL Server (logical) instance.*

This will create a USER in the master DB with "FROM EXTERNAL PROVIDER" option. In fact, we can create additional contained users as follows:

```
CREATE USER <myUser@domain> FROM EXTERNAL PROVIDER;
```

From the client perspective, when we connect to the SQL Database using Azure AD Password authentication, the connection string should be similar as this one below:

```
Data Source; Authentication=Active Directory Password; Initial
Catalog=apress;  UID=user@[domain].onmicrosoft.com; PWD=[password]";
```

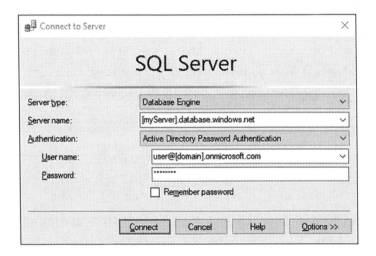

Figure 1-20. *This is how we connect to SQLDB using SSMS and Azure AD Password Authentication*

If we scroll down the Authentication dropdown in the window above (Figure 1-20), we can notice other two options:

- Active Directory Integrated Authentication: another non-interactive authentication method to be used where the client PC is joined to a domain federated with the Azure AD tenant.

- Active Directory Universal Authentication: an interactive, token-based authentication where even complex MFA (Multi-Factor Authentication) workflows are available.

Firewall

SQL Database, through the SQL Server (logical) container is exposed on the public internet with a public DNS name like [myServer].database.windows.net. This means everyone can potentially access the instance to (try to) login into the DB and operate remotely. Thus, it is very important to take a look as soon as possible to the firewall rules (Figure 1-21). By default, no one can access to it, but we should ensure to enable only the required IPs.

Firewall rules and in the IP Range form. This means a rule can be as follows:

RULE NAME	START IP	END IP	
			...
All	0.0.0.0	255.255.255.255	...

Figure 1-21. *The list of server-level firewall rules. The rule above, for example, opens the firewall for every public IP.*

Firewall rules can be set at server-level or at database-level. The order of evaluation of those rules are:

1. First the Database-level rules

2. Then the Server-level rules

Since the rules are only in the form allow (everything is not explicitly allowed is denied by default), this guarantees the server-level rules are broader and win against the database-level ones. This should suggest us to make use of database-level rules first to setup a fine-grained set of access rules.

Database-level firewall rules can be configured only using T-SQL as follows:

```
EXECUTE sp_set_database_firewall_rule N'NWRule','0.0.0.0','1.0.0.0';
```

A summary (Figure 1-22) of the firewall rules can be queried as follows:

- SELECT * FROM sys. firewall_rules - at server-level

- SELECT * FROM sys.database_firewall_rules - at database-level

	id	name	start_ip_address	end_ip_address
1	2	All	0.0.0.0	255.255.255.255
2	1	AllowAllWindowsAzureIps	0.0.0.0	0.0.0.0

Figure 1-22. *This is the result of the sys.firewall_rules query, where the AllowAllWindowsAzureIps rule is a special rule allowing every Microsoft Azure IP range to enabled inter-service communication.*

Encryption

There are two ways (not mutually exclusive) to approach database encryption:

- Encryption at rest: the underlying storage is encrypted.

- Encryption in transit: data from/to the DB travels already encrypted.

Those two methods address the following scenarios:

- Someone has physical access to the storage media where the DB are stored: mitigated with Encryption at rest, the person can obtain the physical media but he/she cannot read it.

- Someone is intercepting the traffic between the client application and the DB: mitigated with Encryption in transit, the person can sniff the traffic but he/she sees only encrypted data.

Transparent Data Encryption

SQL Database offers the TDE (Transparent Data Encryption) to address the first case. A server-generated certificate (rotated automatically and without administrative hassle at least each 90 days) is used to encrypt/decrypt the data.

To enable it on a specific DB, use this query:

```
ALTER DATABASE [myDB] SET ENCRYPTION ON;
```

Every new SQL Database has this option enabled by default. Since we have evidences that the overhead introduced by TDE is minimal, it is recommended to enable it (or leave it enabled) a fortiori if we are subjected to compliance requirement.

Always Encrypted

Always Encrypted is a way to encrypt SQL Database content without ever disclosing the key to SQL Database itself. This approach is the best we can achieve in terms of segregation, since the manager (Azure) cannot read the owner's data.

This approach is more complicated, since SQL Database will deal with encrypted data to be stored, indexed and queried.

Encryption is at column-level, so we can encrypt just a few columns with sensitive data, leaving untouched the rest of the DB. In the screenshot below (Figure 1-23), we are encrypting the CategoryName of the Customer table, specifying Deterministic as the encryption method.

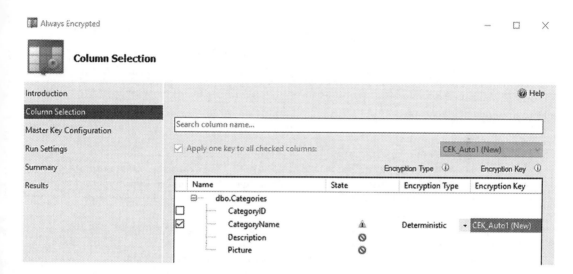

Figure 1-23. *In SSMS, we can right-click the table or the column and select Encrypt Column(s) to start the Wizard process*

Note   Deterministic encryption means that the same source value will generate the same encrypted value. Randomized, instead, will produce different outputs. The first is simpler, but someone can analyze patterns and discover information where data assume a small set of distinct values. The second is less predictable, but prevents SQL Database from performing searching, grouping, indexing and joining. Even with Deterministic encryption there are some missing capabilities, for example the usage of LIKE operator, CASE construct and string concatenation.

In the next step we provide the Encryption Key, which can reside in the Windows Certificate Store of the client computer (during the wizard will be auto-generated) or into Azure Key Vault. In both cases, SQL Database won't know the key content, since it is managed securely. Also, remember that the encryption process is performed of course by the client machine.

After the column has been encrypted, it has been modified as follows:

```
[CategoryName] [nvarchar](15) COLLATE Latin1_General_BIN2 ENCRYPTED WITH
(COLUMN_ENCRYPTION_KEY = [CEK_Auto1], ENCRYPTION_TYPE = Deterministic,
ALGORITHM = 'AEAD_AES_256_CBC_HMAC_SHA_256') NOT NULL
```

From this moment, every client connecting to the Database will see encrypted data (Figure 1-24), except the ones using the special parameter *"column encryption setting=enabled"* in the connection string (and, obviously, having the valid key to decrypt data). Since data types change, application would probably fail if not designed to accommodate those changes gracefully.

	CategoryID	CategoryName	Description
1	1	0x0190032E542220E4C220131E3B0D8FD2159092DB97B671F6...	Soft drinks, coffees, teas, beers, and ales
2	2	0x01FE377E4400B422AD75421FC08A712F8503E2FC1B081D5B...	Sweet and savory sauces, relishes, spreads, and ...
3	3	0x0101EF806BE4B158529ADF14BEF181F8C3479778DBC6AD57...	Desserts, candies, and sweet breads
4	4	0x015AB3407CCAC265AB4DB6A3BC7A99CBCE5AD3E9181D69...	Cheeses
5	5	0x017244C0D091AFC9042B1F1E180588E5275164332FD10B611...	Breads, crackers, pasta, and cereal
6	6	0x01CDBBC7EC9530EFA651EE361C052A11C63FA201DFCF752...	Prepared meats
7	7	0x0102372A930BD229CADDC4169ECA86E8EE71646BC6470D7...	Dried fruit and bean curd
8	8	0x01443F71F0005E7BCD08C06CF6BD64AA5CEF094A6AACE42...	Seaweed and fish

Figure 1-24. *We see the encrypted data into the CategoryName column*

Dynamic Data Masking

If we ever think about the possibility to give access to production database to a developer to investigate a really hard issue in the application/data, we probably run into the even bigger issue of security. Can we grant a (even temporary) access to a specific user, without exposing sensitive data? And, more generally, can we setup users who can fetch the whole data and others who can fetch masked data?

Dynamic Data Masking works by setting up one or more masking rule for each column we would like to mask (Figure 1-25). The rules are simple:

- Administrators and specific users (specified in configuration) will always see unmasked data

- All the other users will see masked data

- For each column we would like to mask, we add a masking rule,
  specifying:

  - The table and the column

  - The masking format

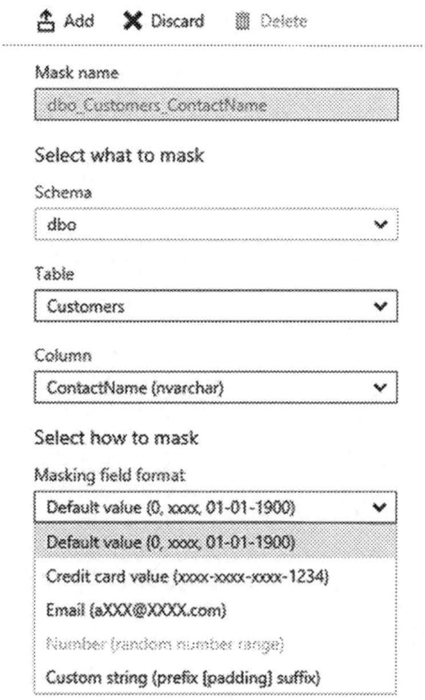

Figure 1-25. *in this example, we apply a Default value (for strings is a sequence of "x")
to the ContactName of the Customers table*

Backup options

Every SQL Database have built-in mechanism which backups the database continuously,
in order to provide the Point-in-time-Restore feature. Depending on the Tier we choose
we can go in the past up to 35 days to restore a copy of the DB in a specific point of time.

The restore process will restore a fully functional online database that can be used
after the restore process is finished. This feature provides us application-level recovery,
letting us recover a DB to copy lost data or to investigate a previous version. In the rare
case we want to switch the recovered DB onto the production DB, we can rename them
through SSMS:

- Rename the production DB "myDB" into something like "myDB_
  old": after that, all connection are lost and your connected systems
  will be down.

- Rename the recovered DB from "myDB_[date]" to "myDB": after that (it takes just few seconds in most cases) existing applications will find again the DB and continue to work.

For whom need to have older backups (after 35 days in the past) Azure provides some other options (Figure 1-26). We can manually export a DB into a BACPAC (by choosing "Export" in the figure below) or we can setup a Long-term backup retention policy.

Figure 1-26. *By clicking Export we setup an Export job, creating a BACPAC of he database at current state*

Note   In the rare case e accidentally delete a DB we want to keep, we can restore it immediately through the Deleted databases blade of the SQL Server (logical) container.

Finally, the Export feature is the common way too to restore locally a database, as the last resort to DR mitigation.

Long-term Retention

Long-term backup retention allows to save backups to a Recovery Services vault to extend the 35 days window of integrated point-in-time backup/restore policy.

We should use long-term as a secondary strategy to backup SQL Database where compliance requirements must be addresses. From the costs perspective, while the integrated backup/restore mechanism is included in the cost of SQL Database, long-term retention is billed through the Recovery Service vault (Figure 1-28), which billing strategy is (at the time of writing) based on storage consumption (Figure 1-27), except some free quota:

Backup Usage

Cloud - LRS	0 B
Cloud - GRS	36.77 GB

Figure 1-27. *This is the tile of the Azure Recovery Services vault blade where we see the GBs consumed by the long-term backup service*

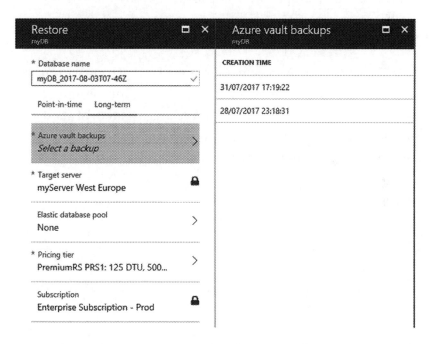

Figure 1-28. *In this image we are restoring the myDB from a Recovery Service vault using one of the recovery points on the right*

Monitoring Options

It's proven that Platform-as-a-Service (managed) services need a fraction of the administrative effort compared to unmanaged services, where everything from the operating system upward needs to be constantly monitored, updated and fixed. However, the residual effort we need to invest on the monitoring area is crucial to have real-time insights on the components we use, especially since managed services are presented as black boxes.

To summarize which the areas we must pay attention to with SQL Database, think about the following:

- Resources monitoring, usage and limits

- Troubleshooting features

- Anomalies/security detection

SQL Database provides most of those value-added features, but it is up to us to enable them and implement proper processes to get the most out of them.

Resources Monitoring, Usage and Limits

One of the most important KPI of consumption is the DTU percentage (Figure 1-29). First, because if 100% is reached, new connections will be probably throttled due to service saturation. Second, because it tells us the usage pattern of our database and it can provide great value to understand the impact from the applications and, consequently, the monitoring/optimization activities to perform.

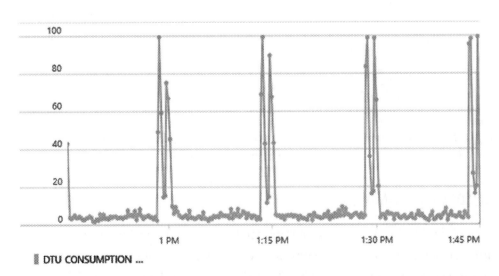

Figure 1-29. *In this figure we can infer there is a recurrent peak in the DB DTU usage, about every 15 minutes. During this short timeframe we notice how the consumed DTU touch the 100% of usage*

The image above tells us the consumption pattern of the last hour for a given Database. In this precise case, we can make some hypothesis:

- During the most of the time, DTUs are about at the 5% of consumption

- If the graph is linear and 5% is without peaks, we could even lower the Performance Level of the DB to a 1/15 tier (if it is a S3-100 DTU, we could even set it to a S0-10DTU.

- However, there are recurrent peaks about every 15 minutes, due to some scheduled/recurrent activities against it from outside (applications, scheduled queries, etc.). Since the usage in those timeframes is very high and completes relatively quickly, it risky to lower the Performance Level because the DB could take more to perform those actions.

- A good option is to investigate which is the application generating those traffic and try to optimize it in order to avoid those burst, to consequently lower the Performance Level with more confidence.

This is just an example, since every DB could have a very different usage pattern.

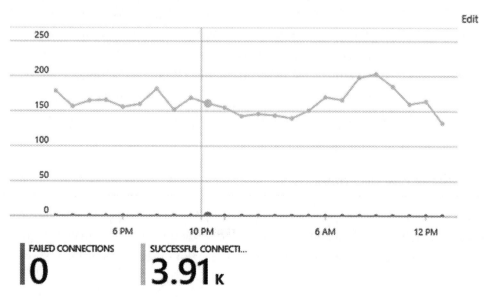

Figure 1-30. *In this other image, we see connections against the DB of the last 24 hours*

In the image above (Figure 1-30), instead, we can have a quick look at the actual state of connections made to the Database. This number is not particular useful itself, since SQL Database has limits on "concurrent" connections. However, we can infer from the line graph there is an average of connections for any given time of about 150-200 connections, that is enough to estimate the Performance Level we should set to avoid throttling.

At the opposite, we see there are no Failed Connections in the last 24 hours, that is good to understand how many times applications were refused to connect.

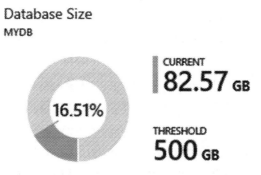

Figure 1-31. *An indicator of the actual storage used and the threshold set for the current DB*

In the image above (Figure 1-31), there is the last of the most important indicators we should monitor. We should expect storage is managed by the platform, preventing us to put effort on administrative task to extend and maintain storage, and that's true. However, there are some hard-limits in SQL Database around storage and, in case those limits are exceeded, DB become unstable and no more writes are allowed.

Of course, in some cases we can Scale Up and provide a greater Performance Level which takes more storage with it. But there are limits too, and it must be constantly monitored.

SQL Database Elastic Pools

An additional layer of attention must be paid with Elastic Pools, since the service type has a cap on maximum DTUs and Storage shared by all the databases inside the pool. Thus, if we place databases inside a pool, we must ensure there enough space and computation power.

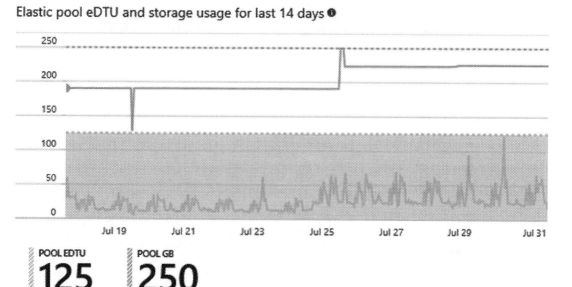

Figure 1-32. *In this image we see a combined view of DTU and Storage consumption for an Elastic Pool*

In the image above (Figure 1-32), we can notice a potential issue. We see, despite DTU consumption is always stable, there is a peak in Storage consumed in the middle of the timeframe. Under those scenario, every DB inside the Pool had certainly stopped to accept writes, with serious consequences on applications and availability.

Even in big applications, the growth rate of standalone DBs is quite predictable. What we need to pay attention to in Elastic Pools, instead, is the fact we can add/remove at runtime a 300GB database in few seconds, filling all the available space of the pool and, consequently, generating serious issues.

Troubleshooting Features

Too many automated alerts can create false alarms but it is important to setup proper automated alerts on every critical resource. An example can be exactly the situation above, where the Storage used of an Elastic Pool reaches the maximum level: we definitely don't want to be notified by the users, instead we would like to proactively take the actions to avoid failures and availability gaps.

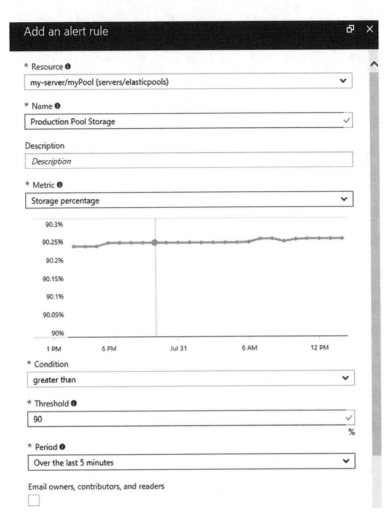

Figure 1-33. *In this image we setup an Alert rule for the Elastic Pool. In case the pool Storage used percentage goes over 90%, an alert is activated and an email is sent to specified emails*

The general rule of thumb is that almost every metric collected by Azure can be used to setup an Alert on it (Figure 1-33). Each service comes with its own metrics (in case of SQL Database we have DTUs, Storage, Connections, etc) and those metrics can be attached to alerts. Therefore, we should setup proper alerts for every critical building block of our infrastructure.

Dynamic Management Views

The metrics exposed in the portal are available directly on the SQL Database instance, through plain T-SQL queries. This approach is recommended when we need to build custom tools and/or catch KPIs without passing from the Azure Portal. An example is the "sys.dm_db_resource_stats" view, as follows:

```
SELECT TOP (10) [end_time]
      ,[avg_cpu_percent]
      ,[avg_data_io_percent]
      ,[avg_log_write_percent]
      ,[avg_memory_usage_percent]
      ,[xtp_storage_percent]
      ,[max_worker_percent]
      ,[max_session_percent]
      ,[dtu_limit]
      ,[avg_login_rate_percent]
  FROM [sys].[dm_db_resource_stats]
```

Which produces the last 10 statistics aggregates (they are ordered using the sampling date, descending) below:

end_time	avg_cpu_percent	avg_data_io_percent	avg_log_write_percent	avg_memory_usage_percent	xtp_storage_percent	max_worker_percent	max_session_percent	dtu_limit	avg_login_rate_percent
2017-07-31 12:48:35.067	3.63	0.14	0.04	58.64	0.00	1.00	0.11	125	NULL
2017-07-31 12:48:20.033	3.89	0.33	0.09	58.57	0.00	1.50	0.11	125	NULL
2017-07-31 12:48:05.003	4.10	0.08	0.11	58.41	0.00	1.50	0.11	125	NULL
2017-07-31 12:47:49.987	4.68	0.10	0.16	58.35	0.00	1.00	0.12	125	NULL
2017-07-31 12:47:34.940	6.86	0.61	0.12	58.25	0.00	1.50	0.11	125	NULL
2017-07-31 12:47:19.907	6.82	0.47	0.14	57.83	0.00	1.50	0.10	125	NULL
2017-07-31 12:47:04.880	5.16	0.14	0.12	57.63	0.00	1.00	0.10	125	NULL
2017-07-31 12:46:49.860	7.33	0.35	0.22	57.53	0.00	1.50	0.10	125	NULL
2017-07-31 12:46:34.810	3.16	0.21	0.06	57.17	0.00	1.00	0.09	125	NULL
2017-07-31 12:46:19.797	7.24	0.07	0.15	57.06	0.00	1.50	0.09	125	NULL

Another useful DMV is about sessions, where knowing WHO is connecting to the Database is a valuable information to troubleshoot problematic queries:

```
SELECT TOP 10 * FROM [sys].[dm_exec_sessions]
```

This view produces the following output (just some columns):

session_id	host_name	program_name	login_name	cpu_time	memory_usage
58	RD000D3A12C460	Application1	app1User	0	6
104	RD000D3A12C460	Application1	app1User	0	6
105	RD000D3A12C460	Application2	app2User	0	6
107	RD0003FF71C768	Application2	app2User	0	6
113	RD000D3A12C460	Application2	app2User	0	6
114	RD000D3A12B52E	ExternalApp	extUser	32	7
115	DESKTOP-LOCAL	SSMS - Query	adminUser	0	3
117	DESKTOP-LOCAL	SSMS - Query	adminUser	0	3
119	RD000D3A12C460	ExternalApp	extUser	0	6
124	RD000D3A12C460	ExternalApp	extUser	0	6

This view is incredibly interesting from the troubleshooting perspective. We see at least:

- The Remote Machine name: 3 unique Azure-hosted machines plus the local DESKTOP machine

- The Application Name: it is strongly recommended to pass the application name in the connection string while connecting to SQL Database, in order to propagate the info here

- The Login Name: useful to know which identities are connecting to the DB

There are a lot of DMVs in SQL Database and they enable advanced monitoring scenarios. SQL Server experts can already be familiar with some of those views and it is an excessive advanced topic to be covered in this book.

Query Performance Insight

Recently in SQL Server was added the Query Store features, that is a sort of flight data recorder of every query passing through the Database. This feature is now enabled by default as mentioned here (https://docs.microsoft.com/en-us/azure/sql-database/sql-database-operate-query-store) and can be enabled on existing databases through the following query:

```
ALTER DATABASE [myDB] SET QUERY_STORE = ON;
```

For whom already has query store enabled by default and they want to know the actual parameters of it, we can right-click the database in SSMS and select Properties:

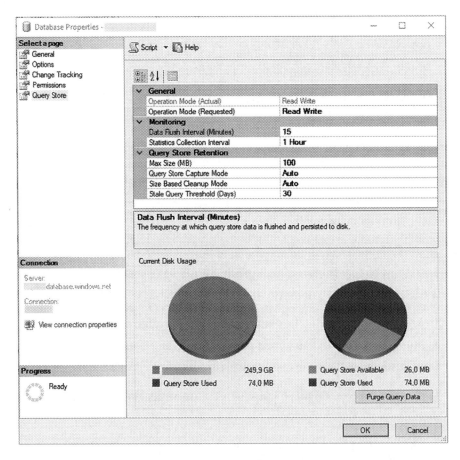

Figure 1-34. *This options window let us configure Query Store parameters*

In the figure above (Figure 1-34) we can fine tune the Query Store service, specifying retention and collection options. This can focus the big picture of Query Store (Figure 1-35) before using it through SSMS or Query Performance Insight.

Note   under certain circumstances, Query Store stops to collect data if the space is full. We can notice this state from the portal. By using the Query Store options we can either change limits or, through T-SQL, clearing the current data.

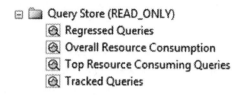

Figure 1-35. *The Query Store node in SQL Server Management Studio*

Query Performance Insight is an online tool to catch the most out of Query Store. It highlights the most consuming queries and provides relevant information to identify them to proceed with optimization:

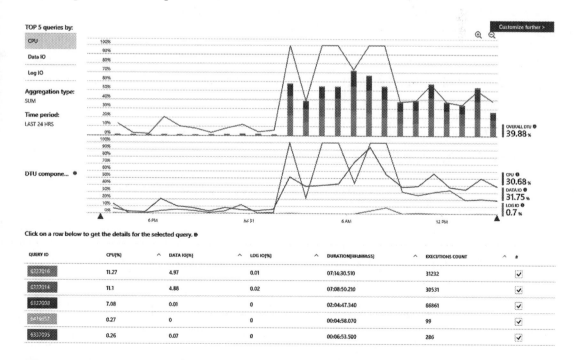

Figure 1-36. *Query Performance Insight showing top 5 consuming queries*

In the figure above (Figure 1-36), we can drill-down in the first row to see which is the query that consumes more. Once identified the query text, we can go upward to the applications and perform further optimization.

Anomalies/Security Detection

As part of every monitoring/management tasks, we should put in place some techniques to prevent security issues or, in case they verify, some logging to inspect and troubleshoot. SQL Database integrates an Auditing feature that collect every event coming into the SQLDB instance and ships it to a remote Storage Account for further analysis.

This feature is useful to the users to investigate problems, to re-build a complex workflow and to have a complete and detailed log of all the operations passing through the database. However, it is useful for Azure too, since Azure itself uses Auditing (if the Threat Detection feature is enabled) to perform real-time proactive detection of potential threats occurring on the DB instance (for example a brute force attack).

Database Auditing

Database Auditing, as mentioned above, is a feature that collects Extended Events occurring on SQL Database for further analysis.

For a reference of what an extended event is and how they are implemented in SQL Database, compared to SQL Server, follow these links:

```
https://docs.microsoft.com/en-us/sql/relational-databases/
extended-events/extended-events
```

```
https://docs.microsoft.com/en-us/azure/sql-database/sql-
database-xevent-db-diff-from-svr
```

After enabling the feature, SQL Database begins to collect .XEL files into the blob storage account specified using this pattern:

```
https://[account].blob.core.windows.net/sqldbauditlogs/[server]/[db]/
SqlDbAuditing_ServerAudit/YYYY-MM-DD/hh_mm_ss_XXX_YYYY.xel
```

XEL files archived with Auditing can be downloaded from the Blob Storage and then parsed with SSMS, with the following experience:

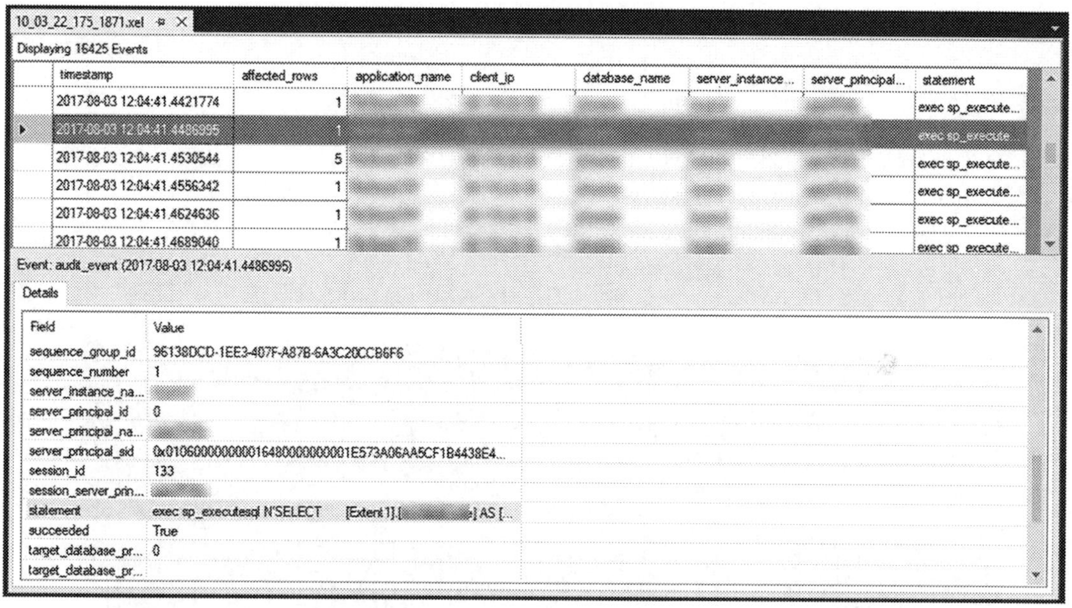

Figure 1-37. *This is how we can read auditing data form inside SSMS*

In the figure above (Figure 1-37) we can have a look of the experience of reading auditing data from within SSMS.

Please note we also have the complete statement executed against SQL Database, comprehensive of sensitive data. Thus, with auditing, keep in mind to protect adequately the Storage Account where the auditing is shipped, since it will contain a huge, despite it is unaggregated, of sensitive data.

Auditing can occur at server-level or at database-level. In the first case, every DB in the SQL Server (logical) instance will inherit the setting and will audit to storage. In the latter, we can fine tune this setting for a single DB.

Threat Detection

With a simple ON/OFF toggle, we can tell Azure to use our auditing data to perform intelligent analysis and detection of issues (Figure 1-38), like:

- SQL Injections

- Brute force attacks

- Unusual outbound data flow

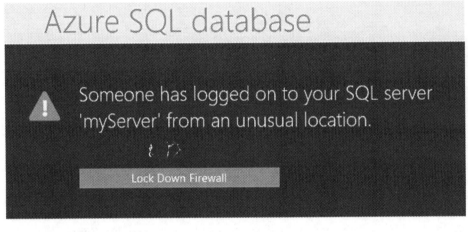

Figure 1-38. *This is a sample email that has been sent from the Threat Detection service*

MySQL and PostgreSQL

The concept behind SQL Database is powerful: use a SQL Server-like Database without any effort to administer its underlying infrastructure and with a lot of value-added services to increase productivity and competition.

In the last years, if someone needed another RDBMS, like MySQL, the only choices were:

- IaaS: building your own Virtual Machine and install/configure/manage MySQL for its entire lifecycle

- Marketplace: buying an existing third-party service offering MySQL as managed service, regardless its underlying infrastructure.

To be clear, those choices are still valid and good, but Microsoft released (now in preview) an Azure Database Service for MySQL and for PostgreSQL, offering a valid alternative to the previous options.

MySQL

Since the vision around Database Services is to provide, regardless the underlying provider, a foundation or services and features in similar, we can expect from MySQL the same high-level features we have with SQL Database. In theory, this is true, but the service is still in preview and (at the time of writing) has limited features.

By the way, a good approach can be to highlight some similarities:

- We create a server to contain one or more database

- Server has firewall rules and encrypted security

- Only a portion or the entire MySQL engine is available, like in SQL Database there are some limitations too. In MySQL, only the InnoDB engine is supported on two versions (5.6.35 and 5.7.17, Community Edition)

- Upgrades (minor patching) is managed by the platform

- There are pricing tiers based on the performance delivered and the storage allocated

- There is the point-in-time restore feature

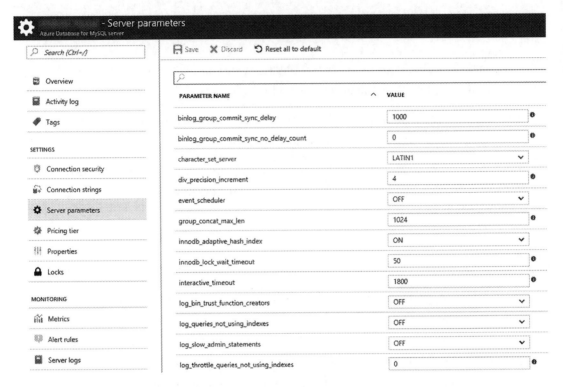

Figure 1-39. *This blade provides the configuration or server-level parameters on the Azure Database Service for MySQL*

And some differences:

- The server is not logical but it hides a real underlying dedicated resource, making it a billable resource itself. In case of MySQL, in fact, pricing tiers are per server and not per database.

- We can explicitly exclude SSL endpoint running on a dedicated port

- The concept of DTU here is called CU (Compute Units)

- The backup/restore operates at server-level

- We can set the MySQL server parameters through the Portal (Figure 1-39)

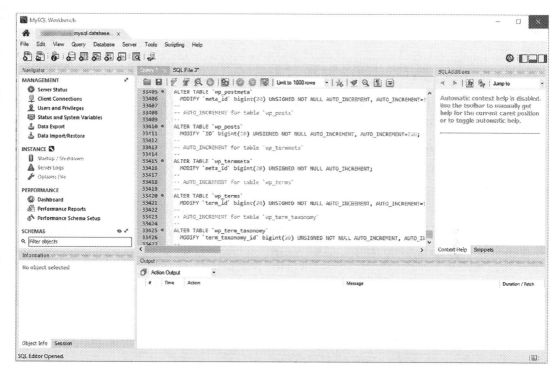

Figure 1-40. *This is MySQL Workbench, one of the most relevant administration tool for MySQL in the market*

In the figure above (Figure 1-40), we see MySQL Workbench connecting to the service. MySQL Workbench is a powerful tool, useful to administer the MySQL instance and to perform various tasks as the Import/Export feature.

PostgreSQL

Azure Database for PostgreSQL service has been built in the same way as MySQL one. Compared to it, we can experiment the same features, the support of two versions on PostgreSQL engine, firewall and SSL support and the same pricing structure.

Summary

In this chapter we learned how to approach SQL Database, the most advanced Database-as-a-Service of the Azure offering and one of the most advanced in the entire Cloud Ecosystem. We learned how to setup a good design process, an evolving maintenance plan and a strategy to monitor it continuously and efficiently. We also learned how to use SQL Database efficiently and how to get the most out of it with its valuable features. We focused on those features useful for a decision maker, as well as for an architect, to plan a project and know in advance the possible approaches to the service.

In the next chapter, we see how to deal with unmanaged RDBMS, with specific support to SQL Server in VMs (IaaS) and how to extend the on-premise topology with the appropriate building block offered by Azure.

## CHAPTER 2

Working with SQL Server on Hybrid Cloud and Azure IaaS

Hybrid Cloud workloads are, without a doubt, among the priorities of many CIOs and CTOs these days. as they can be used in addressing business needs and modernizing IT infrastructures which are key in bringing valuable solutions, often with moderate effort. Data workloads are not exempt from this and SQL Server, the flagship database server of Microsoft, is one the best expressions of the evolution of a server platform from an on-premise only suite to a full-featured and cloud enabled one. SQL Server 2017, recently released in the market, will be used in this chapter to describe both hybrid cloud features and the possibilities to run it in a pure IaaS scenario with Azure. The main topics covered here are the following:

- An introduction to SQL Server 2017, and in particular its ability to run on Linux.

- The features available for hybrid cloud, including backups and high availability options.

- How to migrate a database to Azure IaaS.

- How to run a SQL Server instance on Azure IaaS.

© Francesco Diaz, Roberto Freato 2018
F. Diaz and R. Freato, *Cloud Data Design, Orchestration, and Management Using Microsoft Azure*,
https://doi.org/10.1007/978-1-4842-3615-4_2

Database Server Execution Options On Azure

There are different possibilities to install a relational database server on Azure Virtual Machines. You could:

1. Use the Azure Marketplace to deploy an Azure Virtual Machine image that already contains the database server or deploy a solution template from the Azure Marketplace.

2. Deploy an Azure Virtual Machine with the operating system only, Windows or Linux, and setup the database server yourself, after the deployment.

3. Upload your own database server image to Azure, reusing an on-premises installation.

When you decide to use option 1, you can either select a standalone virtual machine, or use a solution template to deploy a complete configuration of SQL Server. There are many solutions templates already available in the marketplace, and they might be related to a high availability configuration of SQL Server, a setup that includes a Sharepoint farm, etc. Both Microsoft and partners provide several options that implement the Azure Resource Manager (ARM) model for the deployment.

Choosing a database server from the marketplace also has licensing implications. You could use the pay-per-use model and pay SQL Server per-minute, or you could leverage license mobility advantages and bring your own license (BYOL) to the cloud. If you choose BYOL, you are requested to provide to Microsoft the License Mobility Verification form with information of your licenses. In the pay-per-use model, you could also receive a separate bill if the database server you are using is not included. This could happen for example if you deploy a virtual machine with an Oracle database already installed. +

> **Note**   To get additional information on licensing models, we recommend the following links: **Bring your own license** - http://d36cz9buwru1tt.cloudfront.net/ License_Mobility_Customer_Verification_Guide.pdf; **SQL Server licensing on Azure VMs FAQ** - https://azure.microsoft.com/en-us/ pricing/licensing-faq/; **License Mobility Verification Form** - http://www.microsoftvolumelicensing.com/DocumentSearch.aspx? Mode=2&Keyword=License%20verification; **SQL Server 2017 Licensing Guide** - https://download.microsoft.com/download/7/8/C/78CDF005- 97C1-4129-926B-CE4A6FE92CF5/SQL_Server_2017_Licensing_guide.pdf

As you probably noticed, choosing the right option to install a database server on Azure is an important aspect to consider, not only for the technical part, but also for cost estimations. If you are architecting a solution for a customer that includes database workloads, preparing a proper business case for the costs is a very important aspect to consider. Business case preparation of costs on Azure are not the focus of this book, but we recommend that you explore this part in detail in order to better support your customers and partners.

> **Note**   To get more information on Microsoft Azure licensing model, visit: **Azure Pricing** - https://azure.microsoft.com/en-us/pricing/; **Azure Pricing FAQ** - https://azure.microsoft.com/en-us/pricing/faq/

A Quick Overview of SQL Server 2017

As SQL Server 2017 was released while we were writing this book and we utilized it in some of the examples, we thought it was useful to add a very small section to mention some of the most relevant features available.

SQL Server 2017 was released in October 2017, and it arrived not more than one year after the release of SQL Server 2016; this means that you will find many of the features of SQL 2016 in SQL 2017 too, with minor enhancements. This does not mean that SQL 2017 is a minor release. On the contrary there, are some huge additions that represent a substantial change for Microsoft on the direction it is taking with its top product in the database market. The most relevant one is the possibility to run SQL 2017 on a Linux server or a Docker container. Many companies that use Linux as their main server platform can now benefit from this additional option when they need to add a database server platform to a project.

Note 1   Supported versions of Linux are RedHat Enterprise Linux 7.3 or 7.4, SuSE Enterprise Linux v12 SP2 and Ubuntu 16.04LTS. Supported versions of Docker are 1.8+ on Windows, Linux or Mac

Note 2   Not all features and services of SQL Server are available on Linux. Visit this page to see the full list: `https://docs.microsoft.com/en-us/sql/linux/sql-server-linux-release-notes`

SQL Server comes in five different editions:

- **Express**. Available for free, good for entry level workloads that don't require advanced features or more than 10 GB database space.

- **Web**. A basic version, specifically designed for the Service Providers market and to support web applications workloads.

- **Standard**. Fully featured in terms of developer features as, starting from SQL Server 2016 SP1, almost all the advanced features for developers have been included in SQL Server Standard Edition. It misses the advanced features for mission critical scenarios, but it is easy to upgrade to Enterprise version without reinstalling it.

- **Enterprise**. All the features available in Standard Edition, plus enhanced scalability, security, high availability, and advanced analytics capabilities.

- **Developer**. A free edition of SQL Server, for dev/test scenarios, that contains the same features available in the Enterprise Edition.

Note   The following link has the detailed matrix of features available in each edition of SQL Server: `https://docs.microsoft.com/en-us/sql/sql-server/editions-and-components-of-sql-server-2017`

Installation of SQL Server 2017 on Linux and Docker

To run SQL Server on Linux, Microsoft implemented what is called the SQL Server Platform Abstraction Layer (SQLPAL). Having been on the market for decades, SQL Server is strongly integrated with Windows so porting all the codebase to another platform would have been many years of work and at the same time, Microsoft wanted to guarantee excellent performances across all the OS platforms. Thus, Microsoft decided to work on an existing project of Microsoft Research called Drawbridge, to leverage its features focused on providing an abstraction layer between the operating system and the applications, and merge them with the existing SQL Server Operating System (SQLOS). That's how SQLPAL has born and that is what it does: provides an abstraction layer to execute SQL Server with the same functionalities and performances across different operating systems, such as Windows and Linux. At the time of writing, SQL Server database engine, SQL Server Integration Services, and SQL Server Agent are able to run on Linux, but we expect to see more to come in the future.

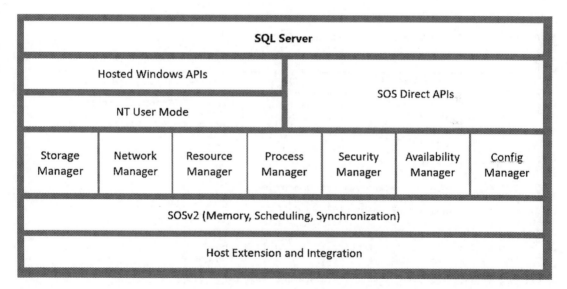

Figure 2-1. *The SQLPAL high level architecture. When SQL Server runs on Linux, a small part of Windows libraries run on Linux.* `https://blogs.technet.microsoft.com/dataplatforminsider/2016/12/16/sql-server-on-linux-how-introduction/`

Note   To get some additional details on SQLPAL read this article on Microsoft Technet: `https://blogs.technet.microsoft.com/dataplatform insider/2016/12/16/sql-server-on-linux-how-introduction/`

SQL Server on Linux

Installing SQL Server on Linux is different than on Windows, and is actually easier as it is based on a command-line utility that requires very few user inputs for the first configuration. Just to give you an idea, below you will find the commands you need to download the 173MB package and to run the setup of SQL Server and the **sqlcmd** tool on an Ubuntu Server.

```
wget -qO- https://packages.microsoft.com/keys/microsoft.asc | sudo apt-key
add -
sudo add-apt-repository "$(wget -qO- https://packages.microsoft.com/config/
ubuntu/16.04/mssql-server-2017.list)"
sudo apt-get update
sudo apt-get install -y mssql-server
sudo /opt/mssql/bin/mssql-conf setup
sudo apt-get update
sudo apt-get install -y mssql-tools unixodbc-dev
```

```
francescodiaz@sqlonlinux:~$ systemctl status mssql-server
● mssql-server.service - Microsoft SQL Server Database Engine
   Loaded: loaded (/lib/systemd/system/mssql-server.service; enabled; vendor pre
   Active: active (running) since Thu 2018-01-25 23:07:07 UTC; 12s ago
     Docs: https://docs.microsoft.com/en-us/sql/linux
 Main PID: 9066 (sqlservr)
    Tasks: 117
   Memory: 479.3M
      CPU: 5.895s
   CGroup: /system.slice/mssql-server.service
           ├─9066 /opt/mssql/bin/sqlservr
           └─9098 /opt/mssql/bin/sqlservr

Jan 25 23:07:13 sqlonlinux sqlservr[9066]: [78B blob data]
Jan 25 23:07:13 sqlonlinux sqlservr[9066]: [84B blob data]
Jan 25 23:07:13 sqlonlinux sqlservr[9066]: [122B blob data]
Jan 25 23:07:13 sqlonlinux sqlservr[9066]: [145B blob data]
Jan 25 23:07:14 sqlonlinux sqlservr[9066]: [66B blob data]
Jan 25 23:07:14 sqlonlinux sqlservr[9066]: [75B blob data]
Jan 25 23:07:14 sqlonlinux sqlservr[9066]: [96B blob data]
Jan 25 23:07:14 sqlonlinux sqlservr[9066]: [100B blob data]
Jan 25 23:07:14 sqlonlinux sqlservr[9066]: [124B blob data]
Jan 25 23:07:14 sqlonlinux sqlservr[9066]: [71B blob data]
lines 1-22/22 (END)
```

Figure 2-2. *SQL Server running on an Ubuntu Server*

SQL Server on a Docker container

Containers use a virtualization concept like virtual machines. The difference is that, with containers, you virtualize the operating system while with Virtual Machines you virtualize the hardware. Microsoft certifies SQL Server 2017 for Docker, the company that leads the market in the containerization platforms. To learn more about Docker, visit: https://www.docker.com/get-docker#/overview

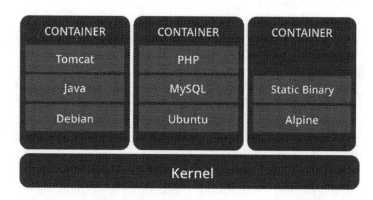

Figure 2-3. *Containers running on Docker, where the OS kernel is virtualized*

Docker provides a repository of SQL Server 2017 ready-to-use container images, both for Windows and Linux, in the Docker Hub, at the following links: Windows (https://hub.docker.com/r/microsoft/mssql-server-windows-express/) and Linux (https://hub.docker.com/r/microsoft/mssql-server-linux/)

PUBLIC REPOSITORY

microsoft/mssql-server-linux ☆

Last pushed: a month ago

Repo Info   Tags

Tag Name	Compressed Size	Last Updated
latest	451 MB	a month ago
2017-latest	451 MB	a month ago
2017-CU2	451 MB	a month ago
2017-CU1	438 MB	2 months ago
2017-GA	479 MB	3 months ago

Figure 2-4. *The Docker Hub repository of Linux container images*

Getting the SQL 2017 container image up and running is a very simple activity:

1. **Download and install Docker on your machine, if you don't have it already, from here:** `https://www.docker.com/get-docker`

2. **Pull** the container image: **`docker pull microsoft/ mssql-server-linux:2017-CU2`** downloads SQL 2017 cumulative update 2 from the Docker Hub. If you want to download the latest version, use the -**latest** tag

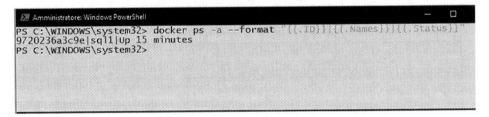

3. **Run** the container image **`docker run -e "ACCEPT_EULA=Y" -e "MSSQL_SA_PASSWORD=P4ssw0rd!" -p 1401:1433 --name sql1 -d microsoft/mssql-server-linux:2017-CU2`**

4. **View** your container using command **`docker ps -a`**

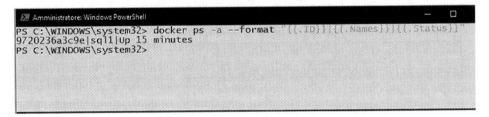

5. **Connect** to SQL Server instance using **sqlcmd** tool, which is also available on Linux. To connect to sqlcmd, you need to first enter bash inside the container using the command **`docker exec -it sql1 "bash"`** . Once inside the container, you can connect using sqlcmd and interact with the SQL instance using T-SQL:

   a. /opt/mssql-tools/bin/sqlcmd -S localhost -U SA -P 'P4ssw0rd!'

   b. SELECT @@version

> **Note**   In our example we are using Powershell in the client to execute commands. Commands on bash are more or less the same. To get additional information read this Microsoft document online: `https://docs.microsoft.com/en-gb/sql/linux/quickstart-install-connect-docker` - it contains also useful information on how to configure Docker minimum requirements in terms of CPU and RAM to execute SQL Server on Docker

SQL Server Operations Studio

For those that are used to working with SQL Server, SQL Server Management Studio (SSMS) is the tool that every DBA knows and loves very much. SSMS is only available on Windows today, therefore if you need to work with an installation on Linux you could use either the command-line tools or use SSMS installed on a Windows machine connected to the Linux server. Microsoft started the development of SQL Server Operation Studio (SSOS), a cross-platform tool based on the code of Visual Studio Code that allows you to work with SQL Server using a Mac or a Linux machine. SSOS is in preview at the time of writing and it contains basic but useful features. It allows you to connect to the database, use the query editor, and perform some administration tasks like backups. One of the features that we find useful is the T-SQL intellisense, which helps a lot of database developers and administrators.

> **Note**   You could download SQL Operations Studio here: `https://docs.microsoft.com/en-us/sql/sql-operations-studio/download`

You can also use it to connect to the docker container that we have just created. You just need to check the IP address (**ipconfig** or **ifconfig**, depending on the platform) assigned to the docker container and use port 1401 in the Advanced of the connect mask, that we mapped with the SQL port 1433 when we started the image.

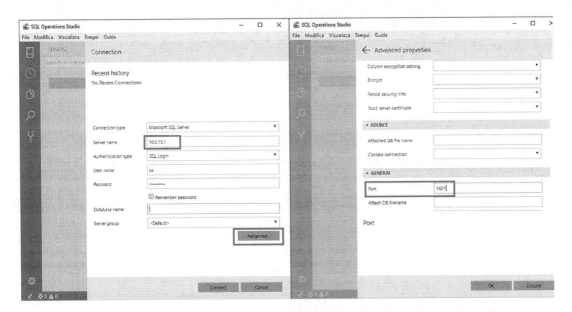

Figure 2-5. *Connect to the docker container using SQL Operations Studio*

Interesting features to highlight are:

- T-SQL intellisense capabilities and code snippets

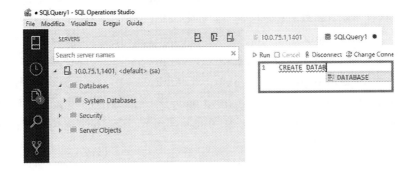

- Backup options that can recognize if the server is installed on Linux, and use file system folders accordingly

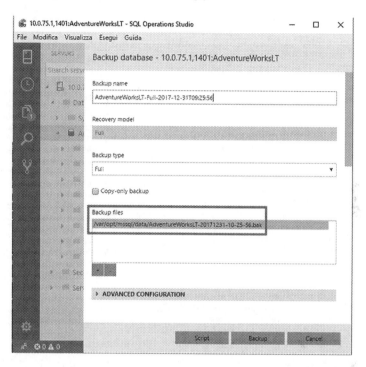

- Enable database dashboard views using the user settings section, editable using JSON. A few widgets are available out of the box, e.g. the table space widget shown in the image below, plus you could add custom widgets for custom insights also. More information is available here: https://docs.microsoft.com/en-us/sql/sql-operations-studio/tutorial-build-custom-insight-sql-server

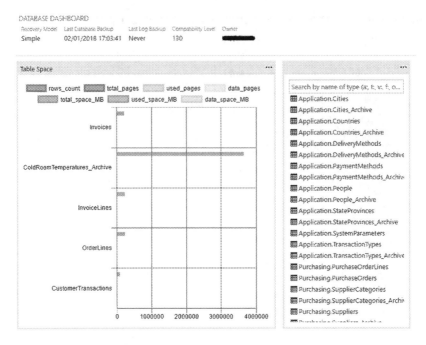

Figure 2-6. *Adding the table space widget to SQL Operations Studio*

Note   We recommend exploring two additional features available in SQL Server 2017. First one is Graph Database, perfect to model hierarchical data or many-to-many relationship. It is available on both SQL Server and Azure SQL Database, and you can get started here: `https://docs.microsoft.com/en-us/sql/relational-databases/graphs/sql-graph-overview`; Second one is SQL Server Machine Learning Services, that allows use of R and Python to develop machine learning scripts, integrated with SQL Server database engine. They are an evolution of SQL Server R Services introduced in SQL Server 2016 and based on R language only on the first release.

Hybrid Cloud Features

In this section of the chapter we will describe some of the features available in SQL Server that allow you to leverage hybrid cloud functionalities with Microsoft Azure. In particular, we will focus on backup scenarios that you will very likely find during your architectural design activities. We will also cover the stretched database feature, which is very interesting to consider as it adds remote positioning of data, managed from a database server on-premises. Later in the chapter, in another section, we will also describe high availability options available in SQL Server that can leverage Microsoft Azure.

Azure Storage

To understand how SQL Server backup to Azure works, we need to dedicate some time to become familiar with Azure Storage and how it works, as it is the layer available on Azure to store data and SQL Server backup features uses it extensively, both from on-premises virtual machines and Azure Virtual Machines.

First thing you need to create is an Azure Storage account that is the endpoint used from the applications to store data and from virtual machines to store operating system and data disks. The connection to Azure storage is done by creating an endpoint; the endpoint name must be unique across all storage accounts on Azure, as it is represented by an FQDN. You can also decide if the Azure storage needs to be exposed on the web, allowing all IPs or the IPs that you prefer, or connected to one or more Azure Virtual Networks of your choice, to remain private. Both options can work together at the same time.

Storage Account Types

In Azure, you could have two types of storage accounts:

1. **General-purpose Storage Accounts**. Creating a general-purpose storage account gives you the ability to use different storage services, such as:

   a. **Tables**. A NoSQL key-value store. In chapter 4 we will go into detail on this service.

   b. **Queues**. A service dedicated to store a large amount of messages, accessible from applications, using a decoupled approach.

    c.   **Files**. A service that allows you to create file shares in the cloud, as a service, without the need to manage it using a file server service installed on a Virtual Machine or a cluster.

    d.   **Blobs**. A service to store unstructured object data. In this chapter we will focus on Blobs only as they are required by SQL Server in Azure Virtual Machines and SQL Server backup features for cloud. Blob object types can be **block** blobs, **append** blobs, and **page** blobs. We will describe them in a minute.

2.   A general-purpose storage account can have two different levels of performance:

    a.   **Standard**. The standard storage can be used by all storage services, based on magnetic disks.

    b.   **Premium**. Designed for high performance and low latency workloads. Premium storage is currently available only for storing operating system disks and data disks of Azure Virtual Machines. They are based on solid state disks.

3.   **Blob Storage Accounts**. Blob storage accounts are a specialized version of storage accounts optimized to store block blobs and append blobs. If you don't need to use page blobs, you should evaluate Blob Storage Accounts as an option for your solution.

In this section, when we talk about General-purpose Storage Accounts, we refer to General-purpose Storage Accounts v2 that include storage tiering possibilities, previously not available in General-purpose Storage Accounts v1, and only available on Blob Storage Accounts. If you have a v1 version of your storage account, you can easily migrate it to v2 using the option available in the Azure Portal.

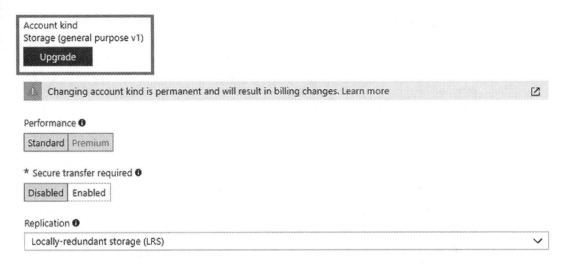

Figure 2-7. *Upgrade option from v1 general-purpose storage accounts to v2*

Storage Access Tiers

Storage tiering helps describe how frequently you will access data in the storage account, with an **access tier** attribute that sets the performances and the accessibility of the storage:

- **Hot** access option indicates that data are frequently accessed.

- **Cool** access option is for data that are less frequently accessed, and stored for at least 30 days.

- **Archive** access option is for rarely accessed data, stored for at least 180 days. This access option is only available at blob access level and not at storage access level. Blob files set to archive are offline, and to read data you need to change the tier to cool or hot again. This process, called rehydration, may take up to 15 hours to complete. Archive tier is very useful for long-term backup and archive scenarios.

Storage Replication

Replication of data is one of the most important aspects to consider when designing a solution. Azure offers out of the box several replication possibilities for data redundancy:

1. **Locally redundant storage (LRS):** This is the basic option available. It provides replicas of data across the sub region of your choice, during storage account creation. If you create the account in the West Europe region, as an example, the replicas of your data will stay there. It is a very good redundancy option, although your data are exposed to sub region failures of Azure. To overcome this limitation, you could either choose another replication option, or, in case this is not applicable, you could add your own replication methodology to the solution. For example, Azure Premium Storage only allows LRS replication, therefore if you want to protect your Azure Virtual Machines disks from sub region failures, you should implement additional services, such as Azure Backup, to have a backup of your data replicated to another region.

2. **Zone-redundant storage (ZRS):** in preview at the time of writing for General-purpose storage account v2; designed to replicate synchronously across multiple availability zones, supporting durability of >= 12 9's. Azure availability zones, in preview too, protect from failures at datacenter level inside an Azure region. Each region that supports this feature has at least three availability zones, with dedicated physical resources such as power source, cooling systems, etc.

3. **Geo-redundant storage (GRS):** this option is very useful to replicate data to a paired Azure region, hundreds of kilometers away from the primary location, asynchronously. The paired region will also have its own local replicas of data, making GRS the right choice to have the highest level of durability of geo-replicated data. Azure regions are geographical areas where one or more datacenters are present. Each region is paired with another region within a same geography, and this is a by-design behavior. For example, Europe geography has North Europe region and West Europe region, and they are paired together. To get additional information on paired region, read this Microsoft document: `https://docs.microsoft.com/en-us/azure/best-practices-availability-paired-regions`

4. **Read-access geo-redundant storage (RA-GRS)**: same as GRS,
   with the addition of read-only capabilities at destination for your
   applications, adding the -**secondary** suffix to the storage account
   name. Storage account `[accountname].blob.core.windows.net` at
   source has a secondary endpoint `[accountname]-secondary.blob.`
   `core.windows.net` at destination, therefore your application could
   read data from this endpoint also. Being an asynchronous copy, not
   all data may be 100% aligned between source and destination.

Storage Account Creation

Most of the options described above to configure Azure Storage accounts are available in
the Azure Portal directly.

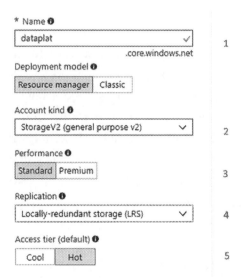

Figure 2-8. *The storage account creation option available in the Azure Portal*

The picture 3-x above contains most of the options that we have discussed, and in
particular:

1. **Name** of the storage account. As you can see from the green tick
   in the image, the portal performs a check to see if the name you
   have chosen is unique across all the Azure accounts that Microsoft
   Azure manages. The `.core.windows.net` suffix will be added
   automatically to the FQDN, after creation.

2. **Account kind**. General-purpose, v1 or v2, or Blob

3. **Performance**. Standard or Premium. Premium storage is only available with General-purpose v1 or v2 storage.

4. **Replication**. Redundancy options. Premium storage only allows Locally-redundant storage (LRS).

5. **Access tier**. Cool and Hot options are available at storage account level, while Archive options are at blob object level.

Blob Objects

In this chapter, we will focus on Blob storage only, both with General-purpose storage and Blob storage accounts. Blob storage, at high level, is organized with the following components:

- Storage Account. It is the endpoint to access data, with HTTP or HTTPS, in public or private mode. Public mode means that your endpoint will be exposed on the internet, therefore each application with need the required access keys or shared access signatures to access it. Private mode means that your applications must reside within an Azure Virtual Network that has been authorized to access the storage account. The application will still need to have the required access keys or shared access signature to access data. Default is set to Public mode.

- Container. A way to group blobs together, like an operating system using folders to group files. A blob needs to reside inside a container, which can have different level of access. By default, a container is created as **Private**, which means that a 512-bit storage access key is required to access blobs inside the container. You could also set the access level to **Blob**, and in that case an anonymous read access is allowed to blob files only. Setting the access level to **Container**, the read-only anonymous access is set at container level.

- Blob. Any type of file. You can have block blobs, append blobs, and page blobs.

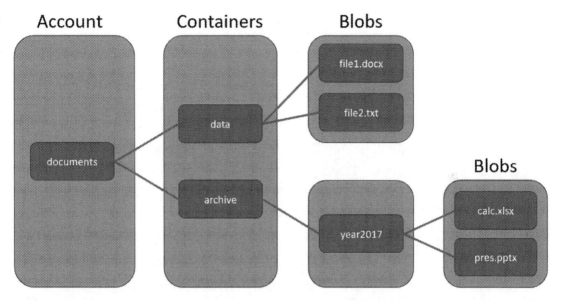

Figure 2-9. *Azure blob account logical structure. In this case, endpoints could be* http://documents.blob.core.windows.net/data/file2.txt, https://documents.blob.core.windows.net/archive/year2017/calc.xlsx

In Azure, you can have Block blobs, Append blobs, and Page blobs:

- **Block blobs**. Ideal to store binary files and text files. You can have up to 50,000 blocks of 100MB each, a total size of 4.75TB per block blob file.

- **Append blobs**. Similar to block blobs, but for append only operations. You can have up to 50,000 blocks of 4MB each, a total size of 195GB per append blob file.

- **Page blobs**. For read/write operations, such as disks of Azure Virtual Machines. Each page blob can have a maximum size of 8TB.

Disks and Managed Disks

So far we have learned that, for our blob files, we can use Standard storage based on HDD disks, and Premium storage based on SSD disks. We also learned that, for operating system disks and data disks, we need to use Page blobs. Let's now focus a bit more on unmanaged disks and managed disks.

- Unmanaged disks. Choosing this option, you manage the storage account. You create it, you add disks to storage accounts, and attach them to virtual machines. You can have unmanaged disks both in the Standard and Premium storage. You can create a disk of the size of your choice, up to 4TB per disk. Depending on the performance of the storage, you could have 500 IOPS in the case of HDD, per disk, and up to 7500 IOPS in the case of SSD, per disk.

- Managed disks. If you choose this option, you let Azure decide how to manage your storage accounts, Premium or Standard. You specify the size of the disk that you need, and Azure will manage the disk for you. When you create a disk of a specific size, Azure will map the size of the disk you created with the closest size available in Azure managed disks. Below you will find the sizes available at the time of writing this book.

Table 2-1. *Sizes available in Premium Managed Disks. If you create a premium managed disk of 100GB, disk is mapped to a P10 managed disk.*

Premium Managed Disk Category	P4	P6	P10	P20	P30	P40	P50
Size	32GB	64GB	128GB	512GB	1TB	2TB	4TB

Table 2-2. *Sizes available in Standard Managed Disks. If you create a standard managed disk of 700GB, disk is mapped to an S30 disk, as Azure maps the size with the most close category available.*

Standard Managed Disk Category	S4	S6	S10	S20	S30	S40	S50
Size	32GB	64GB	128GB	512GB	1TB	2TB	4TB

Managed disks creation is a very simple process and it can be done with Azure Portal also. As you can see from the images below, you don't need to specify the storage account to attach an additional data disk to the SQL Server virtual machine. Azure will manage it automatically.

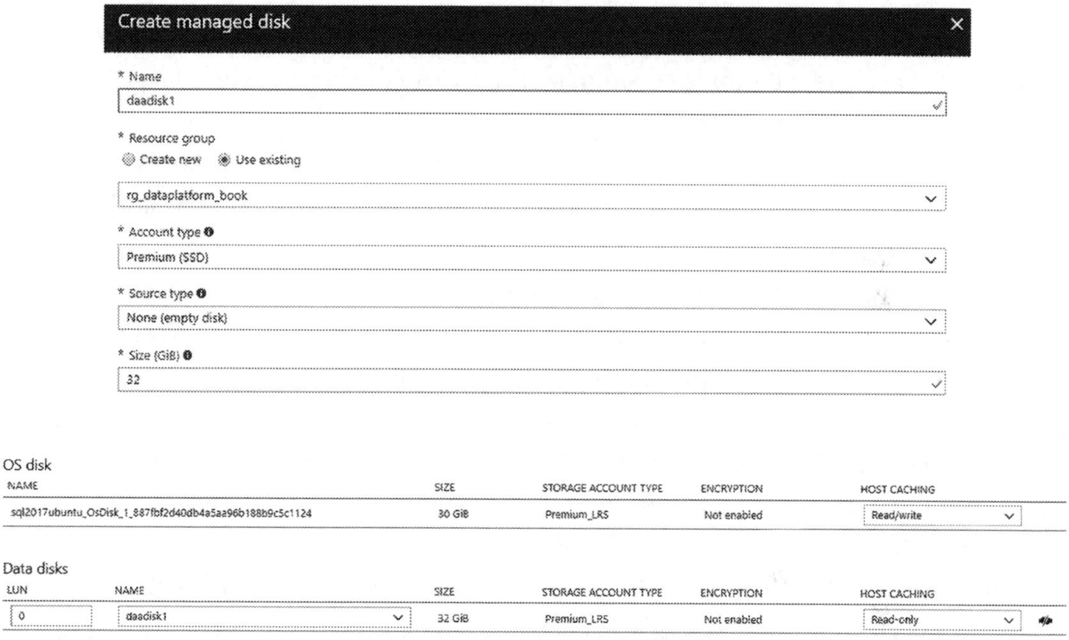

Figure 2-10. *Adding a managed data disk to a SQL Server virtual machine*

Benefits of using Managed Disks become interesting when you need to manage a lot of Virtual Machines and a lot of Storage Accounts. If this is the case you need to deal with when you need to architect a solution for your customer, then we recommend that you explore Managed Disks in detail, as they could give you a lot of benefits in terms of manageability and performance. To read more about managed disks, visit: `https://docs.microsoft.com/en-us/azure/virtual-machines/windows/premium-storage`

Note   Storage performance and scalability numbers are very important when you need to design a proper infrastructure. We leave here a document that can help you to understand scalability limits and performance targets associated with each storage account choice you will make during the design of solutions: `https://docs.microsoft.com/en-us/azure/storage/common/storage-scalability-targets`

Backup to Azure Storage

Now that we have done a quick introduction to Azure Storage, we are ready to understand how SQL Server is able to leverage it to manage backups and restores of data using Azure.

Backing up data to cloud is a very common practice these days, as cloud solves many of the typical backup problems that companies face, and the implementation is usually not difficult to do and to maintain.

Using tapes to move data to a remote location sometimes is not possible for companies that don't have a remote datacenter or a safe location to use. The addition of cloud options is of support in this case. Retention of data is another advantage; space in the cloud is virtually unlimited, and generally cheaper, therefore you will probably be less constrained when designing the retention policies." Basic disaster recovery scenarios in the cloud are also interesting to consider for some customers, as you could backup up data from on-premises and, in case of issues in the main datacenter, use the cloud as a restore option, reducing RTO. Last but not least, storage in the cloud is usually cheaper that on-premises storage, and you can also choose storage tiers optimized to store data with very low frequency access, like backups.

SQL Server, of all the server products that Microsoft makes, is the one with the most advanced features to leverage hybrid cloud possibilities offered by Azure. In this paragraph we will give examples of SQL Server running on-premises and saving data to the cloud. The same examples will work with SQL Server running in an Azure Virtual Machine, with no difference and, due to the positioning of the VM, with even better performances.

SQL Server offers several ways to create backups on Azure:

- SQL Server Backup to URL. The ability to backup data to cloud using an additional option to the Tape and Disk options already available.

- SQL Server Managed Backup to Microsoft Azure. The possibility to backup data to cloud using an automated mechanism provided by SQL Server.

- File-Snapshots Backups. The possibility to take snapshots of data and log files that are placed into Azure Storage.

SQL Server Backup to URL

Using the **SQL Server Backup to URL** feature in SQL Server is very similar to traditional backup possibilities offered by SQL Server. The **TO URL** option is an addition to existing **TO DISK** and **TO TAPE** options already available in SQL Server, starting from SQL Server 2012 SP1. Functionalities are very similar, and below you will find some additional considerations:

- It uses Azure Storage as a destination. You need to create a container to host backups. Recommendation is to set the container as Private, to avoid public access to files, and use HTTPS for the storage endpoint.

- You can use both page and block blobs. Using block blobs gives you the ability to stripe for very large database backups. At the time of writing, Premium Storage is not supported as a destination.

- All the tools and languages commonly used to work with SQL Server are supported, including SQL Server Management Studio, TSQL, PowerShell, and SMO.

Note   Backup To URL requires being part of **db_backupoperator** database role with **Alter any credential** permission.

Backing up data to Azure Storage is a process that requires the following macro steps to be accomplished:

1. Create an Azure Storage Account and a Container, to host backups.

2. Create a SQL Server credential object, to store the authentication information necessary to access the storage account. You can connect to the container URL using a Shared Access Signature token.

3. Execute the backup against the Azure Storage account, using SSMS or code.

In the code snippets and steps below we perform the backup of AdventureWorks to Microsoft Azure.

- CODE SNIPPET 1 - Configure the Storage Account to host backups, including security configuration. We will do that using the storage client library for .NET.

- CODE SNIPPET 2 - Backup AdventureWorks to Azure Storage using TSQL.

- Restore database using SSMS to another virtual machine.

- We will change the storage tier of a backup blob file in order to archive it, using storage tiering possibilities offered by Azure Storage.

CODE SNIPPET 1

We have added the **appSettings** section to the **App.config** file in the console application solution. The **StorageCnn** connection string contains the **protocol**, https in this case, the **account** name, and the account **key**.

```xml
<?xml version="1.0" encoding="utf-8" ?>
<configuration>
    <startup>
        <supportedRuntime version="v4.0" sku=".NETFramework,Version=v4.6.1" />
    </startup>
  <appSettings>
    <add key="StorageCnn" value="DefaultEndpointsProtocol=https;
    AccountName=dataplat;AccountKey=HvZQm2llrFZ6kRxDUJKMdidB9wNJHUPiX
    DdrOu5UUtloKpPRybSNpcROxcvN3ffDBKOwjhVkLsRg4855PfVeQQ==;Endpoint
    Suffix=core.windows.net"/>
  </appSettings>
</configuration>
```

The **Program.cs** file contains:

- References to Microsoft Azure Storage Client Library for .NET (nuget package "**Windows.Azure.Storage**"), and to Microsoft Azure Configuration Manager library for .NET (nuget package "**WindowsAzure.ConfigurationManager**")

- Instances of classes that refer to Storage Account (**sa**), Blob Storage (**cbc**), and Container (**cbco**). The container **backuptourl** is created, if it does not exist already.

- Instances of classes that refer to Shared Access Policy (**sap**). A policy that provides access for one month is created, and then a Shared Access Signature token that inherits the policy is added to the container. The token, **sastoken** string, can now be used from an application, SQL Server in our case, to have access (we gave full access to the container) to the container directly and save backups there. Using Shared Access Signature tokens is a security best practice that is better than giving full access to the entire storage account, using the storage account name and access key, as in this second case you could compromise the security of all the storage account, as security owner. The **Console.Writeline(sastoken);** output should be similar to this one: **?sv=2017-04-17&sr=c&sig=8Yl%2FMF bo%2BWjEYysLJQsXLXK%2BiGzV5XUpSlruSsPlqzE%3D&st=2018-01- 04T18%3A29%3A44Z&se=2018-02-04T18%3A29%3A44Z&sp=racwdl**

```
using System;
using System.Collections.Generic;
using System.Linq;
using System.Text;
using System.Threading.Tasks;

//namespaces for WindowsAzure.Storage and WindowsAzure.ConfigurationManager
nuget packages
using Microsoft.Azure;
using Microsoft.WindowsAzure.Storage;
using Microsoft.WindowsAzure.Storage.Blob;

namespace BackupToURL
{
    class Program
    {
        static void Main(string[] args)
        {
```

```csharp
//reference to storage account using the connection string from
app.config;
string storageCnn = CloudConfigurationManager.GetSetting
("StorageCnn");
CloudStorageAccount sa = CloudStorageAccount.Parse(storageCnn);

//create the container, private by default;
CloudBlobClient cbc = sa.CreateCloudBlobClient();
CloudBlobContainer cbco = cbc.GetContainerReference
("backuptourl");
cbco.CreateIfNotExists();

//create a shared access policy that expires in 1 month; create
a shared access signature on the container;
SharedAccessBlobPolicy sap = new SharedAccessBlobPolicy()
{
    SharedAccessStartTime = DateTime.UtcNow,
    SharedAccessExpiryTime = DateTime.UtcNow.AddMonths(1),
    Permissions = SharedAccessBlobPermissions.
    Add | SharedAccessBlobPermissions.Create |
    SharedAccessBlobPermissions.Delete
    | SharedAccessBlobPermissions.List | SharedAccessBlob
    Permissions.Read | SharedAccessBlobPermissions.Write
};
string saspolicy = "containerpolicy";

BlobContainerPermissions perm = cbco.GetPermissions();
perm.SharedAccessPolicies.Add(saspolicy, sap);
cbco.SetPermissions(perm);

string sastoken = cbco.GetSharedAccessSignature(perm.SharedAcce
ssPolicies[saspolicy]);

Console.WriteLine(sastoken);
Console.ReadLine();
        }

    }

}
```

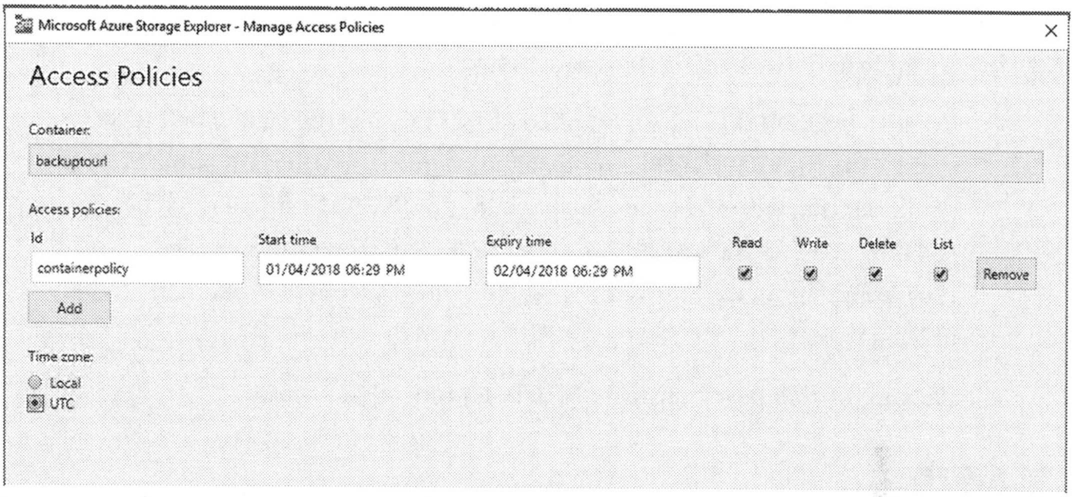

Figure 2-11. *You can use Azure Storage Explorer, a free cross-platform tool, to check if the container, backuptourl, and the shared access policy, containerpolicy, have been created successfully. You can also use the tool to create policies and SAS tokens. You can download Azure Storage Explorer from here:* `https://azure.microsoft.com/en-us/features/storage-explorer/`

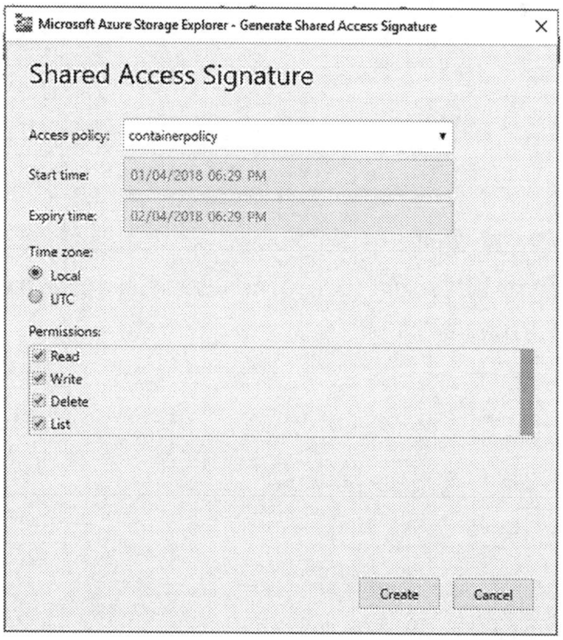

Figure 2-12. *Using the Create button, you can generate a SAS token using the Shared Access Policies created before*

We are now ready to take the first backup to Azure using SQL Server. We will use TSQL to accomplish this task using the script below:

- Create a **CREDENTIAL** object. You need to strictly use the syntax below to set it up; the **CREDENTIAL** name has to contain the URI path to the container that we will use for the backup, the **IDENTITY** name must be **'SHARED ACCESS SIGNATURE'** and the **SECRET** must be the SAS token. Please remember to remove the first character, ?, from the token, to make it work.

- Backup the database using the **TO URL** option

CODE SNIPPET 2

```
USE MASTER
GO

--create credential object using SAS
CREATE CREDENTIAL [https://dataplat.blob.core.windows.net/backuptourl]
WITH IDENTITY= 'SHARED ACCESS SIGNATURE'
, SECRET = 'sv=2017-04-17&sr=c&sig=8Yl%2FMFbo%2BWjEYysLJQsXLXK%2
BiGzV5XUpSlruSsPlqzE%3D&st=2018-01-04T18%3A29%3A44Z&se=2018-02-
04T18%3A29%3A44Z&sp=racwdl'

USE AdventureWorks
GO

BACKUP DATABASE AdventureWorks
TO URL = 'https://dataplat.blob.core.windows.net/backuptourl/advworks.bak'
        WITH COMPRESSION, STATS = 5
GO
```

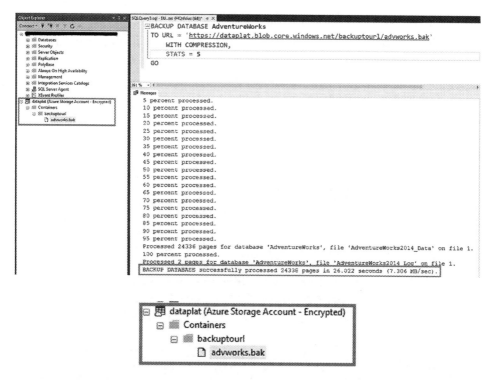

Figure 2-13. *The output of the command in SQL Server Management Studio. You can also see the backup file created in the destination, as SSMS also has the ability to connect, using the Connect button, to Azure Storage, providing the storage account name and the storage access key*

Some of the options that will make your BACKUP TO URL experience better:

- **COMPRESSION**. Enables backup compression; a must use option, especially if your SQL Server instance is located on-premises.

- **FORMAT**. To overwrite backup file, append is not supported.

- **STATS**. To display the percentage of progress. When omitted, 10% is used.

Restore to a different virtual machine

The RESTORE option is also supported, and it is very useful also for dev/test or basic disaster recovery scenarios. Imagine that you want to give a backup of your production database to a developer that needs to test a new feature. You could deploy a SQL Server image from the Azure Marketplace, add the CREDENTIAL object in the same exact way as the script above, and restore the database from the Azure Storage. SQL Server Management Studio includes in the GUI the possibility to manage backups and restores using Azure Storage.

```
RESTORE DATABASE AdventureWorks
    FROM URL = 'https://dataplat.blob.core.windows.net/backuptourl/advworks.bak'
```

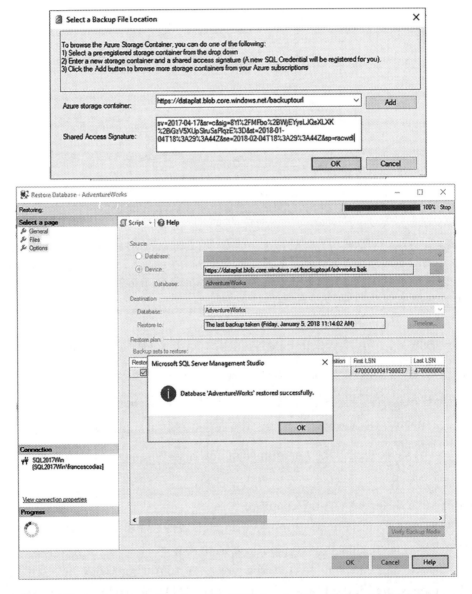

Figure 2-14. *The support to Backup To URL is also available in SQL Server Management Studio*

Use archive tier on blob files for long-term data retention or archiving

As we described earlier in the chapter, general-purpose storage v2 and blob storage have tiers that define how frequently data are accessed. Using archive tiers gives you the ability to achieve long-term retention and archiving options. When a blob is set to archive tier, the blob goes offline and cannot be read again from applications until it goes to cool or hot tiers again. To change the tier property you can use the **SetStandardBlobTier** method contained in the **CloudBlockBlob** class, like in the example below. You can append the C# code that we used before and run it after the T-SQL statement has been executed.

```
CloudBlockBlob blob = cbco.GetBlockBlobReference(blobName);
blob.SetStandardBlobTier(StandardBlobTier.Archive);
```

Azure Portal also has also the ability to change the blob tier property. Consider that changing from archive to cool or hot can take several hours, see the image below that warns before confirming the operation.

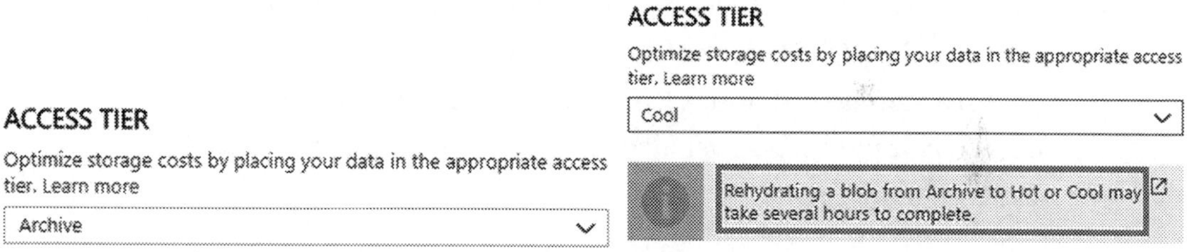

Figure 2-15. *Screenshots taken from Azure Portal, in the container section. Changing the access tier from Archive to Cool/Hot could take several hours to complete*

Note   To try additional scripts that use the Backup TO URL feature, read this document: https://msdn.microsoft.com/library/dn435916(v=sql.120).aspx#credential

---

SQL Server Managed Backup to Microsoft Azure

SQL Server Managed Backup is a very interesting feature introduced in SQL Server 2014, and improved in SQL Server 2016. It basically gives SQL Server the authority to perform backups, based on database usage, using Azure Storage as the destination. Unless advanced options are required to customize the standard behavior of the feature, SQL Server is able to take care of everything without user intervention, managing backups automatically. SQL Server Managed Backup is a feature useful to implement for small workloads, where the DBA intervention required for backups is usually minimal. It is also useful for hosting providers and ISVs that host many small databases in multi-tenant environments, where the backup design is very similar for many workloads or can be clustered in few usage database patterns. A third scenario where SQL Server Managed Backup is an interesting feature is for SQL Server running in Azure Virtual Machines, where the Azure Portal contains options available to enable the feature and define settings.

Main components and features of SQL Server Managed Backup:

- It can be enabled at Database Level or Instance Level. At Database Level, you can override Instance Level Settings. When enabled at Instance Level, SQL Server Managed Backup takes care of newly added databases, also including them in the backup policy.

- Data are saved to Azure Storage, and the way to access it is the same as the Backup TO URL feature, therefore you will need CREDENTIAL objects, a Storage Account, a Container to host blob files (Private access recommended as usual for security reasons), and a Shared Access Signature token.

- SQL Server Agent is required to use SQL Server Managed Backup.

- In the case of SQL Server Managed Backup, the preferred way to do the configuration and monitor the execution is to use T-SQL. Powershell is also supported and cmdlets are available, while SSMS does not contain a GUI to administer SQL Server Managed Backup. SSMS restore database GUI supports restore of databases managed using SQL Server Managed Backup though.

- SQL Server Managed Backup supports backup of user databases. Backup of **master**, **model**, **msdb**, **tempdb** is not supported.

- All metadata and backup history information for SQL Server Managed Backup are stored into **msdb** database.

- Backup files can be encrypted using certificates or asymmetric keys.

> **Note**   SQL Server Managed Backup GUI was available in older versions of SQL Server Management Studio, under the Management node. This is not the case anymore for newer versions, and for on-premises installations we recommend that you use T-SQL to setup SQL Server Managed Backup instead. For Virtual Machines that run SQL Server, you could use both T-SQL and Azure Virtual Machines specific features for SQL Server that we are going to describe later in this section.

As a first step, you need to configure a Shared Access Signature on an Azure Storage blob container, and then create a CREDENTIAL object in SQL Server. This step is the same as we did in the Backup TO URL paragraph previously in this chapter. We will omit this step, as there are no differences.

NAME	LAST MODIFIED	PUBLIC ACCESS LE...	LEASE STATE	
backuptourl	1/4/2018, 7:29:47 PM	Private	Available	...
managedbackup	1/6/2018, 12:17:50 PM	Private	Available	...

Now you have basically two main choices: you could either just enable SQL Server Managed Backup with default settings, or you could set advanced settings first and then enable the feature. You can combine the two options for example, use the default settings at instance level and custom settings for a specific database. In the Transact SQL script below, we will first enable SQL Server Managed Backup using default settings at instance level, then we will use advanced settings for a specific database, overriding default settings. For **database4** we will add encryption and a custom schedule for backups.

```
USE MASTER
GO

--CREATE CREDENTIAL OBJECT USING SAS TOKEN
CREATE CREDENTIAL [https://dataplat.blob.core.windows.net/managedbackup]
WITH IDENTITY= 'SHARED ACCESS SIGNATURE'
, SECRET = 'sv=2017-04-17&si=managedbackup-policy1&sr=c&sig=%2FqcWK6rvceuQr
9DWGz1aVdH49OruUuO1iLXHARqEbvO%3D'
```

```
-- ENABLE SQL SERVER MANAGED BACKUP AT INSTANCE LEVEL WITH DEFAULT SETTINGS
USE MSDB;
GO
    EXEC managed_backup.sp_backup_config_basic
                @enable_backup=1
                ,@container_url =
                'https://dataplat.blob.core.windows.net/managedbackup'
                ,@retention_days=30;
GO
```

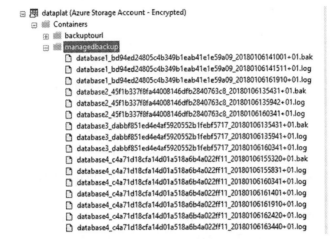

Figure 2-16. *The managedbackup container view from SQL Server Management Studio, where* .bak *(full backups) and* .log *(log backups) files are stored and saved automatically from SQL Server Managed Backup*

```
/*

CONFIGURE ADVANCED OPTIONS AND CUSTOM SETTINGS FOR ADVENTUREWORKS
*/

-- DB MASTER KEY CREATION
USE MASTER;
GO
    CREATE MASTER KEY ENCRYPTION BY PASSWORD = 'P4ssw0rd';
GO
```

```
-- CREATE CERTIFICATE
USE MASTER;
GO
    CREATE CERTIFICATE ManagedBackupCert
        WITH SUBJECT = 'ManagedBackupCert';
GO

-- CUSTOM ADVANCED SETTINGS FOR database4
USE MSDB;
GO
    EXEC managed_backup.sp_backup_config_advanced
        @database_name = 'database4'
        ,@encryption_algorithm ='AES_128'
        ,@encryptor_type = 'CERTIFICATE'
        ,@encryptor_name = 'ManagedBackupCert';
GO

USE MSDB;
GO
EXEC managed_backup.sp_backup_config_schedule
        @database_name =  'database4'
    ,@scheduling_option = 'Custom'
    ,@full_backup_freq_type = 'Daily'
    ,@days_of_week = ''
    ,@backup_begin_time =  '15:50'
    ,@backup_duration = '02:00'
    ,@log_backup_freq = '00:05'
GO
```

Note   Enabling SQL Server Managed Backup at database level, you will receive a message like the following: **SQL Server Managed Backup to Microsoft Azure is configured for the database, 'database4', with container url 'https://dataplat. blob.core.windows.net/managedbackup'**, retention period 5 day(s), encryption is on, backup is on, and a Custom backup schedule has been set.

```
-- FUNCTIONS & PROCEDURES
USE MSDB
GO

SELECT managed_backup.fn_is_master_switch_on () -- 1 = active; 0 = paused
SELECT * FROM managed_backup.fn_backup_db_config (NULL)
WHERE is_managed_backup_enabled = 1 -- managed database status
SELECT * FROM msdb.managed_backup.fn_get_current_xevent_settings() --
extended events settings
EXEC managed_backup.sp_get_backup_diagnostics -- see backup diagnostics
```

	db_name	db_guid	is_ava...	is_d...	is_managed_...	container_url	retention_days	encryption_algorithm	encryptor_type	encryptor_name
1	database1	BD94ED24-805C-4634-9B1E-AB41E1E59A09	0	0	1	https://dataplat.blob.core.windows.net/managedba...	30	NULL	NULL	NULL
2	database2	45F1B337-F8FA-4400-8146-DFB2840763C8	0	0	1	https://dataplat.blob.core.windows.net/managedba...	30	NULL	NULL	NULL
3	database3	DABBF851-ED4E-4AF5-9205-52B1FEBF5717	0	0	1	https://dataplat.blob.core.windows.net/managedba...	5	NULL	NULL	NULL
4	database4	C4A71D18-CFA1-4D01-A518-A6B4A022FF11	0	0	1	https://dataplat.blob.core.windows.net/managedba...	5	AES_128	CERTIFICATE	ManagedBackupCert

Figure 2-17. *The output in SSMS of the* managed_backup.fn_backup_db_
config (NULL) *function. Highlighted the* container_url, retentation_days,
encryption_algorithm, encryptor_type, encryptor_name *fields.*

```
-- DISABLING SQL SERVER MANAGED BACKUP

USE MSDB;
GO
EXEC managed_backup.sp_backup_config_basic
              @enable_backup=0;
GO
```

Conditions that will trigger Full Database backups and Log Database backups:

Below are the standard conditions in which SQL Server Managed backup will run,
unless you decide to customize default settings.

Full Database backup:

- When SQL Server Managed Backup is enabled with default settings at instance level and when SQL Server Managed Backup is enabled for a database

- Log growth since last full backup is >= than 1GB

- 1 week has passed since last full backup

- Log chain is broken, e.g. for a backup launched in T-SQL without using the COPY ONLY option.

Transaction Log backup:

- T-LOG space used is >= 5MB

- 2 hours have passed since last log backup

- No log backup history

- Last log backup timestamp is older than last full backup

Note   We recommend applying at least CU1 for SQL 2017 and CU5 for SQL 2016 SP1, as there is a fix available for SQL Server Managed Backup for custom schedules. More info here: `https://support.microsoft.com/en-us/help/4040535/fix-sql-server-managed-backups-do-not-run-a-scheduled-log-backup-in`

Restore database options available in SQL Server support accessing backups taken using SQL Server Managed Backup. In the image below you can see the SSMS Database Restore GUI accessing backups taken using managed backups.

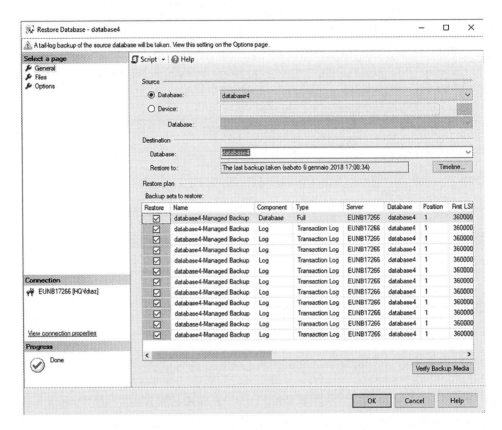

Figure 2-18. *Restore options in SQL Server can access backup data from Azure Storage taken using SQL Server Managed Backup*

If the SQL Server instance is running on a SQL Server Virtual Machine deployed choosing an instance from the Azure Marketplace and the server operating system is Windows, you can enable SQL Server Managed Backup using the Azure Portal, choosing the options that we have explained before, but using a graphical interface. The image below displays the options that you can configure:

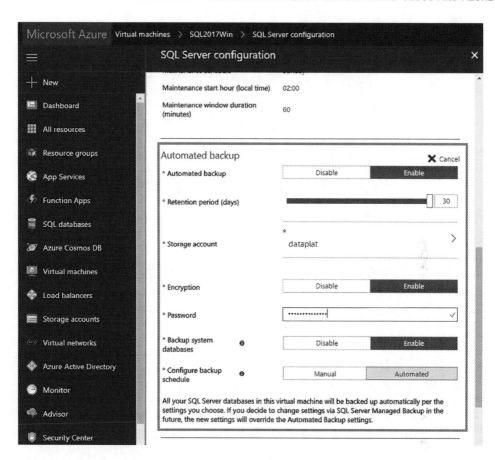

Figure 2-19. *SQL Server Managed Backup can be enabled from Azure Portal, if the SQL Server virtual machine is running on Windows and it has been deployed using a SQL Server image available in the Azure Marketplace*

Using Azure Storage to host SQL Server Database Files and Use Azure Snapshots

SQL Server, starting from SQL 2014, introduces native support to put primary data files (.mdf), secondary data files (.ndf) and log files (.ldf) in Azure Storage directly, instead of using disks. This functionality can be used both for SQL Server running on-premises and SQL Server running on Azure Virtual Machines. Although it is supported to have SQL Server database engine running on-premises and database files on Azure Storage, we recommend that you implement this feature only when SQL Server database engine is running on Azure Virtual Machines.

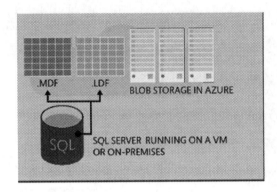

Figure 2-20. *SQL Server engine with database files hosted on Azure Storage high level diagram*

SQL Server 2016 introduced backup possibilities taking File-Snapshot backups for database files hosted in Azure Storage. It is a very interesting possibility as it provides nearly instantaneous backups of data.

The T-SQL script below contains the following:

- CREDENTIAL object creation, with authentication information to access an Azure Storage blob container, using a SAS token, as seen before in chapter

- CREATE DATABASE with SQL Server database files hosted on Azure Storage

- Backup database using the **WITH SNAPSHOT** option

```
CREATE CREDENTIAL [https://dataplat.blob.core.windows.net/databasefiles]
WITH IDENTITY='SHARED ACCESS SIGNATURE',
SECRET = 'sv=2017-04-17&si=databasefiles-policy1&sr=c&sig=teW%2Bf%2FKHinbF6
P7fhwHrs2tXEYApVE2JZIuJBGIN9b8%3D'

CREATE DATABASE filesonazure
ON
( NAME = filesonazure_dat,
    FILENAME = 'https://dataplat.blob.core.windows.net/databasefiles/
    datafile1.mdf' )
 LOG ON
( NAME = filesonazure_log,
    FILENAME = 'https://dataplat.blob.core.windows.net/databasefiles/
    logfile1.ldf')
```

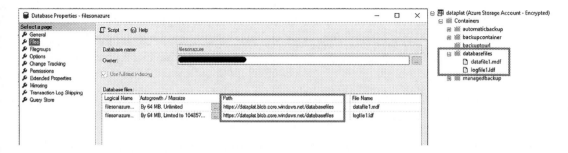

Figure 2-21. *Screenshot taken from SSMS that displays database files hosted on Azure Storage*

```
BACKUP DATABASE filesonazure

TO URL = 'https://dataplat.blob.core.windows.net/databasefiles/
backupwithsnapshot.bak'
WITH FILE_SNAPSHOT;
GO
```

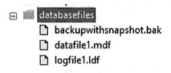

The command above will succeed as the database files that are hosted directly on Azure. Launching the command above on a database hosting files on disks, both on-premises and Azure, will raise an exception like the following:

Msg 3073, Level 16, State 1, Line 16
The option WITH FILE_SNAPSHOT is only permitted if all database files are in Azure Storage.
Msg 3013, Level 16, State 1, Line 16
BACKUP DATABASE is terminating abnormally.

```
-- to view the database snapshots
USE filesonazure
GO
select * from sys.fn_db_backup_file_snapshots (NULL) ;
```

Figure 2-22. *Datafile and log file snapshots*

Note   A snapshot backup consists of one snapshot per each database file (data and log), plus a backup file that contains pointers to snapshot files. In our example, we have two snapshots plus one backup file that is very small, as it only contains pointers. See the image below

---

Figure 2-23. *The backup file that contains pointers to snapshot files, not displayed in the Azure Portal*

A few considerations on SQL Server database files on Azure Storage and backup database WITH FILE_SNAPSHOT option:

Database files on Azure Storage

- Easy to maintain, if you are using a SQL Server running on an Azure Virtual Machine. For example, detach and attach operations from one Virtual Machine to another are very simple, as data and log files are decoupled from the Virtual Machine.

- Simplified HA and DR scenarios for basic workloads. In case of simple scenarios, without SQL Server high availability features enabled such as AlwaysOn, it is very fast to provide a quick restore option of a VM that might crash, simply switching on a new VM and attaching files.

- You can overcome Azure Virtual Machines disk limits. Each VM on Azure has a limit in terms of maximum numbers of disks that can be attached. Using a small VM on Azure could become a limit for databases with big storage requirements. Putting data on Azure Storage excludes this limitation, as you are not attaching disks to VMs but writing to Azure Storage directly

- Support for snapshot backups is only available if you put data and log files on Azure Storage

- If you DROP a database, database files will not be deleted

BACKUP TO URL WITH FILE_SNAPSHOT

- Use the **sys.sp_delete_backup** system stored procedure to delete snapshot backups. Deleting the backup file without using the stored procedure will keep snapshots, as they are directly linked to blob database files. Dropping blobs that have snapshots, the actual database files, is instead prevented.

> **! Failed to delete blobs**   4:40 PM
>
> Failed to delete 1 out of 1 blobs:
datafile1.mdf: This
> operation is not permitted because the blob has snapshots.

- If you have orphaned snapshots because you deleted the backup file, you can use the **sys.sp_delete_backup_file_snapshot** system stored procedure to delete backup snapshots. Database still has to exist to execute the stored procedure. If you deleted the database too, you could still use tools or the Azure API to perform snapshots and blobs deletion, such as the Azure Storage Explorer.

```
sys.sp_delete_backup_file_snapshot @db_name=filesonazure,
@snapshot_url=N'https://dataplat.blob.core.windows.
net/databasefiles/datafile1.mdf?snapshot=2018-01-
13T14:47:28.5749131Z'
```

SQL Server Stretched Databases

So far in this chapter we have worked with data in hybrid cloud scenarios mainly, focusing on backups. SQL Server 2016 introduced a functionality called Stretched Databases that allows us to leverage on Azure to store data used with less frequency while keeping data online for applications. It is a very powerful feature in our opinion, especially for scenarios where you can identify use cases that could benefit from it. The most typical one is related to historical data, like invoices of previous years, that still need to be used inside the ERP and not only via reports. Keeping data live inside the ERP in such scenarios is a huge productivity benefit for users. One cool thing that Stretched Database feature allows is to be transparent for existing applications, as the client connection will still use TDS protocol to connect to the same SQL Server, so the application will not see any change and will continue working as before.

Note   Not all tables are eligible to be stretched to Azure. See this document to understand more on limitations and eligibility criteria for SQL Server tables `https://docs.microsoft.com/en-us/sql/sql-server/stretch-database/limitations-for-stretch-database`

Steps needed to enable SQL Server Stretched Database feature:

- Create an Azure SQL Server Database, if none exist already, to host the Azure SQL Database that will have the stretched tables. Do not forget to open SQL firewall port on Azure SQL Database for the local server IP Address that will use the functionality

- Enable the server for Stretch using **EXEC sp_configure 'remote data archive' , '1';**

- Enable the database for Stretch

Executing the T-SQL script below will enable the Stretch Database feature for the SQL Server instance and a specific database, WideWorldImporters sample database in our case. The script could take a few minutes to complete. What it will do is create a database on the Azure SQL Database server that you created, and this database will be used to stretch your data.

This database will be dedicated to your stretch operations, and its specific storage and performance features; at the time of writing, storage limits for the database is 240TB of data and, depending on the performance that you need for the data that you will stretch, you can choose from different performance levels, measured in Database Stretch Units (DSU).

Note   To get more details on DSU and the pricing model applied to Stretched Databases, we recommend that you visit this document: https://azure.microsoft.com/en-us/pricing/details/sql-server-stretch-database/

```
-- enable the server for stretch
EXEC sp_configure 'remote data archive' , '1';
GO
RECONFIGURE;
GO

-- enable a database for stretch
USE WideWorldImporters;
GO

CREATE MASTER KEY ENCRYPTION BY PASSWORD='P4ssw0rd!';
GO

CREATE DATABASE SCOPED CREDENTIAL sqldbcredential
    WITH IDENTITY = 'francescodiaz' , SECRET = '@@Granturismo6' ;
GO

ALTER DATABASE WideWorldImporters
    SET REMOTE_DATA_ARCHIVE = ON
        (
            SERVER = 'stretchdbs.database.windows.net' ,
            CREDENTIAL = sqldbcredential
        ) ;
GO
```

After command completion, SSMS will display a different icon for the database, to show that the database has been enabled for stretch.

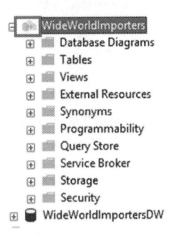

Figure 2-24. *Database icon changes in SSMS when the db is stretched*

Now that the server and the database are ready, you need to identify the tables that could benefit from a stretch scenario. To do that, you can use the Data Migration Assistant (DMA), a separate tool that can help to identify the tables that are eligible for stretching.

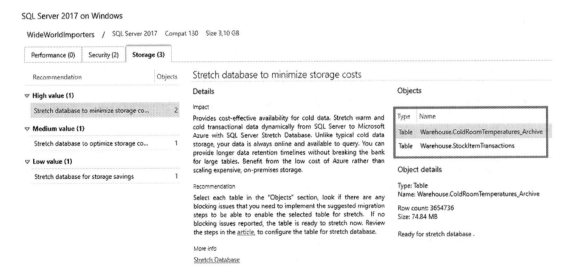

Figure 2-25. *Data Migration Assistant screenshot displays the two tables that are elegible for stretching*

Note   You can download DMA here `https://www.microsoft.com/en-us/download/details.aspx?id=53595`; you can also find a tutorial on how to use the tool here: `https://docs.microsoft.com/en-us/sql/sql-server/stretch-database/stretch-database-databases-and-tables-stretch-database-advisor`

We will move both tables to Azure. **Warehouse.ColdRoomTemperatures_Archive** will be entirely migrated, while rows in **Warehouse.StockItemTransaction** will be moved using a filter criterion, to display a scenario where both cold and hot data are kept in the same table.

```
--enable stretch for table - data will be moved all to Azure
USE WideWorldImporters;
GO
ALTER TABLE Warehouse.ColdRoomTemperatures_Archive
    SET ( REMOTE_DATA_ARCHIVE = ON ( MIGRATION_STATE = OUTBOUND ) ) ;
GO
```

Depending on the amount of data and the internet connection speed, the data movement could take a while to complete. You can use monitor mechanisms such as the Stretch Database Monitor tool available in SSMS, by going to Database/Tasks/Stretch/Monitor. You can also use the data management view **sys.dm_db_rda_migration_status**.

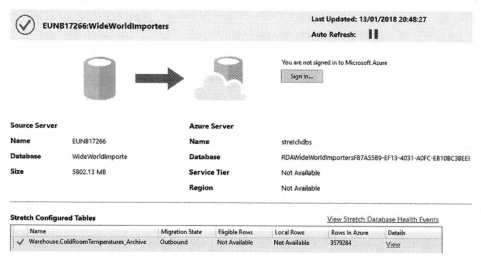

Figure 2-26. *The Stretch Database Monitor tool available in SSMS*

```
SELECT * FROM sys.dm_db_rda_migration_status
```

161 %

	table_id	database_id	migrated_rows	start_time_utc	end_time_utc	error_number	error_severity	error_state
84	1413580074	11	4999	2018-01-13 20:28:29.757	2018-01-13 20:28:34.350	NULL	NULL	NULL
85	1413580074	11	4999	2018-01-13 20:28:34.350	2018-01-13 20:28:38.393	NULL	NULL	NULL
86	1413580074	11	4999	2018-01-13 20:28:38.393	2018-01-13 20:28:43.213	NULL	NULL	NULL
87	1413580074	11	4999	2018-01-13 20:28:43.213	2018-01-13 20:28:47.280	NULL	NULL	NULL
88	1413580074	11	4999	2018-01-13 20:28:47.280	2018-01-13 20:28:51.667	NULL	NULL	NULL
89	1413580074	11	4999	2018-01-13 20:28:51.667	2018-01-13 20:28:55.653	NULL	NULL	NULL
90	1413580074	11	4999	2018-01-13 20:28:55.653	2018-01-13 20:29:00.313	NULL	NULL	NULL
91	1413580074	11	0	2018-01-13 20:29:12.887	2018-01-13 20:29:12.887	NULL	NULL	NULL
92	1413580074	11	4999	2018-01-13 20:29:12.887	2018-01-13 20:29:17.300	NULL	NULL	NULL
93	1413580074	11	4999	2018-01-13 20:29:17.300	2018-01-13 20:29:21.343	NULL	NULL	NULL

Figure 2-27. Monitoring data movement using sys.dm_db_rda_migration_status

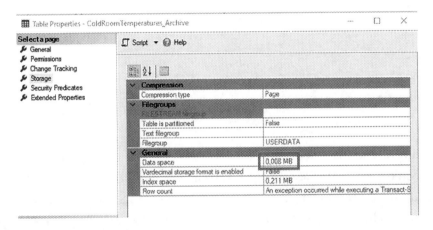

Figure 2-28. Checking the table properties in SSMS, you will see that, after enabling stretched tables, space occupied by tables on-premises will be reduced in case of filters, or freed if all data are moved to Azure

In the script below we are using an inline table-valued function to apply a filter predicate, to keep part of the data on-premises and move the rest to the cloud.

```
-- enable stretch using tvf to filter data
USE WideWorldImporters;
GO

CREATE FUNCTION dbo.fn_filterdata
(
@filter datetime2
)
```

```
RETURNS TABLE
WITH SCHEMABINDING
AS
RETURN   SELECT 1 AS is_ok
         WHERE @filter < CONVERT(datetime2, '1/1/2015', 101)
GO

ALTER TABLE Warehouse.StockItemTransactions
    SET ( REMOTE_DATA_ARCHIVE = ON (
        FILTER_PREDICATE = dbo.fn_filterdata(TransactionOccurredWhen),
        MIGRATION_STATE = OUTBOUND ) ) ;
 GO
```

In case you need to disable Stretch Database for a table, you can use one of the two commands below. You can either decide to bring data on-premises or leave data in the cloud.

```
--disable stretch db and bring data on-premises
USE WideWorldImporters;
GO
ALTER TABLE Warehouse.ColdRoomTemperatures_Archive
   SET ( REMOTE_DATA_ARCHIVE ( MIGRATION_STATE = INBOUND ) ) ;
GO

--disable stretch and leave data on azure
USE WideWorldImporters;
GO
ALTER TABLE Warehouse.ColdRoomTemperatures_Archive
   SET ( REMOTE_DATA_ARCHIVE = OFF_WITHOUT_DATA_RECOVERY ( MIGRATION_STATE
= PAUSED ) ) ;
GO
```

Considerations on connectivity for client applications

SQL Server Stretched Database feature is really an interesting feature, as it allows you to keep live old data and have them stored remotely in the cloud. This architectural change, transparent for applications, however needs some important consideration and, in the real world, applications should actually take care of this change. First of all, connection stability and performance becomes crucial; executing a **[SELECT * …]** query on a big amount of data could become a real performance issue if data are in the cloud. Furthermore, if the connection is not stable, exception handling and retry logic become a priority for the application. To minimize performance issues and exceptions, you can change the scope of the queries using the **sys.sp_rda_set_query_mode** stored procedure, **but please consider that this is a database-wide setting, so you can't achieve user level granularity**. Options are:

- **DISABLED** - All queries against stretched tables will fail

- **LOCAL_ONLY** - Queries are executed on local data only

- **LOCAL_AND_REMOTE** - All data are returned; it is the default option

Another consideration is related to the table-valued function that you will use to filter data when cold and hot data live together in the table. If the function is slow, then performance will degrade. A recommendation here is, when possible, separate archive data in dedicated tables, and use those tables with the stretched feature enabled.

Migrate databases to Azure IaaS

Database migration to Azure Virtual Machine is a task that, depending on the scenario, could be achieved in different ways. There's not a best choice that fits all scenarios, it is important to understand the workload and then decide the most appropriate strategy to perform database migrations. Below you could find the most common scenarios that we experienced in our consulting activities with Azure and SQL Server

1. Backup a database on-premises to disk, move data to Azure Storage and restore it into an Azure Virtual Machine. To perform the copy of the database backup file to Azure, you can use a command-line tool such as AzCopy, available for Windows and Linux. You can use a command like the following to upload a backup file.

   ```
   AzCopy /Source:C:\temp /Dest:https://dataplat.blob.core
   .windows.net/backup /DestKey:[Azure Storage KEY] /Pattern:
   "AdventureWorks.bak"
   ```

```
C:\WINDOWS\system32\cmd.exe                                                    —    □    ×

C:\Program Files (x86)\Microsoft SDKs\Azure\AzCopy>AzCopy /Source:C:\temp /Dest:https://dataplat.blob.core.windows.net/b
ackup /DestKey:                                                                        /Pattern:"Advent
ureWorks.bak"
Finished 1 of total 1 file(s).
[2018/01/19 12:11:21] Transfer summary:
------------------
Total files transferred: 1
Transfer successfully:   1
Transfer skipped:        0
Transfer failed:         0
Elapsed time:            00.00:00:15

C:\Program Files (x86)\Microsoft SDKs\Azure\AzCopy>
```

Figure 2-29. *Use AzCopy to upload a backup file to Azure Storage*

2.   Perform a Backup TO URL and perform a restore in Azure as we
     described in the Backup TO URL section in this chapter.

3.   Put the database files of the on-premises virtual machine on Azure
     Storage, and use a Detach/Attach approach from the source SQL
     Server on-premises to the Azure Virtual Machine at destination,
     described previously in this chapter as well.

4.   Export a data-tier application using SQL Server Management
     Studio or the command line tool **sqlpackage.exe** available in
     [installation folder]/Microsoft SQL Server/140/DAC/bin
     folder, and then import it into the destination SQL Server instance.

5.   Azure Site Recovery (ASR) replication. Azure Site Recovery is a
     disaster recovery (DR) service that enables DR from on-premises
     locations to Azure. On-premises virtual machines could run on
     Hyper-V, VMware or physical hardware. Its replication service
     can also be used for migration purposes, when several virtual
     machines are involved, therefore we recommend exploring this
     feature in case you are facing this scenario. Use this option if you
     want to migrate an entire server to the cloud, not only a database.
     It could be an interesting option in the case where you have the
     database engine plus other services enabled, such as Analysis
     Services. To learn more about ASR, you can visit this page:
     `https://docs.microsoft.com/en-us/azure/site-recovery/`
     `site-recovery-overview`. We will also speak a bit more about
     ASR later in this chapter for an Azure-to-Azure disaster recovery
     scenario.

6. Use the Microsoft Azure Import/Export Service to ship your hard drives with database backups to Microsoft, to deal with very large files that could take too much time to upload to the Azure Storage. Once the files will be available in the Azure Storage, you could restore them from the Virtual Machine on Azure. For further information on this service, you can visit this page: `https://docs.microsoft.com/en-us/azure/storage/common/storage-import-export-service`.

7. In High Availability scenarios, you could also rely on AlwaysOn Availability Groups, Database Mirroring (although deprecated), Log shipping and Transactional replication.

Migrate a Database Using the Data-Tier Application Framework

A data-tier application (DAC) is a self-contained unit of a user database that allows DBAs and developers to package SQL Server objects like tables, stored procedures, etc. inside a package called DACPAC. It is based on the DACfx API, that can run against versions of SQL Server 2008 and later, and Azure SQL Server Database as well. The API exposes several functionalities, and one is useful to export or import schema and data of a database. When we use the import/export functionality we generate a file package with the **.bacpac** extension that is basically a zip file with a set of xml files that contain the schema of the database objects that we have selected for the export, plus the BCP files with the data. The DAC framework can be used by SSMS, and a command line tool called **sqlpackage.exe** is also available with the installation of SQL Server.

To export a database using the DAC framework, you can launch the wizard from the Tasks section of the database you want to export and then select the Extract Data-tier Application option, like in the image below.

Figure 2-30. *To export database objects and data using the DAC framework, you can use SQL Server Management Studio, displayed in this picture*

The .bacpac file can be saved to disk or you can save it directly to an Azure Storage container, which is a good idea if you need to import the file from an Azure Virtual Machine. As you can see from the image below, it can be done using SSMS. In the Advanced tab, you can select the tables' data that you want to be exported during the .bacpac file generation.

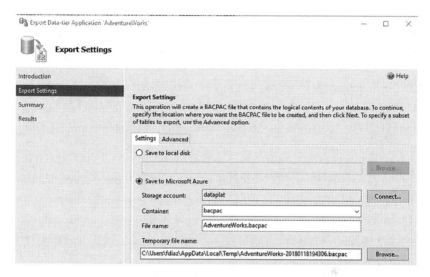

Figure 2-31. *Schema and data export using the DAC framework*

The size of a bacpac file is significantly less than a backup file, even when backup compression is enabled. But it is very important to highlight here that bacpac is just a sort of a snapshot of a database, and it should never be considered as an alternative to backups. It is also important to notice that it is not consistent to a point in time restore, unless modify activities are prevented.

AdventureWorks.bacpac	18/01/2018 19:52	File BACPAC	17.333 KB
AdventureWorks.bak	18/01/2018 19:54	File BAK	195.673 KB
AdventureWorks_compressed.bak	18/01/2018 19:55	File BAK	45.743 KB

Renaming a .bacpac file into a .zip file, you can also notice the contents inside the file, a set of xml files containing the schema plus the bulk import BCP files generated by the API.

[Content_Types].xml	Documento XML	1 KB	No	1 KB	43%	18/01/2018 19:52
DacMetadata.xml	Documento XML	1 KB	No	1 KB	18%	18/01/2018 19:52
model.xml	Documento XML	76 KB	No	1,423 KB	95%	18/01/2018 19:52
Origin.xml	Documento XML	3 KB	No	3 KB	0%	18/01/2018 19:52
TableData-000-00000.BCP	File BCP	4 KB	No	9 KB	64%	18/01/2018 19:52
TableData-001-00000.BCP	File BCP	4 KB	No	8 KB	56%	18/01/2018 19:52
TableData-002-00000.BCP	File BCP	4 KB	No	8 KB	55%	18/01/2018 19:52
TableData-003-00000.BCP	File BCP	4 KB	No	8 KB	55%	18/01/2018 19:52
TableData-004-00000.BCP	File BCP	4 KB	No	8 KB	55%	18/01/2018 19:52
TableData-005-00000.BCP	File BCP	4 KB	No	8 KB	55%	18/01/2018 19:52
TableData-006-00000.BCP	File BCP	4 KB	No	8 KB	55%	18/01/2018 19:52

Figure 2-32. *In this image you can see a portion of the files contained in the .bacpac file, that displays the folder structure above plus part of the contents of the data folder, a set of BCP files to be used in bulk import operations*

Import a .bacpac file at destination is exactly the same operation, and it can be done using SSMS and **sqlpackage.exe** as well. Below you can see the command to restore a .bacpac file from an Azure Virtual Machine at destination.

```
sqlpackage.exe /Action:Import /tsn:tcp:(local),1433 /tdn:AdventureWorksDACPAC
/tu:[user] /tp:[password] /sf:C:\temp\AdventureWorks.bacpac
```

```
Administrator: Command Prompt                                                 —   □   ×
C:\Program Files (x86)\Microsoft SQL Server\140\DAC\bin>sqlpackage.exe /Action:Import /tsn:tcp:(local),1433 /tdn:Adventu
reWorksBACPAC /tu:    /tp:            /sf:C:\temp\AdventureWorks.bacpac
Importing to database 'AdventureWorksBACPAC' on server 'tcp:(local),1433'.
Creating deployment plan
Initializing deployment
Verifying deployment plan
Analyzing deployment plan
Importing package schema and data into database
Updating database
Importing data
Processing Import.
Disabling indexes.
Disabling index 'PK_DatabaseLog_DatabaseLogID'.
Disabling index 'AK_Department_Name'.
Disabling index 'AK_Employee_NationalIDNumber'.
Disabling index 'IX_Employee_OrganizationLevel_OrganizationNode'.
Disabling index 'AK_Employee_LoginID'.
Disabling index 'IX_Employee_OrganizationNode'.
Disabling index 'AK_Employee_rowguid'.
Disabling index 'IX_EmployeeDepartmentHistory_ShiftID'.
Disabling index 'IX_EmployeeDepartmentHistory_DepartmentID'.
Disabling index 'IX_JobCandidate_BusinessEntityID'.
Disabling index 'AK_Shift_StartTime_EndTime'.
Disabling index 'AK_Shift_Name'.
Disabling index 'IX_Address_StateProvinceID'.
Disabling index 'IX_Address_AddressLine1_AddressLine2_City_StateProvinceID_PostalCode'.
Disabling index 'AK_Address_rowguid'.
Disabling index 'AK_AddressType_rowguid'.
Disabling index 'AK_AddressType_Name'.
Disabling index 'AK_BusinessEntity_rowguid'.
```

Figure 2-33. *In this example we are using the sqlpackage.exe tool to import a bacpac file. The path where you can find sqlpackage.exe is c:\program files (86)\ Microsoft SQL Server\[version number]\DAC\bin*

Note   If you are thinking of migrating directly to Azure SQL Database instead, we recommend that you also explore the Azure Database Migration Service, in preview at the time of writing this book. You could find a tutorial here: `https://docs.microsoft.com/en-us/azure/dms/tutorial-sql-server-to-azure-sql`

Run SQL Server on Microsoft Azure Virtual Machines

So far, in this chapter, we spoke mainly of features of SQL Server that can support hybrid configurations for backups and stretched databases. In this section we will focus more on the execution of SQL Server on Azure Virtual Machines, describing when installing SQL Server on Azure Virtual Machines is the best option, the considerations on storage design in IaaS and the performance best practices to implement.

Why Choose SQL Server on Azure Virtual Machines

In the previous chapter we detailed what Azure SQL Database can offer in terms of functionalities for developers and database administrators. As you saw, features available are very rich, so why should we opt for SQL Server installed on Azure Virtual Machines instead? If you had asked us this question a couple of years ago, we would had answered with many points to support the Azure Virtual Machines choice; now that Azure SQL Server database has become a very mature service, reasons to put databases on Azure Virtual Machines are fewer than in the past. Don't get us wrong, we are not saying here that it is a wrong choice to put SQL on Azure VMs, we are just saying that now both SQL Database and SQL Server are mature, real options to choose from and choices are no longer driven by the limitations available in Azure SQL Database. Below are the main reasons, based on our experience, why we recommend SQL Server installed in Azure Virtual Machines as the first choice:

- If you have additional SQL Server services all installed in a single VM, and you want to migrate them to the cloud keeping changes at the application level close to zero. For example, if you are using SQL Server Integration Services in the same box together with SQL Server Analysis Services or SQL Server Reporting Services, plus the database engine, then it is probably better to keep the same structure at destination also, or at least in the first phase of the project. If the workload is small enough to tolerate such configuration, it makes perfect sense to keep it on Azure too, and migrate the image to an Azure Virtual Machine. The second step of the transformation process could be to evaluate additional PaaS services that Azure offers, such as Azure Analysis Services, as an example, or to separate layers in a different way to leverage Azure possibilities.

- If you do an intense usage of Linked Servers, SQL Agent, Filestream, and all the other features of SQL Server that Azure SQL Database doesn't support today. If the migration to an alternative solution requires too much effort, then it is better to stay on Azure Virtual Machines.

- Authentication model. If you have implemented the Windows Authentication model in your application to access SQL Server, you should go with SQL Server as SQL Database supports SQL Authentication and Azure Active Directory, so probably reengineering all database authentication models plus changing the application authentication method would waste too much effort on the first stage.

- Very large databases. For databases bigger than 4TB , at the time of writing, 4TB is the size limit of a database on Azure SQL Database.

- If you want to keep a complete control on the SQL Server instance from the administration point of view, to overcome the level of abstraction that a PaaS solution like Azure SQL Database adds.

- Database design limits. If your database is using schema features that are too old, then it would be better to stay on SQL Server first, and then modify the database before moving to Azure SQL Database. For this aspect, the Data Migration Assistant tool is a very good friend here, to support with the analysis of the features that would need adjustments before the migration.

- Applications limits. If your application is not designed to implement a good retry logic to access the database and it is not designed to work with disconnected datasets, then it is better to keep SQL Server installed on an Azure Virtual Machine, to avoid the Azure SQL Database gateway layer dropping connections.

- Network resource access. Azure SQL Database runs outside the Azure Virtual Network infrastructure, therefore if a database stored-procedure requires access to a network share, for example, then keeping the database on an Azure Virtual Machine becomes a requirement.

Azure Virtual Machines Sizes and Preferred Choice for SQL Server

Talking about Virtual Machine sizes in Azure is a topic that needs constant updates, as Microsoft is continuously increasing the offerings in terms of memory and computing power provided and workload optimization. We like that Microsoft introduced workload categories to simplify choices during architectural design definition, in a way similar to what Amazon AWS does. At the time of writing, there are six categories available, optimized for specific workloads, and for each category you can find optimized virtual machine series and sizes. For each series, you have virtual machines size names to choose from, each one with its specific characteristics. Each virtual machine size has pre-defined characteristics in terms of CPU and RAM and capacity limits in terms of storage that you can add, network throughput, number of network interfaces that you can add, etc.

The Azure Compute Unit (ACU) Concept

Microsoft introduced the concept of ACU to identify in a simple way the CPU performance of each Virtual Machine. It is not an accurate value but just a guideline, but we think it is quite useful to support the architect during the choice of the right VM to execute a database workload. It is standardized to a Standard_A1 virtual machine performances, with a value of 100 and you can find a list of all ACUs per virtual machine sizes here at this link: `https://docs.microsoft.com/en-us/azure/virtual-machines/windows/acu`

Azure Virtual Machines Categories

Category	Typical workloads	Series	VM Sizes	VM Size example name	ACU
General Purpose	Balanced CPU-to-memory ratio, good for dev/test, small to medium databases	B	B1s,B1ms,B2s,B2ms,B4ms,B8ms	Standard_B4ms	
		Dsv3	_v3(D2s,D4s,D8s,D16s,D32s,D64s)	Standard_D32s_v3	160-190
		Dv3	_v3(D2,D4,D8,D16,D32,D64)	Standard_D16_v3	160-190
		DSv2	_v2(DS1,DS2,DS3,DS4,DS5)	Standard_DS3_v2	210-250
		Dv2	_v2(D1,D2,D3,D4,D5)	Standard_D2_v2	210-250
		DS	DS1,DS2,DS3,DS4	Standard_DS1	160
		D	D1,D2,D3,D4	Standard_D4	160
		Av2	_v2(A1,A2,A4,A8,A2m,A4m,A8m)	Standard_A4m_v2	100
		A	A0,A1,A2,A3,A4,A5,A6,A7	Standard_A5	50-100
		A- Basic	Basic(A0,A1,A2,A3,A4)	Basic_A2	
Compute-optimized	High CPU-to-memory ratio, good for network appliances, batch processes, web and application servers	Fsv2	_v2(F2s,F4s,F8s,F16s,F32s,F64s,F72s)	Standard_F64s_v2	195-210
		Fs	F1s,F2s,F4s,F8s,F16s	Standard_F16	210-250
		F	F1,F2,F4,F8,F16	Standard_F16	210-250
Memory-Optimized	High memory-to-CPU ratio, good for relational databases, medium to large cache, in-memory analytics	Esv3	_v3(E2s,E4s,E8s,E16s,E32s,E32s,E64s)	Standard_E2s_v3	160-190
		Ev3	_v3(E2,E4,E8,E16,E32,E64)	Standard_E8_v3	160-190
		M	M64s,M64ms,M128s,M128ms	Standard_M128ms	160-180
		GS	GS1,GS2,GS3,GS4,GS5	Standard_GS3	180-240
		G	G1,G2,G3,G4,G5	Standard_G1	180-240
		DSv2	_v2(DS11,DS12,DS13,DS14,DS15)	Standard_DS13_v2	210-250
		Dv2	_v2(D11,D12,D13,D14,D15)	Standard_D13_v2	210-250
		DS	DS11,DS12,DS13,DS14	Standard_DS12	160
		D	D11,D12,D13,D14	Standard_D12	160
Storage-optimized	Optimized for disk throughput and IO, ideal for BigData, SQL, NoSQL	Ls	L4s,L8s,L16s,L32s	Standard_L4s	180-240
GPU-optimized	Designed for compute-intensive and graphic-intensive workloads. Provided with single or multiple NVIDIA GPUs	NC	NC6,NC12,NC24,NC24r	Standard_NC24	
		NCv2	_v2(NC6,NC12,NC24,NC24r)	Standard_NC24r_v2	
		ND	ND6,ND12,ND24,ND24r	Standard_ND24	
		NV	NV6,NV12,NV24	Standard_NV12	
High-performance compute	Compute and network-intensive applications, including HPC	H	H8,H16,H8m,H16m,H16r,H16mr	Standard_H16mr	290-300
		A	A8,A9,A10,A11	Standard_A11	225

Figure 2-34. *The Azure Virtual Machines categories, Series, VM Sizes, and ACUs available on Azure*

In the table above we tried to put on a single page the complete offering available today for Azure Virtual Machines. Let us tell you first how to read it.

1. Category column. It contains the list of categories available today. Categories are just a logical way to group virtual machines series, it is not something that you will find on Azure but only in the documentation. At the time of writing, there are six categories

    a. General-purpose. They are ideal for dev/test and small and medium databases. They have a balanced CPU-to-memory ratio.

    b. Compute optimized. These virtual machine series have a higher CPU-to-memory ratio, and they are good for batch processing, web and application servers, and network appliances.

c.   Memory optimized. These virtual machines have a higher memory-to-CPU ratio, and are optimized for memory intensive workloads. They are good for relational database servers, medium to large caches, and in-memory analytics services. For database servers like SQL Server and Oracle that, for some workloads, don't have high CPU requirements but have high memory needs, it is possible, for some virtual machine sizes, to constrain the number of virtual CPUs to a lower number compared to the default. This is very important for licensing purposes, when the pricing model is per-core based. To have additional details about the list of the constrained vCPU VM sizes, you can visit this page: `https://docs.microsoft.com/en-us/azure/virtual-machines/windows/constrained-vcpu`

d.   Storage optimized. VMs optimized for storage IO and throughput. Useful for data workload, such as BigData, NoSQL and SQL.

e.   GPU optimized. Perfect for graphics-intensive workloads, these virtual machines come with one or more NVIDIA GPUs.

f.   High performance optimized. Optimized for compute-intensive workloads, such as simulations, HPC clusters, they have last generation Intel Xeon CPUs and in some of them you can also find low-latency and high-performance networking capabilities with RDMA and InfiBand support.

2.   Typical workloads. The main workloads that could run in the specified category.

3.   Series, VM Sizes, VM Size example name. When Microsoft launched IaaS on Azure, only Virtual Machines of the A series were available, with no support to SSD disks and just a few CPU/RAM configurations available. Now, as you can see from this column, there are quite a lot of VM Series available on

Azure. If you look at the column VM Sizes, for each series the corresponding row contains the list of Virtual Machines sizes from where you can choose from. Let's try now to understand something on the naming conventions used.

a. v2,v3...vx: when you find this acronym, it means that the VM series you are looking at is a version 2 or x of the main series, probably with new generation CPUs or in general with some enhancement introduced by the platform. For example, the DSv2 series is an evolution of the DS.

b. When you find the letter S on the second letter of the series name, it means that the series supports Premium storage.

c. Looking at column VM Sizes, we have the actual VM sizes, each one with its own characteristics. For example, if we pick DS2 VM in the General-purpose category, this VM, with the name Standard_DS2 will have: 2 vCPU, 7GB RAM, 14GB of temp SSD storage, max 2 NICs, max 8 data disks, support for Premium Storage.

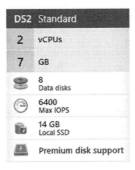

d. The column VM Size example name contains the actual names, one example per row, that Azure uses to identify VMs. When you interact with Azure using the management APIs or the administration tools such as powershell, you need to use that naming convention to create Virtual Machines on Azure.

4.   ACU. The range of ACU that you can expect choosing one of the
     corresponding rows.

Scale-up and scale-down of VM sizes is supported on Azure, but consider that not
all virtual machine series support changing to another virtual machine series, as per
limitations that other VM series might have. You can anyway, in extreme cases where the
VM series is not the right one and you can't migrate to another one, attach data disks to a
newly created virtual machine with the right features that you need.

Note   Biggest VM that you can create on Azure today is the Standard:M128ms,
with 128 vCPUs, 3.8 TB RAM, 8 NICs and 64 data disks

Now, we as data architects don't have an easy life if our customer asks us to
recommend the best VM series and size to host the database server. The good thing
is that with Azure is quite easy to change the design with time and starting with small
workloads and then changing the approach is something that with Azure you do almost
every day. We tried, based on our experience, to create a simple matrix to support these
choices, and please take it as guidance only, as there is not a perfect answer to this
question. What we can say is that the most common adopted VMs that we have seen
for database workloads are in the DS series, as they usually offer a good compromise
between pricing and performance.

Category	Series	VM Sizes	Recommended for SQL	Workloads
General Purpose	B	B1s,B1ms,B2s,B2ms,B4ms,B8ms	NO	
	Dsv3	_v3(D2s,D4s,D8s,D16s,D32s,D64s)	YES	Dev/Test and production workloads
	Dv3	_v3(D2,D4,D8,D16,D32,D64)	YES	Dev/Test and non intensive IO production workloads
	DSv2	_v2(DS1,DS2,DS3,DS4,DS5)	YES	Dev/Test and basic/medium production workloads
	Dv2	_v2(D1,D2,D3,D4,D5)	YES	Dev/Test and non intensive IO production workloads
	DS	DS1,DS2,DS3,DS4	YES	Dev/Test and basic/medium production workloads
	D	D1,D2,D3,D4	YES	Dev/Test and basic DB workloads
	Av2	_v2(A1,A2,A4,A8,A2m,A4m,A8m)	YES	Dev/Test and basic DB workloads
	A	A0,A1,A2,A3,A4,A5,A6,A7	YES	Dev/Test and basic DB workloads
	A-Basic	Basic(A0,A1,A2,A3,A4)	NO	
Compute-optimized	Fsv2	_v2(F2s,F4s,F8s,F16s,F32s,F64s,F72s)	NO	
	Fs	F1s,F2s,F4s,F8s,F16s	NO	
	F	F1,F2,F4,F8,F16	NO	
Memory-Optimized	Esv3	_v3(E2s,E4s,E8s,E16s,E32s,E32s,E64s)	YES	in-memory
	Ev3	_v3(E2,E4,E8,E16,E32,E64)	YES	in-memory, non-intensive IO
	M	M64s,M64ms,M128s,M128ms	YES	Very large enterprise DBs, very high memory request
	GS	GS1,GS2,GS3,GS4,GS5	YES	in-memory workloads
	G	G1,G2,G3,G4,G5	YES	in-memory, non-intensive IO
	DSv2	_v2(DS11,DS12,DS13,DS14,DS15)	YES	production
	Dv2	_v2(D11,D12,D13,D14,D15)	YES	production with non-intensive IO workloads
	DS	DS11,DS12,DS13,DS14	YES	production
	D	D11,D12,D13,D14	YES	production with non-intensive IO workloads
Storage-optimized	Ls	L4s,L8s,L16s,L32s	YES	large databases
GPU-optimized	NC	NC6,NC12,NC24,NC24r	NO	
	NCv2	_v2(NC6,NC12,NC24,NC24r)	NO	
	ND	ND6,ND12,ND24,ND24r	NO	
	NV	NV6,NV12,NV24	NO	
High-performance compute	H	H8,H16,H8m,H16m,H16r,H16mr	NO	
	A	A8,A9,A10,A11	NO	

Figure 2-35. *A simple matrix to help during the choice of the right VM size to use in a database workload configuration*

Note   To see all the details about virtual machine series, you can visit the following pages: General-purpose - `https://docs.microsoft.com/en-us/azure/virtual-machines/windows/sizes-general`; Memory-optimized - `https://docs.microsoft.com/en-us/azure/virtual-machines/windows/sizes-memory`; Compute-optimized - `https://docs.microsoft.com/en-us/azure/virtual-machines/windows/sizes-compute`; GPU-optimized - `https://docs.microsoft.com/en-us/azure/virtual-machines/windows/sizes-gpu`; Storage-optimized - `https://docs.microsoft.com/en-us/azure/virtual-machines/windows/sizes-storage`; High-performance-optimized - `https://docs.microsoft.com/en-us/azure/virtual-machines/windows/sizes-hpc`

Embedded Features Available and Useful for SQL Server

When you install SQL Server using one of the images available in the Azure Marketplace, you get a few helper options that Azure automatically provides to simplify your database administrator work. You can find them under the SQL Server Configuration settings area in the Azure Portal. This area is available because the SQL Server IaaS Agent Extension (SQLIaaSExtension) is provisioned together with the Virtual Machine. It is possible, if you provision a Virtual Machine and you add SQL Server manually, to provision the SQLIaaSExtension, with the following Powershell command:

```
Set-AzureRmVMSqlServerExtension -ResourceGroupName "resourcegroup" -VMName
"vm" -Name "SQLIaasExtension" -Location "West Europe"
```

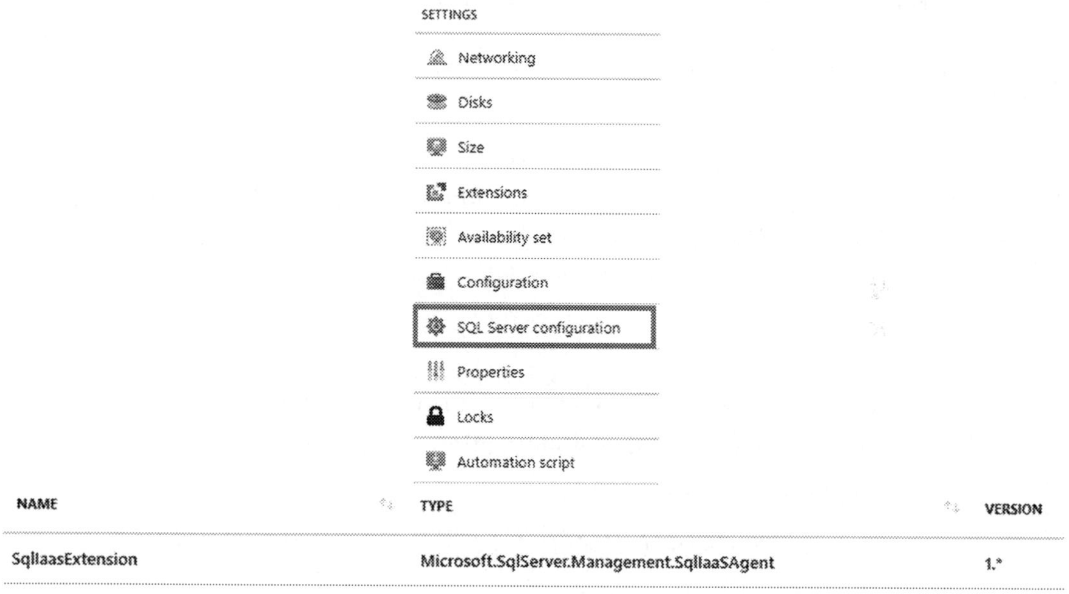

SETTINGS

- Networking
- Disks
- Size
- Extensions
- Availability set
- Configuration
- **SQL Server configuration**
- Properties
- Locks
- Automation script

NAME	TYPE	VERSION
SqlIaasExtension	Microsoft.SqlServer.Management.SqlIaaSAgent	1.*

Figure 2-36. *Each SQL Server virtual machine installed from the Azure Marketplace comes with a SQL Server configuration dashboard. This is because the SQL Server IaaS Agent Extension is installed*

It comes with six configuration options:

1. Storage usage. It contains a dashboard that gives a graphical overview of the storage used by SQL Server, and the possibility to increase the storage size dedicated to SQL Server, adding additional data disks, as you can see from the image below.

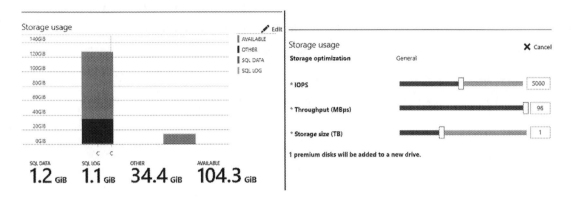

Figure 2-37. *On the left side you can see that the data used by SQL Server is displayed and, using the Edit button, you can open an edit mask where you can add additional storage, IOPSs or throughput to the virtual machine. Maximum limit number depend on the size and the category of the virtual machine that you chose*

2. SQL Connectivity level. Here you define the connectivity options, in case you want to use SQL Authentication, of your SQL Server instance and the scope of accessibility:

   a. Local. The SQL Server instance is not exposed outside the VM.

   b. Private. Scope of access is to the Azure Virtual Network. If there is an application server VM in an Azure Virtual Network that needs to access SQL Server, this option must be selected.

   c. Public. Your SQL Server TCP port will be exposed on the web, so any external client could access it, without any VPN access. This option is only recommended for test purposes, as it represents a security risk. If you choose this option, an inbound rule will be created on the network security group to allow TCP connections on the SQL port, e.g. the 1433. The network security group is associated to the network interface used by the virtual machine, so the inbound and outbound rules are inherited. If you are using a standalone virtual machine, all this part is simplified by the azure portal that exposes many of the features. If you need a more complex scenario, then you need to understand more how Azure Virtual Networks work.

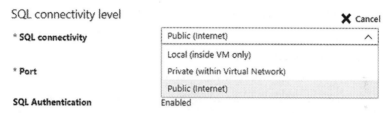

Figure 2-38. *The SQL Connectivity option on the Virtual Machine dashboard*

3. Automated patching. In this area you can define the time window and the preferred day where automatic updates should run.

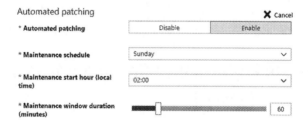

4. Automated backup. We described this part in SQL Server Managed Backup section in this chapter, as this option in the Azure Portal controls this feature.

5. Azure Key Vault integration. It enables the integration with Azure Key Vault service, in case you want to use this service to store the cryptographic keys used by encryption features in SQL Server, such as transparent data encryption (TDE). Configuring this feature installs the SQL Server Connector add-in to the SQL Server virtual machine that enables the interaction between Azure Key Vault and SQL Server.

6. SQL Server Machine Learning Services. Enables them for the SQL Server instance.

Design for Storage on SQL Server in Azure Virtual Machines

At the beginning of this chapter we spoke about Azure Storage and described the main differences between the types of storage accounts available, focusing more on blob storage, both block and page blobs. Then we have described the differences between standard HDD disks and premium SSD disks, and unmanaged and managed disks as well. In this section we will speak a bit more on the storage part, but related to Azure Virtual Machines, which means that we will focus more on Azure Storage page blobs, which are the type of blobs used for disks.

All Azure Virtual Machines come with at least two disks, one for the operating system and one temporary disk, automatically added during provisioning. Then you can add one or more data disks, with the limit of disks that is driven by the size of the virtual machine. Each disk can be up to 4TB and, if the VM Size permits it, you can also add SSD disks.

Operating system and data disks on Azure use the Virtual Hard Disks (.VHD) format, therefore if you want to migrate an image to Azure you need to adhere to this format. You could, in case your image is running on VMware, use Azure Site Recovery that automatically converts to VHD format during migration. The Microsoft Virtual Machine Converter was also available, but support from Microsoft ended on June 2017.

Storage Design and Performance Considerations on Azure Virtual Machine Running SQL Server

Temporary disk. Temporary disks do not reside on the same storage layer that Azure Storage offers; disks data is not replicated and disks are not persistent, as a maintenance event, an unplanned VM failover or redeploy of a VM could make your temporary disk lose data. In essence, do not use this disk to store SQL server data and log files! You could be tempted, as some sizes of VMs come with very large solid state temporary disks, but again do not use it. You could put the TempDB on the temporary disk. We recommend this choice if you are using Standard Storage and your virtual machine is using an SSD temporary disk. But if your application stresses the TempDB a lot and you are using Premium storage, then we recommend putting the TempDB on a Premium data disk as you can know in advance the performances that the disk will provide. In addition, if you don't put the TempDB on the temporary drive, you don't have to add additional windows tasks to manage the failure of the temporary disk in case of failures of the virtual machine. Windows Tasks would be required to give SQL Server the permissions to create the file.

Geo-redundant storage replication. It is not supported to use it with SQL Server if you put data and log files on separate disks, as the replica of data is asynchronous, therefore you could face consistency issues with your database. This means that, for geographical high-availability scenarios, you should not consider it as part of the solution, unless you keep all data in one single data disk, which is a good option only for very small workloads. Using AlwaysOn Availability Groups is instead a good option for geo-replication of data and service availability.

Premium Storage is the recommended choice by Microsoft for production environments with SQL Server. If the VM supports it, you can add up to 256TB of data storage for a VM, if you use a P50 disk: 64 data disks * 4TB = 256TB storage.

Note   At the time of writing, a P60 disk category is also available on Premium storage, and it supports 8TB of storage. You cannot attach to a Virtual Machine as a data disk tough.

Do not use the Operating System disk to store database data and logs.

Disk caching. OS Disks and Data Disks on Azure can have three levels of caching:

- None. Place SQL Server log files here, in one or more data disks, as caching is not needed for write-only workloads such as the log file.

- ReadOnly (default setting for Data Disks on Premium Storage). Place SQL Server data files here, as they are read-heavy workloads.

- ReadWrite (default setting for OS Disk). Leave the operating system disk with this setting. When creating the VM, and if you are using a Premium storage capable VM, consider using Premium storage for the operating system also.

The following Powershell script uses the **Add-AzureRmDataDisk** cmdlet to add a new data disk and sets the caching to none, as this disk will be used for the log file.

```
$rg = 'rg_dataplatform_book'
$vm = 'sql2017win'
$region = 'West Europe'
$storage = 'PremiumLRS'
$datadisk = 'logdatafile'
$diskconfig = New-AzureRmDiskConfig -Location $Region -AccountType $storage
-CreateOption Empty -DiskSizeGB 128
```

```
$disk1 = New-AzureRmDisk -DiskName $datadisk -Disk $diskconfig
-ResourceGroupName $rg

$sqlvm = Get-AzureRmVM -Name $vm -ResourceGroupName $rg
$sqlvm = Add-AzureRmVMDataDisk -VM $sqlvm -Name $datadisk -CreateOption
Attach -Caching None -ManagedDiskID $Disk1.Id -Lun 1

Update-AzureRmVM -VM $sqlvm -ResourceGroupName $rg
```

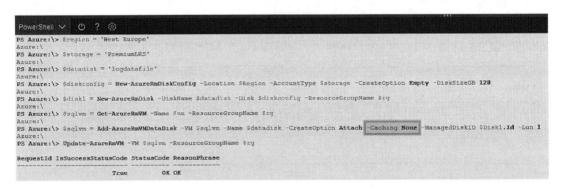

Figure 2-39. *The script above is executed using the Azure Cloud Shell from the Azure Portal, an interactive console that allows you to use Powershell or Bash to do scripting on Azure resources. Lo learn more about the Azure Cloud Shell, visit this page:* `https://docs.microsoft.com/en-us/azure/cloud-shell/overview`

After launching the script, the Azure Portal Disk section of the Virtual Machine will look like the following:

OS disk

NAME	SIZE	STORAGE ACCOUNT TYPE	ENCRYPTION	HOST CACHING
SQL2017Win_OsDisk_1_2fd476c74be84d5aa5841ac466fa2d0b	128 GiB	Premium_LRS	Not enabled	Read/write

Data disks

LUN	NAME	SIZE	STORAGE ACCOUNT TYPE	ENCRYPTION	HOST CACHING
0	SQL2017Win_disk2_5148ef7569794699b0f912a60147d724	1023 GiB	Premium_LRS	Not enabled	Read-only
1	logdatafile	128 GiB	Premium_LRS	Not enabled	None

Figure 2-40. *The Disks section in the Azure Virtual Machines dashboard in the Azure Portal*

Now you also need to ensure that newly created databases will use the new disks as the default path for data and log files, like in the simple T-SQL script below, that changes

SQL Server Instance property to the default data and log location, using registry keys in Windows. This change requires you to restart the SQL Server instance.

```
USE MASTER
GO
EXEC xp_instance_regwrite
      N'HKEY_LOCAL_MACHINE',
      N'Software\Microsoft\MSSQLServer\MSSQLServer',
      N'DefaultData',
      REG_SZ,
      N'F:\DataFiles'
GO
EXEC xp_instance_regwrite
      N'HKEY_LOCAL_MACHINE',
      N'Software\Microsoft\MSSQLServer\MSSQLServer',
      N'DefaultLog',
      REG_SZ,
      N'G:\LogFiles'
GO
```

Move System Databases to Data Disks. System databases, after the Virtual Machine provisioning using the Azure Marketplace, will reside in the operating system disk. To change this, follow the steps described in this document: https://docs.microsoft. com/en-us/sql/relational-databases/databases/move-system-databases

Multiple data disks. Using multiple data disks can help you to increase the number of IOPS available. Like we described earlier in the chapter, depending on the size of the disk that we will choose on Premium disks, they will be associated with a Premium Disk Type. For example, in the script above, we have created a 127GB disk, which means that the disk will become a P10 Premium Disk Type. Each disk type has specific IOPS associated with it and specific throughput. See the table below to see IOPS and throughput associated to different premium disk types.

Premium Disks Type	P4	P6	P10	P20	P30	P40	P50
Disk size	32 GB	64 GB	128 GB	512 GB	1 TB	2 TB	4 TB
IOPS	120	240	500	2300	5000	7500	7500
Throughput	25 MB/s	50 MB/s	100 MB/s	150 MB/s	200 MB/s	250 MB/s	250 MB/s

Figure 2-41. *Premium Disks and related IOPS and throughput*

When adding multiple disks to a VM to increase performances, take into account the limits that the VM itself has in terms of IOPS and storage throughput that it can manage, to avoid your performance limit being constrained to the lower value. As an example, the Standard_DS2_v2 virtual machine is limited to 6,400 IOPS, therefore adding a P50 disk will give you 4TB of storage, but you will not be able to achieve 7500 IOPS. This is something that requires an application performance requirement analysis to get the best performance results in your production environment. To go more in depth on this aspect, we recommend reading this Microsoft document: `https://docs.microsoft.com/en-us/azure/virtual-machines/windows/premium-storage-performance`

Note   You can read additional performance tips for SQL Server running on Azure Virtual Machines here: `https://docs.microsoft.com/en-us/azure/virtual-machines/windows/sql/virtual-machines-windows-sql-performance`

Considerations on High Availability and Disaster Recovery Options with SQL Server on Hybrid Cloud and Azure IaaS

Let's start the last section of the chapter with a table that lists the options available for SQL Server for high availability and disaster recovery in both hybrid cloud configurations and full Azure IaaS configurations.

Solution scope	Solution name	HA and/or DR	Enterprise ready (Yes or No)	Requires external tools
Hybrid Cloud	Log Shipping	DR	Y, if combined with other options	N
Hybrid Cloud	AlwaysOn AG	HA/DR	Y	N
Hybrid Cloud	Backup To Azure Storage	DR	Y, if combined with other options	N
Hybrid Cloud	Azure Site Recovery	DR	Y, if combined with other options	Y
Azure IaaS	AlwaysOn AG	HA/DR	Y	N
Azure IaaS	AlwaysOn FCI	HA	Y	Y
Azure IaaS	Backup To Azure Storage	DR	Y, if combined with other options	N
Azure IaaS	Log Shipping	DR	Y, if combined with other options	N
Azure IaaS	Azure Site Recovery	DR	Y, if combined with other options	Y

Figure 2-42. The list of options available for HADR SQL Server configurations in both hybrid cloud and public cloud scenarios. Note that database mirroring has not been included in the list as it has been deprecated by Microsoft, which means that it will disappear in future versions of SQL Server

Note   If you decide to run SQL Server on a standalone Azure Virtual Machine, you can get a 99.9% SLA provided by Microsoft, a new option available since November 2016. It is not of course a high availability option, but having a SLA on a single VM could be an option for small and non-critical databases, maybe adding SQL Server Backup to URL as an additional insurance option.

Hybrid Cloud HA/DR Options

In hybrid cloud configurations, you usually have the main workload running on-premises, and you use Azure for high availability and disaster recovery purposes. This means that you first need to design your HADR solution to be highly available on-premises, and then leverage the possibilities offered by the Azure platform. Not doing so will make the solution weak as it could often trigger into a disaster recovery scenario as the on-premises is not well designed. So, whether you decide to use high availability at the virtualization layer or to use high availability options available in SQL Server such as AlwaysOn, either way this is a must when you need to design your HADR scenario that involves Azure too.

SQL Server Backup to URL or SQL Server Managed Backup

We have extensively described these two options in this chapter. If used alone, they represent a basic disaster recovery scenario as, in case of failure on-premises, you need to have another virtual machine on Azure to restore backups and bring the database online. Things could become more complex if you need to guarantee access to clients after the disaster happens on-premises.

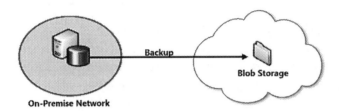

Figure 2-43. *SQL Server backup to Azure Storage*

We would like to make a couple of recommendations, in case you choose this solution as the only one for disaster recovery:

- On-premises. Have a local high availability solution. Active is, of course, recommended.

- On Azure. To reduce the impact on clients and reduce the time to recover the server, we recommend having a VPN Site to Site configured with Azure, and a virtual machine with SQL Server installed and connected to the virtual network, able to communicate with the on-premises datacenter. You could keep the virtual machine turned off to save compute costs, and turn it on only for system and SQL Server updates, restore tests, and in case of a disaster. This is not an enterprise DR solution if used alone, and it is a decent option only in case of very small workloads where it is acceptable to have some downtime. In addition, having the SQL Server machine on Azure and the clients on-premises could result in performance issues, and this must be considered during analysis and accepted by the customer as a compromise.

Log Shipping

The configuration of Log Shipping with Azure is the same as you do the configuration with a Secondary SQL Server on-premises. Since it requires access to a shared folder, you need to have a VPN Site-to-Site active, and the Secondary SQL Server must reside in a Virtual Network and Subnet that is able to communicate with your Primary SQL Server. It is possible to combine it with other HADR solutions, such as AlwaysOn Availability Groups, in case you want to enrich the solution you want to propose to the customer. It is not good enough to keep it alone as the only DR solution available, as it requires manual intervention in case of disasters that make the on-premises site unavailable.

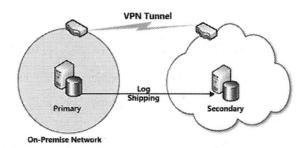

Figure 2-44. *Log shipping configuration using Azure. A VPN tunnel is required*

AlwaysOn Availability Groups

In this scenario you have a complete HADR solution provided by SQL Server, where you have different replicas, synchronous and asynchronous of your databases. Using a Listener you can also setup automatic failover in case of a disaster on-premises. On top of that, you could also set the Secondary Replica on Azure to be readable, and you could use it to offload some on-premises workloads, such as reporting and backups. As a requirement, you need to have a VPN Site-to-Site active and a Domain Controller on the Azure side is strongly recommended to avoid continuously querying active directory on-premises and in case the Primary site becomes unavailable. This is the HADR option that we recommend for enterprise scenarios, as it is the most complete.

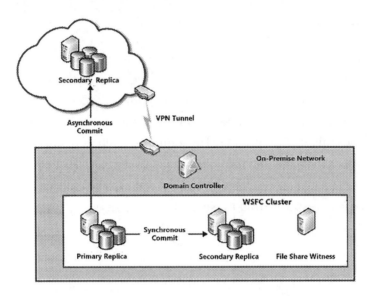

Figure 2-45. *SQL AlwaysOn AG configuration using Azure for a secondary replica*

Azure Site Recovery

Azure Site Recovery (ASR) is one of the most interesting services that Microsoft offers in Azure. After the acquisition of InMage in 2014, a company focused on developing disaster recovery tools, Microsoft gave a boost to its DR technology that today is probably the most advanced across all the public cloud vendors.

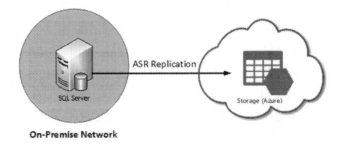

Figure 2-46. *Azure Site Recovery replicates data to Azure Storage*

ASR allows implementation of a disaster recovery configuration starting from an on-premises virtualized environment with VMware, Hyper-V, or an installation on physical hardware. Data are replicated to Azure and the virtual machines remains offline unless you want to do a test failover or a real disaster recovery is necessary. Having only the storage replica on the cloud and the VMs that are not active makes Azure Site Recovery a cost-effective solution to implement, as you don't have to pay for the compute power, but only for the storage occupied and the ASR cost of each protected virtual machine.

The replica does not require a VPN to work as an HTTPS connection is sufficient. To implement the most complete DR configuration, and to allow connections from on-premises virtual machines, it is better to setup a VPN tunnel too. IT will not be used for the replica, but it will make your life easier in case of a disaster recovery in scenarios of hybrid cloud.

Replica works with both Windows and Linux, and for some server application, such as SQL Server, application consistency is also guaranteed. This is the reason why we decided to cover ASR in this book, because if you are involved as an architect in a broader discussion that touches other workloads, it is possible that ASR will become part of the conversation for SQL Server too.

It is also important to highlight that ASR can be combined with SQL Server high availability features, such as AlwaysOn Availability Groups, AlwaysOn Failover Cluster Instances and Database Mirroring. It can also work with a standalone installation of SQL Server, in case you are implementing virtual machine availability through the hypervisor.

At the time of writing, Microsoft added in preview the support of ASR between two Azure sites. We will describe it the next section.

Azure only HA/DR Options

Now we will describe the options available for Azure only scenarios that are more or less the same here.

AlwaysOn Availability Groups

Like on hybrid configurations, AlwaysOn availability groups provide both a high-availability and a disaster recovery solution when running on Azure. In the case of high availability, the configuration has all nodes in the same Azure Region, including the Domain Controller.

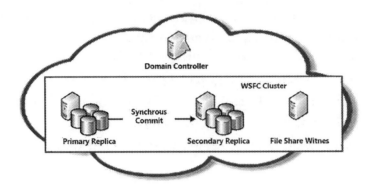

Figure 2-47. *AlwaysOn Availability groups synchronous replicas running on the same Azure Region*

When you want to add disaster recovery, you can setup AlwaysOn Availability Groups across different regions, using a VPN site-to-site configuration between the two virtual networks using either the Azure VPN Gateway or a firewall virtual appliance of your choice.

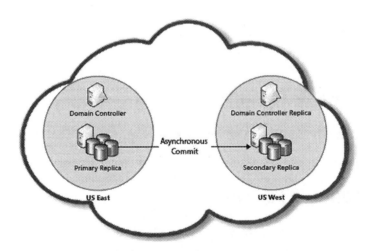

Figure 2-48. *AlwaysOn Availability Groups running on different Azure Regions using asynchronous replicas across datacenter*

AlwaysOn Failover Cluster Instances

In the case of AlwaysOn Failover Cluster Instances, you can setup a high availability solution using a shared virtual storage, for example using a software storage clustering solution available in the Azure Marketplace or Windows Server Storage Spaces.

Azure Site Recovery

We have presented ASR in the previous paragraph. Microsoft has enhanced the service adding the support for Azure-to-Azure replications, in preview at the moment of writing.

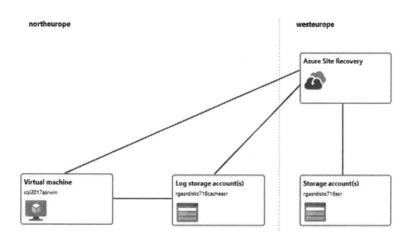

Figure 2-49. *ASR supports replication between two Azure regions*

You can configure and Azure-to-Azure ASR at service level, in case you need to design DR for an entire infrastructure or you can enable it at virtual machine level, for standalone virtual machines. We will describe this second option here, protecting a SQL Server 2017 Virtual Machine running on Windows Server 2016.

First thing you need to setup is the ASR service, which is a one step operation, where you basically define the Azure Region where the service will run. It is an important choice as the ASR service must reside in a different region than the source servers that you want to protect. In our example, our service is called **AzureSiteRecovery**, located in West Europe region, and we will protect a VM located in the paired Azure region, in North Europe.

Now we need to setup the ASR service for a specific virtual machine, in our case the VM name is **sql2017asrwin**. To do that, you need to go to the **Disaster recovery** section. You will need to configure the options described in the image below.

Configure disaster recovery - PREVIEW

Welcome to Azure Site Recovery
You can replicate your virtual machines to another Azure region for business continuity and disaster recovery needs. You can conduct periodic DR drills to ensure you meet the compliance needs. The VM will be replicated with the specified settings to the selected region so that you can recover your applications in the event of outages in source region. Learn more about Azure Site Recovery.

* Target region   1
West Europe

Target settings

	SOURCE	TARGET	
VM resource group	rg_asr	(new) rg_asr-asr	
Availability set	Not Applicable	Not Applicable	
Virtual network	rg_asr-vnet	(new) rg_asr-vnet-asr	3

Storage settings   [-] Hide details

SOURCE STORAGE	TARGET STORAGE	CACHE STORAGE	
rgasrdisks716 [PremiumLRS]	(new) rgasrdisks716asr [Premium_L...	(new) rgasrdisks716cacheasr [Stand...	4

Replication settings   [-] Hide details

Recovery services vault	AzureSiteRecovery	
Vault resource group	rg_azuresiterecovery	
Replication policy	(new) 24-hour-retention-policy	

5

♥ Source region (North Europe)
♥ Selected target region (West Europe)
♥ Available target regions

Figure 2-50. *The ASR configuration dashboard of Azure Virtual Machines*

Setting the options above you define:

1. Target region. The destination region where you want to replicate the source VM.

2. It displays the source and the target region in the map.

3. The source Virtual Network with the destination Virtual Network
    that in this example will be created during the setup.

4. Storage. It maps the source storage with the target storage, and
    it uses cache storage, located on the source region, for caching
    purposes.

SOURCE STORAGE	TARGET STORAGE	CACHE STORAGE
rgasrdisks716 [PremiumLRS]	(new) rgasrdisks716asr [Premium_L... ⌄	(new) rgasrdisks716cacheasr [Stand... ⌄

5. Replication policy. You can define it in advance or you can
    customize it later. You can define the retention period (up to 72
    hours) of each recovery point and the frequency of application-
    consistent snapshots, which is a very important feature for SQL
    Server workloads.

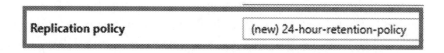

The first configuration plus the first full replication process could take from 30
minutes to a few hours, in cases where you are replicating a lot of data.

When the first full replica is completed, you will see a dashboard like the one below,
that displays the status of replication, RPO, and recovery points details, including
application consistent recovery points.

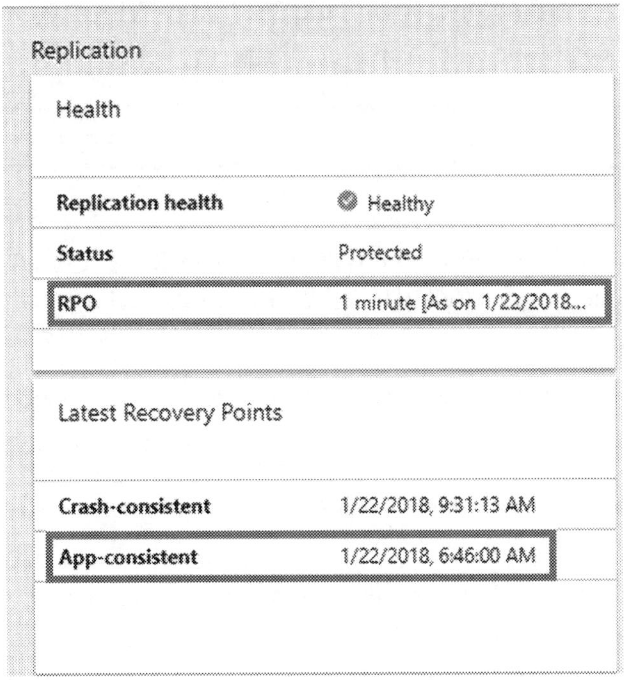
Replication
Health
Replication health
Healthy
Status
Protected
RPO
1 minute [As on 1/22/2018...
Latest Recovery Points
Crash-consistent
1/22/2018, 9:31:13 AM
App-consistent
1/22/2018, 6:46:00 AM

Figure 2-51. *Status of RPO and app-consistent recovery points on the ASR section in the Virtual Machine Dashboard*

It is worth mentioning that you can do some customization on the configuration that will be configured in the target site. As an example, if you don't want to guarantee the same performances at destination because you think that it would be acceptable for a temporary downtime to have reduced performances, you could choose a different virtual machine series and size. Of course, keep in mind that VMs at destination must be able to meet minimum requirements, for example the possibility to attach Premium storage and the number of data disks that the source VM has.

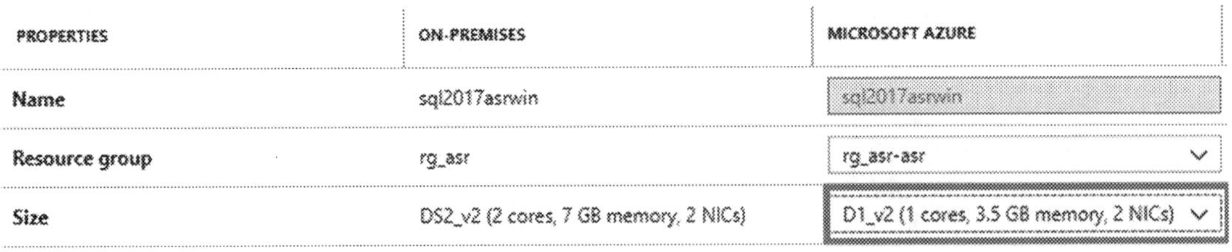
PROPERTIES
ON-PREMISES
MICROSOFT AZURE
Name
sql2017asrwin
sql2017asrwin
Resource group
rg_asr
rg_asr-asr
Size
DS2_v2 (2 cores, 7 GB memory, 2 NICs)
D1_v2 (1 cores, 3.5 GB memory, 2 NICs)

Figure 2-52. *You can select different VMs sizes and series at destination*

Test Failover

Once the first full replica is completed, you have two options available. The first one is to perform a **Test Failover**, which will simulate everything at destination, keeping the production active and turning on all the resources at destination. In this simple example, basically it will create the virtual machine at destination using the selected configuration and using the disks in the target storage. Test Failover is a very helpful feature and a recommended one to use, as it guarantees your customer the ability to periodically check if the disaster recovery infrastructure is healthy. The second one is to run an actual **Failover** that can also be triggered manually. This will make the failover site the active one. In case of failover of multiple virtual machines, you need to set a Recovery plan, which is not covered here in this book. A recovery plan will give you the ability to define the rules that you want to give to your disaster recovery strategy. For example, you could define dependencies that set the boot sequence of VMs, and you can also define very sophisticated scripts using Azure Automation runbooks, your Swiss Army Knife for complex scenarios. To learn more about ASR Recovery Plans, you can visit this page: `https://docs.microsoft.com/en-us/azure/site-recovery/site-recovery-create-recovery-plans`.

To perform a failover test, you just need to select two options. The first one is to choose the recovery point. The dropdown list will provide you with the list of all recovery points available including, as in the case of the picture, the app-consistent recovery points. The second choice is related to the Azure Virtual Network that you will use to place objects. It is recommended, like in the example, to avoid using the Azure Virtual Network that you chose for the actual disaster recovery.

Figure 2-53. *The failover test mask*

The Test Failover took just five minutes in this case, as we had to test one virtual machine only. Once the failover is completed, you have a virtual machine at destination with a different name, running in parallel with the source virtual machine. After verifying that everything is working as expected, you can delete the Test Failover environment using the **Cleanup test failover** option.

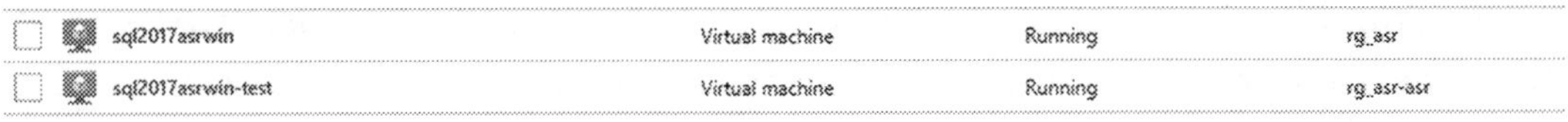

☐	sql2017asrwin	Virtual machine	Running	rg_asr
☐	sql2017asrwin-test	Virtual machine	Running	rg_asr-asr

Figure 2-54. *The two virtual machines running in parallel, both source with production and target with the DR in test*

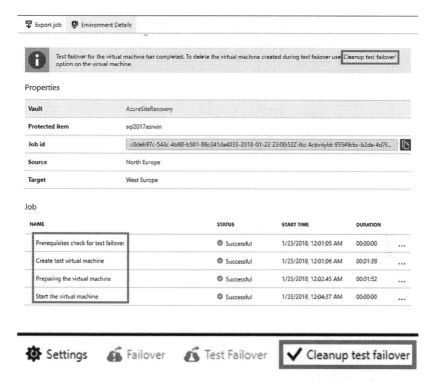

Figure 2-55.   *The steps executed during the test failover and the Cleanup test failover to delete the objects created during tests.*

Failover

The Failover follows the same approach, with the difference being that steps will be executed against the target Azure Virtual Network that you chose during the configuration. You also have the opportunity to turn-off the source VM, in case it is still accessible, which is a recommended option if you are performing the Failover for real reasons. This ASR feature is often used to migrate workloads from on-premises to cloud. Failover is always a manual task that you trigger; it is not an automatic action.

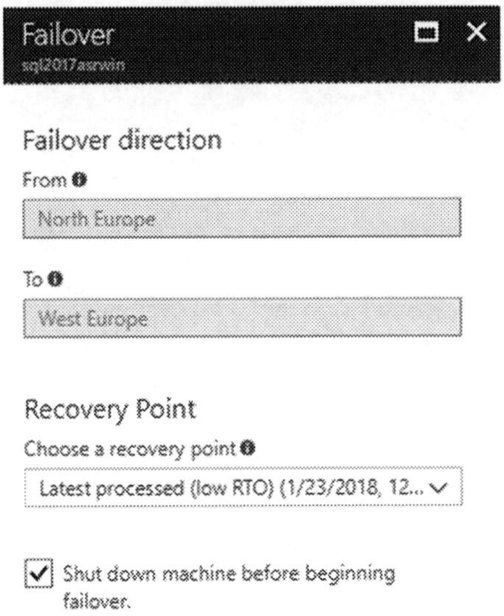

Figure 2-56. *Failover procedure*

To close this section, and considering that Azure Site Recovery is not a common tool that data architects use, we decided to put some additional information and links below, to go more in depth on this service:

- Azure Site Recovery Q&A: `https://docs.microsoft.com/en-us/azure/site-recovery/site-recovery-faq`

- In case you want to script ASR configuration and management, you can use the Azure Site Recovery Powershell, cmdlets here: `https://docs.microsoft.com/en-us/powershell/module/azurerm.siterecovery/?view=azurermps-5.1.1`

- Failback. After the Failover from one Azure region to another, the virtual machine goes on an unprotected state. If you want to do a failback to the source region you need to protect the VM again using the Re-protect dashboard and then do another failover. This is how the failback works at the moment on an Azure-to-Azure DR with ASR

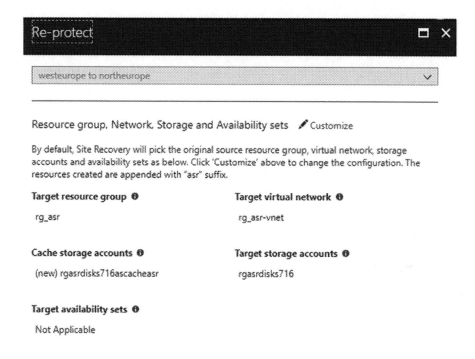

- Add Azure Automation runbooks to recovery plans: `https://docs.microsoft.com/en-us/azure/site-recovery/site-recovery-runbook-automation`

Summary

This concludes the chapter where we spoke about SQL Server running on Azure in both hybrid and Azure-only configurations, covering aspects like backups and the setup of SQL Server in Azure IaaS, including disaster scenarios. We move now to chapter 3, where the focus is on NoSQL workloads that you can run on Azure.

CHAPTER 3

Working with NoSQL Alternatives

We often deal with projects which have not involved anything outside the "plain-old" RDBMS as the storage engine. Fortunately, the law saying SQL should be the primary data source of enterprise application, is a guideline belonging to the past, and it's been few years we can see NoSQL alternatives around the corner in almost every complex project.

In this chapter, we are going to understand how much value we can get from NoSQL alternatives of Microsoft Azure, designing usage patterns and highlighting useful tips to catch out the most from the composition of those services.

Understanding NoSQL

We would avoid to write "yet-another-what-is-NoSQL-paragraph" but unfortunately, we have to, since we need to set a baseline. Let's try with an example as shown in Figure 3-1.

© Francesco Diaz, Roberto Freato 2018
F. Diaz and R. Freato, *Cloud Data Design, Orchestration, and Management Using Microsoft Azure*,
https://doi.org/10.1007/978-1-4842-3615-4_3

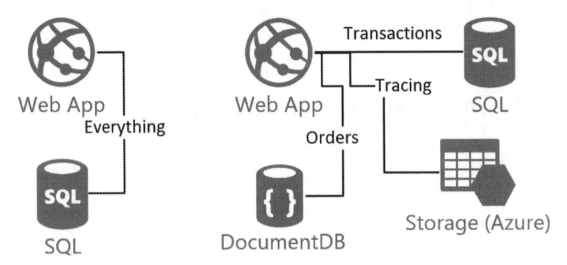

Figure 3-1. *We should read NoSQL as "not-only-SQL", since there are a lot of products with specific features very useful to address small (but important) pieces of our applications*

Suppose we have an e-commerce with online transactions with different payment gateways, where users can choose one at runtime, depending on their preference. Each payment gateway has its own protocol and message formats; even the payload exchanged between the e-commerce and the gateway is different. One broker may include in the payload some credit card data; another one may return additional information about the merchant and/or the acquirer.

It doesn't matter what the information exchanged is: we want to trace everything exchanged between those actors for further eventual analysis.

A first design approach would analyze the various gateways, finding a sort of common fields of the entire set, and designing the appropriate SQL table to put those data into. Additional fields, the ones related to a specific gateway, can be either skipped (bad!) or aggregated in a special field like in the structure below:

```
CREATE TABLE [tracing].[PaymentsTracingData]
(
        [ID] INT NOT NULL PRIMARY KEY IDENTITY,
        [Type] INT NOT NULL,
        [Timestamp] INT NOT NULL,
        [Amount] DECIMAL(8,2) NULL,
```

```
[TransactionID] VARCHAR(100) NULL,
[AdditionalData] VARCHAR(MAX)
)
```

This approach normalizes the basic subset of information in common for the various gateways (but in fact only the ones known at the state of the art) and delegates the additional information to a "catch-all" field, in a free-text fashion.

We can extract all the tracing data by an Amount filtering, with the following query:

```
SELECT * FROM tracing.PaymentsTracingData
WHERE Amount IS NOT NULL AND Amount > 5000
```

This leads to the following facts:

- We can use well known SQL to perform queries on the tracing data

- We can use SQL the perform advanced grouping or filtering techniques

- We have all the advantages of using an RDBMS, like: transactions, referential integrity, foreign keys, etc.

All this stuff is, for tracing data, kindly useless. It is very unlikely we need integration logs over a tracing table nor we need to enforce some referential integrity rules between this table and other. We may, of course, but we think it is and edge-case.

More important: what if we eventually need to query every tracing entries of type X, filtering on the specific field that type has, for the limitation of the design, in the AdditionalData field?

This simple scenario does not justify NoSQL alternatives, it just emphasizes the limitation of the RDBMS option in front of a simple problem of saving eterogeneous tracing data.

Actually, there are some ways to accommodate the need of eterogeneous data in traditional RDBMS. In SQL Server as well as Azure SQL Database, we can also use the native support for JSON fields, in conjunctions with the indexing and querying support.

Simpler Options

It not uncommon to see enterprise application making use of the File System. Yes, the same file system we use to store files and folders, but to save business critical data which is not a traditional BLOB.

In the previous sample, every tracing "row", can be either a "file" in a folder on the file system. We can store message payloads in the content of a plain text file and name it to represent basic properties, for instance:

- /
    - /[brokerType]
        - /[brokerType]/[transactionID]_[timestamp].json

With some instances (files) as follows:

- /2/999AA12019_1505060089.json

- /4/A00-12019-EE-1_1505060190.json

With this basic files and folder structure, we can "query" every transaction occurred for the broker "2", with a simple directory listing API.

The "query options" of this very simple strategy are three (corresponding to the segments of the path):

1. Query by the broker type

2. Query by the transaction ID

3. Query by the timestamp value

Of course, we are not able yet to query by the actual information inside the payloads; in fact, we are in a worse condition as the SQL alternative, since there is no way to get this query working:

```
SELECT * FROM tracing.PaymentsTracingData
WHERE Amount IS NOT NULL AND Amount > 5000
```

Except by writing custom code like the following:

```
var basePath = "[path]";
Func<T, bool> predicate = T=> true; //Specify a predicate
var files = Directory.EnumerateFiles(basePath, "*.json", SearchOption.
AllDirectories)
    .Select(p => JsonConvert.DeserializeObject<T>(File.ReadAllText(p)))
    .Where(predicate);
```

So we got those downsides:

- Every file should deserialize in a common format to "read" the common property we are expecting

- The code is very time consuming since it reads and deserializes every single file of the tracing folder (which is growing continuously)

- If the T definition changes, that code is useless and we are at the same point as we were with the RDBMS solution

We can expand the Path pattern to include more fields to query on, but this seems very awkward and it only moves the problem from SQL to file-system.

Thus, from those two distinct experiences, we learned:

- SQL isn't the only way to solve the tracing problem and it has limitations

- File System can be an alternative, but it has other limitations

We finally should find something useful to solve the problems above, in the optimal way.

Document-oriented NoSQL

In the previous section, we learned RDBMS isn't the only option to save tracing data. However, a file system alternative can be poor too, and we would like to highlight which are the requirements of our scope. Let's try to focus on those three documents:

Type "2"	Type "4"	Type "5"
```json { "Type": "2", "Timestamp": 1505061982, "mpTrxAmount": 100, "mpTrxID": "999AA12019", "mpTrxCardHolder": "Roberto Freato", "mpTrxMaskedPan": "XXXX-XXXX-XXXX-XXXX", "mpTrxResult": "OK" } ```	```json { "Type": "4", "Timestamp": 1505061982, "Amount": 12.34, "TransactionID": "A00-12019-EE-1", "Account": "Wallet", "Status": "Refused" } ```	```json { "Type": "5", "Timestamp": 1505061982, "PaymentCurrency": "EUR", "PaymentNetAmount": 34, "PaymentTaxAmount": 7, "TransactionRef": "BB15827287391872" } ```

Every document can be the serialization of the payload resulting from a message exchanged with a specific payment gateway. In some cases, we have some information and in other cases we have not. We notice we have the same information (the Amount of the operation) in each document, but in different format, since specific providers can have different naming conventions.

The only two fields in common are Type and Timestamp, since we assume this information is mandatory for every tracing entry and can be either autogenerated by the system itself.

If those documents were files, we have already said we should read the files one by one, parse them and find the appropriate values: all this nightmare just for a basic filtering query!

In a document-oriented NoSQL engine, we instead assume we can put the documents as they are, and then query them per their actual fields. Assuming a SQL-like language, we can setup a query as follows:

```
SELECT * FROM Documents
WHERE mpTrxAmount > 20 OR Amount > 20 OR
(PaymentNetAmount+PaymentTaxAmount) > 20
```

With this approach we now can easily save documents in different formats and query them according to their actual structure, without thinking in advance to normalized tables of well-defined structures to contain all the fields we need. This moves the problem on the query itself, which has to be defined to deal with multiple types of document.

Be aware this is only a concept explained, since the underlying technology which can handle this type of query, efficiently, is to be discussed later in the chapter.

NoSQL is not related only on this property/feature, which is commonly known as "schemaless". NoSQL products often break some of the classic RDBMS assumptions, like to ACID ones (Atomicity-Consistency-Isolation-Durability) in order to provide scalability scenarios which are not easy to achieve in the pure relational ecosystem.

NoSQL alternatives in Microsoft Azure

Assuming we have got just the minimal knowledge of the NoSQL initiative, we are going to explain which services of the Microsoft Azure platform are NoSQL-oriented and how to use them in our solutions, paying attention to the specific features they provide to maximize the efficiency and to provide much value to applications.

In the rest of the chapter we are exploring:

- Azure Storage: mainly Blobs and Tables

- Azure Redis Cache: the managed key-value store, acting like a fast in-memory cache

- Azure Search: a document-based store, similar to the open-source Elastic Search engine

There also Azure Data Lake, a repository for Big Data: but it has a dedicated chapter later in the book.

We are strong supporters of polyglot persistence, meaning we strongly encourage architects to use the appropriate technology to save persistent data, according to the business requirements and using/maximizing the specific features of the individual components instead normalizing all the data operations into a single-type repository.

Using Azure Storage Blobs

The Blob Storage (Figure 3-2) is one of the 4 services associated to a Storage Account, where the other three are:

- Table storage: we are going to discuss it later

- Queue storage: a container of FIFO queues to integrate systems

- File storage: a SMB-like file service to be mounted remotely from inside and outside Azure

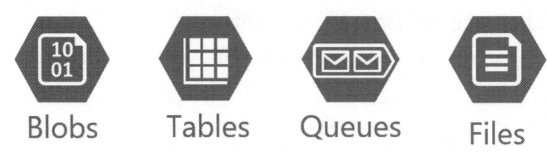

Figure 3-2. *Those are the four services/endpoints of a storage account. Some services may overlap in features with other Azure services*

In the next pages we will talk about a specific type of Blob, the block blob.

Azure Storage Blobs can be of two main types: Block Blobs and Page Blobs. We think Page Blobs, used to provide random access features and mainly to be used as the backing technology for virtual disks (VHD), are out of the scope of this chapter since they are not really fitting NoSQL scenarios.

Understanding Containers and Access Levels

Block Blobs (Figure 3-3) are generally large objects representing unstructured data, accessed for read/write through a REST API. Once a Storage Account is created, the location of the Blob service is at the following URL pattern:

```
http(s)://[account].blob.core.windows.net
```

A sample structure for a Blob storage account can be the following:

- `http(s)://[account].blob.core.windows.net`
  - /container1
  - /container1/images/small/P001.jpg
  - /container1/images/small/P002.jpg
  - /container1/js/jquery.js
  - /container2/configuration.json
  - /$root
  - /$root/index.html

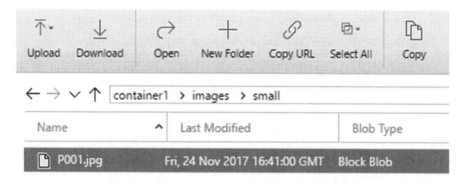

Figure 3-3. *This is taken from the Microsoft Azure Storage Explorer client application, one of the most comprehensive applications to operate against the Azure Storage service*

In the simple scenario above there a lot of concept explained. First, we do not create folders in the Blob storage but "containers". A container is like a first-level folder, defining an Access Level between those three options:

- No public access (aka "Private"): despite the contained blobs have unique URLs, they cannot be accessed publicly, without the proper access key. This is the most restrictive option (Figure 3-4).

- Public read access for container and blobs (aka "Container"): every object inside the container is publicly accessible through its URL and the container itself exposes its information and metadata to the public. This is the less restrictive option.

- Public read access for blobs only (aka "Blobs"): as the previous option, every blob contained here is public, but the container information is kept private (we cannot, for instance, ask the container to list its blobs).

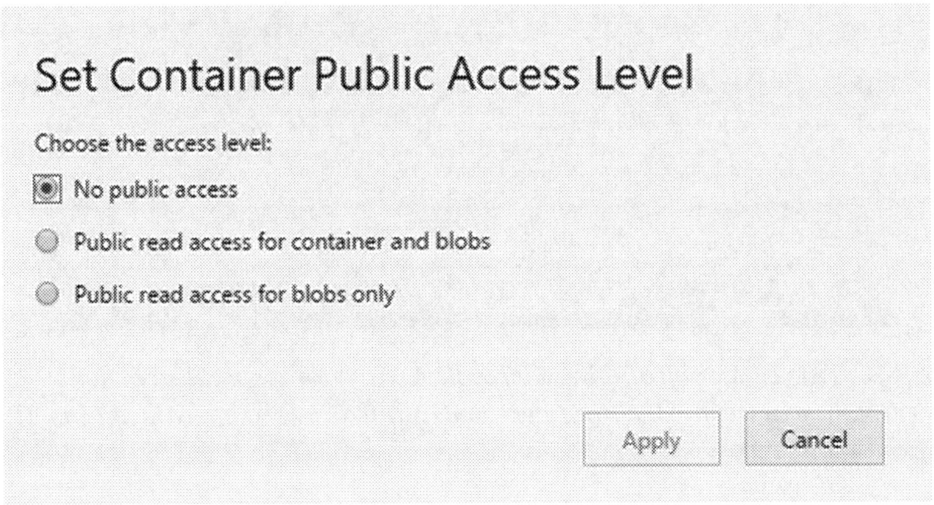

Figure 3-4. *This dialog (taken from Microsoft Azure Storage Explorer) lets us change the access level of a container among the three options explained*

In the sample above we can suppose "container1" is Public for blobs. Everyone can access the P001 image through its public URL:

```
http(s)://[account].blob.core.windows.net/container1/images/small/P001.jpg
```

The same stands for "P002.jpg" and the "jquery.js" JavaScript file. However, "images", "small" and "js" are not real folders. There is not an API on the Blob Storage to create those folders nor to assign them permissions and/or ACLs. Those segments of the URL are just prefixes of the blobs or, if we would like to see it differently, the blob names are comprehensive of the entire "path", beginning just after the container name (Figure 3-5):

- images/small/P001.jpg

- js/jquery.js

This concept is also known as "Flat namespace" and it exists only for querying purposes.

Coming back to the previous sample, we can instead suppose "container2" is Private. This means that despite "`http(s)://[account].blob.core.windows.net/container2/configuration.json`" is a valid URL, only authenticated clients will connect to it and, in case someone tries to access it anonymously, the service returns a generic not found error message.

Name	▲	Last Modified	Blob Type	Content Type	Size
📄 Saml.txt		Mon, 18 Sep 2017 13:41:57 GMT	Block Blob	text/plain	8.7 KB
📄 saml.txt		Mon, 18 Sep 2017 13:41:51 GMT	Block Blob	text/plain	8.7 KB

Figure 3-5. *Blob storage is case sensitive and we need to pay attention to this in order to avoid the situation above. In that case, we have the same file persisted two time with different case but the same name and content*

A special mention for the "$root" container. As the name suggests, it is the special container that is mapped to the root of the Blob Storage account. This means the blob "/$root/index.html" can be accessed through the "`http(s)://[account].blob.core.windows.net/index.html`" URL. All the considerations about Access Level are still valid for the $root container, since it must be explicitly created from the user along with its Access Level.

Understanding Redundancy and Performance

As solution architects, we must know in advance the limits of the services we use, to design proper relationships between all the components of the solution.

Just to make a concrete example, at the time of writing, a single storage account has a target bandwidth of about 20-30Gbps for egress (data "coming from" the storage account) and about 10-20Gbps for ingress (date "going to" the storage account). In practical, this means we need to plan the capacity in order to avoid bottlenecks or, worse, service interruption.

Let's think about a Blob storage account containing tons of Images for a B2C website. The pages of the website, hosted on any web server, can include <img> tags referencing the storage account, to release resources form the Web Server and instead loading the content Tier, which can be the Blob storage itself. In case the average page loads about 20 images of 10KB each, we can achieve about 20K pageviews/second to reach the maximum throughput of the Storage Account (30Gbps ~ 30.000.000.000bits/sec - 10KB ~ 81920bits - 366.210 images/sec - 18310 pages/sec).

This is a high-end number and it is more likely we encounter issues on the Web Tier first (to serve this number of simultaneous request) before the Storage Account can be saturated. However, it is a limit we should consider, to plan our infrastructure accordingly.

To understand the point of view we should adopt to design robust applications, there is an interesting checklist for Performance and Scalability of Storage Accounts here:

https://docs.microsoft.com/en-us/azure/storage/common/storage-performance-checklist?toc=%2fazure%2fstorage%2fblobs%2ftoc.json

---

Another good example of how a service limit can influence the behavior of an application is explained by the following story: let's think about an e-learning system where students can get courses and labs independently but concurrently. A course about Azure VM could tell the student to import a VHD from the Blob Storage into his/her private account, to use it for the lab environment. Well, given that we know there is a cap on the bandwidth for a single Blob of about 60MB/sec or 500requests/sec, we realize students will download their VHD with a variable speed, depending on the current traffic on that specific Blob. For instance, with 100 students downloading, they will experience a "slow" speed of about 614KB/sec, resulting in a 60-hours download for a VHD of about 127GB.

Even this example happened in the real world.

In addition to the checklist above, we should also consider the Scalability Targets of the Storage Accounts, as mentioned here:

https://docs.microsoft.com/en-us/azure/storage/common/storage-scalability-targets?toc=%2fazure%2fstorage%2fblobs%2ftoc.json

In the previous reference link, we can understand of the Service Tier and the Region can influence those limits: knowing them before going in production can be extremely valuable.

A comprehensive checklist about performance of the Storage, is available here:

https://docs.microsoft.com/en-us/azure/storage/common/storage-performance-checklist?toc=%2fazure%2fstorage%2fblobs%2ftoc.json

Service Tiers

At the time of writing, those are the Service Tiers of the Storage Account:

- LRS (Locally redundant storage): data is replicated three times but in the same datacenter (~ facility). This can ensure the best in terms of performance and the worst in terms of availability.

- ZRS (Zone redundant storage): data is replicated across datacenters and then replicated three times as the LRS. This ensures a higher availability with a cost increase.

- GRS (Geo-redundant storage): data is replicated to a secondary region, according to the matching table available here (`https://docs.microsoft.com/en-us/azure/storage/common/storage-redundancy?toc=%2fazure%2fstorage%2fblobs%2ftoc.json`). This option costs more, but ensures the best level of availability in case of service interruption of an entire region.

- RA-GRS (Read-access Geo-redundant storage): it the same as GRS with the plus that the replica on the secondary region is readable (with the URL pattern [myAccount]-secondary.blob.core.windows.net).

The latest option is a hidden gem, since provides us a replica of the Storage endpoint, which is unable to write by design. This can be extremely useful to use in read-only scenarios or, as mentioned above, as the frontend tier for static resources of high-end web applications.

In addition to the Service Tiers we can define an "access tier", between those three options:

- Hot access tier: this is the default one and the behavior is exactly what expected from blobs.

- Cold access tier: it is like a reduced-availability option, where it is suggested to use it for data less frequently accessed, compared to the data stored in the Hot mode.

- Archive access tier: this is, at time of writing, a preview feature, letting us archive blobs with the lowest price, at the cost of availability. In fact, an archive Blob cannot be read or modified: to do this, it must be rehydrated changing its tier to Hot or Cold, using the Set Blob Tier API, which is itself also a preview feature.

181

The Set Blob Tier API, aka Blob-Level Tiering, let us decide blob-by-blob which policy to apply, providing a flexible management without the need to physically separate blobs by their access patterns.

At the time of this writing, there are two General Purpose versions of the Storage Account: GPv1 and GPv2. Currently, new features like tiering are available only in the GPv2 version. We do not enter too much in those versions specifications since it may change over time.

Backup and Disaster Recovery

The underlying infrastructure of Azure Storage guarantees availability as long as durability of its Storage Accounts, with a very high SLA. Since the Storage is one the foundation services for the whole Azure infrastructure, it is very likely that a great focus is around it to prevent service disruption and unavailability.

For a complete reference about SLA for Storage, follow this link: `https://azure.microsoft.com/en-us/support/legal/sla/storage/v1_3/`

In the unlikely case a service disruption occurs on the infrastructure side, there are no options to make a user-initiated transparent failover against a secondary replica. Instead, we need to use the RA (Read-Access) endpoint of the RA-GRS account to bulk copy the entire contents into a new Storage Account for both read/write operations. To do that, at the time of this writing, we can use manual tooling (AzCopy, PowerShell) of the Azure Data Movement library (which is manual too, but it saves some time in coding).

The Azure Storage Data Movement library is explained here: `https://docs.microsoft.com/en-us/azure/storage/common/storage-use-data-movement-library`.

However, the real issue is not on the Azure side, which we expect is managed by Microsoft, but on the user side, where the focus is on the necessary measures to prevent damages on the storage account themselves, made by the user using them.

Let's suppose those kind of incidents:

- A blob has been overridden with the wrong content

- A user accidentally deletes the entire storage account (or a container)

- A blob has been deleted

Unfortunately, Azure does not help us under those circumstances, and we need to setup a recovery plan immediately before going in production.

AzCopy is a good cross-platform (Windows/Linux) command-line utility to perform multiple downloads/uploads from/to storage accounts.

In this example we are downloading all the blobs of a container to a local folder:

```
AzCopy /Source:https://[account].blob.core.windows.net/[container]
/Dest:[localPath] /SourceKey:[key] /S
```

However, we must keep in mind that we may put in place some infrastructure code to achieve resiliency, in order to orchestrate the data movement appropriately.

Azure Storage Data Movement Library has been released to implement exactly those scenarios, using the same core data movement framework that powers AzCopy.

Implement a Simple-but-resilient Backup Service

There are several online Software-as-a-Service solutions to manage the backups of Azure Blob Storage, each one involving those three building blocks:

- A source Blob Storage account

- A destination Blob Storage account (or another storage type)

- A compute tier which should perform the data movement

Take a look at CherrySAFE (https://www.cherrysafe.com), which is a SaaS solution to backup to and from various Azure data sources.

In case we would give a try by yourselves, we can use the Azure Storage Data Movement Library, which offers a managed SDK over the robust AzCopy features.

Here there are the requirements:

- Write a job that copies the entire content of a Blob Storage account inside another one

- In the destination storage account, map each source account to a specific container (which would permit a many-to-one backup relationship)

- Perform the copy using the fastest method but minimizing the overall costs

- Ensure the job is resilient and robust

The Copy Process

Let's go straight to the point:

```
var task = TransferManager.CopyDirectoryAsync(
    sourceBlobDir: sourceDirectory,
    destBlobDir: destinationDirectory,
    isServiceCopy: true,
    options: new CopyDirectoryOptions() { Recursive = true },
    context: context,
    cancellationToken: tokenSource.Token);
```

In this code snippet, we use the TransferManager class to ask the library to initiate the copy process from the sourceBlobDir Blob Directory to the destBlobDir Blob Directory. The TransferManager, in fact, can copy blobs one-by-one or in a per-directory basis.

We know directories are just aliases in the Blob Storage, so we can point the source to the first-level directory of a given container (the "" -empty directory):

```
var sourceDirectory = container.GetDirectoryReference("");
```

While the destination can be a prefix representing the source container:

```
var destinationDirectory = destinationAccountContainer
    .GetDirectoryReference(container.Name);
```

The "isServiceCopy" flag indicates TransferManager will use the integrated service-level copy feature of a storage account. This feature provides us with a convenient way to initiate a copy process without physically downloading the resource on the compute tier. This will increment copy performance and, at the same time, will save a lot of money since minimal outbound bandwidth is used.

Since we are pointing to the "root" of a source container, we implement a "Recursive" copy, using the CopyDirectoryOptions object. Finally, a cancellation token is passed to the TransferManager to gracefully end the process in case of termination (think about a high-level signal that indicates a shutdown attempt of the compute tier is doing the job).

The DirectoryTransferContext Object

The context parameter can be passed as a null value (bad), or can we take advantage of assigning it explicitly. This will be a context object keeping several interesting information around our copy process:

- Bytes transferred

- Blobs transferred, failed, or skipped

- Callback logics for conflict management

- Checkpointing features to resume a copy process previously aborted

This is a sample implementation of this context object:

```
DirectoryTransferContext context = new DirectoryTransferContext
(lastCheckpoint);
var collectFailed = new List<TransferEventArgs>();
var collectSkipped = new List<TransferEventArgs>();
context.FileFailed += (sender, e) =>
{
    collectFailed.Add(e);
};
context.FileSkipped += (sender, e) =>
{
    collectSkipped.Add(e);
};
context.ProgressHandler = new Progress<TransferStatus>((progress) =>
{
```

```
    Console.WriteLine($"OK: {progress.NumberOfFilesTransferred} " +
        $"- Skipped: {progress.NumberOfFilesSkipped} " +
        $"- Failed: {progress.NumberOfFilesFailed} " +
        $"- Bytes transferred: {progress.BytesTransferred}");
});
context.ShouldOverwriteCallback = new ShouldOverwriteCallback((source,
destination) =>
{
    return true;
});
```

We are collecting the EventArgs of the FileFailed and FileSkipped events, for further statistics. We are attaching a callback to the ProgressHandler property to inform the user of the progress of the operation and, for reference purposes, we are using the ShouldOverwriteCallback property to perform decisions about conflicts (in the case above, we always overwrite an existing destination blob).

Some Other Context

We decided to setup a transfer between two Storage Account, dumping the entire source storage account (container-by-container) into a single destination container. To do this, it is useful to track progress and make the job resilient, since it could be interrupted by several actors (internal or external) and it should restart/resume from the point it stopped.

The Azure Storage Data Movement library helps us on this task but we need to add some custom logic too:

- The library continuously updates a TransferCheckpoint object which represent the status of a single TransferManager operation. In case we are copying an entire Directory, it will contain the status of the copy process.

- We need to track the containers we have already copied, to resume from the correct one in case of stop/start.

To save those two state item, we use a Storage Account too, with two distinct blobs representing the serialization of this states:

```
var checkpointBlob = CloudStorageAccount
        .Parse(cAccount)
        .CreateCloudBlobClient()
        .GetContainerReference("dm-operations")
        .GetBlockBlobReference($"{sAccountName}.checkpoint.json");
var containersCheckpointBlob=checkpointBlob.Container
        .GetBlockBlobReference($"{sAccountName}.containers.json");
```

We assume those files could exists and, in case, we deserialize them into real objects:

```
var lastCheckpoint = default(TransferCheckpoint);
var processedContainers = new List<string>();
if (checkpointBlob.Exists())
{
    lastCheckpoint = JsonConvert.DeserializeObject<TransferCheckpoint>
(checkpointBlob.DownloadText());
}
if (containersCheckpointBlob.Exists())
{
    processedContainers = containersCheckpointBlob.DownloadText()
        .Split(',').ToList();
}
```

In the previous step, we saw a lastCheckpoint object passed into the constructor of the DirectoryTransferContext class. With this switch, the TransferManager will initiate the transfer at the correct point. Additionally, when we cycle the source containers to copy one-by-one, we can avoid the ones already processed:

```
var containers = sourceAccount.ListContainers()
    .Where(p => !processedContainers.Contains(p.Name)).ToArray();
foreach (var container in containers)
{
    //...
}
```

At the end of a single container iteration, we can have two possible status:

- The iteration was stopped by the cancellation token, so we need to save the current checkpoint

- The iteration finished due to its natural completion (i.e. every blob of the container was copied to the destination), so we need to update the processedContainers state variable.

```
if (!tokenSource.IsCancellationRequested)
{
    processedContainers.Add(container.Name);
    containersCheckpointBlob.UploadText(string.Join(",",
processedContainers));
}
else
{
    var checkpoint = JsonConvert.SerializeObject(context.LastCheckpoint);
    checkpointBlob.UploadText(checkpoint);
}
```

For reference purposes, we attach the entire snippet, including some minor infrastructure code:

```
var sourceAccount = new CloudStorageAccount(
    new StorageCredentials(sAccountName,sAccountKey),true)
    .CreateCloudBlobClient();
var destinationAccountContainer = CloudStorageAccount
    .Parse(dAccount)
    .CreateCloudBlobClient().GetContainerReference($"dm-{sAccountName}");
destinationAccountContainer.CreateIfNotExists();

var lastCheckpoint = default(TransferCheckpoint);
var processedContainers = new List<string>();
if (checkpointBlob.Exists())
{
    lastCheckpoint = JsonConvert.DeserializeObject<TransferCheckpoint>
                (checkpointBlob.DownloadText());
}
```

```
if (containersCheckpointBlob.Exists())
{
    processedContainers = containersCheckpointBlob.DownloadText()
        .Split(',').ToList();
}

var containers = sourceAccount.ListContainers()
    .Where(p => !processedContainers.Contains(p.Name)).ToArray();
foreach (var container in containers)
{
    if (tokenSource.IsCancellationRequested) break;

    DirectoryTransferContext context = new DirectoryTransferContext(last
    Checkpoint);
    var collectFailed = new List<TransferEventArgs>();
    var collectSkipped = new List<TransferEventArgs>();
    context.FileFailed += (sender, e) =>
    {
        collectFailed.Add(e);
    };
    context.FileSkipped += (sender, e) =>
    {
        collectSkipped.Add(e);
    };
    context.ProgressHandler = new Progress<TransferStatus>((progress) =>
    {
        Console.WriteLine($"OK: {progress.NumberOfFilesTransferred} " +
            $"- Skipped: {progress.NumberOfFilesSkipped} " +
            $"- Failed: {progress.NumberOfFilesFailed} " +
            $"- Bytes transferred: {progress.BytesTransferred}");
    });
    context.ShouldOverwriteCallback = new ShouldOverwriteCallback((source,
    destination) =>
    {
        return true;
    });
```

```
Console.WriteLine($"Processing container: {container.Name}");
var sourceDirectory = container.GetDirectoryReference("");
var destinationDirectory = destinationAccountContainer
    .GetDirectoryReference(container.Name);

try
{
    var task = TransferManager.CopyDirectoryAsync(
        sourceBlobDir: sourceDirectory,
        destBlobDir: destinationDirectory,
        isServiceCopy: true,
        options: new CopyDirectoryOptions() { Recursive = true },
        context: context,
        cancellationToken: tokenSource.Token);
    while (!task.IsCompleted)
    {
        if (Console.KeyAvailable)
        {
            var keyinfo = Console.ReadKey(true);
            if (keyinfo.Key == ConsoleKey.Q)
            {
                tokenSource.Cancel();
            }
        }
    }
    task.ConfigureAwait(false).GetAwaiter().GetResult();
}
catch (Exception e)
{
    //Actual type would be OperationCanceledException
}
finally
{
    if (!tokenSource.IsCancellationRequested)
```

```
    {
        processedContainers.Add(container.Name);
        containersCheckpointBlob.UploadText(string.Join(",",
        processedContainers));
    }
    else
    {
        var checkpoint = JsonConvert.SerializeObject(context.
        LastCheckpoint);
        checkpointBlob.UploadText(checkpoint);
    }

  }
}
```

Using Snapshots

Each Blob stored into the Blob Storage can be versioned using the Snapshot mechanism.
A Snapshot is a read-only version of the Blob taken at the time of the snapshot request.
A typical snapshot URL is in the following form:

```
https://[myAccount].blob.core.windows.net/[container]/blob.
txt?snapshot=[dateTime]
```

We can take an indefinite number of snapshot (except for Premium Storage VHDs,
which the limit for them is 100 per blob) and they are related to the base blob until it will
be deleted. We must know in advance this requirement, since there is no way to preserve
only the snapshots while deleting the base blob instead.

As a further measure of control, we need to explicitly delete snapshots before
deleting the corresponding base blob. If a blob has one or more snapshots on it, we can't
delete it until they have gone.

Pay attention to the pricing model for snapshots. As we can imagine, we are
billed just for the blocks changed from a snapshot to the next one. However,
what is a block? For non-page blobs (a.k.a. the Block Blobs) a blob is made of
blocks and, in case we are updating a portion of the blob, we can update just
one or few block. In that case, the next snapshot will capture just the difference

between state 0 and state 1, so only the updated blocks will generate additional costs. However, under some conditions (for example using the UploadFromText methods of the SDK), the intended behavior is the replace the entire blob contents, which will trigger a complete re-dump of the new content in case of a Snapshot. Thus, it is very important to understand this to accurately plan how to deal with snapshots.

Understanding Concurrency

Let's say we have two or more concurrent clients impacting the same blob, for example a single blob containing an index, populated from various sources in different timeframes. We would like to avoid this scenario:

1. Client A gets the blob content, read it and add some information

2. In the meantime, Client B does the same

3. Client A save the changes by rewriting the blob contents

4. Client B does the same, eventually

This is the trivial situation of a "Later writer wins" that is often unsuitable for most scenarios.

We can approach the problem in two ways:

- Optimistic concurrency: Client B writes the updated content if, and only if, the actual blob content has not been changed since its read.

- Pessimistic concurrency: Client B cannot even read the blob content until Client A releases the resource, with a lock.

Optimistic Concurrency

Suppose we have initiated a Blob Container as follows:

```
var container=CloudStorageAccount
    .Parse("[connString]")
    .CreateCloudBlobClient().GetContainerReference("private");
container.CreateIfNotExists();
```

And we created a TXT file containing a number "0" in it. We can now build a sample console application like this:

```
var counter = container.GetBlockBlobReference("counter.txt");
var random = new Random(DateTime.Now.Millisecond);

while (true)
{
    var counterInt = int.Parse(counter.DownloadText());
    var etag = counter.Properties.ETag;

    counterInt++;

    try
    {
        counter.UploadText(counterInt.ToString(), null,
            AccessCondition.GenerateIfMatchCondition(etag));
        Console.WriteLine($"Success while saving: {counterInt}");
    }
    catch (Exception)
    {
        Console.WriteLine($"Error while saving: {counterInt}");
    }
    Thread.Sleep(random.Next(100));
}
```

Which tries to get the counter, increment it and upload it again to the same source. A Blobk Blob comes with a ETag property, which is very useful to track changes while re-write it against the store. Specifically, during the UploadText phase we specify a conditional access, based on the ETag obtained during the reading phase. This ensures, on the service side, that the write will occur if and only if the target ETag is the same as the one declared in the write operation. If we run two or more instances of the application (Figure 3-6), we can notice this result:

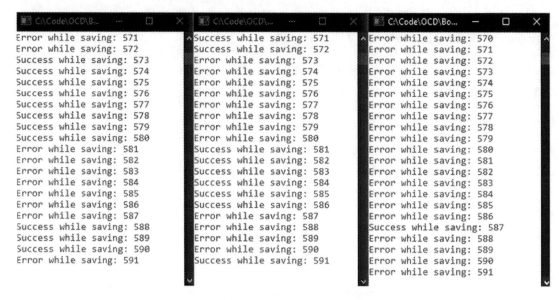

Figure 3-6. *We see three concurrent jobs trying to change/increment the same content on Blob Storage. Only ones per increment is successfully, since the others fail due to the conditional access policy (Optimistic Concurrency)*

Pessimistic Concurrency

Now we work in a scenario where we do not want to "try", but we need the guarantee our operation will succeed. This is the case where, instead of incrementing a number, we need to perform a time/resource-consuming job.

We can modify the code above as follows:

```
while (true)
{
    string lease = null;
    try
    {
        lease = counter.AcquireLease(TimeSpan.FromSeconds(15), null);
    }
    catch (StorageException)
    {
        Console.WriteLine("Error while obtaining the lease. Waiting...");
        Thread.Sleep(random.Next(1000));
        continue;
    }
```

```
var counterInt = int.Parse(counter.DownloadText());
counterInt = Process(counterInt);

try
{
    counter.UploadText(counterInt.ToString(), null,
        AccessCondition.GenerateLeaseCondition(lease));
    Console.WriteLine($"Success while saving: {counterInt}");
    counter.ReleaseLease(AccessCondition.GenerateLeaseCondition
    (lease));
}
catch (StorageException ex)
{
    if (ex.RequestInformation.HttpStatusCode ==
        (int)HttpStatusCode.PreconditionFailed)
        Console.WriteLine($"Error while saving: {counterInt}");
    else
        throw;
}
Thread.Sleep(random.Next(1000));
}
```

First, we try to get the Lease (a sort of lock) on the blob before reading it, for a maximum duration of 15 seconds (after that, the lease will be released automatically). In case of failure, we simply wait without perform the actual work, while in case of success, we download the contents, perform the long-running job and then release the lease.

Notice that, in this second example, we used the strong-typed StorageException, to catch exactly the case where precondition has failed.

In this second scenario (Figure 3-7), the result is quite different:

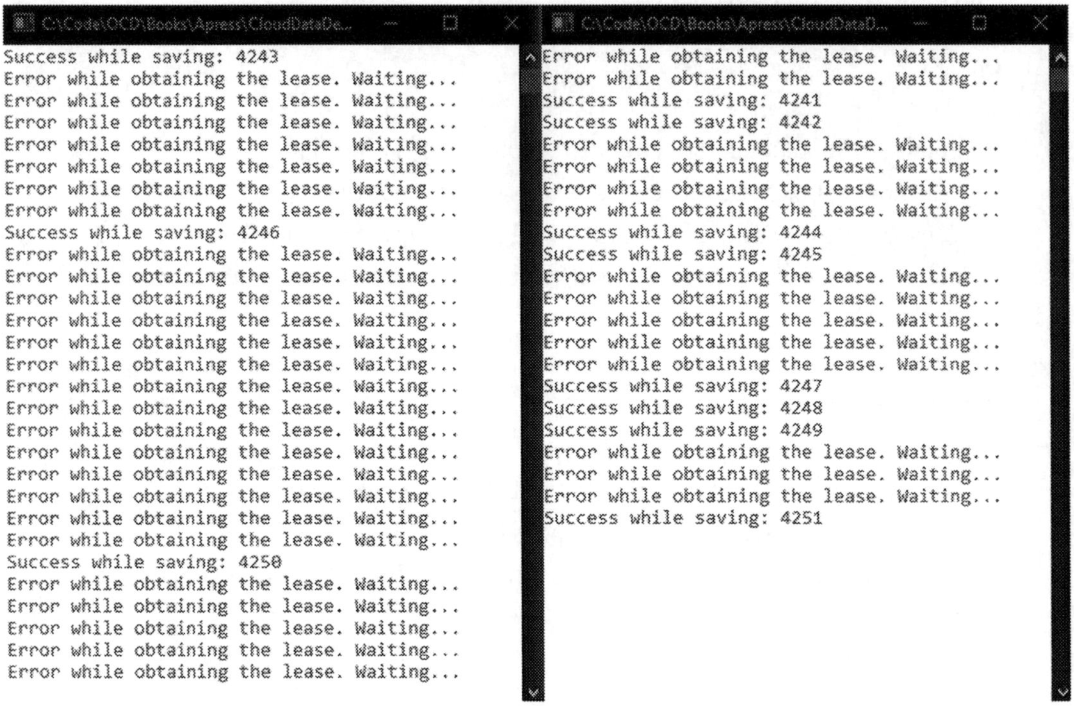

Figure 3-7. *We see two concurrent jobs trying to acquire a lease to perform a job. Only one worker can get the lease and enter the critical section. Finally, in case someone else has changed/released/re-acquired the lease under-the-hood, the write action will fail due to the conditional access policy*

So we have two ways to deal with concurrency, even if I would like to emphasize to reduce its usage at minimum, since we are dealing with HTTP stack and network latency, which is not the best choice to use them for high-performance synchronization patterns. Instead, we suggest to define distributed architectures to use immutable Blobs, in order to avoid (where possible) the need of changing them.

Understanding Access and Security

Every blob in the Blob storage (also Page blobs, which are not covered in this book) is represented by an URL that uniquely identifies it worldwide:

```
http(s)://[account].blob.core.windows.net/[container]/[blob]
```

This URL is the fully qualified name of the blob itself and, in case the blob stays in a "Public" container, this URL also gives others access to its content publicly.

For most situations where Blob storage is used to store public assets (i.e., products imagery, web content, scripts) this is a ready-to-go solution; at the other side, users are prevented from directly access blobs contained in a "Private" container.

We now focus on a third option which is very useful in many scenarios. Let's think about a common Web Application providing bookings to users (flight bookings, e-commerce orders, hotel bookings) where the "order" can be often represented by a PDF with the transaction data plus some sensitive data about the user.

We want to focus on the workflow starting when a user clicks on the Download button in his/her profile page, to download the transaction summary. We also suppose this PDF is not generated on-the-fly and it is stored somewhere in the Blob storage.

In the first approach we can assume PDFs are stored into a "Public" container and we can embed the public URL into the page:

```
<a link=https://[account].blob.core.windows.net/pdfs/ORDXXXXXX.pdf
>Download</a>
```

This approach is the simplest but exposes the entire PDF set to the Internet. A user can easily infer another order number to try download other's content. Some real-world applications use to prepend a GUID somewhere in the URL to make guessing harder, but in our opinion, it is not a real solution:

```
<a link=https://[account].blob.core.windows.net/pdfs/[random-number-or-
guid]/ORDXXXXXX.pdf >Download</a>
```

We can now protect the Blob using a "Private" container, but this prevents the browser form directly download it. In a first attempt, we can proceed as follows:

1. The Web Application displays an internal URL like "/DownloadPDF"

2. A handler inside the web app, using the Storage Account keys, first downloads the contents into a temporary file and it serves it as a download stream to the browser

This approach forces two distinct transfers, one for the server-to-storage download and one for the server-to-browser push. Even in case we are not paying for the intra-region bandwidth, it represents a waste of resources.

The ideal solution is the one we are now approaching, using the Shared Access Signature feature of the Storage Account itself.

Shared Access Signatures

With SAS, we can generate a signed URL based on a private resource, to let it be available to end-users without knowing the administration key of the entire storage. The process is quite simple:

1. Identify the private blob we want to "share"

2. Identify some parameters:

    a.   The timeframe the share link will be valid

    b.   The type of operations permitted (read, read/write, only write, etc.)

3. Using a public algorithm and one of the Access Keys, generate a signature for that blob with the parameters above, in order to generate a deep link to the secured resource

If we had a blob like this:

```
https://apress.blob.core.windows.net/private/counter.txt
```

A SAS-enabled URL can be as follows:

```
https://apress.blob.core.windows.net/private/counter.txt?st=2017-12-
01T14%3A26%3A00Z&se=2017-12-02T14%3A26%3A00Z&sp=rl&sv=2015-12-11&sr=b&sig=%
2FUdYYlH%2B36swEINIaExizietG%2FWTS9TlFckR89kykrU%3D
```

This URL embeds the timeframe of validity of the URL itself (form 12/01/2017 to 12/02/2017) with the appropriate permission set (sp=rl stands for "Read" and "List" permissions).

This could be the link we can provide to end-users, to be downloaded directly from the browser.

If SAS are used more often, we can rely on the SAPs (Shared Access Policies) to define a single policy which can be applied to multiple resources. For example, if we define a Policy with fixed parameters, we can apply it to multiple blobs to centralize the revocation of the permissions. In case of a single SAS is setup, revocation is available only through changing the Access Key used for the signature generation.

To generate SASs and SAPs we can use:

- the REST API directly

- the Azure Storage managed library

- Azure Storage Explorer (https://azure.microsoft.com/it-it/features/storage-explorer/) - Free

- Azure Management Studio (https://www.cerebrata.com/products/azure-management-studio) - Commercial

- CloudBerry Explorer (https://www.cloudberrylab.com/explorer/microsoft-azure.aspx) - Free/Commercial

Encryption Options

We can (to read "must") use HTTPS instead the plain HTTP to access blobs. It is strongly recommended to enforce this behaviour in the client applications, even if a recent service upgrade introduced this option (Figure 3-8):

Figure 3-8. *We can set the option on Enabled, in the Configuration blade of the storage account, to prevent clients to connect using plain HTTP (for the blob service) or using SMB without encryption (for the file service)*

The previous option is also known as Encryption-in-transit, since prevents the contents be intercepted in the middle of the connection. Another option is the Encryption-at-rest (Figure 3-9), which includes an encryption pass when the data is stored on the underlying media.

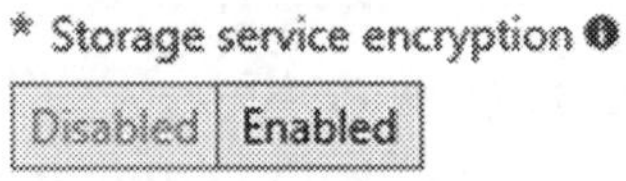

* Storage service encryption ❶

| Disabled | Enabled |

Figure 3-9. *The encryption option will encrypt all the new contents arriving to the account after its enablement. Old content won't be encrypted (except it is overwritten) and this option cannot be reverted once enabled*

At the time of this writing, encryption key is managed, secured, and rolled by Microsoft itself. There is a preview feature letting customers choose their keys using Azure Key Vault.

Security Perimeter

Since the beginning of the Azure Storage Service, every Storage Account have been available on the Internet by default. There was no way to prevent specific users to access the account or, conversely, to enable just few IPs or VNets to access it securely.

Recently, Microsoft introduces a Firewall capability similar to the one used in SQL Database, with the additional benefit to include one or more Virtual Networks in the trusted ring of permitted clients (Figure 3-10). In this last case, it is also guaranteed that the path followed by the clients, inside a VNet, will not pass through the public internet. For more information of this feature, known as Virtual Network Service Endpoints, you can follow this link: `https://docs.microsoft.com/en-us/azure/virtual-network/virtual-network-service-endpoints-overview`.

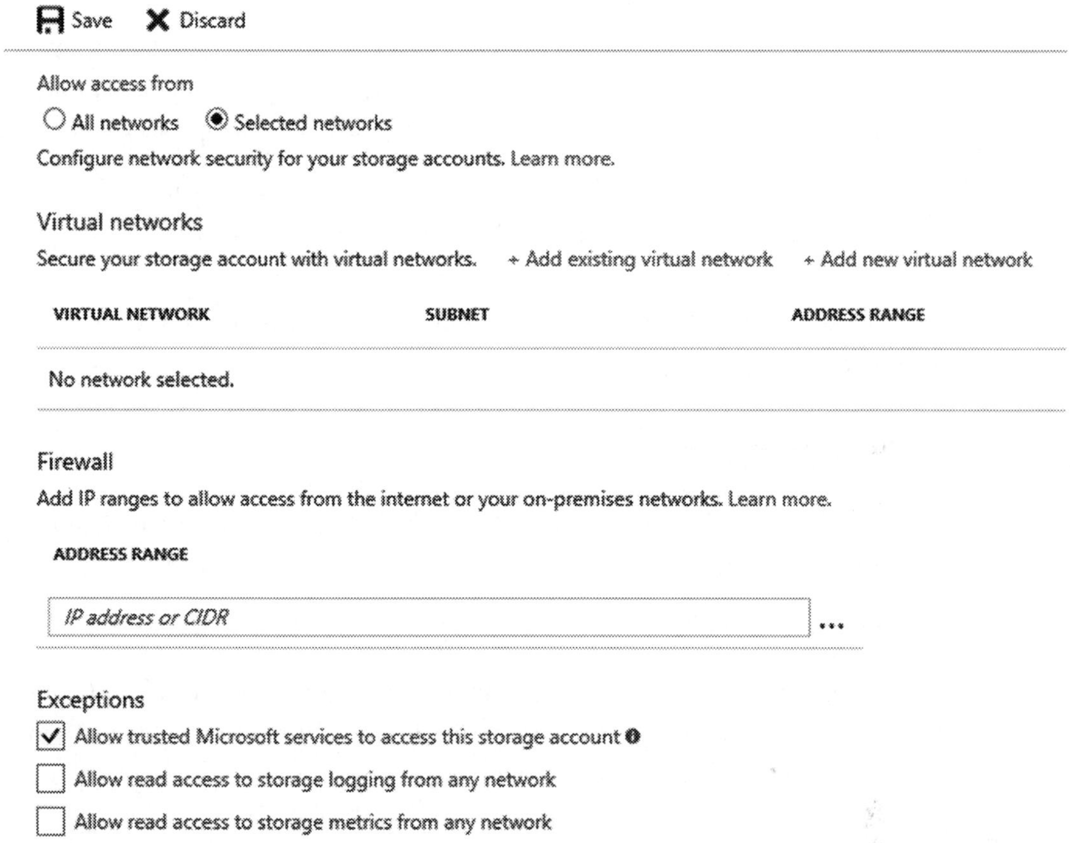

🖫 Save   ✕ Discard

Allow access from
○ All networks   ⦿ Selected networks
Configure network security for your storage accounts. Learn more.

Virtual networks
Secure your storage account with virtual networks.   + Add existing virtual network   + Add new virtual network

VIRTUAL NETWORK	SUBNET	ADDRESS RANGE

No network selected.

Firewall
Add IP ranges to allow access from the internet or your on-premises networks. Learn more.

ADDRESS RANGE

IP address or CIDR	•••

Exceptions
☑ Allow trusted Microsoft services to access this storage account ❶
☐ Allow read access to storage logging from any network
☐ Allow read access to storage metrics from any network

Figure 3-10. *We see how to include new or existing VNets to the allowed clients for the Storage Account, as well as specific IPs on the public internet. In case we have external monitoring software using the logging and metrics features of the storage account, we can check the last two options above*

Using Azure Storage Tables

Azure Storage Tables have been one of the first services offered in the Azure Platform from the beginning. For many reasons, its adoption has not been as huge as the blob storage or SQL Database, but it represents a great NoSQL alternative for whom looking for a simple but performant key-value storage service with minimal indexing capabilities.

Now, the new growing trend is to emphasize the usage of the Storage Account for Blobs only, moving the need of Storage Tables to Cosmos DB. In fact, since Storage Tables are available only for General Purpose storage accounts (which often are not included in new features), it can be read as an implicit suggestion to invest on the Blob Storage endpoint or, for Tables, on the Table API of CosmosDB.

But what is the Table service? Despite the name resembles the relational world, we are not dealing with tables at all.

Planning and Using Table Storage

One of the biggest misconception about Table Storage is the query capability of it. Since there are client libraries which let us write code as follows:

```
context.CreateQuery<Order>("MyQuery").Where(p=> p.LastName.Equals("Doe"))
```

It is a very common misconception to think about Table Storage as an indexed data store. In fact, this is not true, and the only indexed fields, mandatory for each entity and to be explicitly populated, are those three:

- PartitionKey

- RowKey

- Timestamp (it is populated by the service and it cannot be modified)

This means the query above will perform an explicit Scan on the table, so records will be fetched in bulk from the storage to clients until the condition has been satisfied.

As stated above, we are enforcing the schema of the query/table on the client side. In fact, on the service side, there is no concept of Order and, as mentioned before, we can have two completely different entities in the same table as well.

Understanding PartitionKey, RowKey, Timestamp, and Fields

The PartitionKey can be a string value up to 1KB in size. The purpose of the PartitionKey, under the hood, is to let the service partition the storage across storage nodes.

The RowKey is the unique identifier of an entity of a given partition. Together with the PartitionKey, it represents the primary key of an entity in a table. The RowKey can be also a string value up to 1KB.

The Timestamp is a server-maintained fields with the time an entity was last updated.

As mentioned above, other fields are defined at entity-level, meaning that two entities can define the field "Amount" as string and double, respectively.

The supported data types are:

EDM (OData) Data Type	CLR Type	Description
Edm.Binary	byte[]	An array of bytes up to 64KB
Edm.Boolean	Bool	A boolean
Edm.DateTime	DateTime	A 64-bit datetime in UTC format
Edm.Double	Double	A 64-bit floating point value
Edm.Guid	Guid	A 128-bit GUID
Edm.Int32	Int32 (int)	A 32-bit integer
Edm.Int64	Int64 (long)	A 64-bit integer
Edm.String	String (string)	A UTF-16 encoded string up to 64KB

Since the PartitionKey and RowKey fields are often used in the resources URLs, there are some restrictions applied. We can even use the common sense, avoiding slash, backslash, question mark and special characters. Here a sample of a URL for a PUT request updating and entity:

```
PUT https://[account].table.core.windows.net/[table](PartitionKey='Heatmaps',
RowKey='591769:2:015beb5f-8e67-426b-93d7-e3e8e4536269')
```

We use "Heatmaps" as PartitionKey to group the sampling by its type; in the RowKey field, instead, we make a concatenation of different fields to use them while querying later.

In Table service, we cannot index any fields explicitly. The only two usable fields in queries are PartitionKey and RowKey. If we want to retrieve data in a certain order, it is very important to design the values of those fields appropriately.

PartitionKey is designed to suggest the engine to partition unrelated data; so it is important to keep related data in the same partition to improve performance of queries. On the other side, the RowKey is the actual primary key of the entity inside a given partition, ad it can be composed to fill as much information as we can.

Ordering is important too and Table Service automatically orders the entity retrieved by its PartitionKey and then by the RowKey. This means, in case we would like to order the results by the most recent, we should format the RowKey appropriately. Let's take a concrete case:

PartitionKey	RowKey
Orders	EW002341;00034;636483420626403391
Orders	AC120013;00125;636483421493850048

The two orders in the table above have a RowKey composed as follows:

`ORDERID;AMOUNT;DATETIME_TICKS`

We can easily see how the second is the latter one, since the Ticks value is higher. However, while querying the Table Service with the query "PartitionKey eq 'Orders'" this would be the result:

PartitionKey	RowKey
Orders	AC120013;00125;636483421493850048
Orders	EW002341;00034;636483420626403391

Because the Table storage will order the result by the RowKey value. Let's say we always want a reverse chronological ordering in place (meaning the first result should be the last order arrived). We cannot say the key composition above will satisfy the requirement, since another order can change the result set:

PartitionKey	RowKey
Orders	AC120013;00125;636483421493850048
Orders	EW002341;00034;636483420626403391
Orders	WW12999;00014;636483424083654861

We now have a third order which is the most recent (with higher Ticks value). Let's change the RowKey composition pattern as is:

`REVERSE_DATETIME_TICKS;ORDERID;AMOUNT`

For REVERSE_DATETIME_TICKS we mean the subtraction HIGHEST_NUMBER-DATETIME_TICKS or, in C#:

```
DateTime.MaxValue.Ticks-DateTime.Now.Ticks
```

Under this strategy, we produce decreasing numbers while the time flows, guaranteeing the latter order will have the lowest number:

PartitionKey	RowKey
Orders	2518895551916345138;WW12999;00014
Orders	2518895554506149951;AC120013;00125
Orders	2518895555373596608;EW002341;00034

GUIDELINES FOR TABLE DESIGN

As explained in the previous section the most important advice while implementing a Table Storage solution is the choice of the right RowKey composition. Choosing the right strategy for this can workaround the limitation of the Table Storage itself missing secondary indexes on custom fields.

It is also important to use PartitionKey to effectively group unrelated data. In conjunction with this, it is recommended to always specify both PartitionKey and RowKey in queries; otherwise, if just the RowKey is specified, the query will perform the lookup across partitions, which is slower and more expensive.

If a single RowKey pattern is not enough to speed up the query process, think about storing the same value multiple times, using different RowKey composition patterns. Also, consider to de-normalize data, since Table Storage was intended to be used for Big Data purposes.

Finally, consider asking for the only fields needed in the query, by using projection, to avoid unnecessary bandwidth consumption and to improve the overall performance of the query itself.

Dealing with CRUD Operations

A single Table Storage endpoint can contain several tables and, in each one, there can be several different PartitionKey values and entities. Starting from the recommendations above, we should place related data into the same table and using the same PartitionKey. This will ensure we can join multiple entities in an Entity Group Transaction, which is the transaction type supported in Table Storage.

Entity Group Transactions are batch transaction applied to entities in the same table and with the same PartitionKey value. The supported operations are the following:

- Insert (Or Replace, Or Merge) Entity

- Update Entity

- Merge Entity

- Delete Entity

However there are some limitations around EGT, with on the top the maximum number of entities involved into a single transaction (100) and the request max size (4MB).

Those limitations suggest to use some patterns to deal with common scenarios. Let's take one as an example:

PartitionKey	RowKey	Coordinates
Locations	000121;00001	45.464204:9.189982
Locations	000121;00002	41.902783:12.496366
Locations	000121;00003	40.851775:14.268124

As shown above, the DeviceID '000121' generates some coordinates samples to be captured for further maps pinning. A single entity is written for each sample. Using EGT, we can save a bulk of 100 samples in a single transaction, which seem okay. However, in case of deletion of an entire DeviceID, we need to cycle a lot around entities.

We can avoid this by proceeding in two distinct ways:

- Aggregate multiple coordinates samples in a single entity: we can store up to 1MB for a single entity and we can reduce the number of total entities with the consequent reduction of the total operations needed to insert/update/delete them.

- Use a different table for each DeviceID: this will not save by itself time while inserting/updating data but, in case of deletion, we can delete the entire table in a single shot and recreate it later.

Besides those considerations, here it is a simple Point Query to get a range of results:

```
TableQuery<MyEntity> rangeQuery = new TableQuery<MyEntity>().Where(
    TableQuery.CombineFilters(
        TableQuery.GenerateFilterCondition("PartitionKey", Query
        Comparisons.Equal, "Locations"),
        TableOperators.And,
        TableQuery.GenerateFilterCondition("RowKey", QueryComparisons.
        LessThan, "000121;99999")));
```

This is SDK-based code, where MyEntity is a POCO with strong-typed properties, decorated with Attributes mapping to Table fields.

OData and Supported Queries

Table Service uses REST to operate with resources. The base endpoint is in the following form:

```
http(s)://[account].table.core.windows.net
```

A single table is expressed as follows:

```
http(s)://[account].table.core.windows.net/Samples() - It returns all the
entities
```

Not the whole OData clauses are supported; actually just those three:

- $filter: used to apply conditions (max 15 per query)

- $top: used to take the first N results

- $select: used to project only the desired fields

The $filter clause supports the following operators:

- eq - ne: Equal, NotEqual

- gt - lt: GreaterThan, LowerThan

- ge - le: GreaterOrEqual, LessThanOrEqual

- and, not, or

For whom are already familiar with OData the encoding we must apply to queries is probably well known. Since the query string is part of the URL itself, a starting query like this:

```
$filter=LastName eq 'Freato' and FirstName eq 'Roberto'
```

Must be encoded as follows:

```
$filter=LastName%20eq%20'Freato'%20and%20FirstName%20eq%20'Roberto'
```

LIMIT THE BANDWIDTH CONSUMED

By default, the Table Service echoes the request body payload in a successful response of insertion methods like Insert Entity. We can set the HTTP header "Prefer" to "return-no-content", to avoid this default behavior. This is particularly useful in scenarios where massive data is inserted from "outside" the Azure DCs. In those cases, while every ingress byte is free, every egress one is paid. This strategy also saves time while requests are generated from inside the same Region of the Table Service.

Understanding Monitoring

This part applies also to Blob Storage, but it is covered here since Tables are involved. Azure Storage is one of the core services of the Azure platform and there is an extensive approach to monitoring, diagnosing and troubleshooting it (Figure 3-11).

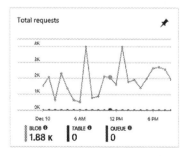
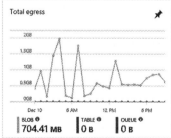
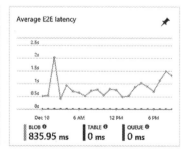

Figure 3-11. *This is a quick view into some of the collected metrics of Azure Storage. We see the Total Request metric, the Total Egress traffic (which is the paid traffic related to the service account), the Average End-to-End latency, which is the time taken to process the request and send back the response to the clients. We see those metric for the three services "Blob, Table, Queue"*

Apart from the quick look on your Storage account, Azure Storage Analytics performs logging and provides metrics for a storage account (Figure 3-12). Storage Analytics is not a standalone service: instead, it is related to a given Storage Account and we should opt-in explicitly while creating a new one.

Figure 3-12. *As we see, there are some metrics to enable. For each service, there are the aggregates metric and the API metrics. Instead, for logging, Azure Files is not yet supported at time of writing*

Metrics and Logging can be also enabled via REST API and, consequently, via the SDK and C# code. In the following excerpt, we enable Logging and hourly Metrics:

```
//Creating the Blob Client
var connStr = "DefaultEndpointsProtocol=https;AccountName=[name];AccountKey
=[key]";
var account = CloudStorageAccount.Parse(connStr);
var blobClient = account.CreateCloudBlobClient();

//Enable logging
var properties = new ServiceProperties();
var retention = 7;
var version = "1.0";
properties.Logging = new LoggingProperties()
```

```
{
    LoggingOperations= LoggingOperations.All,
    RetentionDays=retention,
    Version=version
};

//Enable metrics
properties.HourMetrics = new MetricsProperties()
{
    MetricsLevel=MetricsLevel.ServiceAndApi,
    RetentionDays=retention,
    Version=version
};

properties.MinuteMetrics = new MetricsProperties()
{
    MetricsLevel = MetricsLevel.ServiceAndApi,
    RetentionDays = retention,
    Version = version
};

blobClient.SetServiceProperties(properties);
```

Exploring Metrics and Logging

At one side, we have metrics, which represents aggregate measures for a given KPI (RequestTime, E2ELatency, etc.); in other words, statistics. At the other side, we have logging, which includes the details of successful/failed requests. To avoid recursion, all request made by the Storage Analytics itself are not logged.

Metrics go to Table Storage, while Logs go to Blob Storage. Both generates billable traffic and capacity consumption.

There are special tables for the metrics, for example:

- $MetricsTransactionsBlob

- $MetricsTransactionsTable

- $MetricsTransactionsQueue

Actually, those three tables are the "old" tables containing hourly metrics. Now, the recommendation is to use the specific tables:

- $MetricsHour[Primary|Secondary]Transactions[Blob|Table|Queue|File]

- $MetricsHour[Primary|Secondary]Transactions[Blob|Table|Queue|File]

- $MetricsCapacityBlob

As stated above, we have the $MetricsCapacityBlob table containing statistics of capacity and actual size of the Blob Storage. However, this useful information is not yet available for the other sub-services (Tables/Queues/Files).

If enabled, a rich set of data is collected for each service and API operation in a per-hour and per-minute basis. Metrics are not supported for the Storage Account of Account Kind "Storage", since there are no tables where Storage Analytics could rely on.

$MetricsCapacityBlob

This tables contains the metrics of size occupancy of Blob storage. Data is collected daily with the retention specified in configuration. An example is shown below (Figure 3-13):

PartitionKey ∧	RowKey	Timestamp	Capacity	ContainerCount	ObjectCount
20171205T0000	analytics	2017-12-05T01:23:30.555Z	58	1	0
20171205T0000	data	2017-12-05T01:23:30.670Z	695235535163	62	5388938
20171206T0000	analytics	2017-12-06T01:21:05.449Z	58	1	0
20171206T0000	data	2017-12-06T01:21:05.119Z	695940940017	62	5389532
20171207T0000	analytics	2017-12-07T01:24:53.948Z	58	1	0
20171207T0000	data	2017-12-07T01:24:53.700Z	696604921508	62	5390302
20171208T0000	analytics	2017-12-08T01:24:16.489Z	58	1	0
20171208T0000	data	2017-12-08T01:24:16.478Z	697093363776	62	5391080
20171209T0000	analytics	2017-12-09T01:23:36.321Z	58	1	0
20171209T0000	data	2017-12-09T01:23:36.081Z	697211853929	62	5391240
20171210T0000	analytics	2017-12-10T01:22:24.387Z	58	1	0
20171210T0000	data	2017-12-10T01:22:24.131Z	697332157313	62	5391434
20171211T0000	analytics	2017-12-11T01:24:04.496Z	1515142	1	15
20171211T0000	data	2017-12-11T01:24:03.770Z	697427231925	62	5391444

Figure 3-13. *This is an excerpt of the $MetricsCapacityBlob table, showing capacity for the Blob Storage account. In the case above, we have an average of about 5.390.000 object of an average size of 12-13KB*

We see two distinct rows for each of the last (at time of capturing) 7 days of retention, with the fields:

- PartitionKey: determines the day of sampling

- RowKey: determines if the row is user data (data) or analytics data (analytics)

- Timestamp: indicates the actual time of sampling

- Capacity: the size in bytes of the used Blob storage

- ContainerCount: the number of containers

- ObjectCount: the number of objects

$MetricsHourPrimaryTransactionsBlob

This table contains a lot of useful information about the activity generated on the Blob storage (and there are other ones respectively for Tables/Queues/Files).

PartitionKey ^	RowKey	Timestamp	TotalRequests	TotalBillableRequests	TotalIngress	TotalEgress	Availability	AverageE2ELatency
20171211T0100	system;All	2017-12-11T02:24:35.534Z	28	28	303266	5130	100	46.392857
20171211T0100	user;ListBlobs	2017-12-11T02:24:35.534Z	7	7	3028	1997365	100	263
20171211T0200	system;All	2017-12-11T03:21:55.511Z	27	27	817017	4970	100	51.777778
20171211T0200	user;All	2017-12-11T03:21:55.516Z	1424	1424	661306	2436858922	100	1124.341377
20171211T0200	user;GetBlob	2017-12-11T03:21:55.511Z	552	552	157646	148647283	100	707.521415
20171211T0200	user;ListBlobs	2017-12-11T03:21:55.511Z	871	871	502162	2288194823	100	1382.598163
20171211T0200	user;ListContainers	2017-12-11T03:21:55.511Z	1	1	382	15002	100	15
20171211T0300	system;All	2017-12-11T04:24:17.264Z	27	27	590606	4905	100	73.444444
20171211T0300	user;All	2017-12-11T04:24:17.845Z	1156	1156	401779	568910348	100	556.335371
20171211T0300	user;GetBlob	2017-12-11T04:24:17.264Z	941	941	299147	196134118	100	466.078495
20171211T0300	user;GetBlobProperties	2017-12-11T04:24:17.264Z	10	10	2855	4034	100	6.7
20171211T0300	user;GetBlockList	2017-12-11T04:24:17.264Z	10	10	4065	5184	100	88.4
20171211T0300	user;ListBlobs	2017-12-11T04:24:17.264Z	195	195	95163	372766149	100	1038.974359
20171211T0400	system;All	2017-12-11T05:22:36.755Z	26	26	396239	4745	100	59.653846

Figure 3-14. *We notice the table is similar to the previous one. In this case we have hourly sampling aggregated and pivoted for each API service call (i.e., GetBlob, ListBlobs, etc.)*

We have a lot of metrics available here (Figure 3-14), each one in a row aggregated for the whole account and the whole service API call:

- PartitionKey: determines the time of sampling

- RowKey: determines if the row is user data (user) or analytics data (system)

- Timestamp: indicates the actual time of sampling

- TotalRequests: includes the successful and failed requests

- TotalBillableRequests: indicates how many billable requests among the total request are registered. Azure can self-demote some requests to the non-billable status, if it classifies them ineligible.

We analyze each request received and then classify it as billable or not billable based upon our ability to process the request and the request's outcome.

(from MSDN)

- TotalIngress: the amount of (free) ingress data to the account

- TotalEgress: the egress (subject to billing) data from the account

- Availability: indicates the calculated availability of the system, by dividing the TotalBillableRequests on the TotalRequests.

- AverageE2ELatency: as mentioned earlier, it is the time to Read the request, Send the response, Receive ack of the response.

- PercentSuccess: indicates the percentage of successful request. If not, requests are made to the account, the value will be zero.

  - Success metrics will provide the related number (not percentage)

- PercentThrottlingError, PercentTimeoutError, PercentServerOtherError, PercentClientOtherError, PercentAuthorizationError, PercentNetworkError

  - Indicates a percentage of failed request for a given Error

The complete list is available here:

```
https://docs.microsoft.com/it-it/rest/api/storageservices/Storage-
Analytics-Metrics-Table-Schema?redirectedfrom=MSDN
```

Exploring Logging

There is a special container in the Blob Storage named $logs. This is the candidate container for the logs of the account, which are organized as follows:

```
[service-name]/YYYY/MM/DD/hhmm/[counter].log
```

Inside each Log entry, we should expect a semicolon(;)-separated file in this format:

<version-number>;<request-start-time>;<operation-type>;<request-status>;
<http-status-code>;<end-to-end-latency-in-ms>;<server-latency-in-ms>;
<authentication-type>;<requester-account-name>;<owner-account-name>;
<service-type>;<request-url>;<requested-object-key>;<request-id-header>;
<operation-count>;<requester-ip-address>;<request-version-header>;
<request-header-size>;<request-packet-size>;<response-header-size>;
<response-packet-size>;<request-content-length>;<request-md5>;<server-md5>;
<etag-identifier>;<last-modified-time>;<conditions-used>;
<user-agent-header>;<referrer-header>;<client-request-id>

The first four fields have the following semantics:

- Version number: it is important if we plan to automatically parse those logs

- Request start time (trivial) and Request type (API type)

- Request status: the various status a request can have, like to AnonymousSuccess or failures

A complete list is available here:

```
https://docs.microsoft.com/it-it/rest/api/storageservices/storage-
analytics-log-format
```

To give an example of using this dataset, we can pivot on the <request-url> fields to calculate how much a single blob would costs in terms of transactions and bandwidth.

Another interesting piece of information about logs comes from the Blob metadata itself. Each log blob is saved with the following Metadata:

- StartTime: the time of the earliest entry of the log

- EndTime: the time of the latest entry of the log

- LogType: write/read/delete, or a combination of the three

- LogVersion: it is the same version number as the first fields of the blob content

Since the various log files are organized by the [counter] number and it is not predictable how many entries and of which timeframe they consist of, we can use the StartTime and EndTime to lookup for specific content. Specifically, we can list blobs of a specific day range using the ListBlob API (with prefix), specifying to fetch the Metadata attributes, in order to understand the only relevant files to download actually.

Using Azure Monitor

Azure Monitor is the central point of discovery of the metrics coming from the whole of the Azure Platform services. While some features are still in preview, it enables to consume metrics from a variety of Azure services in a central location, providing the capability of filtering, drilling and pinning the results to the Dashboard (Figure 3-15).

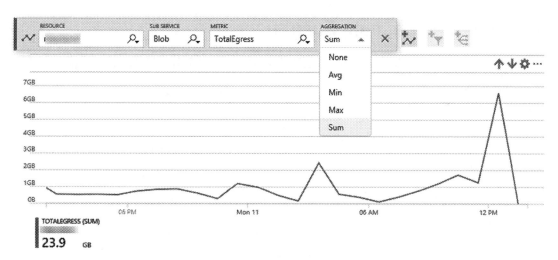

Figure 3-15. *This is a view of the TotalEgress metric of a production Storage account for Blobs in the last 24 hours*

Azure Monitor can integrate to OMS to ship every metric collected for further analysis inside Log Analytics. Data can be consumed by REST API to setup custom action or, through the Alerts feature, can notify the administrators in case a condition is satisfied. Alerts can also be re-used inside the Azure Platform itself to trigger some platform events, like autoscaling.

Using Azure Redis Cache

Redis is an open source (BSD licensed), in-memory data structure store, used as a database, cache and message broker. It supports data structures such as strings, hashes, lists, sets, sorted sets with range queries, bitmaps, hyperloglogs and geospatial indexes with radius queries. Redis has built-in replication, Lua scripting, LRU eviction, transactions and different levels of on-disk persistence, and provides high availability via Redis Sentinel and automatic partitioning with Redis Cluster.

From the official site "Redis.io"

However this chapter is not about Redis itself, but on caching and its declination onto the Azure Platform. The distributed cache problem is the final point of a series of considerations about performance. Let's investigate this point in the next section.

Justifying the Caching Scenario

Suppose we have a simple, custom Blog engine which serves blog posts to the users. The simplified editorial workflow can be the following:

- An author writes the piece for further review from the editor

- After performing one or multiple editorial passes, the content is published

- Anonymous users read blog posts

- Authenticated users can comment the posts

- Authors and Editors can change the contents whenever

From the technical point of view, let's suppose we have an ASP.NET application (just for the minimal code snippets we need in the chapter) with a SQL Database as the data store. The simplest system design can be the following (Figure 3-16):

- When an author/editor writes/edits a blog post, it is saved into a row of a table in the SQL Database

- When a user (either authenticated or not) navigates to a blog post page, the contents are fetched from the SQL Database and displayed

This first approach is very trivial but effective and correct. Let's now suppose some metrics:

- Pageviews: 100/sec

- SQL queries (read): 300/sec

- SQL queries (write): 5/sec

Those are realistic metrics for a given Blog website with moderate traffic. We notice immediately the write operations are less than read ones and, on an average, we have about 3 SQL queries for each web request.

Having a high ratio of queries/request is a normal pattern. Since we need to build the page aggregate (the post content, the comments, the UI configuration, other elements, etc.) we can imagine each piece generates its own query. It's not bad by itself but it can be optimized for sure.

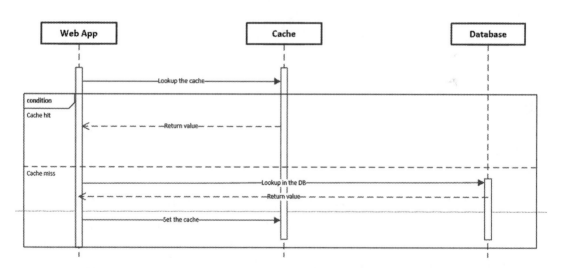

Figure 3-16. *In this first step, we actively feed the cache with data (if not already present) from the fresh DB*

From the development perspective, using C# and the StackExchange.Redis library (we can connect to Redis using several libraries as well), the approach is near to the following:

```csharp
var conn = ConnectionMultiplexer.Connect("[connStr]");
var db=conn.GetDatabase(10);

try
{
    IEnumerable<BlogPost> posts = null;
    var res = db.StringGet("GetBlogPosts");
    if (!res.HasValue)
    {
        res = JsonConvert.SerializeObject(posts=GetBlogPosts());
        db.StringSet("GetBlogPosts", res);
    }
    else
    {
        posts = JsonConvert.DeserializeObject<BlogPost[]>(res);
    }

}
catch (Exception)
{
    throw;
}
```

As we can see, we create a connection to the Redis cache and to a given Database (in Redis we deal with the concept of Databases that are logical groups of keys isolated between each other. We then try to get the value from the key "GetBlogPosts". In case of a cache miss, we proceed to the active materialization through the GetBlogPosts() method, to further serialize the results and feed the cache for the next lookup. In case of a cache hit, we proceed to the deserialization to use the results.

Unit of Caching

One of the biggest problem in caching is what to cache. In the previous sample we cached the generic GetBlogPosts method, that is provocatory, since it's very unlikely there is a Database query to get all the blog posts in a single shot.

But think about it for a moment: wouldn't be great to take in-memory all the blog posts to serve them directly from the memory, instead looking one by one on the DB?

It is completely up to the developer/architect what to cache in terms of aggregate. In the case above is probably wrong to cache the entire blog posts collection since, in case of new posts, a complete refresh of the entire cache item is needed. Instead, we can work on a per-posts caching pattern.

```
var res = db.StringGet("GetBlogPost_12142312");
if (!res.HasValue)
{
    res = JsonConvert.SerializeObject(post = GetBlogPost(12142312));
    db.StringSet("GetBlogPost_12142312", res);
}
```

In the modified code, we have a new data method fetching a single post, based on the post ID passed as parameter. We can use that ID to construct the proper key to lookup the Redis cache and to feed it.

This approach can be useful in the Blog Post page, where a single post is shown full page. But what about the Homepage? If we had to show the latest 10 posts in a preview fashion? Let's discuss it in the next section.

Cache Invalidation

One of the biggest problems around caching is its invalidation, that can be explicit (someone deletes the specific Key from the cache, or replaces it with a new value) or implicit (by defining a timeout while inserting the Key, after that the item is removed automatically from the caching engine).

Thinking about the discussed scenario, we identified those two cases:

- Homepage: we need an excerpt of the latest 10 blog posts

- Blog post page: we need the complete blog post to show

As for the initial specifications, we need to invalidate the cache every time an author/editor will re-publish the post. This means, as a first attempt, we need to write code in the blog engine, to link the publishing action with a cache invalidation statement, like this one:

```
db.KeyDelete("[key]");
```

This tells Redis to remove immediately the key and, as we setup before, at the next attempt to read that blog post, the cache would be refreshed with the new value.

We can also work on the requirements to find the perfect fit of our caching pattern. Think about the real world: is it really important to have the very latest updated content on a blog website? We mean, it is mandatory for the company to push updates in real time? If the response is yes, the pattern above is okay; however, some optimization can be made.

Supposing we can tolerate a delay of maximum 30 minutes between the post has changed and the result is live, we can feed the cache specifying an explicit timeout, to tell Redis to keep that key for the timeout specified:

```
db.StringSet("[key]", res,TimeSpan.FromMinutes(30));
```

Under this constraint, we can dramatically improve the performance of page views of a blog post.

Caching is an open theme. A variety of mixed approach exist and they are working well. In a hybrid solution, where Editorial edits must be propagated immediately to the end-users, while the author edits can wait the 30 minutes, the Blog Engine can use both approaches altogether.

Now it is clear that the Homepage requirements can easily fit the caching pattern with timeout. Smaller units of cache are preferable since they require few resources for the round-trip and storage. Bigger units are preferable when we need an aggregate where we are confident it's not changing frequently. To summarize, we need to focus on the frequency of our data and, based on this, tune the caching pattern appropriately.

Why a Distributed Cache

We explained (by over-simplifying) why we should need a cache into our applications. But now it is important to understand with we need a distributed cache and why Redis, eventually.

Let's suppose we have just the VM hosting the Web Application and the DB server. We can change the previous sequence diagram accordingly (Figure 3-17):

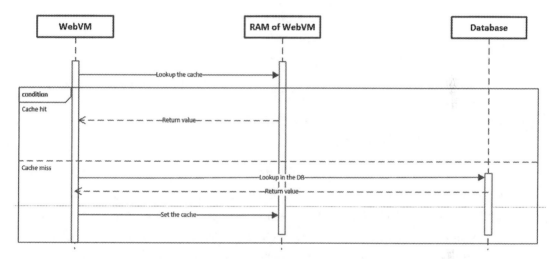

Figure 3-17. *We see the scenario is the same, with the difference that we go to the local memory of the Web Application instance*

We can obviously work on the assumptions above and make our own cache using the local memory of the Web VM. However, this approach tends to lead to some issues. The first is about scalability: since we can have hundreds of VM serving our requests (even 2 are okay for this demonstration), keeping the cached objects inside a single VM's memory can produce a waste of memory (the same data occupies, at the same time, the size of the object multiplied by the number of VM).

This waste can be however accepted most of time. The other issue, instead, is not well accepted at all. How about the Cache Invalidation discussed above? Let's see how the explicit invalidation fails (Figure 3-18):

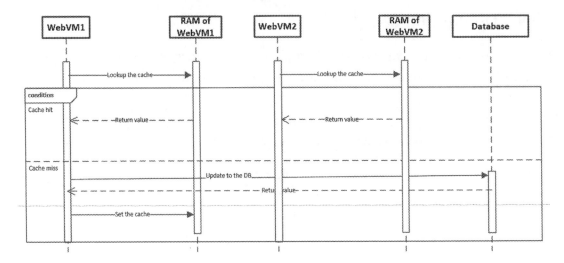

Figure 3-18. *In this sequence, we notice disalignment between the two instances hosting the web application*

It's clear we have two instances with a different view on data. In the first instance, a user publishes an update that refreshes the DB and the cache (we can either remove the Key or replace its value with the refreshed one). However, the second instance will not receive an update and it continues to serve the old cached data from its local memory.

But also, timeout invalidation fails (Figure 3-19):

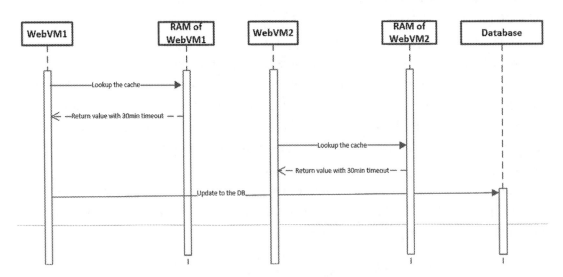

Figure 3-19. *In this sequence too, we notice disalignment between the two instances hosting the web application*

Now we have an instance that is updating the Database during the validity timeframe of the cache item of a second instance. WebVM2 is again misaligned with the real data, since there is no propagation of updates to it.

We can bypass those issues by externalizing the state outside of the running machine, using an actor which serves as a cache server as a single central point.

Why Redis

But Why Redis? We would say performance. Since we are externalizing hot data into a single central datastore, we need a software capable of:

- Working in-memory with the best efficiency and performance

  - Which means less latency, less bandwidth consumption, less CPU and VM resources

- Scale up/down as the traffic increase

  - Redis scales extremely well

Is proven there are various options to solve the problems above with other than Redis, but it is also a de-facto standard for caching and many companies use it in production for huge workloads. Apart its amazing performance, its capability to scale, through replication, enables complex scenario where we need huge resources.

In conjunction with PaaS, where replication is performed automatically, Redis (used as a Cache) can be an effective solution for the application's in-memory needs.

Understanding Features

Azure Redis Cache is a fully featured Platform-as-a-Service for Redis. Azure manages everything, from the VMs to the Storage, Network and the underlying Redis installation and configuration. The main metric of choice of a Redis instance is obviously the memory size, since is primarily an in-memory data store.

Currently there are three different tiers of Redis Cache:

- Basic: the simplest offer with no SLA and limited features, ideal for dev/test scenarios.

- Standard: suitable for the most of scenarios, with various sizes and SLA.

- Premium: suitable for the most intensive scenarios, with advanced features, sharing and private deployment options.

Those three tiers, in conjunction with the various memory sizes they support, provide users with a comprehensive set of options to build even high-end in-memory applications.

Eviction

We often deal with memory (the persistent, HDD/SSD-based one) as something that can grow in an indefinite way. Compared to volatile memory, this is still true, since the limits of persistent data stores are very high compared to the (often physical) limits of the maximum RAM we can install on a computing unit. We can have nodes with up to hundreds of GB of RAM, but no more, generally.

In an in-memory solution, we cannot simply "swap-to-disk" what is not fitting anymore in the main memory. This would invalidate at all the main purpose of products like this, like Redis. So, we need to define what happens if the memory is full: this policy is often known as Eviction Policy.

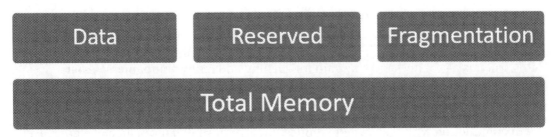

Figure 3-20. *This is how the total memory of a Redis instance is allocated. Despite the graphic does not suggest proportions, we should consider we have not the total amount of memory available for data*

As shown in the figure above (Figure 3-20), if we have, for instance, a Redis Cache of 6GB, we must reserve a portion of this space to two dedicated slots:

- Maxmemory-reserved: the amount of memory reserved for non-cache operations, like the replication overhead and more.

- Maxfragmentationmemory-reserved: the amount of memory reserved to deal with fragmentation. Fragmentation occurs mainly when eviction occurs.

Figure 3-21. *This is how we configure the reserved memory of our Redis instance. This section is available under the Advanced Settings page of the Redis instance blade on the Azure Portal*

In both the cases above (Figure 3-21), there is no the magic number or percentage to allocate for those values. It depends entirely on the data, the load and the usage patterns.

So, let's take this flow as an example:

1. We create a Redis instance of 1GB with 100MB reserved memory (50MB + 50MB)

2. We start to feed memory with data up to cache exhaustion

3. Three things can happen:

    a. One or more items have been saved with expiration and, by expiring, they are freeing up some resources.

    b. If the configuration does not allow eviction, the cache is full and cannot accept any more writes.

    c. If the configuration allows eviction, the cache picks one or more existing keys and deletes them to free up some space.

We can configure eviction in those six ways (there is no Azure in the middle of this, it's entirely a Redis-level option):

- noeviction: an error is raised when the memory reaches its full size.

- allkeys-lru: tries to remove the less-recently-used keys.

- volatile-lru: tries to remove the less-recently-used keys, but only among the ones which have an expiration set by the user.

- allkeys-random: removes random keys.

- volatile-random: removes random keys, but only among the ones which have an expiration set by the user.

- volatile-ttl: in conjunction with providing TTL when creating cached object, it tells Redis to evict first objects with shorter TTL and a valid expiration set by the user.

Generally, the allkeys-lru could be the best option in most cases.

Please note that the default option, volatile-lru, works as noeviction is there are no candidate keys matching the eviction condition.

Local Caching and Notifications

In the "Why a distributed cache" section, we see why a distributed cache is good to avoid inconsistency between multiple nodes. However, a drawback of this outsourcing, is that for each cache request (either hits or misses) we are involving an external actor (the distributed cache), which always introduces network latency.

Additionally, that's a pity, for the same source node, to subsequently request the same data to the cache server, if it has not changed. Therefore, we can "cache-the-cache", by introducing a first-level cache in the in-process memory of the application itself.

The actual scenario of this "final" workflow, can be the following (Figure 3-22):

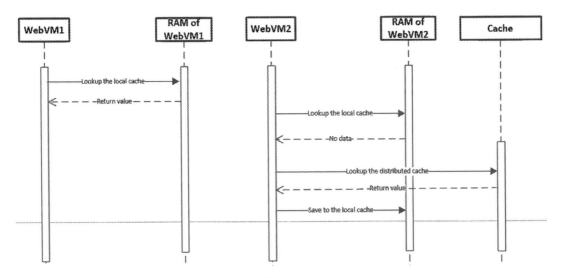

Figure 3-22. *In this last scenario, two nodes with local first-level cache behave differently. The first finds the value in its local cache, while the second needs to look it up into the distributed cache first, to then set its returning value to its local cache too*

This solution seems optimizing, but it still leads to the same issues we had before. In case one of the nodes updates/deletes a key during the timeframe it is materialized on the local cache side, there is no way for the nodes to know that, introducing serious inconsistencies.

However, Redis is, other than a Cache server, also an in-memory Message Broker. It is not actually a reliable message broker, but a good option to be notified in a Pub/Sub manner, for those events related to the usage of the keys of the data store.

This feature is known as Keyspace events notifications (Figure 3-23), as explained here:

```
https://redis.io/topics/notifications
```

There are two types of events (Figure 3-24) in Redis:

- keyspace: it is the channel from the "key" point of view. It notifies all the events occurring for a given key. The form of the notification is "__keyspace@[dbNumber]__:[key]"

- keyevent: it is the channel form the "operation" point of view. It notifies all the keys related to a given operation. The form of the notification is "__keyevent@[dbNumber]__:[operation]"

  - Operations are represented by the commands of Redis, like DEL, EXPIRE, SET

```
Welcome to secure redis console!

This console connects to your live redis server and all commands are run on the server.

WARNING: Use expensive commands with caution as they can impact your server load!

>CONFIG SET notify-keyspace-events KEA
>
```

Figure 3-23. *We are enabling the KEA notifications from the Redis Console integrated in the Azure Portal. KEA stands for "K-Keyspace channel, E-Keyevent channel, A-all commands*

notify-keyspace-events ❶

KEA

Figure 3-24. *We are enabling the same settings from within the Advanced Settings page of the Redis Cache blade in the Azure Portal*

Simple Local Cache Provider

By using the notification engine above, we can write the proper code to use a faster, in-process, local cache and also be notified from the remote Cache in case something has changed.

We can do this as follows:

```
public class SimpleLocalCacheProvider
{
    private MemoryCache localCache = null;
    private string cachePrefix = "slcp:";
    private ConnectionMultiplexer connection = null;
    private IDatabase database = null;
    private int dbNumber = 10;
    public SimpleLocalCacheProvider()
    {
        connection=ConnectionMultiplexer.Connect("[connStr]");
        database = connection.GetDatabase(dbNumber);
        localCache = MemoryCache.Default;
        Task.Run(() =>
        {
            connection.GetSubscriber()
            .Subscribe($"__keyevent@{dbNumber}__:*", (channel, value) =>
            {
                localCache.Remove(value.ToString());
            });
        });
    }
}
```

With the code above, we are saying to be notified on the Keyevent channel, for a given DB Number for every (*) commands. The local invalidation policy removes the key from the local first-level cache in reaction to any event on that key (a simple assumption).

The method feeding the cache can be the following:

```csharp
public T GetOrAdd<T>(string key,Func<(T,TimeSpan)> resolve)
{
    try
    {
        T res = default(T);
        //Local lookup
        var local = localCache.Get($"{cachePrefix}{key}");
        if (local != null) return (T)local;
        else
        {
            //Remote lookup
            var str = database.StringGet($"{cachePrefix}{key}");
            if (!str.HasValue)
            {
                var solution = resolve();
                str = JsonConvert.SerializeObject(res = solution.Item1);
                database.StringSet($"{cachePrefix}{key}", str, solution.
                Item2);
            }
            else
            {
                res = JsonConvert.DeserializeObject<T>(str);
            }
            localCache.Set($"{cachePrefix}{key}", res,null);
            return res;
        }
    }
    catch (Exception)
    {
        throw;
    }
}
```

In this method, we:

- Try to perform a local lookup

- If failed, we try to perform a remote lookup

- If failed, we materialize the data from the underlying lambda

It is a simplistic scenario, but it gives the sense of the problem we are trying to solve.

In those samples, we used the StackExchange.Redis C# library.

Persistence

Do not think about persistence as a consistent, real-time, filesystem replication of what is in memory. This isn't possible and is contrary to the purpose a Cache has. Redis cache must be in-memory and very fast, so we now discover how persistence is made and for what purpose.

Redis Persistence is a Premium feature (available in the Premium tiers of the Azure Redis Cache), which can be enabled to save, periodically, the state of the cache into Azure Storage. We must think about persistence if and only if we are working in the following assumptions:

- The Cache is not really a cache, but a reliable data store

- The Cache is so hard to build (hours, days, weeks) that a full refresh operation is not to be considered

In the first case, suppose we use the Cache as the data store to accept incoming Orders in an e-Commerce platform. An order cannot simply go to an in-memory store, but it is common to save it immediately into a reliable store like a DB, a Queue or a persistent NoSQL product. With Redis, every cache object is stored in-memory: a system failure will result in a loss of data.

In the second case, we are working in a scenario where the actual cache population has come from weeks of materialization and tuning and we do not want to lose this grace state and restart from the point zero.

In the Premium Tier, we have two options to persist the Redis state:

- RDB

- AOF

With the RDB method (Figure 3-25), Redis persists snapshots of the entire Redis instance at specific intervals (15/30/60 mins, 6/12/24 hours). The advantage of this method is the portability of the backup item, which is a self-contained file easy to store, move and restore. The main disadvantage is the frequency of the operation: even under the shortest frequency, there could be a gap between the last snapshot and the actual cache data.

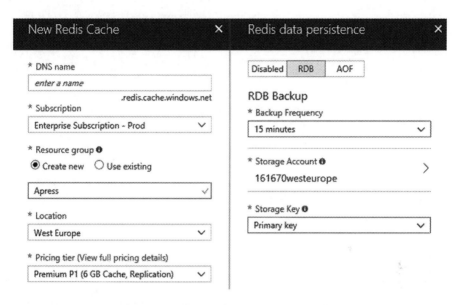

Figure 3-25. *We are configuring the Redis Persistence of a Premium Tier, with RDB method and 15 minutes frequency*

With the AOF method (Figure 3-26), a write log is continuously appended to the backup file, in order to replicate writes in case of restart. That log is saved at least once per second, which guarantees a good trade-off between performance and durability. The main disadvantage is that AOF is much more resource-intensive compared to RDB and, in case of restart, the restore process would be slower.

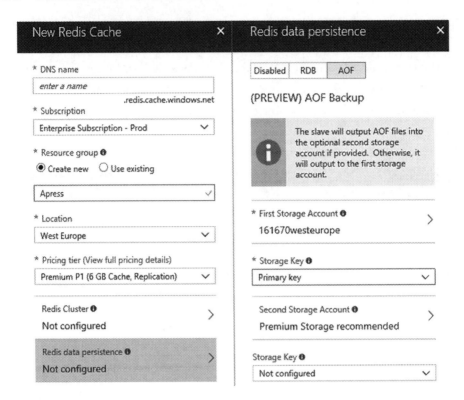

Figure 3-26. *We are configuring the Redis Persistence of a Premium Tw2ier, with AOF method using the master only*

In a plain Redis installation outside Azure, we can mix the two methods (RDB and AOF) to provide the greater flexibility and reliability of the backups, which is often the same backup strategy used by relational databases.

RDB and AOF methods use Page Blobs, so it is advised to use Premium Storage, to boost up the backup process by using the fastest storage option we have in Azure.

Private Deployments

Recently Azure started to invest a lot into private deployments, to enable customers to deploy PaaS directly inside their VNets, in order to gain endpoint protection and to be compliant with company policies.

There are two types of scenarios currently available in some Azure services:

- Public deployment with Firewall and VNet bridging

- Private deployment

When we say "private" we don't want to mean "dedicated". It's different since in the public cloud resources are, almost always, shared between tenant. Instead, "private" means the actual deployment is made into a private SDN (Software defined network) of the tenant itself.

Azure Redis Cache applies to the second scenario: a Premium Tier is deployable into a private customer VNet in order to prevent to be publicly addressable.

Understanding Management

Redis Cache is a Platform-as-a-Service, so minimal administrative effort is required to govern it in production. It is important, however, to know in advance its limitations to provide the most effective usage patterns.

Clustering and Sharding

The Standard Tier of Redis Cache is a high SLA tier, but with a Master/Slave relationship. In the Premium Tier instead, we can enable Clustering (Figure 3-27), which is completely managed by Azure. Redis Clusters are used both to scale-out/sharding (and have bigger caches) and to provide reliability.

When working with a Redis Cluster, we must know some limitations in advance:

- After a cluster is created, the action cannot be reversed

- We cannot "upgrade" a cache to a cluster, we can do it only during the creation phase

- Clustering is not supported by all the clients. StackExchange.Redis supports it.

- We can create up to 10 shards with self-provisioning (and more by asking to Microsoft) of a max size of 53GB (so 530GB total)

- When clustering is enabled on a Redis Cluster, we can only use the Database number 0.

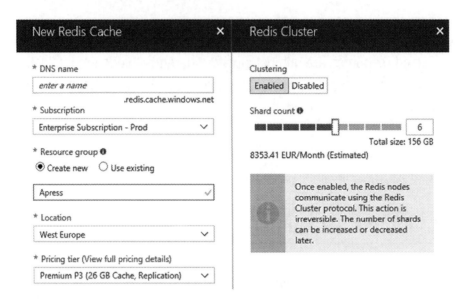

Figure 3-27. *We define a cluster of a shard size of 26GB, scaled to 6 nodes, to provide an overall cache size of 156GB. Actual prices may vary. Each shard is a primary/replica cache pair managed by Azure*

Advanced Options

In Premium Tier, we can enable a series of features (currently in preview) which makes the Tier the most appropriate for Enterprise scenarios.

Geo-replication

Geo-replication is a Premium Tier feature that enable to replicate the cache across two different Azure Regions, in order to have a read-only copy accessible for a remote location or for disaster recovery purposes.

Import/Export

In Premium Tiers, we can take the RDB file from any Redis cache inside or outside Azure and restore it on the Azure Redis Cache seamlessly. The process uses the storage account, on which we need to load the RDB files in advance, with one or more Page or Block blobs.

For Export, however, only Page Blobs are supported, which makes the Premium Storage a great option in terms of performance.

Scaling and Limitations

As the majority of PaaS, Redis Cache can scale up and out, under some constraints. As we see in the previous paragraph, scale out is available only, through sharding, on Premium Tiers. Scale up however is available, with limitations, between those Tiers:

- Basic:
    - Scaling between sizes of the same Tier results in a shutdown and reboot. This means availability can be interrupted and all data cache is lost.
    - It is possible to scale to the Standard Tier, which results in a data copy and no downtime is generated. However, we cannot change the cache size at the same time. We can do this after the first scaling process is done.
- Standard:
    - Scaling between sizes will preserve hot data
    - It is possible to scale up to the Premium Tier, but it's not possible to scale down back to Basic
- Premium:
    - It is not possible to scale back down to Standard or Basic tiers

Premium Tier is not just about sizes, it is a completely new Tier which used, under the hood, much more powerful VMs and hardware. As we mentioned earlier, we can use Persistence, Clustering, Isolation, Geo-Replication, Import/Export with Premium, which makes it the most appropriate choice for high-end, enterprise systems.

Finally, Premium instances let us reboot them (to test resiliency) and define the maintenance windows preferred.

Security, Monitoring, and Performance

Security management in Redis is very important. In cached object applications usually store sensitive data, either voluntarily or not. Think about in case we are redirecting the ASP.NET Sessione State to Redis. This is possible by just appending those lines in the Web.config file, without the developer even know that (it is almost transparent):

```
<sessionState mode="Custom" customProvider="MySessionStateStore">
    <providers>
    <!--
    <add name="MySessionStateStore"
            host = "127.0.0.1" [String] - The cache endpoint
        port = "" [number] - The cache endpoint's port
        accessKey = "" [String] - One of the two access keys
        ssl = "false" [true|false] - Connect with SSL or not (depends on
        the port)
        throwOnError = "true" [true|false] - Choose to silently fail or not
        retryTimeoutInMilliseconds = "0" [number] - Millis to retry an
        operation (0=no replies)
        databaseId = "0" [number] - Which database to use for Session State
        applicationName = "" [String] - Useful to build a good key
        "appName_sessionID_Data"
        connectionTimeoutInMilliseconds = "5000" [number] - equivalent to
        connectTimeout
        operationTimeoutInMilliseconds = "5000" [number] - equivalent to
        syncTimeout
    />
    -->
    </providers>
</sessionState>
```

It's not uncommon to think about the Session State as an in-process store where to save any information like it is in volatile memory. However, in the case we inadvertently save sensitive data, this would go to the Redis cache and it can be read from the console or by any clients having the proper Access Keys.

In short, we have three security hot spots in the "managed" Redis:

- Public addressability: anyone in the internet can try to access the cache

- Ports: we should disable the plain non-SSL port (Figure 3-28) of the service

- Keys: we have, as many services provide, two independent keys, to accommodate rolling strategies

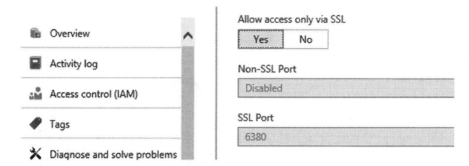

Figure 3-28. *This let us disable the non-SSL port, which may permit man in the middles to read the traffic from/to the cache*

Understanding Metrics

Let's start from one of the most important metric in a cache. The ratio Hits/Misses (Figure 3-29), which determines the health state and the good/bad caching pattern we setup.

A higher ratio is always preferred, since the main purpose of a cache is to serve frequently accessed data. At the opposite, a ratio near, equal or less than 1, shows a wrong usage pattern, where there are too many misses compared to the hits.

This can happen in short-expiration scenarios, as explained here:

1. The code looks up for the cached information

2. If it does not find it (that's a miss), it populates it

   a. However, since it is a core information which has to be updated near realtime, it sets an expiration of 5 seconds

3. The subsequently request arrives at second 6, resulting in a cache miss, plus the point 2 executed again.

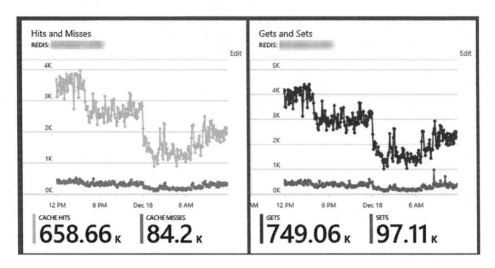

Figure 3-29. *On the left, we see the Hits and Misses (with a ratio of 7.8 about, good but not best). On the right, we see operations splitted by Gets/Sets. Gets is the approximate sum of Hits/Misses*

But it is very common to fall under these conditions, even while implementing microcaching:

1. The user is navigating to the 3rd information tab of a product page on an e-commerce website

2. Developers decided to micro-cache that specific information with a normal expiration (it does not matter how, short/long is irrelevant)

3. Since the specific piece of information is very less accessed, it would expire without being hit once

The second scenario will raise the questions again: "What should I cache? Smaller object? Bigger ones?". We notice a smaller piece of cache may be useful to micro-cache a specific portion to avoid waste. However, in the case above, it is very likely that caching the whole product page had better results.

Those metrics are useful to understand if the caching approach was developed correctly. But in any case, we must ensure the performance of the instance is not compromised by the usage itself. In those cases, we need a scaling strategy. In the figure below, we see a "relaxed" condition of a real Redis instance:

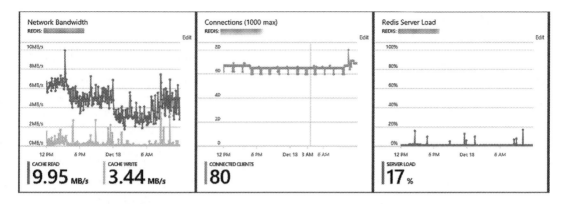

Figure 3-30. *We notice a good number of connected clients, a quiet server load and bandwith usage*

Despite the metric above (Figure 3-30) are the main ones to have a quick look on the service, we can investigate in:

- Used Memory: the memory used by actual data object

- User Memory RSS: the actual memory footprint (Resident Set Size) of the process, which may be higher than "User Memory" due to delays in memory releasing

- Total operations: it is self-explaining

- Total/Expired/Evicted Keys: the number of the keys in the given state

As any other Azure service, we can export Diagnostics to the Storage Service for further analysis.

Using Azure Search

There are a lot of applications which are almost entirely a SERP (Search Engine Result Page). Think about an eCommerce portal (Figure 3-31), where there are usually these common areas:

- Homepage: which is a SERP with default options (most-wanted, cheapest, offers)

- Search page: accessed by a canonical search text box on the top of the page, it shows the results of a specific search criteria. In addition to the entry point of the search (the text query) in the Search page it is very common to have advanced filters to refine the current search

- Category pages: if the user navigates by category, the result is a SERP "filtered" on that specific category, with a very similar result as the Search page

- Product page: despite it does not seem a SERP, it could be a "TOP 1" Search page, where the search filter is the specific Product we want to show

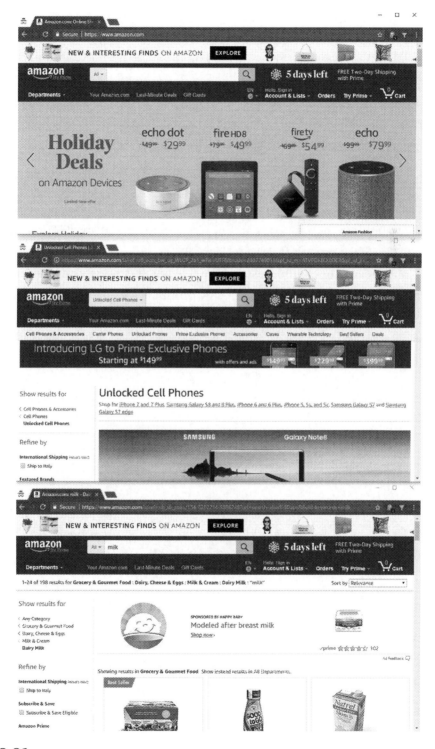

Figure 3-31.

Starting from these assumptions, for the eCommerce scenario, as well as for many others, the search component is central, so it is its importance for the business too. Better the search is, better experience and, eventually, sales are.

Traditionally, since the majority of the applications runs with a relation DB as the Data Tier, developers and or DB specialists used to adapt (or try to) the DB to serve well as a search engine. There are a lot of articles and discussions about Full-text Search in SQL Server, as well as other strategies to accommodate the same requirements for other RDBMSs.

Using SQL to Implement Search

A first attempt to implement full-text search can be made on SQL itself. There are a lot of people that state SQL Server is far enough for full-text search. We do not agree with this opinion, not because of an underestimation of what SQL Server can do and does, but since we believe that today there are specific products/services to solve specific problems in a very deep and advanced way.

However, let's suppose we are working on this subset of the AdventureWorksLT database (Figure 3-32):

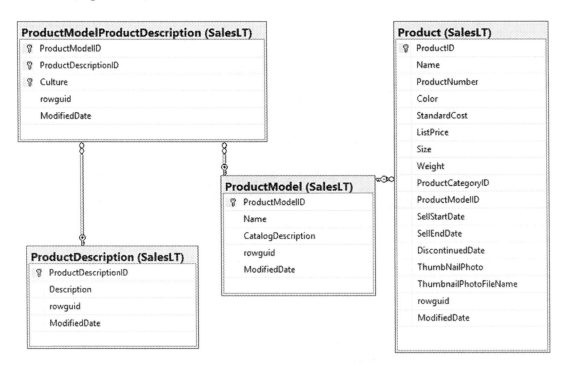

Figure 3-32. *We can create a Sample instance of this database in the Azure Portal, during the creation wizard of a new SQL Database instance*

Now suppose we want to search terms "leather" and "aluminium" into the Description field of the ProductDescription table and, at the same time, we want to produce the output dataset composed by the Name and Description of the Product. This can be the query:

```
SELECT p.[Name], pd.[Description]
FROM SalesLT.ProductDescription pd
JOIN SalesLT.ProductModelProductDescription pmpd ON
pd.ProductDescriptionID=pmpd.ProductDescriptionID
JOIN SalesLT.Product p ON p.ProductModelID=pmpd.ProductModelID
WHERE pd.[Description] LIKE '%alluminium%' OR pd.[Description] LIKE
'%leather%'
```

We think this approach is very basic, since there are no specific optimizations involved, except indexes, if any. When the rows are many (more that millions) we would see a sensible performance degradation, which would lead us to introduce FTS (Full-text Search) capabilities.

With FTS, we need first to create a catalog:

```
CREATE FULLTEXT CATALOG awCatalog AS DEFAULT;
```

Then we create a full text index that indexes the Description field:

```
CREATE FULLTEXT INDEX ON SalesLT.ProductDescription([Description]) KEY
INDEX ui_PD ON awCatalog;
```

FTS needs a UNIQUE index on the table where FTS is enabled. If not defined, define it as follows:

```
CREATE UNIQUE INDEX ui_PD ON SalesLT.ProductDescription(Product
DescriptionID);
```

Once created, the index needs to be enabled:

```
ALTER FULLTEXT INDEX ON SalesLT.ProductDescription ENABLE;
```

And populated:

```
ALTER FULLTEXT INDEX ON SalesLT.ProductDescription START FULL POPULATION;
```

We can check the population status with 'SELECT * FROM sys.dm_fts_index_population'

The result is an index like this (Figure 3-33):

	keyword	display_term	column_id	document_count
523	0x006C00650061006B002D00700072006F00...	leak-proof	2	1
524	0x006C00650061007400650800650072	leather	2	3
525	0x006C00650067	leg	2	2
526	0x006C006500670065007200000020E	léger	2	14
527	0x006C0065006700650072006500000020E020F	légère	2	5
528	0x006C006500670065007200650073000002...	légéres	2	1
529	0x006C006500670065007200730000020E	légers	2	1
530	0x006C006500670073	legs	2	1
531	0x006C00650073	les	2	27
532	0x006C006500730073	less	2	2
533	0x006C006500740073	lets	2	1
534	0x006C006500760065006C	level	2	9
535	0x006C006500760065006C0073	levels	2	1
536	0x006C0065007600650072073	levers	2	1
537	0x006C006500760065006500720073	leviers	2	1
538	0x006C00690061006900730006F006E	liaison	2	2
539	0x006C0069006700680074	light	2	7
540	0x006C006900670068007400020D0077006500...	light-weight	2	2
541	0x006C0069006700680074006500720072	lighter	2	1
542	0x006C0069006700680074002500720074	lighted	2	1

Figure 3-33.   *This is the generated index with keywords, available through the query: 'SELECT * FROM sys.dm_fts_index_keywords(DB_ID('ADWorks'), OBJECT_ID('SalesLT.ProductDescription'))'*

We believe relational DBs are not really suited for these kind of approaches, not from the performance point of view, where someone could say that they can rock. Instead, from these points:

- Effort: the overall effort in building and maintaining the FTS structure is high

- Structure: an RDBMS table is designed to be normalized, effective and optimized. So, each search will probably involves multiple JOINs to build the appropriate aggregate

- Load: since search is often a "client-requested" feature, we are not really fans of the exposure a SQL database may have to the B2C traffic

Now, we are investigating on Azure Search, a Platform-as-a-Service product that acts like a search-as-a-service.

Understanding How to Start with Azure Search

The main issues while starting a search-as-a-service solution come from the inexperience with the specific area. So, instead to provide the method, let's start immediately with an example.

Let's define this query:

```
SELECT *
FROM SalesLT.ProductDescription pd
JOIN SalesLT.ProductModelProductDescription pmpd ON
pd.ProductDescriptionID=pmpd.ProductDescriptionID
JOIN SalesLT.Product p ON p.ProductModelID=pmpd.ProductModelID
```

Now refine it to get explicit fields and avoid name duplication:

```
SELECT CONCAT(pd.ProductDescriptionID,'-',pmpd.Culture) as [SearchKey],
pd.ProductDescriptionID,pd.Description,pd.ModifiedDate as
[pdModifiedDate],pmpd.ProductModelID,pmpd.Culture,pmpd.ModifiedDate as
[pmpdModifiedDate],
p.ProductID,p.Name,p.ProductNumber,p.Color,p.StandardCost,p.ListPrice,p.Size,
p.Weight,p.ProductCategoryID,p.SellStartDate,p.DiscontinuedDate,
p.ThumbnailPhoto,p.ThumbnailPhotoFileName,p.ModifiedDate as [pModifiedDate]
FROM SalesLT.ProductDescription pd
JOIN SalesLT.ProductModelProductDescription pmpd ON
pd.ProductDescriptionID=pmpd.ProductDescriptionID
JOIN SalesLT.Product p ON p.ProductModelID=pmpd.ProductModelID
```

We now have a resultset of the entire projection of the 3 tables joined together. We make a view based on this query as follows:

```
CREATE VIEW SalesLT.vProducts AS (
[...]
)
```

We added the computed SearchKey field to create the view in order to have a unique field.

Now we would like to make full-text search on these fields:

- Description, Name

- ProductNumber *, Color *

Additionally, we would like to filter on the fields with the star (*) plus the following:

- ProductModelID, ProductID, ProductCategoryID

- Culture

- StandardCost, ListPrice

- Size, Weight

- SellStartDate, DiscontinuedDate

Finally, we create an Index on a Search Service instance, using the wizard, as follows (Figure 3-34):

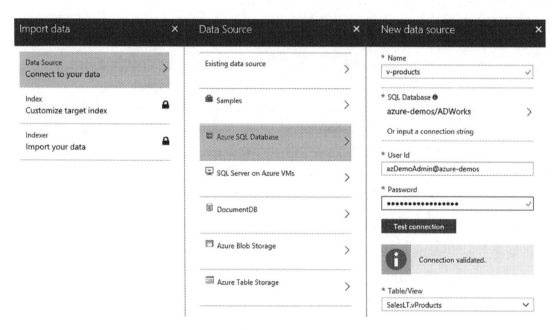

Figure 3-34. *With this wizard, we can connect an existing Azure resource (among the supported ones) to Azure Search. The operation creates three items: an Index, a Data Source and an Indexer*

During the creation process, we can customize the mappings between the fields of the View and the index, to accommodate specifications (Figure 3-35):

* Index name ❶

v-products

* Key ❶

SearchKey

Basic	Analyzer	Suggester

🗑 **Delete**

FIELD NAME	TYPE	RETRIEVABLE ☑	FILTERABLE ☐	SORTABLE ☐	FACETABLE ☐	SEARCHABLE ☐
SearchKey	Edm.String	☑	☐	☐	☐	☐
ProductDescriptionID	Edm.String	☑	☑	☐	☐	☐
Description	Edm.String	☑	☐	☐	☐	☑
pdModifiedDate	Edm.DateTim...	☑	☐	☐	☐	
ProductModelID	Edm.Int32 ⌄	☑	☑	☐	☐	
Culture	Edm.String	☑	☑	☐	☐	☐
pmpdModifiedDate	Edm.DateTim...	☑	☐	☐	☐	
ProductID	Edm.Int32	☑	☐	☐	☐	
Name	Edm.String	☑	☐	☐	☐	☑
ProductNumber	Edm.String	☑	☐	☐	☐	☑
Color	Edm.String ⌄	☑	☐	☐	☐	☑

Figure 3-35. *We define, for each field of the view, what Data type on Azure Search will have and the field properties. Based on the Index definitions, the underlying engine of Azure Search will organize the data structure to accommodate search*

We now have a working index, updated periodically with fresh data, available for full-text queries like this one:

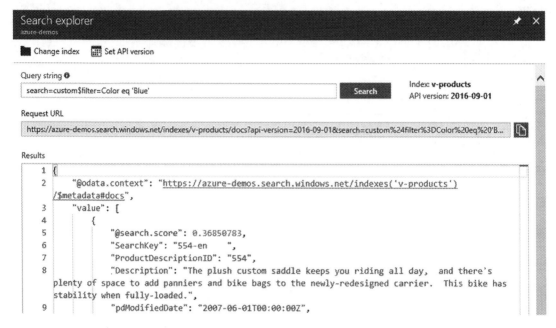

Figure 3-36. *We see a query against an HTTP endpoint which returns documents matching the FTS plus the filters*

In this REST query (Figure 3-36), we are not loading the DB; instead, we are working on a document-based, denormalized, cached copy of the DB structures involved.

Planning Azure Search

Since it is a PaaS, we need to understand which Tier we need considering the requirements of our scenario. Let's understand Azure Search has a pricing model based on size limits, like these main ones as follows:

- Storage size: the actual storage consumption by the index data and metadata

- Number of Indexes/Indexers: the total number of different indexes we can have concurrently

- Number of total documents: the total documents we can store in the account (not in a single index)

Table 3-1. *This table (taken from* https://docs.microsoft.com/en-us/azure/ *search/search-sku-tier) shows the actul limits for each tier of the Azure Search*

Resource	Free	Basic	S1	S2	S3	S3 HD
Service Level Agreement (SLA)	No	Yes	Yes	Yes	Yes	Yes
Index limits	3	5	50	200	200	1000
Document limits	10,000 total	1 million per service	15 million per partition	60 million per partition	120 million per partition	1 million per index
Maximum partitions	N/A	1	12	12	12	3
Partition size	50 MB total	2 GB per service	25 GB per partition	100 GB per partition (up to a maximum of 1.2 TB per service)	200 GB per partition (up to a maximum of 2.4 TB per service)	200 GB (up to a maximum of 600 GB per service)
Maximum replicas	N/A	3	12	12	12	12

They are exclusive, so if we have a S1 with just one index of 26GB, we are out. The same happens for a solution of 60 indexes with an overall consumption of 10Million documents and 10GB of storage space.

We need to plan accurately the tiers to use according to the solution we need to implement.

In late 2017, new Azure Search instances were provisioned using a more powerful hardware and without some limits as above, this blog post can explain better what's changed: https://azure.microsoft.com/en-us/blog/azure-search-unlimited-document-counts/.

Multitenancy with Azure Search

One of the first question in Azure Search is often "How to deal with multi-tenancy?". A single S1 deployment of two nodes costs around 0,5k$/month, so it is a legitimate to achieve density and maximize its usage by tenant. In fact, if we can deal with the problem of noisy neighbourhood (where a heavy tenant will consume much resources degrading the others' performance), we can definitely use a single deployment for even a huge number of different tenants.

Initially, Azure has set the approximate point around the performance target of a Search Tier. For example, defined that a given Tier would serve around N QPS (Queries per second). However, since it depends entirely on the index topology, the document size and factors 100% related to its usage, there are no official statements around this, actually. And it is correct there aren't.

There are some platform limits, like:

- Max request size: 16MB

- Max request URL length: 8KB

- Max number of documents indexed in a batch: 1000

- Max fields included in an $orderby clause: 32

- Max length of a search term: 32KB (minus 2 bytes)

The complete and comprehensive list and tables of service limits by Tiers, is available here:

```
https://docs.microsoft.com/en-us/azure/search/search-limits-quotas-capacity
```

So, let's think about this scenario: we have an e-commerce solution with 1000 customers. Each customer has a catalog of around 5000 items (2KB each) and we need to design the proper Azure Search topology. Each catalog is updated by two distinct sources, one for the nightly update, and another one for 5-minute price changes update.

So we have:

- 1000 indexes, one per customer

- 5M of documents, considering 5000 items x 1000 customers

- ~9,5GB of space, considering 2KB x 5M documents

- 2000 indexers, considering 2 distinct indexers for each index (1000)

Let's try to evaluate tier one by one to identify the most appropriate one:

- Free: it is just for testing purposes, next.

- Basic: every limit is under our requirements, next.

- S1: documents and storage size is okay (15M/p and 25GB/p) but we can have just 50 indexes per service, next

- S2: indexes are now 200, but it is a per-service limit, so we cannot have all the 1000 indexes in a single service.

- S3: the same as S2, since the only changes are in documents and total size, next.

- S3 HD: it has been designed to achieve density and, in fact, it supports up to 1000 indexes per partition and 3000 per service (since 3 is the maximum number of partitions we can have). This would ensure us the capability to grow without changing the service or pooling elsewhere. However, there is no support for indexers in the S3 HD, so we must implement our own technology to index data.

This example wanted to show how to setup a planning phase around Azure Search by starting from service limits which is, in Platform-as-a-Service, a standard pattern to evaluate the compatibility of a service with a given scenario.

Finally, we suggest to mix patterns to achieve the best option, between the most popular models "one-index-per-tenant" and "one-service-per-tenant". Effective solutions can have multiple service pools with many tenants, as already discussed in previous chapters.

Security and Monitoring

As usual for the PaaS service, in Azure Search we have two Keys with full rights on the service itself. The two administrative keys (whose job is to permit their rolling) can create indexes, delete them as long as any other operation against the service.

However, it's not uncommon (but we do not suggest it) to expose the search API on the frontend of the application. Think about this scenario:

1. User navigates to the e-commerce store frontend

2. He/she types some words in the search bar, resulting in a series of ajax calls to the frontend tier of the web application

3. The web application, for each request, acts as a proxy and makes the request against the search service using the administrative key

To reduce the involved actors, we can even modify the scenario as follows:

1. User navigates to the e-commerce store frontend

2. He/she types some words in the search bar, resulting in a series of ajax calls to the Search service directly, using the Azure Search library for javascript. No web tier is involved anymore.

Despite we do not like this scenario (it is always better to have the complete control over the backend resources, even to apply traffic limiting and throttling, in case), it is possible to achieve. However, we should disclose, in the frontend page's code, a key which has just the capability of query data, in a read-only mode (Figure 3-37).

NAME	KEY
<empty>	86DD018A04ABACB785C093167D817C93
Tenant01	3D6326149F8256BB8AABCE0597870795
Tenant02	765476431A30BCFCD91420487687CF5B
Tenant03	A41D802D1471ADD043A831C75D651158
TestApplication	E78249863FD8FE6A677F09573A8BEA8E
AngularFE	A16CA42271C63C946DD82659A113AD45

Figure 3-37.   *Here we define the "query keys", which are special read-only keys. Despite it is supported, nothing will prevent a user from fiddlering the traffic or reading the client's code and crawling the entire Search Service*

The three metrics exposed by Azure Search are: Search Latency (which indicates both the complexity of search queries and the load on the search node), Search Queries (which is an aggregate number of the total queries against the service) and Throttled Queries (which is an aggregate number of the queries which are refused by the service).

Azure Search can throttle queries in order to preserve its general status of availability. For instance, is a user submits a query, specifying the target minimum coverage of 100%, the Search engine will return the result only if the target coverage has completed. If the service is not able to fit that coverage, since it would require a loss of overall performance or an unacceptable degradation, the query would be throttled and refused.

At the other side, much the concurrent queries are, much more we would expect the latency will be and, possibly, the throttled queries (Figure 3-38). Those three metrics are obviously related and, considering those, we can have a quick look at the health state of our instance.

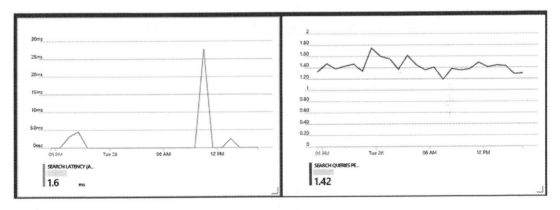

Figure 3-38. *These are the Search Latency metric and the Search Queries metric for the same period. We see a peak around 11PM that can be a sudden, isolated event of load, since the corresponding metric about queries is normal*

Implementing Azure Search

We believe Azure Search should not be the primary copy of your data. RDBMS are usually involved into transactions, concurrent operations from multiple sources on the same destination, punctual updates of fields and constraints checks among tables. Those are just a few of the things we cannot guarantee with a Search service.

A search service can be easily seen as a document-oriented, multi-indexed cache of our data, with a specific set of features related to full-text search.

However, differently from an ordinary cache, we cannot achieve the "on-demand" caching pattern, since the consumer want to rely on the availability of the entire search set upon search and it does not want (and know how) to actively populate it. The general suggestion is to then maintain some idempotency around the state of the search nodes: a set of scripts that bring the search nodes to the desired state, can be a good example.

Establishing the Search

A good "search establisher" is a component which does the following tasks:

- Index definition:

    - Creation in case it does not exists

    - Drop/creation in case of missing fields (Azure Search does not support index changes)

- Index contents:

    - Active population with the desired data set

    - Configuration of the appropriate jobs to populate it further

We can write a C# method, using the Microsoft.Azure.Search NuGet package, to drop/create an index, as follows:

```
private static void BuildIndex
    (string searchService, string searchKey, string indexName)
{
    var search = new SearchServiceClient(searchService,
        new SearchCredentials(searchKey));
    search.Indexes.Delete(indexName);
    var index = new Microsoft.Azure.Search.Models.Index()
```

```
    {
        Name = indexName,
        Fields = CommonFields.ToList()
    };
    index.ScoringProfiles = new List<ScoringProfile>() {
        new ScoringProfile()
        {
            Name = "Relevance",
            TextWeights = new TextWeights(new Dictionary<string, double>()
            { { "CategoryName", 5 }, { "Description", 3 }, { "Brand", 1 }
    })
        }
    };
    index.DefaultScoringProfile = "Relevance";
    search.Indexes.CreateOrUpdate(index);
}
```

In this snippet, we first drop the existing index and we create the definition of a new one along with a scoring profile to attach to it. A scoring profile is an attribution model of scores to the search result, based on custom properties and logics. By default, Azure Search has a balanced score profile, which awards equally search results, based on the "natural relevance" of the input keywords.

In case we are searching "milk" in a document set like this (with all the three fields "searchable"):

```
{
        CategoryName: "Bath products",
        Description: "Active Shampoo with Nuts Milk"
        Brand: "F&D Milk Products"
},
{
        CategoryName: "Milk",
        Description: "Organic Milk"
        Brand: "F&D Dairy Products"
}
```

Azure Search can place the two documents in the result set with a very similar score. It is even possible two consecutive searches shows those results in a different order, since the default attribution model spans equally between the two occurrences of "milk" in, relatively, Description and Brand for the first product and CategoryName and Description for the second.

However, in the e-commerce scenario, we would like to boost the relevance of a product based "first" on its category, leaving the brand as the least important. Why this decision? It is obviously a domain-based decision, but it makes sense, since many brands can have specific keywords in their claims which are not relevant at all with sold products (i.e. "Nuts and Co." can be a family name, not a company selling nuts).

Therefore we created, along with the index, the Scoring Profile:

```
new ScoringProfile()
        {
            Name = "Relevance",
            TextWeights = new TextWeights(new Dictionary<string, double>()
            { { "CategoryName", 5 }, { "Description", 3 }, { "Brand", 1 } })
        }
```

We are telling Azure to give specific weights to text matches on fields. With the model above, a single match on the CategoryName can win over two matches on Description and Brand which, in the case above, will award the second product always.

Defining Fields and Properties

We can notice that, in the index definition, we used the CommonFields property, which encapsulates all the field definition as follows:

```
public static IEnumerable<Field> CommonFields
{
    get
    {
        return new Field[]
        {
            new Field("SearchId",DataType.String){IsKey=true},
            new Field("Brand",DataType.String)
```

```
            { IsSearchable=true, IsFilterable=true,IsFacetable=true},
            new Field("Description",DataType.String)
            { IsSearchable=true,IsSortable=true,
                Analyzer =AnalyzerName.ItMicrosoft},
            new Field("CategoryName",DataType.String)
            { IsSortable=true, IsFilterable=true,IsFacetable=true,
            IsSearchable=true,
                Analyzer =AnalyzerName.ItMicrosoft},
            new Field("IsPromo",DataType.Boolean)
            { IsFilterable=true,IsSortable=true,IsFacetable=true},
            new Field("PromoStart",DataType.DateTimeOffset)
            { IsFilterable=true},
            new Field("PromoExpiration",DataType.DateTimeOffset)
            { IsFilterable=true,IsSortable=true},
            new Field("Price",DataType.Double)
            { IsSortable=true,IsFilterable=true,IsFacetable=true},
            new Field("Tags",DataType.Collection(DataType.String))
            { IsSearchable=true }
        };
    }
}
```

A field defined in a search index, can be decorated with the following properties:

- IsKey: it is reserved to the key field. Inside a single index, every document must have a unique value for the field defined with the IsKey flag.

- IsSearchable: only DataType.String values can be defined searchable and, when enabled, the field is marked to be indexed for the full-text search.

- IsFilterable: we can specify which fields can be included in a filtering clause, to optimize the index. Not every field is involved by default, to avoid waste of resources and degradation of performance.

- IsSortable: it works like the IsFilterable, except it denotes a sortable capability on that specific field.

- IsFacetable: this is very interesting, since it denotes "attributes". Usually, a "facetable" field is a field where we want to group our results for a search refinement. Every field decorated with that flag, is returned in the search results with an occurrence counter, to refine the search later. It involves computation and storage resource, so we need to use this only if necessary.

- IsRetrievable: it marks a field to be included in the result set of a search query. This is not enabled by default because we can even search among fields we do not want in results. This is probably uncommon, but it is a supported scenario.

Along with these flags, we see we decorated some fields with the Analyzer attribute. Azure Search supports text analyzers, to make more effective the search query with the destination language we choose. In the case above, we specify the contents of the Description and CategoryName are to be interpreted as Italian-localized (ItMicrosoft) strings, which gives us some interesting features out-of-the box:

- Lemmatization

- Decompounding

- Entity recognition

To make a simple example, the default analyzer (the language-agnostic one) will just remove punctuation, normalizes upper/lower casing, rooting, while the language-specific will be the foundation to implement even Phonetic search.

Populating Index

A search index can be populated via REST API, so it is possible to let several sources feed it as they want.

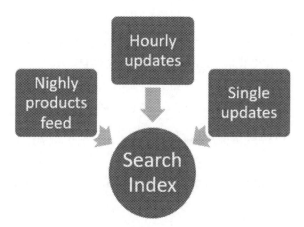

Figure 3-39. *We can feed an index from different sources, each one using the REST API autonomously*

However, there is an integrated mechanism to provide contents to the indexes. Azure Search can instantiate, in the same nodes of the search engine, some jobs, called Indexers, which can perform a fetch against some supported sources (like SQL Database, Cosmos DB, Blob Storage) and populate the indexes accordingly (Figure 3-39).

We can define an Indexer through the portal or the REST API or, via C#, as follows:

```
search.Indexers.CreateOrUpdate(
new Indexer(name:indexerName, dataSourceName:dsName, targetIndexName:
indexName)
{
    Schedule = new IndexingSchedule(TimeSpan.FromMinutes(minutes),
DateTimeOffset.UtcNow),
    Parameters = new IndexingParameters()
    {
        Configuration = new Dictionary<string, object>() { {
        "queryTimeout", "00:20:00" } }
    }
});
```

This will create a job that, every "minute" interval (minimum 5 minutes) will execute against the DataSource defined in "dsName" populating the "indexName" index.

We are also specifying a queryTimeout, which is a custom property telling the indexers to use that timeout in case of SQL Connections.

The Data Source, in case of SQL Database, can be something like that:

```
search.DataSources.CreateOrUpdate(new DataSource(dsName, DataSourceType.
AzureSql,
    new DataSourceCredentials(connStr), new DataContainer(viewName))
{
    DataChangeDetectionPolicy =
new HighWaterMarkChangeDetectionPolicy("SearchUpdate"),
    DataDeletionDetectionPolicy =
new SoftDeleteColumnDeletionDetectionPolicy("SearchDelete", "True")
});
```

With this Data Source we are specifying the DB through the "connStr" parameter and the "viewName" view where to fetch data. Finally, we are defining two important properties, which are discussed now in the next section.

Change and Delete Detection

The update process of an indexer cannot be defined a synchronization process.

First, it is one-way: there is no update in the search-datasource direction and it shouldn't, since the first is generally an aggregate produced for the only purpose of a full-text search.

Second, there is no an automatic way to track changes and items deletion. For example, if we are running an indexer that, in first execution produces 1000 items and, at the next execution produces just 998 items, there is no way to tell the Search to remove the "missing items".

If we think about it, it is correct. Since we can have multiple indexers around the same Index and also external sources which feeds the index by API, it is obvious we cannot just think a single indexer will make the rule of what is to be deleted or not. An indexer may index just a subset of items or an external job may enrich the saved documents with extended properties (i.e., the Tag field in the example above).

However, a common scenario to realize is to provide a sort of synchronization, guaranteeing the indexer will both insert/update and delete the missing items. To be smarter, the update should occur only on the changed items and not on the entire subset.

Therefore, the supported data sources of Azure Search have these two properties:

- HighWaterMarkChangeDetectionPolicy: it marks a column of the source Table/View of the SQL Database as the change tracking field. The indexer will save the highest value of this field encountered during the first execution, to execute the next ones in this form:

  - SELECT * FROM [ViewName] WHERE [HighWatermark]>[highest ValuePreviouslyEncountered]

- SoftDeleteColumnDeletionDetectionPolicy: since there is no way to remove missing items (on the Data source side) from the index, we must mark a column/field with a flag (or value) indicating if the actual item is to be preserved or deleted. This is also known as "soft deletion" since this requires, on the data source side, to avoid deleting items. Instead, we should consider to keep them and producing a View/Table where a proper field indicates its validity state.

If we implement those two search-specific fields in the View/Table, we can have a pseudo-synchronization in place, sure we are updating only the changed items and deleting the old ones.

The HighWaterMark field can be a field of DateTime, Rowversion or another type, updated by the business logic when a record is updated too. This makes the above query work with the compare operator.

Summary

In this chapter, we learned how to maximize the usage of NoSQL alternatives and how to fit them into scenarios often monopolized by RDBMS products. We learned how to use Blobs efficiently for basic storage requirements and how to use Tables for basic filtering requirements.

We introduced Redis Cache to speed up existing solutions or setup a fast and volatile storage alternative and Azure Search where the application is really focused on searching features.

In the next chapter, we look into data orchestration with Azure Data Factory.

CHAPTER 4

Orchestrate Data with Azure Data Factory

In this chapter you will learn how to architect an integration service solution using Azure Data Factory (ADF), starting from the most common adopted solutions up to the customization scenarios. The aim of this chapter is to give the data architect an overview of the options available with ADF to move and transform data using this service, providing some practical example. To do that, we will use, like in other parts of the book, the *AdventureWorksLT* sample database.

The chapter will cover three sections:

- An introduction to Azure Data Factory, focused on the advantages of using this service, the terminology we need to become familiar with, and the options to administer the service

- Designing an Azure Data Factory solution. This is the longest part, where we will see how to author a solution, working with the tools and with cloud and on-premises data

- Considerations on performance and scalability, with suggestions and best practices

Azure Data Factory Introduction

Even though Azure Data Factory is not one of the oldest services available in the Azure platform, it is already quite a powerful service, rich in functionalities to help the data architect and the developer in designing an orchestration solution. It is aimed to support both extract-transform-load (ETL) and extract-load-transform (ELT) projects. It is designed with the cloud in mind and to support modern and traditional data sources, and accessing data on-premises is possible as well.

© Francesco Diaz, Roberto Freato 2018
F. Diaz and R. Freato, *Cloud Data Design, Orchestration, and Management Using Microsoft Azure*,
https://doi.org/10.1007/978-1-4842-3615-4_4

For those of you that, like us, are coming from work experience with SQL Server Integration Services (SSIS), you will find similarities in the concepts, with an additional "as a service" approach and a native support for modern cloud data stores, such as big data stores, machine learning, and high performance computing services. Furthermore, comparing ADF with SSIS, the Transform part is different, as ADF works more with external compute services and it is not focused much on transforming data directly. It is more of a **cloud orchestrator engine** rather than a compute engine. Another difference is that ADF is focused on processing time series of data, instead of having a control flow system like in SSIS.

Other services in the market that adopt a similar as-a-service approach to Azure Data Factory are Informatica Cloud or Amazon AWS Data Pipeline, just to mention a few.

Note   You may find additional information on **SQL Server Integration Services**, **Informatica Cloud** and **Amazon AWS Data Pipeline** at the following links: `https://docs.microsoft.com/en-us/sql/integration-services/ sql-server-integration-services`; `https://www.informatica.com/ products/cloud-integration/integration-cloud.html` ; `https:// aws.amazon.com/datapipeline/`

Figure 4-1 below displays the typical workflow on an Azure Data Factory solution, where you can **ingest** and **prepare** data coming from several data sources, **transform** and **analyze** them with the support of external compute services, and **publish** results to a sink data store, ready to be consumed by a report, an application, etc.

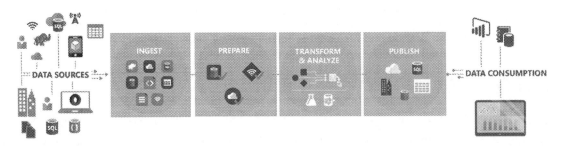

Figure 4-1. *The typical flow of an Azure Data Factory implementation*

Main Advantages of using Azure Data Factory

We will now explore the main advantages of relying on Azure Data Factory as your **data movement** and **data transformation** service.

- It is a cloud based service that runs on Microsoft Azure, and it doesn't require having anything installed locally. Potentially, the authoring part can all be done using Data Factory Editor provided out of the box.

- It is a PaaS service; therefore, the surface of administration you need to do it is much lower, and you can focus on the design of the solution instead. Azure Data Factory SLAs guarantee that *"at least 99.9% of the time will successfully process requests to perform operations against Data Factory resources,"* and that *"at least 99.9% of the time, all activity runs will initiate within 4 minutes of their scheduled execution times."*

- Numerous data stores are supported and the number grows regularly. They can be on-premises and on cloud, from text files up to big data.

- Everything you design with Azure Data Factory generates JSON (JavaScript Object Notation), therefore maintaining a solution becomes easy, and it is also supported by a visual designer to display workflows.

- It is open to be tailored by writing custom code, when the functionalities provided out of the box are not sufficient.

- Copy activities, very common in ETL scenarios, are simplified thanks to a tool provided within the platform.

- To verify that workflows are working as expected, a monitor and manage tool is also provided by Azure Data Factory.

Terminology

It is now important to become familiar with the terminology used by Azure Data Factory, to understand the aim of each functionality included herein. An Azure Data Factory workflow is built upon **four main components**, which we are going to cover in detail in the pages below:

1. **Linked Service**. A connection to a data store

2. **Dataset**. A representation of the structure of the data

3. **Activity**. They consume, transform, and produce data

4. **Pipeline**. A group of one or more activities

In Figure 4-2 below you can find a visual illustration of how the four components interact with each other. First you create a linked server to **connect to a data store**, and then you create a dataset with the **representation of the data**, e.g. a table, contained in the data store. Then you run an activity on the linked service that can **consume data** using the dataset and **produce data** putting them in another dataset. If you need to **group** a number of activities that are designed with the same scope, you can use a pipeline.

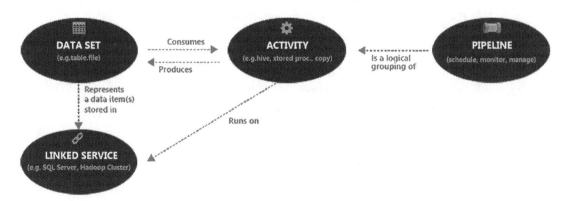

Figure 4-2. *Shows the relationship between the main features of Azure Data Factory*

There is a fifth component, the **Data Management Gateway** (DMG), which is fundamental when the linked service needs to access data from an on-premises data store. We will cover the DMG in a specific section later in this chapter.

Linked Services

Linked Services represent the information needed by Azure Data Factory to connect to a specific datasource. A linked service is basically the connection string to the data store or to a compute resource. Linked Services can be:

- A connection to a **data store**, a container of data, used for **data movement** activities. The data store can reside in the cloud or on-premises.

- A connection to a **compute** resource that can host the execution of a **data transformation** activity. The compute resource can be on cloud or, if it is a stored procedure activity, on-premises.

Every linked service is provided with a JSON template. The script below represents the way to connect to an Azure Machine Learning service. We will get deeper in the authoring and coding part later in the chapter.

```
{
    "name": "AzureMLLinkedService",
    "properties": {
        "type": "AzureML",
        "description": "",
        "typeProperties": {
            "mlEndpoint": "<Specify the batch scoring URL>",
            "apiKey": "<Specify the published workspace model's API key>",
            "updateResourceEndpoint": "<(Optional) Specify the Update
            Resource URL >",
            "servicePrincipalId": "<(Optional) Specify the ID of the
            service principal >",
            "servicePrincipalKey": "<(Optional) Specify the key of the
            service principal >",
        }
    }
}
```

Datasets

A dataset is simply the representation of the structure of the data you want to access from a data store. The datasets can be used as an input or as an output of an activity.

The JSON template below contains an example of an Azure SQL Database table.

```
{
    "name": "AzureSQLDatasetTemplate",
    "properties": {
        "type": "AzureSqlTable",
        "linkedServiceName": "<Name of the linked service that refers
        to an Azure SQL Database. This linked service must be of type:
        AzureSqlDatabase>",
        "structure": [],
        "typeProperties": {
            "tableName": "<Name of the table in the Azure SQL Database
            instance that linked service refers to>"
        },
        "availability": {
            "frequency": "<Specifies the time unit for data slice
            production. Supported frequency: Minute, Hour, Day, Week,
            Month>",
            "interval": "<Specifies the interval within the defined
            frequency. For example, frequency set to 'Hour' and interval
            set to 1 indicates that new data slices should be produced
            hourly>"
        }
    }
}
```

Activities

An activity is the minimal unit of operation of Azure Data Factory. It may be a copy task from a source to a destination, or it may be a transformation task executed by a compute resource, like the Azure Data Lake Analytics.

Azure Data Factory has two categories of activities:

1. **Data movement** activities

2. **Data transformation** activities

An activity can have zero or more datasets in input, a **source**, and one or more datasets in output, a **sink**. In Table 4-1 you will find a matrix of all data stores that can be manipulated by Azure Data Factory, and if it is available as a source, as a sink, and if it requires the Data Management Gateway.

Table 4-1. *Data stores available for data movement activities*

Data store name	Available as source	Available as sink	Data Management Gateway required
Azure Blob	YES	YES	NO
Azure Cosmos DB	YES	YES	NO
Azure Data Lake	YES	YES	NO
Azure SQL Database	YES	YES	NO
Azure SQL Data Warehouse	YES	YES	NO
Azure Search Index	NO	YES	NO
Azure Table Storage	YES	YES	NO
AWS Redshift	YES	NO	NO
AWS S3	YES	NO	NO
HTTP/HTML	YES	NO	NO
OData	YES	NO	NO
Salesforce	YES	NO	NO
FTP/SFTP	YES	NO	NO

(continued)

Table 4-1. (*continued*)

Data store name	Available as source	Available as sink	Data Management Gateway required
DB2	YES	NO	YES
MySQL	YES	NO	YES
Oracle	YES	YES	YES
PostgreSQL	YES	NO	YES
SAP BW / HANA	YES	NO	YES
SQL Server	YES	YES	YES
Sybase	YES	NO	YES
Teradata	YES	NO	YES
Cassandra	YES	NO	YES
MongoDB	YES	NO	YES
File System	YES	YES	YES
HDFS	YES	NO	YES
ODBC	YES	NO	YES
GE Historian	YES	NO	YES

Note   Azure Search Index is only supported as a sink **and not as a source**.

In Table 4-2 you can find the list of the data transformation activities supported by Azure Data Factory. We will go in to detail later in the chapter.

Table 4-2. *Compute resources for data transformation activities*

Transformation activity	Compute environment
Hive	HDInsight
MapReduce	HDInsight
Hadoop Streaming	HDInsight
Pig	HDInsight
Spark	HDInsight
Azure Machine Learning	Azure Machine Learning
U-SQL	Azure Data Lake Analytics
Stored Procedure	Azure SQL Database, Azure SQL Data Warehouse, SQL Server*
DotNet	Azure Batch, HDInsight

* SQL Server requires that the Linked Service connects via Data Management Gateway

Pipelines

Pipelines allow grouping of activities together. Each activity can share the same window of execution and, in general, the logical task for which it has been designed. You can have one or more activities in each pipeline, and you can have many pipelines in an Azure Data Factory workflow. A JSON template for a pipeline is as follows:

```
{
    "name": "PipelineTemplate",
    "properties": {
        "description": "<Enter the pipeline description here>",
        "activities": [],
        "start": "<The start date-time of the duration in which data
        processing will occur >",
        "end": "<The end date-time of the duration in which data processing
        will occur>"
    }
}
```

Azure Data Factory Administration

The administration of Azure services can be done in several ways, many of them available also for Azure Data Factory. As a reference, in Table 4-3 you can find the possibilities you have to manage Azure Data Factory; in the *Link to tutorial* column you can also find a getting started document.

Table 4-3. *Administration options available in Azure Data Factory*

Tool/API	Available for ADF	Link to tutorial
Azure CLI	NA	NA
Azure Powershell	YES	https://docs.microsoft.com/en-us/azure/ data-factory/data-factory-build-your-first-pipeline-using-powershell
Azure Portal	YES	https://docs.microsoft.com/en-us/azure/ data-factory/data-factory-build-your-first-pipeline-using-editor
.NET API	YES	https://docs.microsoft.com/en-us/azure/ data-factory/data-factory-create-data-factories-programmatically
Powershell Core	NA	NA
REST API	YES	https://docs.microsoft.com/en-us/azure/ data-factory/data-factory-copy-activity-tutorial-using-rest-api

Designing Azure Data Factory Solutions

So far, we have explored the terminology and the main advantages of using Azure Data Factory. This section of the chapter is the longest one, and we will focus on the authoring of ADF solutions.

Like other services in the Azure platform, ADF is available in different regions. At the time of writing, the service is available in four Azure regions: **East US**, **North Europe**, **West Central US**, **West US**, but data can be taken from all the Azure regions where the supported data sources are distributed. In the case of on-premises data or VMs located in a cloud or service provider, it is enough to install the Data Management Gateway, if the data store is supported.

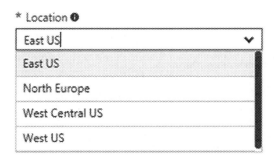

Figure 4-3. *The list of Azure locations where an Azure Data Factory service can be published*

Note   It is important to highlight that, while the Azure Data Factory service will run in the regions above, the regions where the copy tasks may be executed **are available globally**. To ensure data movement efficiency, Azure Data Factory automatically chooses the location close to the data store destination. You may also specify it manually, using the **executionLocation** parameter in the copy activity JSON definition file.

Exploring Azure Data Factory Features using Copy Data

To explain how Azure Data Factory works, we will play with the **Copy data** feature, a visual tool available in the Azure Data Factory dashboard that permits the movement of data from a source to a destination. Walking through the steps below, we will describe what Azure Data Factory generates under the hoods, and we will modify the code to upgrade our solution. Figure 4-4 displays how to launch the Copy data tool from the Azure Portal.

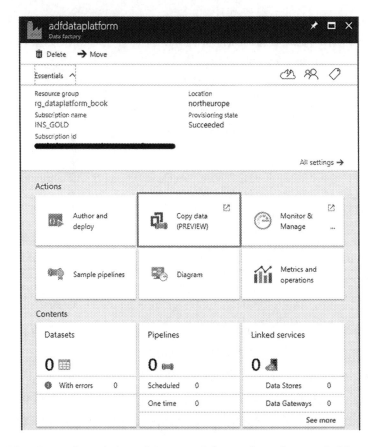

Figure 4-4. *The Copy data wizard is one of the web tools available in the Azure Data Factory management dashboard*

During the exercise, we will cover the following parts:

- How to move data from a source to a destination, using a relational database

- Understand how Pipelines work

- Understand how Datasets and slices work

- Understand monitoring and retry logic

- Become familiar with tooling

We will move data between two Azure SQL Databases. The source, the *AdventureWorksLT* sample database, is in the West Europe datacenter, while the destination is hosted in the West US datacenter.

dataplatform	Available	West Europe
dataplatformwestus	Available	West US

We will move the data contained in the *SalesLT.Customer* table of the source to the destination table, which is empty, but has the same schema. On the source database, we have slightly modified the data of the sample database, in order to have a bit of partitioning of information, useful in explaining how ADF Datasets work. The column *ModifiedData*, *which we will use in a moment,* is a *datetime* column where we have changed data in order to have slices at intervals of three hours each. You can see it in Figure 4-5 below:

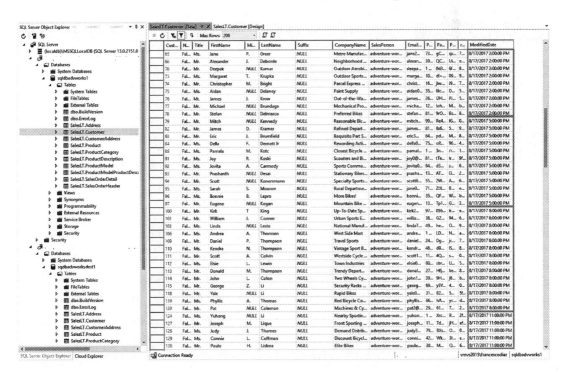

Figure 4-5. *SalesLT.Customer has been modified to have ModifiedData data partitioned with a 3hrs interval*

Now we will explore a bit more of what the Copy data wizard allows you to do, focusing on the main options, with the objective being to better understand the service. Figure 4-6 represents the first step, where we can type the name of the pipeline and if it should run once or on scheduled mode. We select the scheduled option, and the *Start date time* and *End date time*, in combination with the *Recurring pattern*, are important options because they define how data movements will be segmented.

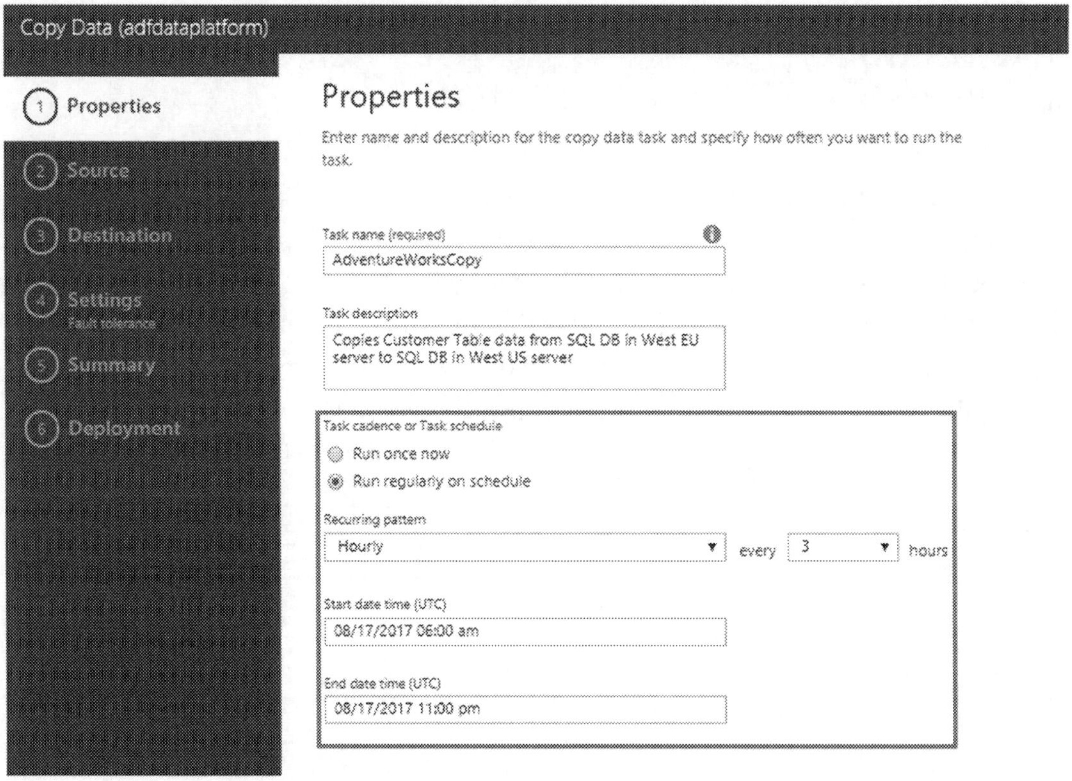

Copy Data (adfdataplatform)

Properties

Enter name and description for the copy data task and specify how often you want to run the task.

① Properties

② Source

③ Destination

④ Settings
Fault tolerance

⑤ Summary

⑥ Deployment

Task name (required)

AdventureWorksCopy

Task description

Copies Customer Table data from SQL DB in West EU
server to SQL DB in West US server

Task cadence or Task schedule

○ Run once now
◉ Run regularly on schedule

Recurring pattern

Hourly ▼   every   3   ▼   hours

Start date time (UTC)

08/17/2017 06:00 am

End date time (UTC)

08/17/2017 11:00 pm

Figure 4-6. *Pipeline name definition and scheduling options*

The pipeline will be active within the Start date time and End date time interval, between 6AM and 11PM on 08/17/2017. The recurring pattern will define a scheduler that will execute the activities inside this pipeline every three hours within the Start date time and End date time interval. This option requires that you also create an output dataset, in order to contain the data generated by the activity. Every three hours, in our example, the activity run will produce what Azure Data Factory calls a data **slice**.

This is a bit of a tricky concept to digest at the beginning, so we will elaborate more on this part. Let's have a look at Figure 4-7 to explain what is happening in this step of the wizard. The pipeline, in the center of the image, will run from 6AM to 11PM, if not paused. We said that a pipeline can contain one or more activities. In our case we are creating only one activity. The activity, a copy activity, has what Azure Data Factory calls activity windows, tumbling windows with contiguous invervals of execution that we are defining using the Recurring pattern option. In our case we chose Hourly, every three hours. That means that we will have six activity window intervals in total, therefore the activity will run six times. The input dataset and the output dataset will undergo this option, and six slices of data will be produced when the activity runs.

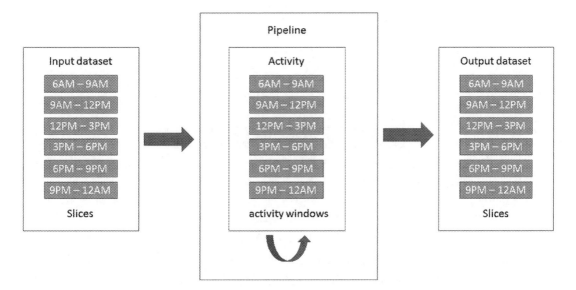

Figure 4-7. *How data slices are produced by activity runs*

We are now ready to choose the source dataset. You can see from Figure 4-8 that we have the list of available sources displayed here. In our example, we select Azure SQL Database, the one highlighted. The next step, omitted here to save space, asks for the connection string information. What the tool is doing under the hood is to define a Linked Service for us.

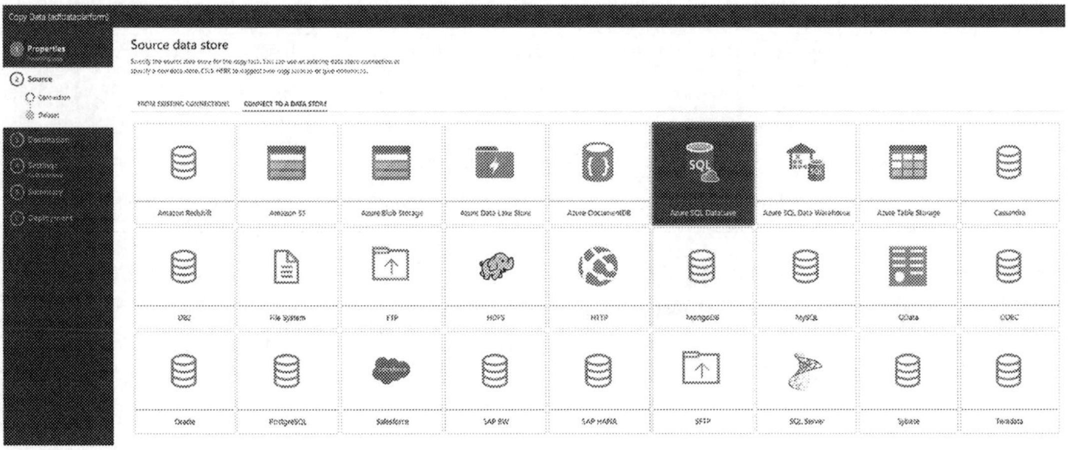

Figure 4-8. *Now we need to select the source, some of them will require the DMG*

In the second part of step 2 of the wizard, we can select tables, views, or use a custom query; we will select *SalesLT.Customer* table, therefore we will generate one dataset and one activity.

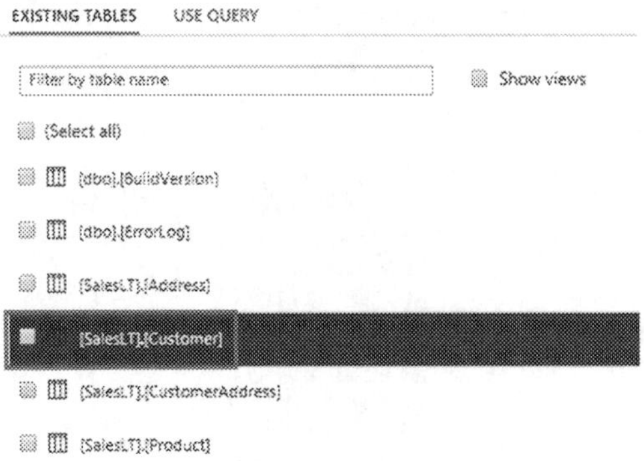

It is also useful to see in real time a preview of the data that we are selecting. As you can see from Figure 4-9, the data in the ModifiedData field are within the timeline range that we defined in the first step of the wizard, where we specified the options for the pipeline. We will tell the tool how to use this field later.

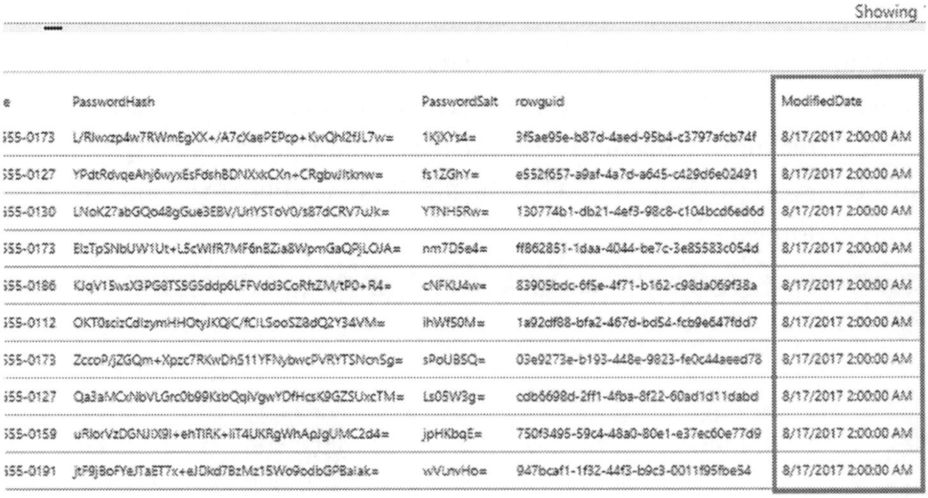

Showing

e	PasswordHash	PasswordSalt	rowguid	ModifiedDate
55-0173	L/Rlwzp4w7RWmEgXX+/A7cXaePEPcp+KwQhl2fJL7w=	1KjXYs4=	9f5ae95e-b87d-4aed-95b4-c3797afcb74f	8/17/2017 2:00:00 AM
55-0127	YPdtRdvqeAhj6wyxEsFdshBDNXxkCXn+CRgbvJItknw=	fs1ZGhY=	e552f657-a9af-4a7d-a645-c429d6e02491	8/17/2017 2:00:00 AM
55-0130	LNoK27abGQo48gGue3EBV/UrlYSToV0/s87dCRV7uJk=	YTNH5Rw=	130774b1-db21-4ef3-98c8-c104bcd6ed6d	8/17/2017 2:00:00 AM
55-0173	ElzTpSNbUW1Ut+L5cWlfR7MF6nBZia8WpmGaQPjLOJA=	nm7D5e4=	ff862851-1daa-4044-be7c-3e85583c054d	8/17/2017 2:00:00 AM
55-0186	KJqV15wsX3PG8TSSGSddp6LFFVdd3CoRftZM/tPO+R4=	cNFKU4w=	83905bdc-6f5e-4f71-b162-c98da069f38a	8/17/2017 2:00:00 AM
55-0112	OKT0scizCdIzymHHOtyJKQjC/fCILSooSZ8dQ2Y34VM=	ihWf50M=	1a92df88-bfa2-467d-bd54-fcb9e647fdd7	8/17/2017 2:00:00 AM
55-0173	ZccoP/jZGQm+Xpzc7RKwDh511YFNybwcPVRYTSNcn5g=	sPoUB5Q=	03e9273e-b193-448e-9823-fe0c44aeed78	8/17/2017 2:00:00 AM
55-0127	Qa3aMCxNbVLGrc0b99KsbQqiVgwYDfHcsK9GZSUxcTM=	Ls05W3g=	cdb6698d-2ff1-4fba-8f22-60ad1d11dabd	8/17/2017 2:00:00 AM
55-0159	uRlorVzDGNJIX9I+ehTlRK+IIT4UKRgWhApIgUMC2d4=	jpHKbqE=	750f3495-59c4-48a0-80e1-e37ec60e77d9	8/17/2017 2:00:00 AM
55-0191	jtF9j8oFYeJTaET7x+eJDkd7BzMz15Wo9odbGPBalak=	wVUnvHo=	947bcaf1-1f32-44f3-b9c3-0011f95fbe54	8/17/2017 2:00:00 AM

Figure 4-9. *Step 2-b of the wizard, that allows us to select one or more views/ tables or to write a custom query*

There is the ability to define a custom query, displayed in Figure 4-10, and this is the option that we choose. Azure Data Factory provides a set of **system variables** and **functions** that can be used to define filter expressions. In the *Query* textbox, we use the *$$* keyword to invoke an Azure Data Factory function, *Text*, to format the datetime field in the query. We also use two system variables, *WindowStart* and *WindowEnd*, to filter data with the same timeline range expressed when we have defined the pipeline execution period, in the first step of the wizard.

Note   To learn more about system variables and function, visit the official Azure Data Factory documentation, here: `https://docs.microsoft.com/en-us/ azure/data-factory/data-factory-functions-variables`

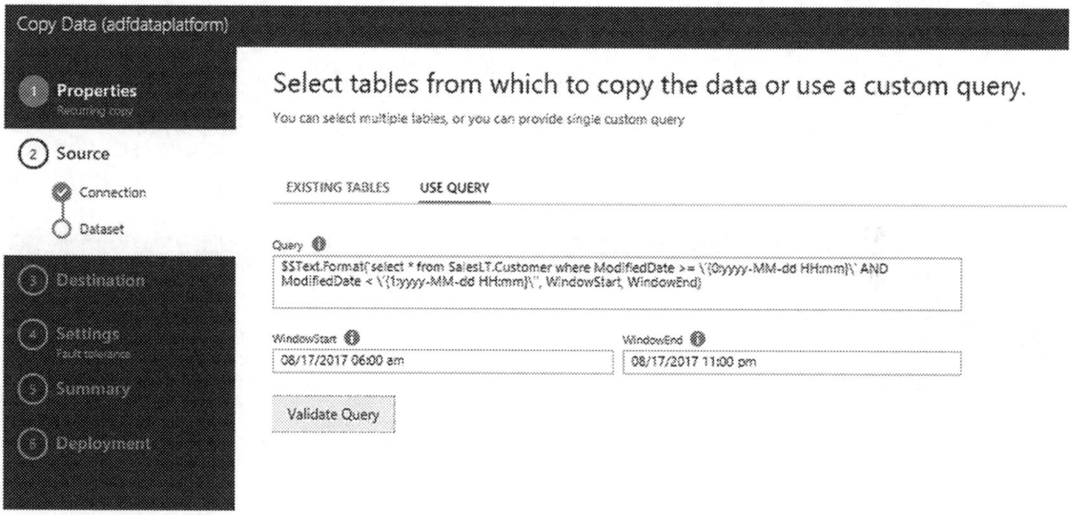

Figure 4-10. *We can define a custom query, using system variables and functions provided by Azure Data Factory*

After defining the source Linked Server and the source dataset, we can define the sink data store, Figure 4-11. In this case we will specify the connection string to access the Azure SQL Server database available in the West US datacenter.

Figure 4-11. *We need to select the sink data store*

Table mapping and schema mapping are represented in Figure 4-12 and 4-13. In Figure 4-12 we are mapping our custom query with the destination table, and in Figure 4-13 we are mapping the columns of the source and sink.

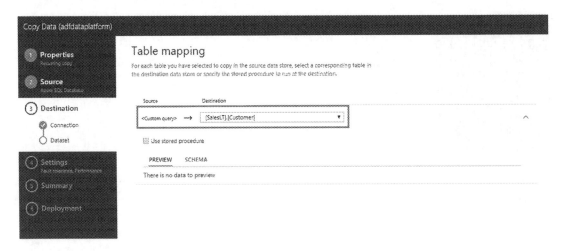

Figure 4-12. *Table mapping*

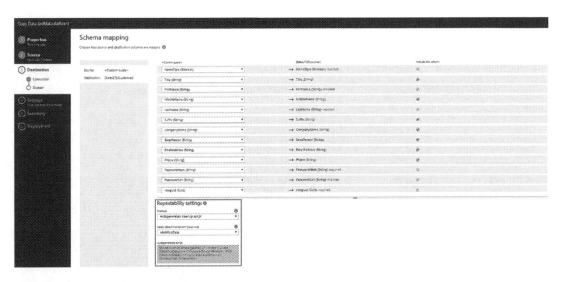

Figure 4-13. *Table mapping*

Let's zoom-in on Figure 4-13 for a second, on the red rectangle, and look at Figure 4-13b. This section contains the *Repeatability settings* options. These are very important to manage how Azure Data Factory will behave when working with relational data stores, in the case of a rerun of a slice, or if you apply a retry-logic that needs to be triggered in case of failures. In both cases you want data that are read again and written to the destination, without creating any duplicates and forcing an UPSERT semantics. You have four options:

- None: no action will be taken by ADF.

- Autogenerated cleanup script: you can let Azure Data Factory generate a script for you to clean up data before the rerun or the retry-logic.

- Custom script: same as above, but you provide your own script.

- Slice identifier column: it corresponds to the sliceIdentifierColumnName in the JSON file. In this case you specify a column dedicated to Azure Data Factory that it will use to uniquely identify the slice, in order to clean up data in case of a rerun.

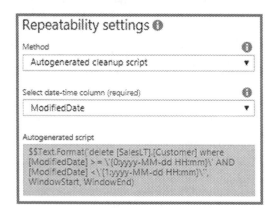

Figure 4-13b. *Repeatability settings options for relational data stores*

Figure 4-14 is also a relevant part to discuss. It basically covers two things:

1. **Error handling.** The red rectangle on the top; it contains the options that we can set to decide what happens if an exception is raised during the copy activity, like a constraint violation. We can stop the copy, and copy fails, or we can skip errors, and copy succeeds. In this second option, we can write logs to an Azure Storage Account for further analysis.

2. **Performance settings.** Please visit the *Considerations on performance, scalability and costs section*, later in this chapter

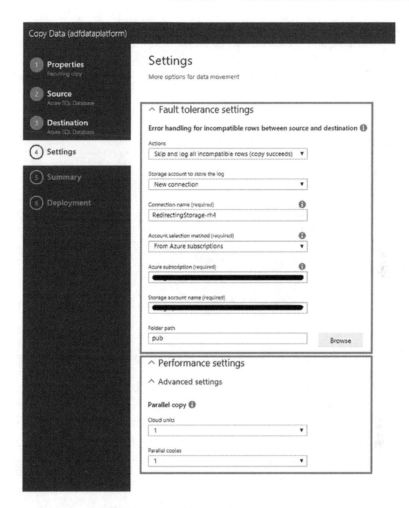

Figure 4-14. *Error handling settings and performance settings*

Figure 4-15 displays the summary and invites us to visit the **Monitor & Manage** tool, to check how the tasks are going on.

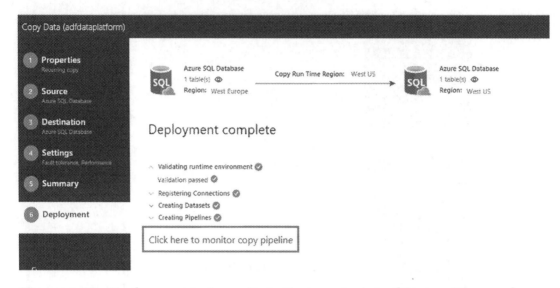

Figure 4-15. Deployment to Azure Data Factory starts in this step. We can also monitor it using a tool

In Figure 4-16 we have highlighted three parts of the *monitor and manage* tool:

1. The wizard produced a diagram that contains the source table, the copy activity, and the sync table.

2. The status of the activity windows, where we can see that the first **slice** (3 hours, from 6AM to 9AM) has been executed.

2

3. Information on the attempts. We can see that the activity worked on first attempt, and that nine records have been moved from source to sink.

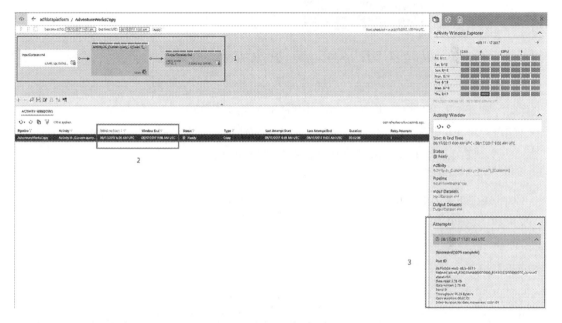

Figure 4-16. *The monitor and manage tool, useful to track progress of a pipeline or to troubleshoot errors*

The **Monitor and Manage** tool will become your best friend; you can also find it in the Azure Data Factory dashboard.

You can setup email alerts, like shown in Figure 4-17

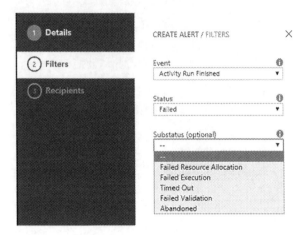

Figure 4-17. *Email alerts in the Monitor and Manage tool*

Note   To learn more on how to use the Monitor and Manage tool, you can read this document: `https://docs.microsoft.com/en-us/azure/data-factory/data-factory-monitor-manage-app`

Coming back to the copy activity, records with `ModifiedDate` data modified at 8AM have been added, and the range ties with the first slice, so the task worked as expected.

CustomerID	NameStyle	Title	FirstName	Middl...	LastNa...	Suffix	Com...	SalesPe...	EmailAddress	Phone	PasswordHash	Pas...	rowguid	ModifiedDate
31020	False	Mr.	Jim	NULL	Geist	NULL	Two B...	adventu...	jim1@adventur...	724-555-0161	cvqeC4fJcKwJ9j...	ot8...	c6ebb2...	8/17/2017 8:00:00 AM
31021	False	Ms.	Betty	M.	Haines	NULL	Finer ...	adventu...	betty0@advent...	867-555-0114	Q/nGAVzOO1Z...	6lvc...	e5eda3f...	8/17/2017 8:00:00 AM
31022	False	Ms.	Sharon	J.	Looney	NULL	Fitnes...	adventu...	sharon2@adve...	377-555-0132	Uo3kAuNh936...	uHg...	6808b1e...	8/17/2017 8:00:00 AM
31023	False	Mr.	Darren	NULL	Gehring	NULL	Journ...	adventu...	darren0@adven...	417-555-0182	kqptixZ7LqTuO...	Xe7g...	aa5e28f...	8/17/2017 8:00:00 AM
31024	False	Ms.	Erin	M.	Hagens	NULL	Dista...	adventu...	erin1@adventu...	244-555-0127	92Sfw/bI0dUJO...	8sol...	e1ba20e...	8/17/2017 8:00:00 AM
31025	False	Mr.	Jeremy	NULL	Los	NULL	Healt...	adventu...	jeremy0@adve...	911-555-0165	jLMkpmNutZFz...	JK9/...	64acd30...	8/17/2017 8:00:00 AM
31026	False	Ms.	Elsa	NULL	Leavitt	NULL	Fruga...	adventu...	elsa0@adventu...	482-555-0174	BmJaM+147Gr...	YAD...	9e449d3...	8/17/2017 8:00:00 AM
31027	False	Mr.	David	O	Lawrence	NULL	Gear-...	adventu...	david19@adve...	653-555-0159	HyZexVTTLfKfh...	/kc6...	21849ec...	8/17/2017 8:00:00 AM
31028	False	Ms.	Hattie	J.	Haemon	NULL	Great...	adventu...	hattie0@advent...	141-555-0172	RLemw9BUkhy...	8n38...	0d9abe...	8/17/2017 8:00:00 AM
NULL	NULL	NULL	NULL	NULL	NULL	NULL	NULL	NULL	NULL	NULL	NULL	NULL	NULL	NULL

Figure 4-18. *Records within the range of the first slice have been moved to the destination table*

If we wait for the second slice to be executed, then the records within the timeline range will be moved to the second table. If we look at Figure 4-19 below, we can see that the wizard created six slices, the second has been also executed therefore we can now see the new records have been added, Figure 4-20.

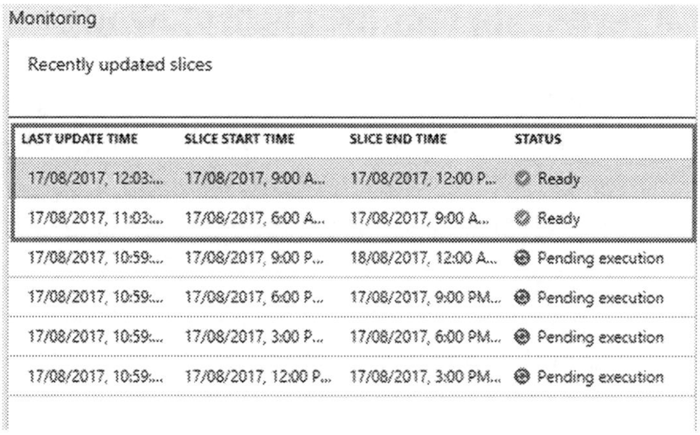

Figure 4-19. *The list of slices with the related status*

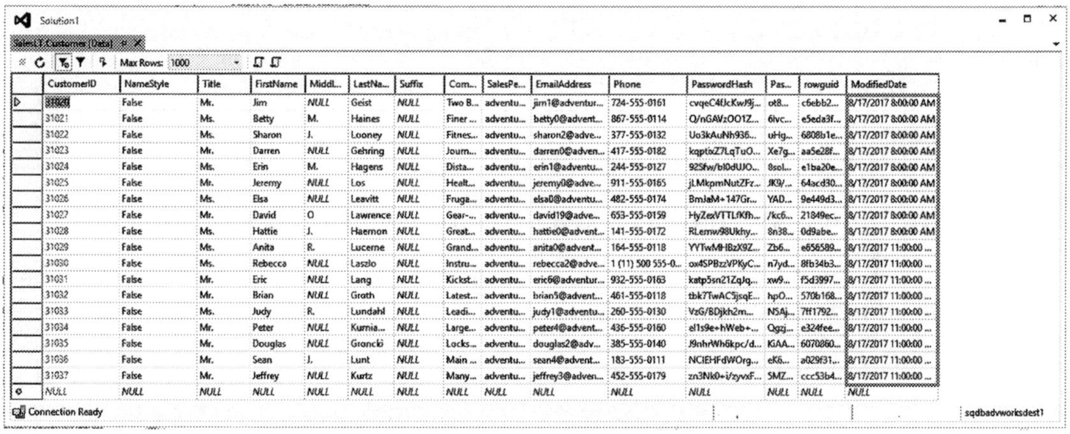

Figure 4-20. *Records of the second slice have been added*

We are now ready to move to the next passage, where we will use the JSON scripts to continue exploring Azure Data Factory.

Note   Copy Data options and masks change depending on the data store source and sink that you select.

Anatomy of Azure Data Factory JSON Scripts

We have now populated the SQL Database table on the sink data store, and our Azure Data Factory deployment has a pipeline, datasets, and linked services that we can explore to see how ADF uses JSON to store information.

We will also apply some changes to explain additional functionalities available in ADF.

You may recall that the authoring part can be done using the **Data Factory Editor** that you can launch using **Author and deploy action**, Figure 4-21.

Figure 4-21. *The author and deploy option launches the Data Factory Editor*

The Data Factory Editor contains two main areas:

1. A treeview on the left that contains the list of linked services, datasets, pipelines, and gateways that we created. In our case we have six JSON documents, and there are dependencies between them. I cannot delete a dataset if it is referenced by a pipeline. I cannot delete a linked service if it is referenced by a dataset. On the menu on the top left, we may add additional objects to our solution.

2. The JSON editor on the right and a menu on the top allows us to do actions like **Add activity**, **Deploy** actions, etc.

Figure 4-22. *The Data Factory Editor on the Azure Data Factory portal*

Linked Services Script

A linked service is basically a connection to a data store or a compute resource; the JSON definition file is structured as follows:

1. name (*): linked service name

2. properties: this section includes several options, most relevant are:

    a. type (*): the type of the dataset, such as AmazonRedshift, Hdfs, etc. In our example below, type is set to AzureStorage

    b. typeProperties (*): it depends on the data store or compute you are using. In our example is connectionString

Let's look at the code generated to access an Azure Storage account to store activity logs, the JSON file named RedirectingStorage-rh4.

```
{
    "name": "RedirectingStorage-rh4",
    "properties": {
        "hubName": "adfdataplatform_hub",
        "type": "AzureStorage",
        "typeProperties": {
```

```
            "connectionString": "DefaultEndpointsProtocol=https;Account
            Name=********;AccountKey=**********"
        }
    }
}
```

`* = required`

Dataset Script

Defining a dataset file requires us to fill some important information in the JSON file, such as:

1. `name` (*): name of the dataset

2. `properties`: this section includes several options, most relevant are:

    a. `type` (*): the type of the dataset, such as `AzureSQLTable`, `AzureBlob`, etc.

    b. `typeProperties` (*): in our example is the name of the table, but they are different for each data store or compute you may choose

    c. `linkedServiceName` (*): name of the linked service

    d. `structure`: the schema of the dataset, that includes `name` and data `type` of the column

    e. `availability` (*): defines the data activity window, in terms of `frequency` (*) and `interval` (*). Supported values for frequency are `Minute`, `Hour`, `Day`, `Week`, and `Month`. In our example the **slice** is produced every three hours, as the frequency is set to Hour and interval is set to 1.

    f. `policy`: the rules that each dataset slice must adhere to. If you are working with an Azure Blob storage, you can set the `minimumSizeMB` policy that defines the minimum size in megabytes of the slice. If you are working with Azure SQL Database or Azure Table, you can set the `minimumRows` policy, which defines the minimum number of rows allowed by the slice.

g. external: defines if the dataset is not produced as an output
    of an activity. "external":true means that data are not
    produced by Azure Data Factory. It usually applies to the first
    input dataset in the workflow. In the case of external datasets,
    you may also apply an ExternalData policy, in case you need
    to apply a retry logic to the workflow.

    * = required

Note   In case the frequency is set to Minute, the interval should be at least
15. You also have the ability to set the style property, which defines if the slice
should be produced at the beginning of the interval, StartOfInterval, or at the
end of the interval, EndOfInterval. If you set frequency to Day and you set
style to StartOfInterval, the slice is produced in the first hour.

Now we are ready to read the datasets JSON scripts created with the Copy Data
wizard, in the case below we have the output dataset OutputDataset-rh4.

```
{
    "name": "OutputDataset-rh4",
    "properties": {
        "structure": [
            {
                "name": "NameStyle",
                "type": "Boolean"
            },
            {
                "name": "Title",
                "type": "String"
            },
            {
                "name": "FirstName",
                "type": "String"
            },
```

```
{
    "name": "MiddleName",
    "type": "String"
},
{
    "name": "LastName",
    "type": "String"
},
{
    "name": "Suffix",
    "type": "String"
},
{
    "name": "CompanyName",
    "type": "String"
},
{
    "name": "SalesPerson",
    "type": "String"
},
{
    "name": "EmailAddress",
    "type": "String"
},
{
    "name": "Phone",
    "type": "String"
},
{
    "name": "PasswordHash",
    "type": "String"
},
{
    "name": "PasswordSalt",
    "type": "String"
},
```

```
        {
            "name": "rowguid",
            "type": "Guid"
        },
        {
            "name": "ModifiedDate",
            "type": "Datetime"
        }
    ],
    "published": false,
    "type": "AzureSqlTable",
    "linkedServiceName": "Destination-SQLDB-Customer",
    "typeProperties": {
        "tableName": "[SalesLT].[Customer]"
    },
    "availability": {
        "frequency": "Hour",
        "interval": 3
    },
    "external": false,
    "policy": {}
    }
}
```

Pipeline and Activity Script

Pipelines and activities files often require a higher amount of information. The structure of the JSON schema includes:

1. name (*): name of the pipeline

2. properties: this section includes several options, most relevant are:

    a. activities (*): contains the description of all activities, one or more

        i.   name (*): name of the activity

        ii. type (*): type of the activity, e.g. a Copy activity

293

     iii. `typeProperties`: they depend on the activity we are
using. We are using Azure SQL Database, and there
are several parameters that we can specify, such as
`SqlSource` to specify the source, `SqlSink` to specify the
destination, `sqlReaderQuery` to define the query string,
`columnMappings` to map columns of the two tables,
`enableSkipIncompatibleRow` to define the error
handling, etc.

     iv. `policy`: used to define how the pipeline should behave
during runtime. When an activity is processing a table
slice, you can define the `retry` logic applied to it, the
`concurrency`, and execution processing order of slices as
well, `executionPriorityOrder`. In our example the value
is set to NewestFirst, which means that if more than
one slice is pending execution, the newest will be
processed first

     v. `inputs` (*): input objects used by the activity

     vi. `outputs` (*): same as above, but for output objects

  b. `start`: start date and time for the pipeline

  c. `end`: end date and time for the pipeline

  d. `isPaused`: set true if you want to pause it

  e. `pipelineMode`: `Scheduled` if you specify start and end, `Onetime`
if it only runs once

     `* = required`

We are now able to read the JSON script that we generated for the `AdventureWorks`
`Copy` pipeline:

```
{
    "name": "AdventureWorksCopy",
    "properties": {
        "description": "",
        "activities": [
```

```
{
    "type": "Copy",
    "typeProperties": {
        "source": {
            "type": "SqlSource",
            "sqlReaderQuery": "$$Text.Format('select *
            from SalesLT.Customer where ModifiedDate >=
            \\'{0:yyyy-MM-dd HH:mm}\\' AND ModifiedDate
            < \\'{1:yyyy-MM-dd HH:mm}\\'', WindowStart,
            WindowEnd)"
        },
        "sink": {
            "type": "SqlSink",
            "sqlWriterCleanupScript": "$$Text.Format('delete
            [SalesLT].[Customer] where [ModifiedDate] >=
            \\'{0:yyyy-MM-dd HH:mm}\\' AND [ModifiedDate]
            <\\'{1:yyyy-MM-dd HH:mm}\\'', WindowStart,
            WindowEnd)",
            "writeBatchSize": 0,
            "writeBatchTimeout": "00:00:00"
        },
        "translator": {
            "type": "TabularTranslator",
            "columnMappings": "NameStyle:NameStyle,Title:Title,
            FirstName:FirstName,MiddleName:MiddleName,LastName:
            LastName,Suffix:Suffix,CompanyName:CompanyName,Sale
            sPerson:SalesPerson,EmailAddress:EmailAddress,Phone
            :Phone,PasswordHash:PasswordHash,PasswordSalt:Passw
            ordSalt,rowguid:rowguid,ModifiedDate:ModifiedDate"
        },
        "parallelCopies": 1,
        "cloudDataMovementUnits": 1,
        "enableSkipIncompatibleRow": true,
        "redirectIncompatibleRowSettings": {
            "linkedServiceName": "RedirectingStorage-rh4",
```

```
                                "path": "pub"
                        }
                },
                "inputs": [
                        {
                                "name": "InputDataset-rh4"
                        }
                ],
                "outputs": [
                        {
                                "name": "OutputDataset-rh4"
                        }
                ],
                "policy": {
                        "timeout": "1.00:00:00",
                        "concurrency": 1,
                        "executionPriorityOrder": "NewestFirst",
                        "style": "StartOfInterval",
                        "retry": 3,
                        "longRetry": 0,
                        "longRetryInterval": "00:00:00"
                },
                "scheduler": {
                        "frequency": "Hour",
                        "interval": 3
                },
                "name": "Activity-0-_Custom query_->[SalesLT]_[Customer]"
            }
        ],
        "start": "2017-08-17T06:00:00Z",
        "end": "2017-08-17T23:00:00Z",
        "isPaused": false,
        "hubName": "adfdataplatform_hub",
        "pipelineMode": "Scheduled"
    }
}
```

Note   In order to go more in depth with JSON scripting in Azure Data Factory, you can visit the **Azure Data Factory - JSON Scripting Reference** page: `https://docs.microsoft.com/en-us/azure/data-factory/data-factory-json-scripting-reference`

Azure Data Factory Tools for Visual Studio

Azure Data Factory tools for Visual Studio provide a rich set of tools to accelerate authoring productivity using the power of Visual Studio.

It is a plug-in fully integrated with the Visual Studio IDE, therefore you can manage the solution using Solution Explorer, like in Figure 4-22 below, and benefit from all of the other options available, including the Azure SDK.

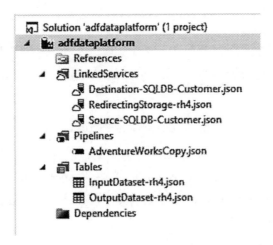

Figure 4-23.   *ADF tools for Visual Studio are seamless integrated with Visual Studio IDE*

You can write your JSON scripts using Visual Studio, see a Diagram view in real time, and deploy the solution to ADF, when ready to go in to production, like in Figure 4-24 below.

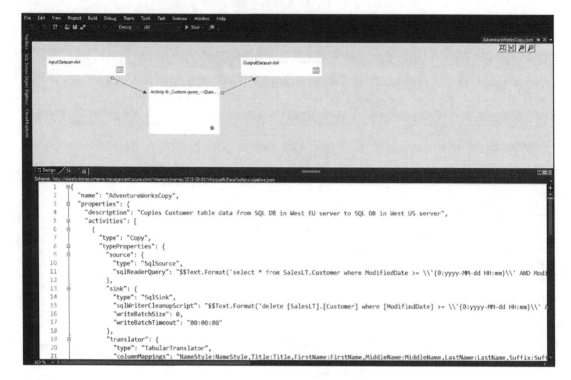

Figure 4-24. *JSON editor in Visual Studio also includes a Diagram view of our projects*

ADF tools add two project templates to Visual Studio:

1. **Data Factory templates.** You can use it to start from a use case template that can help you to familiarize yourself with the service, or you can launch a Copy Data template to implement an assisted data movement activity.

2. **Empty Data Factory Project**. Self explanatory, you can start from an empty solution and start authoring your project from scratch.

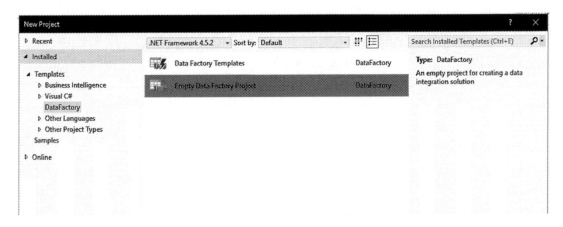

Figure 4-25. *Azure Data Factory tools for Visual Studio 2015 project templates*

Good Practices for Authoring ADF solutions

Authoring online only using the Data Factory Editor is not properly a best practice. Let's see why:

- Data Factory Editor does not have a versioning system embedded in the platform, therefore any change made on the Data Factory Editor goes straight to production, and you lose the previous version of the document.

- Azure Data Factory does not have a cloning option embedded in the portal. Imagine you have designed a solution, but you are not sure of the changes you are about to apply. Today you can only clone a single object, like a Dataset, but it would remain part of the production solution. Therefore in some cases you risk creating a result that could be worse than the original one.

  - Or imagine you want to start a new project reusing a previous solution, without repeating each step again. The Data Factory Editor doesn't permit that, at the moment. You could, but this is different scenario, migrate an existing ADF project from one subscription to another subscription or to another resource group.

Luckily there is an easy solution to overcome the considerations above and we recommend, like in all good families, to have a test environment, with a dedicated Azure Data Factory service for testing purposes, and data stores and compute resources specifically for this. To do that, one of the best solutions is to use Azure Data Factory tools for Visual Studio to have at least one project for testing and one for production, to edit JSON files offline, to use a source control if needed, and to deploy to the right environment when ready.

Using, as example, our *adfdataplatform* solution, we could open it in Visual Studio as a new Azure Data Factory Project, make required changes, and deploy to another Azure Data Factory provisioned service, as displayed in Figure 4-26.

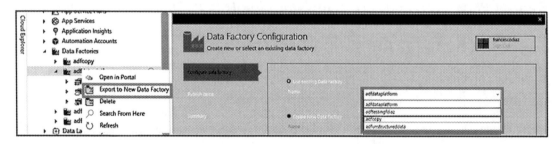

Figure 4-26. *Export the production to a New Data Factory project and deploy it to a test environment after changes*

Note 1   Azure Data Factory tools for Visual Studio are available to download from the Visual Studio marketplace: `https://marketplace.visualstudio.com/items?itemName=AzureDataFactory.MicrosoftAzureDataFactoryToolsforVisualStudio2015`

Note 2   Azure Data Factory tools are not yet available for Visual Studio 2017, so you will need to install Visual Studio 2015 (or Visual Studio 2013 Update 4) to use them. There is a request for change open on the Azure forums, you can read it here and support it with your vote, if you would like to: `https://feedback.azure.com/forums/270578-data-factory/suggestions/18773008-support-adf-projects-in-visual-studio-2017`

Working with Data Transformation Activities

We explored data movement activities earlier in the chapter. In this section we will work with **data transformation activities**, modifying the ADF solution we used so far.

To execute a data transformation activity, we need a **compute environment**. A data transformation activity can be added to an existing pipeline and live together with other activities, or it can be part of a new pipeline, depending on the need.

Azure Data Factory supports the following data transformation activities:

- **Hive**, **Pig**, **MapReduce**, **Streaming**, **Spark** (*) Activities: they can run in an existing or on-demand HDInsight cluster, Windows or Linux based.

- Azure **Machine Learning** activities:

    - **Batch Execution Activity**: used to invoke an Azure ML web service to make predictions - "type": "AzureMLBatchExecution"

    - **Update Resource Activity**: to update the web service with Azure ML newly trained models - "type": "AzureMLUpdateResource"

    - **Batch Scoring Activity**: use Batch Execution Activity instead, as newer

- **Stored Procedure Activity**: used to invoke a stored procedure in an Azure SQL Database, Azure SQL Data Warehouse or a SQL Server**

- **Data Lake Analytics U-SQL Activity**: used to run a U-SQL script in Azure Data Lake Analytics

- **.NET Custom Activity**: for any transformation not included out of the box in Azure Data Factory, you may rely on custom activities, and write your .NET code that can run inside Azure Batch or Azure HDInsight

    * Spark Activities do not support on-demand HDInsight clusters

    ** Data Management Gateway required

Note   **On-demand HDInsight** clusters are managed by Azure Data Factory. They are a very good solution when the cluster doesn't have to be persistent and it is only needed to execute activities. Azure Data Factory will create the cluster just before the activity execution, and the cluster will be removed after the task completion. On-demand clusters are a very good practice to leverage the power of public cloud services like Microsoft Azure, especially because they often can help to reduce the costs of the project.

Stored Procedure Activity

We will now upgrade adfdataplatform to insert a **Stored Procedure Activity**. We want to see how multiple activities can work together and how to chain them, when needed.

We have added four objects to Azure SQL Database sqldbadvworksdest1, the sink store in the Copy Data activity used before in this chapter. Objects are:

1. The stored procedure dbo.spAppendToArchive: it contains a very simple business logic, just needed to explain how a data transformation activity can be invoked. It basically copies the records modified in the current day from the table SalesLT. Customer to the dbo.Archive. After that, it inserts a record in the table dbo.LogArchive to store the number of inserted records in dbo.Archive. The stored procedure runs once per day, in the time interval of the last slice, from 9PM to 12AM, to be able to move all the records inserted during the day. The time interval will be provided by the activity using two parameters, @hourstoadd1 and @hourstoadd2

2. The table dbo.Archive: used by dbo.spAppendToArchive to archive records with the ModifiedData field data that match the current day

3. The table dbo.LogArchive: used by dbo.spAppendToArchive to force one execution per day, at most, to track the execution and the total number of records inserted in dbo.Archive

4.   The table dbo.dummyTable: empty, used only because a Stored
     Procedure Activity requires an output dataset

Let's now have a look at the T-SQL code

```
/****** Object:   Table [dbo].[Archive]******/

CREATE TABLE [dbo].[Archive](
        [id] [int] IDENTITY(1,1) NOT NULL,
        [FirstName] [nvarchar](50) NOT NULL,
        [LastName] [nvarchar](50) NOT NULL,
        [CompanyName] [nvarchar](128) NULL,
        [EmailAddress] [nvarchar](50) NULL,
        [ModifiedDate] [datetime] NOT NULL,
 CONSTRAINT [PK_Archive] PRIMARY KEY CLUSTERED
(
        [id] ASC
)WITH (PAD_INDEX = OFF, STATISTICS_NORECOMPUTE = OFF, IGNORE_DUP_KEY = OFF,
ALLOW_ROW_LOCKS = ON, ALLOW_PAGE_LOCKS = ON) ON [PRIMARY]
) ON [PRIMARY]
GO
/****** Object:   Table [dbo].[LogArchive]******/

CREATE TABLE [dbo].[LogArchive](
        [id] [int] IDENTITY(1,1) NOT NULL,
        [archiveexecuted] [datetime] NOT NULL,
        [numofrows] [int] NOT NULL,
 CONSTRAINT [PK_Log] PRIMARY KEY CLUSTERED
(
        [id] ASC
)WITH (PAD_INDEX = OFF, STATISTICS_NORECOMPUTE = OFF, IGNORE_DUP_KEY = OFF,
ALLOW_ROW_LOCKS = ON, ALLOW_PAGE_LOCKS = ON) ON [PRIMARY]
) ON [PRIMARY]
GO

****** Object:   Table [dbo].[dummyTable]******/
```

```sql
CREATE TABLE [dbo].[dummyTable](
        [dummyColumn] [char](1) NULL
) ON [PRIMARY]
/****** Object:   StoredProcedure [dbo].[spAppendToArchive]******/

CREATE PROCEDURE [dbo].[spAppendToArchive]

@hourstoadd1 int,
@hourstoadd2 int
AS
BEGIN
        SET NOCOUNT ON;

        DECLARE @base datetime = CONVERT(date,GETDATE())
        DECLARE @minDate datetime = DATEADD(HOUR, @hourstoadd1,@base)
        DECLARE @maxDate datetime = DATEADD(HOUR, @hourstoadd2,@base)

        IF (GETDATE() >= @minDate AND GETDATE() <= @maxDate)
        BEGIN
                IF NOT EXISTS(SELECT archiveexecuted FROM dbo.LogArchive
                WHERE archiveexecuted = @base) --only one run permitted
                per day
                BEGIN
                INSERT INTO dbo.Archive -- inserts all the records of the
                current day

                        SELECT FirstName, LastName, CompanyName,
                        EmailAddress, ModifiedDate
                                FROM SalesLT.Customer
                                WHERE ModifiedDate >= @base AND
                                ModifiedDate <= @maxDate;

                INSERT dbo.LogArchive VALUES (@base,@@ROWCOUNT) -- tracks
                operation and number of records

                END
        END
END
```

We can now have a look at the additional JSON scripts that we have used to implement the Stored Procedure Activity.

Output dataset: only needed because it is mandatory to have an output dataset linked to an activity. We have added it just to make the activity work, which is why the structure property is empty.

```
{
  "$schema": "http://datafactories.schema.management.azure.com/
  schemas/2015-09-01/Microsoft.DataFactory.Table.json",
  "name": "OutputDatasetDummy",
  "properties": {
    "type": "AzureSqlTable",
    "linkedServiceName": "Destination-SQLDB-Customer",
    "structure": [],
    "typeProperties": {
      "tableName": "dummyTable"
    },
    "availability": {
      "frequency": "Hour",
      "interval": 3
    }
  }
}
```

Pipeline: in this first example we are deploying the activity in a new pipeline, not connected to the other one. Therefore, an input dataset is not required. We will explore additional options in the next paragraph. The typeProperties section contains the name of the stored procedure and the parameters. Below you can find only the relevant portion of code related to the pipeline object.

```
{
  "$schema": "http://datafactories.schema.management.azure.com/
  schemas/2015-09-01/Microsoft.DataFactory.Pipeline.json",
  "name": "AdventureWorksArchive",
  "properties": {
    "description": "",
    "activities": [
```

```
    {
      "name": "ArchiveActivity",
      "type": "SqlServerStoredProcedure",
      "outputs": [
        {
          "name": "OutputDatasetDummy"
        }
      ],
      "typeProperties": {
        "storedProcedureName": "dbo.spAppendToArchive",
        "storedProcedureParameters": {
          "@hourstoadd1": "6",
          "@hourstoadd2": "24"

        }
      },
      "policy": {
        "concurrency": 1,
        "executionPriorityOrder": "OldestFirst",
        "retry": 3,
        "timeout": "01:00:00"
      },
      "scheduler": {
        "frequency": "Hour",
        "interval": 3
      }
    }
  ],
  "start": "2017-08-19T06:00:00Z",
  "end": "2017-08-19T23:00:00Z",
  "isPaused": false,
  "pipelineMode": "Scheduled"
 }
}
```

After the execution of both activities, we can query the three tables in the sink datastore to verify results. As you can see from Figure 4-27 below, 13 customer records have been copied to the archive and the activity has been logged.

```
select * from dbo.LogArchive
select * from dbo.Archive
select * from SalesLT.Customer
```

id	archiveexecuted	numofrows
1	7 2017-08-19 00:00:50.000	13

	id	FirstName	LastName	CompanyName	EmailAddress	ModifiedDate
1	1	Kathleen	Garza	Rural Cycle Emporium	kathleen0@adventure-works.com	2017-08-19 09:00:00.000
2	2	Katherine	Harding	Sharp Bikes	katherine0@adventure-works.com	2017-08-19 09:00:00.000
3	3	Johnny	Caprio	Bikes and Motorbikes	johnny0@adventure-works.com	2017-08-19 09:00:00.000
4	4	Christopher	Beck	Bulk Discount Store	christopher1@adventure-works.com	2017-08-19 09:00:00.000
5	5	David	Liu	Catalog Store	david20@adventure-works.com	2017-08-19 09:00:00.000
6	6	John	Beaver	Center Cycle Shop	john8@adventure-works.com	2017-08-19 09:00:00.000
7	7	Jean	Handley	Central Discount Store	jean1@adventure-works.com	2017-08-19 09:00:00.000
8	8	Jinghao	Liu	Chic Department Stores	jinghao1@adventure-works.com	2017-08-19 09:00:00.000
9	9	Linda	Burnett	Travel Systems	linda4@adventure-works.com	2017-08-19 09:00:00.000
10	10	Kerim	Hanif	Bike World	kerim0@adventure-works.com	2017-08-19 09:00:00.000
11	11	Kevin	Liu	Eastside Department Store	kevin5@adventure-works.com	2017-08-19 09:00:00.000

	CustomerID	NameStyle	Title	FirstName	MiddleName	LastName	Suffix	CompanyName	SalesPerson	EmailAddress	Phone	PasswordHash	PasswordSalt	rowguid	ModifiedDate
1	31092	0	Ms.	Kathleen	M	Garza	NULL	Rural Cycle Emporium	adventure-works\jose1	kathleen0@adv	150-55..	Qa3aNCxNbVl..	Ls05W3g=	CDB9658..	2017-08-19 09:00:00.000
2	31093	0	Ms.	Katherine	NULL	Harding	NULL	Sharp Bikes	adventure-works\jose1	katherine0@adv..	526-95..	uR0rVzDGNJiX..	joHKqE=	750F3495..	2017-08-19 09:00:00.000
3	31094	0	Mr.	Johnny	A.	Caprio	Jr.	Bikes and Motorbikes	adventure-works\garrett1	johnny0@adven..	112-55..	jtF9jBoFYeJTaE..	wVLnwHo=	947BCAF..	2017-08-19 09:00:00.000
4	31095	0	Mr.	Christopher	R.	Beck	Jr.	Bulk Discount Store	adventure-works\jae0	christopher1@a..	1 (11) ..	sK9daCzEEKW..	8KfYx/4=	C938158..	2017-08-19 09:00:00.000
5	31096	0	Mr.	David	J.	Liu	NULL	Catalog Store	adventure-works\michael9	david20@adven..	440-55..	61zeTkO+el5g8..	c7Thvv0=	C04D6B4..	2017-08-19 09:00:00.000
6	31097	0	Mr.	John	A.	Beaver	NULL	Center Cycle Shop	adventure-works\pamela0	john8@adventur..	521-55..	DzbqWX7B3EK..	zXNgrJw=	69AE5D4..	2017-08-19 09:00:00.000
7	31098	0	Ms.	Jean	P.	Handley	NULL	Central Discount Store	adventure-works\david8	jean1@adventur..	582-55..	o1GVo3vExeNz..	uMe4Ido=	EB10C10..	2017-08-19 09:00:00.000
8	31099	0	N...	Jinghao	NULL	Liu	NULL	Chic Department Sto...	adventure-works\jillian0	jinghao1@adve..	928-55..	laD5AeqK9mRIr..	p8pOqKc=	564E0B4..	2017-08-19 09:00:00.000
9	31100	0	Ms.	Linda	E.	Burnett	NULL	Travel Systems	adventure-works\jillian0	linda4@adventu..	121-55..	23AwhvqCoXYS..	SmyIPjE=	9774AED..	2017-08-19 09:00:00.000
10	31101	0	Mr.	Kerim	NULL	Hanif	NULL	Bike World	adventure-works\ahu0	kerim0@advent ..	216-55..	d0WSjosAd7Y3..	33g5co8=	733F8250..	2017-08-19 09:00:00.000
11	31102	0	Mr.	Kevin	NULL	Liu	NULL	Eastside Department..	adventure-works\linda3	kevin5@advent..	926-55..	yiTpkIOHKLqjh..	TgZnUOg=	C111E51..	2017-08-19 09:00:00.000
12	31103	0	Mr.	Donald	L.	Blanton	NULL	Coalition Bike Comp ..	adventure-works\ahu0	donald0@adven..	357-55..	pKYDelLBOZM..	jKeOaOw=	31D0354..	2017-08-19 09:00:00.000
13	31104	0	Ms.	Jackie	E.	Blackwell	NULL	Commuter Bicycle St..	adventure-works\jose1	jackie0@advent..	972-55..	wqhgMfOTfef4Z..	SZ+6Go=	988A04A..	2017-08-19 09:00:00.000

Figure 4-27. Data in the destination database after the execution of the Stored Procedure Activity

Chaining Azure Data Factory Activities

Figure 4-28 below shows three different deployment options we have tested, each one of them can be a good solution depending on the need.

1. Stored Procedure Activity is deployed within a new pipeline, not connected the other one. There is no dependency between the two. It may be a good solution if the data transformation activity doesn't need to wait for the copy activity to run. In our case we don't need to have a dataset in input, as the stored procedure will consume the data directly accessing tables without the help of Azure Data Factory. The output dataset is required instead, not because the Stored Procedure will use it, but because the Stored Procedure Activity needs it, since it controls the scheduling. So, it is sufficient to create a dummy table, with no records, and use it as an output dataset for the Stored Procedure Activity.

2. Stored Procedure Activity is deployed to a new pipeline, chained
    to the other pipeline. To be more accurate, the activities are
    chained. To implement such a solution it is sufficient to set the
    output dataset of the Copy Activity as input dataset of the Stored
    Procedure Activity, and after the deployment the dependency
    between the two will be displayed in the diagram.

```
"inputs": [
    {
        "name": "OutputDataset-rh4"
    }
],
"outputs": [
    {
        "name": "OutputDatasetDummy"
    }
```

3. Same as above, with the difference that the Stored Procedure
    Activity will be deployed inside the same pipeline.
    Implementation is the same as point two, setting the output of
    Copy Activity as input of SP Activity.

Choosing the best solution really depends on how the workflow should behave. In
the case of options 2 and 3, in general it is a good practice to group activities within the
same pipeline, if they are designed to run within the same `start` and end `time` of the
pipeline and if they are designed to share the same logical part of the workflow.

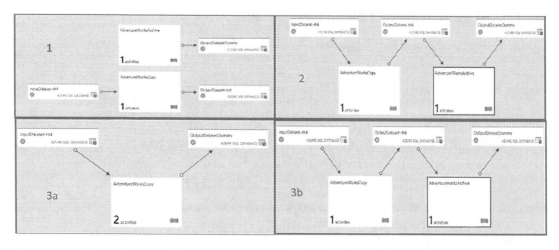

Figure 4-28. *3 different deployments of the Stored Procedure Activity. 3b is the
same as 3a, with the difference that in 3b you have the detail view of the activities
contained in the pipeline.*

Custom Activities

Custom activities are a type of **data transformation activities** that consist of code written in .NET and executed in a compute environment based on an **HDInsight** cluster or an **Azure Batch** pool of virtual machines. HDInsight can also be an on-demand cluster provisioned by Azure Data Factory before the activity execution and removed after the conclusion. In this section we will provide the high-level information needed to implement a custom activity in .NET.

High level requirements are:

- **A .NET Class Library**. A reference to the `Microsoft.Azure.Management.DataFactories` assembly is required, and the installation can be done via NuGet. The design of the class that contains the application logic must implement the `IDotNetActivity`. It contains one method, `Execute()` and four parameters:

  - `linkedServices: IEnumerable<LinkedService>` - linked servers

  - `datasets: IEnumerable<Dataset>` - input and output datasets

  - `activity: Activity` - the current activity

  - `logger: IActivityLogger` - used to write debug comments

```
namespace ADF
{
    public class customActivity:IDotNetActivity
    {

        public IDictionary<string, string> Execute(
            IEnumerable<LinkedService> linkedServices,
            IEnumerable<Dataset> datasets,
            Activity activity,
            IActivityLogger logger)
```

After implementing the business logic all you need to do is compile it and create a zip file with the files contained in the **bin\release** or **bin\debug** folder, depending on how you have compiled the solution. This file will be uploaded to an Azure Storage account and it will be consumed by the compute environment.

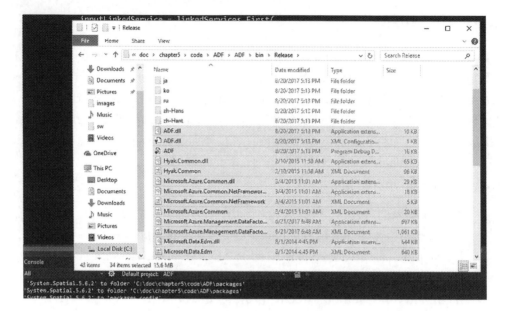

- A compute environment. In our case we are using **Azure Batch**.
  Azure Batch is a service able to run intensive jobs in parallel across a
  pool of virtual machines. Azure Batch is a PaaS service, therefore the
  administration surface is very much reduced compared to a standard
  high performance computing (HPC) solution. Files that need to be
  processed can be uploaded to Azure Storage, and our .NET library
  will be executed by the nodes in the pool. We do not need to launch
  tasks from Azure Batch, because Azure Data Factory will manage this
  aspect for us. To get information on how to create a Batch account
  you can read this document: https://docs.microsoft.com/en-us/
  azure/batch/batch-account-create-portal.

- An **Azure Storage Account** is used to store the zip file that contains
  the .NET code and to log in a file the results from the execution.

The code inside the .NET Class library does nothing but write a string inside a text
file which is stored in Azure Storage, to confirm that the execution has been successfully
completed by Azure Batch.

```
CloudStorageAccount outputStorage = CloudStorageAccount.Parse(connectionString);
Uri outputUri = new Uri(outputStorage.BlobEndpoint, path);
logger.Write("URI: {0}", outputUri.ToString());
CloudBlockBlob outputBlob = new CloudBlockBlob(outputUri, outputStorage.Credentials);
logger.Write("output blob", output);

outputBlob.UploadText("ADF executed by Azure Batch");
```

The JSON code of the Azure Batch linked server is below. The batchUri specifies the datacenter where the Azure Batch has been deployed, and together with the accountName, hidden here, represent the FQDN of the service. linkedServiceName parameter points to the linked services that contain the Azure Storage Account connection string. We also specify the pool that will be used, using the poolName parameter.

```
{
    "name": "AzureBatchLinkedService",
    "properties": {
        "description": "",
        "hubName": "adftestingfdiaz_hub",
        "type": "AzureBatch",
        "typeProperties": {
            "accountName": "********",
            "accessKey": "*********",
            "poolName": "adf_jobs",
            "batchUri": "https://northeurope.batch.azure.com",
            "linkedServiceName": "AzureStorageLinkedService"
        }
    }
}
```

The portion of code of the pipeline below contains the most relevant information.

- assemblyName: contains the name of the .NET assembly

- entryPoint: ADF.customActivity, where ADF is the namespace name and customActivity is the name of the class

- packageFile: container/filename, the path where the zip file is stored in the Azure Storage account

```
"activities": [
        {
            "type": "DotNetActivity",
            "typeProperties": {
                "assemblyName": "ADF.dll",
                "entryPoint": "ADF.customActivity",
                "packageLinkedService": "AzureStorageLinkedService",
                "packageFile": "customactivity/ADF.zip",
```

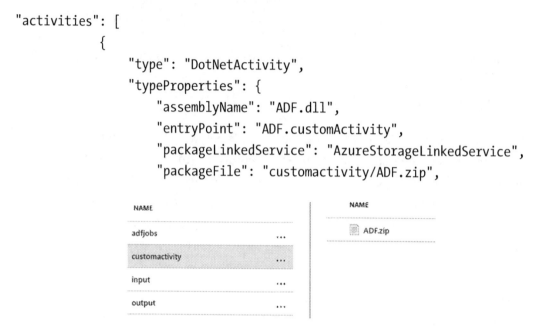

Figure 4-29. *Containers inside the storage account. The ADF.zip file contains the .NET class library*

After the provisioning of all services, results are as follows:

- An Azure Data Factory service that contains a custom .net activity

- Slices on the output have all been processed.

Recently updated slices

LAST UPDATE TIME	SLICE START TIME	SLICE END TIME	STATUS
20/08/2017, 8:13:51...	16/08/2017, 4:00 A...	16/08/2017, 5:00 A...	● Ready
20/08/2017, 8:13:10...	16/08/2017, 3:00 A...	16/08/2017, 4:00 A...	● Ready
20/08/2017, 8:13:10...	16/08/2017, 2:00 A...	16/08/2017, 3:00 A...	● Ready
20/08/2017, 8:12:19...	16/08/2017, 1:00 A...	16/08/2017, 2:00 A...	● Ready
20/08/2017, 8:12:18...	16/08/2017, 12:00 A...	16/08/2017, 1:00 A...	● Ready

- Virtual Machines in the Azure Batch pool have changed status from idle (the two grey squares in the picture below) to running (green squares) each time Azure Data Factory triggered a slice processing. Each square represents a virtual machine.

- Each execution has been tracked by the application, saving a new file in Azure Storage.

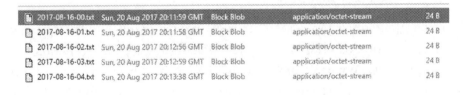

Note   To execute an Azure Data Factory custom activity, the nodes in the HDInsight cluster and the virtual machines in the Azure Batch pool must run a Windows operating system to run the .NET Framework.

Microsoft Data Management Gateway

Copying data from and to on-premises locations requires the Data Management Gateway (DMG) installation, an agent that enables the communication between the source and the sink data store, using a secure HTTPS channel.

Some considerations for the Data Management Gateway:

- It runs on Windows, 32-bit and 64-bit MSI packages are available. It can be installed on the same machine where the data store resides, or in a separate machine.

- One instance can serve more data stores.

- One instance can be tied with only one Azure Data Factory instance. If you need to use a DMG with another Azure Data Factory, you need to install it in a separate virtual machine, as two instances of DMG can't coexist.

- Outbound ports in the corporate firewall must be open. In particular: *.servicebus.windows.net:443,80; *.core.windows. net:443; *.frontend.clouddatahub.net:443. And, of course, the DMG must be also able to communicate with the ports of the data store source and sink, for the copy operations, e.g. TCP 3306 for MySQL default listening port.

When a copy activity is performed between two cloud data stores, the service that is performing the Copy Activity handles it, including type conversions, column mappings etc. When a Copy Activity involves an on-premises data store, **DMG manages the Copy Activity**, and most of the logic resides on the client side, including compression and serialization/deserialization. This is a very important aspect to consider, as the machine running DMG could have peaks of resource usage, therefore it is better to have it installed in a dedicated machine, in case of production environments, or in any case consider the additional resource power required, in coexistence scenarios. Microsoft recommends at least a 2GHz, 4 cores, 8-GM RAM configuration.

Note   **The Data Management Gateway** is also used by **Azure Machine Learning** to access on-premises data sources. To avoid confusion on the tools used to access on-premises data, it is important to highlight that gateways like DMG are also used by other Microsoft services, such as Power BI; the concept is basically the same, but tools are different, with a different setup too. You can learn more about the **On-Premises data gateway** (e.g. for Power BI) here: `https:// powerbi.microsoft.com/en-us/documentation/powerbi-gateway- onprem/`.

After installing the client and registering it using the key provided by the portal, the DMG definition file generates JSON too, and you can look in the portal and on the client using the **Microsoft Data Management Gateway Configuration Manager,** to check if everything is working fine.

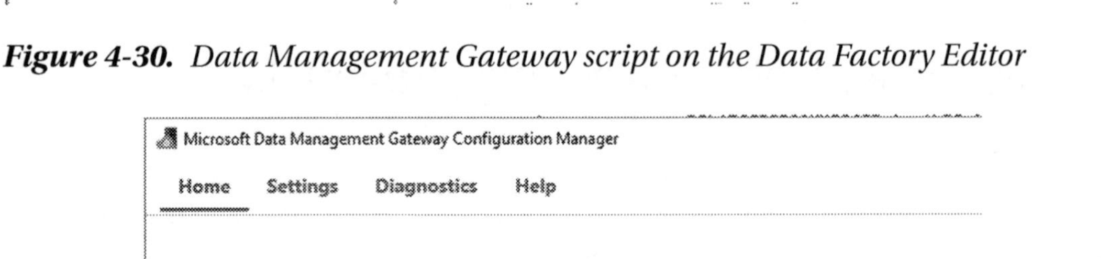

Figure 4-30. *Data Management Gateway script on the Data Factory Editor*

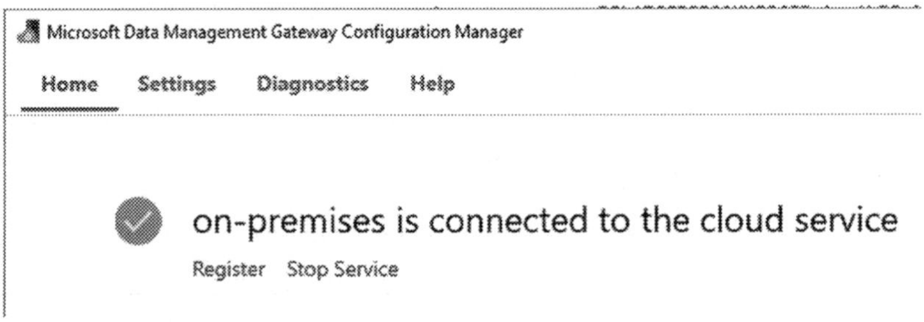

Microsoft Data Management Gateway Configuration Manager

Home   Settings   Diagnostics   Help

on-premises is connected to the cloud service

Register   Stop Service

Figure 4-31. *Microsoft Data Management Gateway Configuration Manager*

The Linked Service definition must include a reference to the gateway name, using the gatewayName parameter. The JSON below represents the connection to an on-premises MySQL development VM.

```
{
    "name": "Source-MySQL-oct",
    "properties": {
        "hubName": "adfdataplatform_hub",
        "type": "OnPremisesMySql",
        "typeProperties": {
            "server": "localhost",
            "database": "world",
            "schema": null,
            "authenticationType": "Basic",
            "username": "",
            "password": "**********",
            "gatewayName": "on-premises",
            "encryptedCredential": "***"
        }
    }
}
```

Considerations of Performance, Scalability and Costs

When designing a solution with Azure Data Factory, you need to have performance and scalability in mind. Answering the *how long the activity will take to finish* question depends, at least, on three aspects:

1. Copy activities between data sources that do not use a Data Management Gateway. In this case, you need to tweak the solution more on the activity itself, working on the parameters to control parallelism. Of course, how fast the data store source and sink are reading and writing data, is also very important.

2. Copy activities that include linked services that use the Data Management Gateway. In this case, the performances at DMG level becomes relevant, so you may check if scaling is required on the client side, adding more instances of the DMG that can execute copies in parallel.

3. Data transformation activities. As seen earlier in the Stored Procedure Activity section, in this case the execution depends heavily on the compute resources that are outside Azure Data Factory, each one of them with dedicated performance and scalability options. You may have an HDInsight cluster running a Hive script on several nodes, Azure Batch running a .NET custom code distributed across several VMs in the pool, or a U-SQL script used by Azure Data Lake Analytics to perform jobs on an Azure Data Lake Store. It is important to check the Monitor and Manage area to wee if the bottleneck is on one data transformation activity. If so, likely you may have to check the performances of the compute resource also. For this reason, we will focus more on points 1 and 2 here.

Copy Activities

Copy activities are designed to be optimized for terabytes of data loading per day. Microsoft tested several copy activities in-house and has produced the table in Figure 4-32 below that can be used as a reference to plan an ADF solution.

	(Unit: MBps)	# of cloud DMUs OR gateway nodes	Azure Blob (GRS)	Azure Data Lake Store	Azure SQL Data Warehouse (6000 DWU) — PolyBase	Bulk Insert	Azure SQL Database (P11)	Azure Table	Azure Cosmos DB (DocDB API, 2500RU) (single partition)	On-prem SQL Server	On-prem File System
Cloud Sources	Azure Blob (GRS)	1	17	16	1250	0.3	2	0.1	0.04	11	129
		8	105	105		*	9	0.2	*		
	Azure Data Lake Store	1	13	16	1060	0.3	1	0.1	0.04	10	114
		8	120	108		*	9	*	*		
	Azure SQL Data Warehouse (2000 DWU)	1	4	3	3	0.4	3	0.2	0.05	11	*
		4	9	8	6	1	8	0.3	*		
	Azure SQL Database (P11)	1	4	4	3	0.5	4	0.1	0.04	14	*
		4	9	8	6	1	8	0.3	-		
	Azure Table	1	1	1	*	0.7	1	0.4	0.07	1	*
		4	2	2	*	2	2	1	*		
	Azure Cosmos DB (DocDB API, single partition)	1	1	1	*	0.6	1	0.3	*	*	*
		4	2	2	*	2	2	*	*		
	Amazon S3	8	107	101	69	*	*	*	*	*	*
	Amazon Redshift	4	*	*	7.2	*	*	*	*	*	*
On-prem Sources	On-premises SQL Server	1	7	7	18	0.4	7	0.2	0.04	*	*
	On-premises File System	1	195	192	102	0.3	6	0.2	0.04	*	*
		4	505	510	*					*	*
	On-premise HDFS	1	179	183	83	0.3	3	0.2	0.04	*	*
		4	500	525	*					*	*

Unit: MBps
*: The throughput numbers for this source-sink combination will be published later.
**: For copying from cloud sources to on-prem sinks, single gateway node was used.

Figure 4-32. *Performance table for data store sources and data store sinks of a Copy Activity*

Data Movement Units (DMU), Parallel Copies, Concurrency, Compression and DMG

Data Movement Units are useful when source and sink are both on cloud, as the copy is not driven by the Data Management Gateway. DMU is a way to measure the power of each unit of execution in Azure Data Factory. They are a combination of network, CPU, and memory resources associated to ADF. You may find a similar concept in other Azure services, such as Azure SQL Database, where you define performances using Data Transaction Units (DTU). You can set the number of DMUs using the cloudDataMovementeUnits parameter in the Activity script. Default is 1, and you can have 2,4,8,16,or 32. You can ask for more, if needed, by contacting Microsoft Azure Support.

Parallel copies represent the ability to execute a single activity run in parallel. The parallelCopies parameter affects the single activity run, such as the processing of a specific slice. Parallel copies configuration touches both cloud data stores and DMG data stores, and you could set up to 32 parallel copies simultaneously.

You define both parallelCopies and CloudDataMovementUnits inside the typeProperties section of the JSON file.

```
"parallelCopies": 1,
"cloudDataMovementUnits": 2,
```

Concurrency gives you the ability to improve performances executing in parallel activities that affect different activity windows, like the processing of different slices of data. You can define it using the concurrency parameter, under the policy section of the activity file.

```
"policy": {
    "timeout": "1.00:00:00",
    "concurrency": 2,
```

Compression is also an important aspect of a copy activity. You can configure compression using the compression parameter under the typeProperties section of the activity definition file. You can define the type (GZip, BZip2, Deflate, ZipDeflate) and the level of compression, considering the balance between the additional compute resources needed to compress data at optimal levels plus the reduced amount of data copied (Optimal) and, on the other side, a higher amount of data due to the lower compression ratio, with less impact on the CPU (fastest).

```
"compression": {
    "type": "GZip",
    "level": "Fastest"
```

Note   Azure Data Factory supports several file format types, such as **Text** format, **JSON** format, **Avro** format, **ORC** format, **Parquet** format. The compression setting is not supported by file format types Avro, ORC, and Parquet, as Azure Data Factory chooses the default compression codec for that format. To understand more about file format types, you can visit Microsoft documentation here: https://docs.microsoft.com/en-us/azure/data-factory/data-factory-supported-file-and-compression-formats

---

Data Management Gateway also has the ability to scale. You can scale it up, adding more resources to the VM if you see that it is suffering on the CPU or memory component, or you can scale it out, configuring a multi-node environment, part of a one **logical gateway** connected to an Azure Data Factory service. In a scale-out scenario, you can add **up to four nodes**, all active, each one installed in a different virtual machine, that you can also use for fault tolerance reasons, in case one node goes down. In Figure 4-33 below you will find a diagram on how a multi-node gateway works:

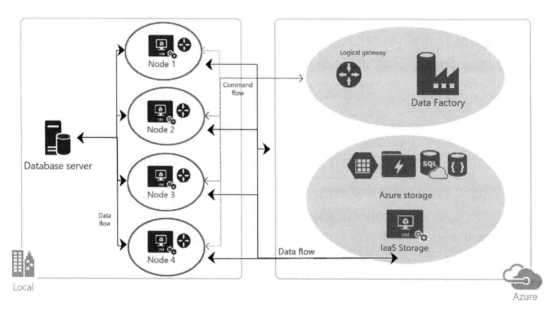

Figure 4-33. *How to design DMG for high availability and scalability*

Note   You can find a detailed Microsoft document on the performance aspects of copy activities here: `https://docs.microsoft.com/en-us/azure/data-factory/data-factory-copy-activity-performance`. A tutorial on how to configure a multi-node logical gateway is available here: `https://docs.microsoft.com/en-us/azure/data-factory/data-factory-data-management-gateway-high-availability-scalability`

Costs

There are only a few considerations of costs, before ending this chapter. This section doesn't aim to be exhaustive, but to give the main factors used by Microsoft Azure to calculate costs of Azure Data Factory usage.

Costs of Azure Data Factory are calculated based on:

- The Region where the service is deployed

- Where the activity runs, on-premises or on cloud

- The frequency of activities. They can be LOW or HIGH; LOW is when an activity runs not more than once per day, while HIGH is when an activity runs more than once per day. Cost is calculated in activity per month. For example, if you are in a LOW scenario and you execute an activity per day in December, you will pay 31 units.

- Data movement of data. In this case you pay depending on the amount of time, as the cost is per hour of execution. For example, if your data movement activities last two hours for the execution, you pay for two hours.

- An inactive pipeline also generates costs, and in this case you pay per pipeline per month.

- Re-running activities has a fixed cost, based on units of 1,000 re-runs.

- External resources invoked by Azure Data Factory have their own pricing models, like Azure Batch, HDInsight, Azure Machine Learning, Azure Storage, data transfers, etc.

Note   We have not included costs numbers here, as they change from time to time. We recommend, for a more comprehensive and updated view on costs, visiting the official page of Azure Data Factory, here: `https://azure.microsoft.com/en-us/pricing/details/data-factory/`. You can also practice with the Azure Pricing Calculator online, available here: `https://azure.microsoft.com/en-us/pricing/calculator/?service=data-factory`

Azure Data Factory v2 (Preview)

Note   While writing this chapter, Microsoft released a Public Preview of Azure Data Factory v2. As it contains significant changes compared to the previous version, we decided to add a very short introduction to the service here, and some extra pages in the next chapter to demonstrate how it works with Azure Data Lake.

Azure Data Factory v2 Key Concepts

Azure Data Factory v2 (ADFv2) adds the following implementation scenarios, features, and components:

1. Authoring. The designer has been enriched with the ability to do all authoring parts using the visual tool. JSON is still there, as the result of what is done visually, but this new addition could simplify the learning curve and give an immediate representation of what the workflow will look like. The copy wizard is still available in v2, and it has pretty much the same masks, only with different options related to the new features of ADFv2.

Figure 4-34. *ADFv2 comes with a login page that helps you to launch the Create Pipeline to design you workflows, launch the Copy Data wizard, Configure SSIS Integration Runtime (we'll come to that in a second), and to Configure Git Repository to implement source control.*

2. Branching of activities. We now have the ability to better manage error handling and in general the flow of activities, for example, because each activity now has the ability to be linked to another activity, but are based on events such as execution failures.

3. Parameters. When you link two pipelines together, you can pass parameters between them. Parameters will be also available to activities to read information inside it, which enriches the workflow design process.

4. Triggers. This is one of the most relevant additions, as it allows the introduction of additional use cases, without the need to rely on custom activities only to handle specific events, like in v1. The time dimensions and slices approach used in v1 will add additional use cases scenarios now. You can trigger the start of a workflow on-demand or based on a schedule, or based on watching for file and folders on storage sources.

5. Control flow tasks. The designer contains a graphical toolbox and you now have the ability to use activities like **ForEach** and **If Condition**, to control the iteration or to verify specific conditions inside a workflow.

6. Working with ADFv2 on Linux is now possible not only calling the REST APIs, but also using the Python package for Data Factory: **pip install azure-mgmt-datafactory**. You also have new powershell cmdlets available for Windows; you can find some here: **Set-AzureRmDataFactoryV2** (create a datafactory); **Set-AzureRmDataFactoryV2LinkedService** (create a Linked Service); **Set-AzureRmDataFactoryV2Dataset** (create a Dataset); **Set-AzureRmDataFactoryV2Pipeline** (create a Pipeline).

7. Integration Runtime. This is also new in ADFv2, a very important addition too. An Integration Runtime (IR) is a compute engine, and there are three types of IR:

    a. **Azure:** Useful for data movement activities or to dispatch the execution of a task to an external service, such as Azure HDInsight.

    b. **Self-hosted:** Same concept as above, with the ability to work with data movement activities and to dispatch them externally, with the addition of being able to communicate with services that typically are on-premises or behind a virtual network. Conceptually this does the same job as the Data Management Gateway in v1.

c. **Azure-SSIS:** SSIS package execution: Thanks to this IR you can natively execute SQL Server Integration Services packages inside ADFv2, which provides the execution engine in combination with Azure SQL Server Database that hosts the SSIS package in the SSISDB database catalog. A typical scenario is related to the migration of on-premises SSIS packages to an Azure SQL Server Database; when you deploy an Azure-SSIS integration runtime, you choose the size of the compute node (an Azure Virtual Machine) and the number of nodes that will be used to perform package execution.

In the next chapter we will use the v2 of the service to move data to Azure Data Lake Store.

Summary

In conclusion, we can say that Azure Data Factory is a service rich in functionalities; it gives data architects and developers the ability to orchestrate data movement and data transformation workflows using a platform fully managed by Microsoft Azure. Solutions are easy to manage during time, thanks to the fact that everything produces JSON files. We have spent the majority of the time working with the authoring part, and we have also seen how Visual Studio can improve our productivity and support in designing more elegant and robust solutions. In the last section of the chapter we also considered the impacts on performances and costs. We also introduced the changes coming in the next version of Azure Data Factory, now in preview.

In the next chapter we will present Azure Data Lake, an Azure PaaS service designed to store and analyze big data.

CHAPTER 5

Azure Data Lake Store and Azure Data Lake Analytics

Microsoft Azure has done a lot to support data administrators and developers to provide a rich platform for big data workloads. Historically, Microsoft Azure, as a platform, was born being a PaaS offering solution only, and in this area we have always seen a more comprehensive offering compared to its competitors. On big data services, we must say that the effort Microsoft is providing in making the tools and technology rich and simple is remarkable. Azure Data Lake is one of the most ambitious services Microsoft is working on, and there is quite a lot of background and experience on which Microsoft is basing the design of the service, thanks to internal big data projects called Cosmos and Scope. This chapter is focused on Azure Data Lake Store, a PaaS big data store service, and Azure Data Lake Analytics, a PaaS big data compute service. We will cover the key concepts of each service, the different possibilities to work with them, and some considerations on how to optimize performances and design.

> *A data lake is a method of storing data within a system or repository, in its natural format, that facilitates the collocation of data in various schemas and structural forms, usually object blobs or files.*

If you look at this definition, it says that a data lake is a place where you can put different types of data in their natural format, and it is designed to store a large amount of information.

A data lake repository usually is aligned with the concept of Extracting and Load first, and then Transform later, if needed (ELT); this is because the storage and the compute are designed to work with any form of data. In a data lake project, you usually

327

don't spend much time in doing the transformation phase at the beginning, while focusing instead on how to access sources in a simple way and on giving tools the ability to load data in its original form. You could use a data lake to ingest and analyze tons of logs coming from servers, as a repository for IoT events raw data, to extend your data warehouse capabilities, etc.

In Figure 5-1, you can see the high-level description of what Azure Data Lake offering is. It includes two categories of services, one for the storage, based on HDFS and is able to store unstructured, semi-structured, and structured data, and one for the analytics, that includes a managed version of Hadoop clusters, called HDInsight, and a PaaS service called Azure Data Lake Analytics. In this chapter we will focus on Azure Data Lake Store (ADLS) and Azure Data Lake Analytics (ADLA) only, both released after HDInsight, at the end of 2016.

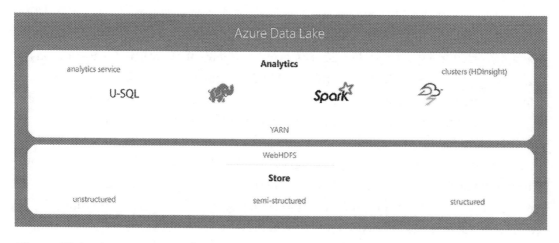

Figure 5-1. *Azure Data Lake services*

Azure Data Lake components:

- Azure Data Lake Store (ADLS): a repository for big data, capable of storing a virtually infinite amount of data.

- Azure Data Lake Analytics (ADLA): an on-demand analytics service able to execute jobs on data stores to perform big data analysis.

- HDInsight: A managed Hadoop cluster service, where the provisioning and the maintenance of cluster nodes is done by the Azure Platform.

How Azure Data Lake Store and Analytics were Born

Microsoft has several years of experience with big data, including the internal management of the data related to their business and consumer services available in the market, such as Bing, Skype, XBOX Live, and on the business side, the experience that Microsoft has with providing services on a massive scale through Azure is also part of the game.

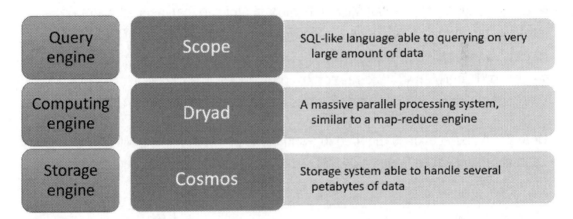

Figure 5-2. *Azure Data Lake Store and Analytics are based on the experience that Microsoft has with internal projects, aimed to manage and analyze huge amounts of data coming from their services largely adopted worldwide*

At a very high level, we can summarize the three projects that Microsoft used as a base to design Azure Data Lake as the following:

- Cosmos [Storage]. An append-only file system, optimized for large sequential I/O. The system contains a replication engine to make data tolerant to failures. Files stored in Cosmos can be very large and they are divided in blocks called extents. Extents reside in the cluster nodes managed by Cosmos.

- Dryad [Computing]. A system able to distribute jobs across multiple execution engine nodes, responsible for accessing and manipulating data in storage. Dryad also contains the logic able to manage failures of nodes.

- Scope [Querying]. A query engine that is able to combine SQL scripting language with C# inline code. Even if the data on Cosmos can be structured and unstructured, Scope is able to return rows of data, made of typed columns.

Mapping internal projects with the now public and commercial services, Cosmos is related to Azure Data Lake Store, while Dryad and Scope are the base on which Azure Data Lake Analytics has been built.

Note 1   To learn more about Microsoft internal projects that inspired Azure Data Lake, we recommend reading the following documents: SCOPE and COSMOS - `http://www.vldb.org/pvldb/1/1454166.pdf` ; DRYAD - `https://www.microsoft.com/en-us/research/project/dryad/?from=http%3A%2F%2Fresearch.microsoft.com%2Fen-us%2Fprojects%2Fdryad%2F;`

Note 2   A clarification is required to avoid confusion with names: Microsoft internal project called Cosmos **IS NOT** Azure CosmosDB, formerly DocumentDB that is instead a NoSQL database engine service available on Azure.

Azure Data Lake Store

Azure Data Lake Store (ADLS) is a repository designed to store any type of data, of any size. It is designed to be virtually unlimited in terms of the storage available for a single file and for the entire repository.

Key Concepts

- It is a pure PaaS service; therefore the administration effort required is nearly zero. You only need to focus on the design of the solution that includes ADLS.

- ADLS can store data in its native format, without any restrictions in terms of size and structure

- It is a file system, compatible with the Hadoop Distributed File System, accessible by all HDFS compliant projects, and that supports POSIX-compliant ACL on file and folders.

- It exposes WebHDFS via REST API, that can be used by Azure HDInsight or any other WebHDFS capable application.

- It is highly available by design, with built-in replication of data, and it provides 'read-after-write' consistency. Three copies of data are kept within a single Azure region.

- It is designed and optimized to support parallel computation.

- It supports encryption at rest, with support for Azure Key Vault too.

- It is natively integrated with Azure Active Directory, with support for OAuth 2.0 tokens for authentication.

In the image below, you can see the list of open source applications, installed in an HDInsight cluster that can work with Azure Data Lake Store using a WebHDFS interface. Any application able to work with HDFS file system can benefit from ADLS too.

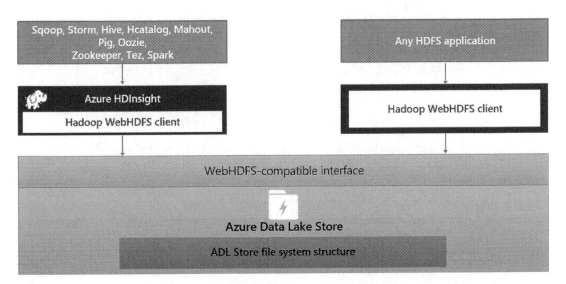

Figure 5-3. *To see a detailed matrix of the versions of open source applications and HDInsight supported, you can visit this page:* `https://github.com/ MicrosoftDocs/azure-docs/blob/master/articles/data-lake-store/ data-lake-store-compatible-oss-other-applications.md`

Note   The WebHDFS REST API exposes access to client using the namespace
webhdfs://<hostname>:<http_port>/<file_path>, and you can find a
description here: `https://hadoop.apache.org/docs/r1.0.4/webhdfs.html`

Hadoop Distributed File System

Before jumping into the details of ADLS, let's spend some time describing what H`DFS is first, as it is important to understand how ADLS implementation behaves behind the scenes, even if, being a full PaaS service, everything can be more or less ignored as Azure takes care of most of the aspects.

Some of the features of HDFS that are worth mentioning are:

1. It is part of Apache Hadoop family of services.

2. It is designed to run on low cost hardware, and it is designed to quickly react to hardware failures.

3. It is best in batch processing of data, while the interactive low-latency access to data is not the best scenario to implement an HDFS file system.

4. It is designed using a Master-Slave architecture, with a single NameNode and several DataNodes, usually one per cluster node:

    a. NameNode main functions:

        i.   It exposes the HDFS namespace, used by clients to access data. Files are organized in hierarchical way

        ii. Executes operations on files and directories of the file system - opening, closing, and renaming

        iii. Contains the map of the file blocks assigned to data nodes

    b.   DataNode main functions:

        i.   Each file is split in blocks, and blocks are stored in datanodes. Blocks have the same size, and data are replicated for fault tolerance. Customization is granular so you could define, at file level, the size of the block and the number of replicas you want to have

        ii.   Datanode servers read and write requests from clients

        iii.   Performs block creation, deletion, and replication

        iv.   It sends replica hearthbeats to NameNode

Changes that occur in the file system metadata are stored in a log file called **EditLog**, in the server hosting the NameNode application. The file system is stored in a file called **FsImage**, stored in the NameNode server too. Of course, being **EditLog** and **FsImage** critical, it is possible to have multiple copies of these files.

Create an Azure Data Lake Store

To create an Azure Data Lake Store, you need to provide the following information:

- Name. It has to be unique as the service is exposed on the web, and it uses the suffix **.azuredatalakestore.net**.

- Resource Group. It can be an existing one or a new one.

- Location. It defines the Azure Region where ADLS will be and, at the time of writing, ADLS is available in **Central US**, **East US 2**, **North Europe, and West Europe** regions.

- Encryption [optional parameter]. You can specify if the account will be encrypted using keys managed by ADLS (default if nothing is specified) or Azure Key Vault. You can also decide not to use encryption.

- Tier [optional parameter]. Represents the payment plan of your preference for the account. You can choose to have a **Consumption** (pay-as-you-go) based commitment, or you could use a monthly commitment plan for a specific amount of storage, using the following options: **Commitment1TB**, **Commitment10TB**, **Commitment100TB**, **Commitment500TB**, **Commitment1PB**, **Commitment5PB**. Monthly commitments give the ability to have a discount on the cost of the storage.

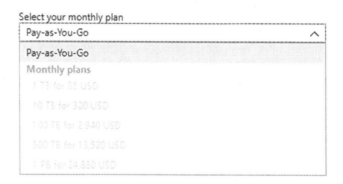

To create an Azure Data Lake Store, you have different options, including Azure Portal, Powershell, Azure CLI, and SDKs. Below is an example of how to create an Azure Data Lake Store using Powershell.

The **Get-AzureRmDataLakeStoreAccount** Powershell cmdlet returns the list of existing ADLS accounts already available in the active Azure subscription.

```
PowerShell ∨    ⏻    ?    ⚙

Type "help" to learn about Cloud Shell

VERBOSE: Authenticating to Azure ...
VERBOSE: Building your Azure drive ...
Azure:\
PS Azure:\> Get-AzureRmDataLakeStoreAccount


Identity                       :
EncryptionState                :
EncryptionProvisioningState    :
EncryptionConfig               :
FirewallState                  :
FirewallRules                  :
TrustedIdProviderState         :
TrustedIdProviders             :
DefaultGroup                   :
NewTier                        :
CurrentTier                    :
FirewallAllowAzureIps          :
ProvisioningState              : Succeeded
State                          : Active
CreationTime                   : 4/21/2017 2:53:55 PM
LastModifiedTime               : 4/21/2017 2:53:55 PM
Endpoint                       :           .azuredatalakestore.net
```

Figure 5-4. *Screenshot taken from the Azure Cloud Shell tool, with the output of the Get-AzureRmDataLakeStoreAccount cmdlet. The Azure Cloud Shell can be invoked directly from the Azure Portal, and can use both PowerShell and BASH scripting engines.*

To create a new ADSL account, we use the **New-AzureRmDataLakeStore Account -ResourceGroup "rg_dataplatform_book" -Name "book" -Location "North Europe"** cmdlet. To test the existence of an ADLS account, you can use the **Test-AzureRmDataLakeStoreAccount**, that returns a Boolean value, **True** or **False**.

```
PowerShell ∨ | ⏻ ? ⚙

Azure:\
PS Azure:\> New-AzureRmDataLakeStoreAccount -ResourceGroup "rg_dataplatform_book" -Name "book" -Location "North Europe"
WARNING: No Encryption type passed in, defaulting to Service managed encryption. To opt out, explicitly pass in -DisableEncryption

Identity                      : Microsoft.Azure.Management.DataLake.Store.Models.EncryptionIdentity
ProvisioningState             : Succeeded
State                         : Active
CreationTime                  : 2/3/2018 8:19:10 AM
LastModifiedTime              : 2/3/2018 8:19:10 AM
Endpoint                      : book.azuredatalakestore.net
AccountId                     : 1d2d86e8-60db-4cab-9933-66bc56b43706
EncryptionState               : Enabled
EncryptionProvisioningState   :
EncryptionConfig              : Microsoft.Azure.Management.DataLake.Store.Models.EncryptionConfig
FirewallState                 : Disabled
FirewallRules                 : {}
```

Figure 5-5. The New-AzureRmDataLakeStoreAccount cmdlet creates a new ADLS account

The ADLS creation will take just a couple of minutes. Being a public PaaS service, it is also important to define security access rules to the service, and using the **Add-AzureRmDataLakeStoreFirewallRule** or the Azure Portal, you can define the IP ranges that can access the service. Using the two cmlets below, you can first enable the firewall in ADLS, and then add a firewall rule to allow access to the service from the IP of your choice.

```
Set-AzureRmDataLakeStoreAccount -Name "book" -FirewallState "Enabled"
Add-AzureRmDataLakeStoreFirewallRule -AccountName "book" -Name myip
-StartIpAddress "82.84.125.110" -EndIpAddress "82.84.125.110"
```

```
Azure:\
PS Azure:\> Add-AzureRmDataLakeStoreFirewallRule -AccountName "book" -Name myip -StartIpAddress "82.84.125.110" -EndIpAddress "82.84.125.110"

Name StartIpAddress EndIpAddress
---- -------------- ------------
myip 82.84.125.110  82.84.125.110
```

Common Operations on Files in Azure Data Lake Store

After the account creation and the firewall configuration, you will have an empty data lake where you can store your data organizing them in folders and subfolders with related ACLs in POSIX format. Do not forget that names are case sensitive, for example using DataFolder is different than using datafolder.

Now we introduce the Azure CLI that we will use to do some operations like copy sample files, change permissions, and so on. Commands for ADLS are in preview at the time of writing and they are divided in two subgroups of commands, one dedicated to manage the account (**az dls account**), and one dedicated to manage the file system (**az dls fs**).

```
Group
    az dls account  (PREVIEW) Manage Data Lake Store accounts.

Subgroups:
    firewall        : (PREVIEW) Manage Data Lake Store account firewall rules.
    trusted-provider: (PREVIEW) Manage Data Lake Store account trusted identity providers.

Commands:
    create          : Creates a Data Lake Store account.
    delete          : Delete a Data Lake Store account.
    enable-key-vault: Enable the use of Azure Key Vault for encryption of a Data Lake Store account.
    list            : Lists available Data Lake Store accounts.
    show            : Get the details of a Data Lake Store account.
    update          : Updates a Data Lake Store account.

Group
    az dls fs  (PREVIEW) Manage a Data Lake Store filesystem.

Subgroups:
    access          : Manage Data Lake Store filesystem access and permissions.

Commands:
    append          : Append content to a file in a Data Lake Store account.
    create          : Creates a file or folder in a Data Lake Store account.
    delete          : Delete a file or folder in a Data Lake Store account.
    download        : Download a file or folder from a Data Lake Store account to the local machine.
    join            : Join files in a Data Lake Store account into one file.
    list            : List the files and folders in a Data Lake Store account.
    move            : Move a file or folder in a Data Lake Store account.
    preview         : Preview the content of a file in a Data Lake Store account.
    remove-expiry:  Remove the expiration time for a file.
    set-expiry      : Set the expiration time for a file.
    show            : Get file or folder information in a Data Lake Store account.
    test            : Test for the existence of a file or folder in a Data Lake Store account.
```

Figure 5-6. *The list of commands available in the Azure CLI to manage Azure Data Lake Store. The first group manages the account (first red square), and the second one manages the file system (second red square)*

The ADLS dashboard in the Azure Portal contains a visual explorer for the storage called **Data Explorer**. It can work with many of the settings available with the APIs exposed by ADLS. We will display some screenshots of the Data Explorer to clarify some of the commands that we will use in the script below.

Note   The Azure CLI script below uses csv files that are part of the Ambulance sample dataset available here on github: `https://github.com/Azure/usql/tree/master/Examples/Samples/Data/AmbulanceData`

```
# login to Azure
az login

#sets the active subscription
az account set -s [subscription name]

# lists the ADLS accounts
az dls account list
```

```
# creates a folder called "folder1"
az dls fs create --account book --path /folder1 --folder

# uploads a file in /folder1/
az dls fs upload --account book --source-path C:\adls\AmbulanceData\
vehicle1_09142014.csv --destination-path /folder1/vehicle1_09142014.csv

# uploads all files in a specified folder to /folder1 - overwrites existing
files
az dls fs upload --account book --source-path C:\adls\AmbulanceData\*.csv
--destination-path /folder1/ --overwrite

# checks if a specified file exists (returns TRUE or FALSE)
az dls fs test --account book --path /folder1/vehicle4_09172014.csv

# returns information on a file or a folder
az dls fs show --account book --path /folder1
az dls fs show --account book --path /folder1/vehicle1_09142014.csv
# output1
{
    "accessTime": 1517672964545,
    "aclBit": false,
    "blockSize": 0,
    "group": "dbd51d38-bd51-4b57-ae3d-de1d41667495",
    "length": 0,
    "modificationTime": 1517674017744,
    "name": "folder1",
    "owner": "dbd51d38-bd51-4b57-ae3d-de1d41667495",
    "pathSuffix": "",
    "permission": "770",
    "replication": 0,
    "type": "DIRECTORY"
}
# output2
{
    "accessTime": 1517674008507,
    "aclBit": false,
```

```
    "blockSize": 268435456,
    "group": "dbd51d38-bd51-4b57-ae3d-de1d41667495",
    "length": 1561082,
    "modificationTime": 1517674010629,
    "msExpirationTime": 0,
    "name": "folder1/vehicle1_09142014.csv",
    "owner": "dbd51d38-bd51-4b57-ae3d-de1d41667495",
    "pathSuffix": "",
    "permission": "770",
    "replication": 1,
    "type": "FILE"
}
```

```
# previews the content of a file. If you want to preview a file that is
greater than 1048576 bytes you need to use the --force option
az dls fs preview --account book --path /folder1/vehicle1_
09142014.csv --force
```

```
# moves a file from a folder to another inside ADLS
az dls fs move --account book --source-path /folder1/vehicle1_
09142014.csv --destination-path /folder2/vehicle4_09172014.csv
```

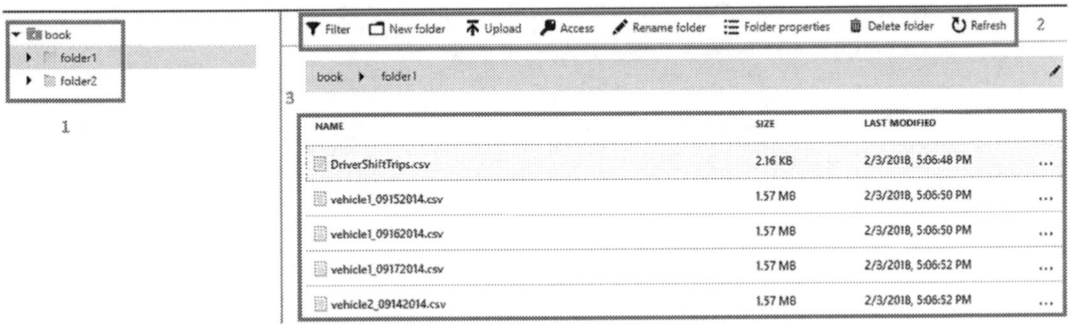

Figure 5-7. *The Data Explorer tool available in the ADLS dashboard in the Azure Portal. In evidence: 1 - the folder structure of the account; 2 - the action bar that allows to do actions on the ADLS account; 3 - a subset of the files available in folder1*

```
# downloads a file or a folder locally
az dls fs download --account book --source-path /folder1/
--destination-path c:\adls\downloads\

# displays permissions in a file or a folder
az dls fs access show --account book --path /folder1
az dls fs access show --account book --path /folder1/vehicle1_09152014.csv

# output1 - output2, both  are the same
{
  "entries": [
    "user::rwx",
    "group::rwx",
    "other::---"
  ],
  "group": "dbd51d38-bd51-4b57-ae3d-de1d41667495",
  "owner": "dbd51d38-bd51-4b57-ae3d-de1d41667495",
  "permission": "770",
  "stickyBit": false
}

# gives write access privileges to a file to a specific Azure AD User
az dls fs access set-entry --account book --path /folder1/ --acl-spec
user:e511cdaa-3496-4077-8bde-0137d5815c9b:-w-
```

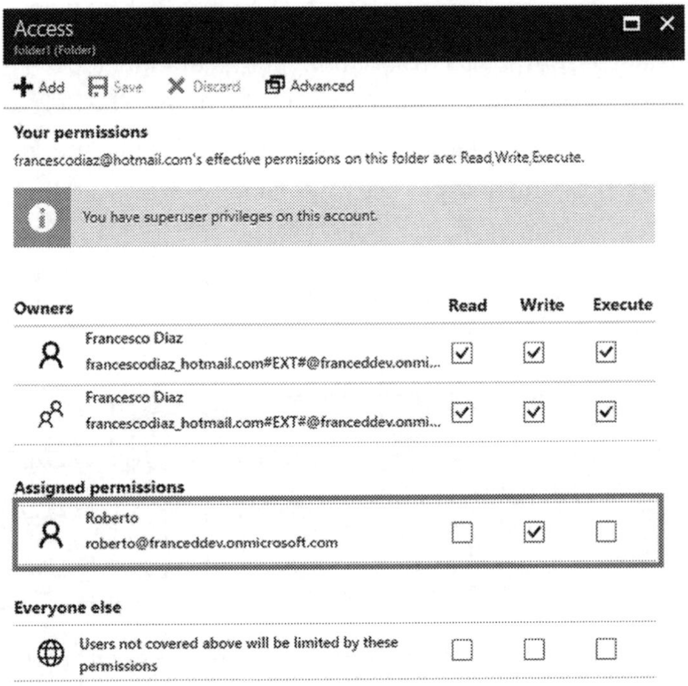

Figure 5-8. *The command above assigns Write permissions to folder1 to the Azure AD user Roberto, using his Object ID property*

Copy Data to Azure Data Lake Store

Copying data to and from big data stores is one of the most common activities to become familiar with. There are many ways to copy data to ADLS and many factors determine the method used, such as:

- The copy performance that you want to achieve. This depends also on the capability of the service, in this case ADLS, to achieve specific storage copy performance targets, and of course on the solution that you are using, that might require some degree of parallelism.

- If you need to transform data while moving them from source to destination. If it is not just a pure copy, then a tool designed for data transformation and orchestration might be the right choice.

- The distance between the service that performs the copy activity and the data at source and destination. For an architect it is extremely important to recommend to the customer the best way to position services, especially on cloud solutions. Having the services performing copy and analysis activities close to data is a design best practice.

In the table below you can see some of the possibilities you have to copy data to Azure Data Lake Store.

Tool	Requirements	Notes
SSIS	Azure Feature Pack for SSIS	Good for orchestration scenarios
Azure CLI or Powershell		Not for large amounts of data
Azure Data Factory	ADF service	Good for orchestration scenarios
AdlCopy		It can be combined with ADLA
Distcp	HDInsight cluster	
Sqoop	HDInsight cluster	Good to copy data from relational DBs
Azure Data Lake Store SDK		Good for heavy customizations

Figure 5-9. *In the picture you can see some of the options that you could use to copy data to Azure Data Lake Store*

- SSIS. SQL Server Integration Services, with the Azure Feature Pack for SSIS, is a good option, in case you need to orchestrate and modify data between source and destination. It is important to consider where you put the SSIS engine, as it is important, for performance reasons, to have it close to the data you need to move and, if you are installing it on an Azure Virtual Machine, to choose the right size of the VM in order to have the right throughput required.

- Azure Data Factory. As in SSIS, ADF is good in case you need to orchestrate and transform data before moving them to and from Azure Data Lake Store.

- Azure CLI, Powershell. In the previous paragraph we have seen some of the possibilities offered by the Azure CLI to upload or move data to ADLS. Powershell has similar cmdlets to perform the same operations. We recommend using these tools in case you don't have a big amount of data to transfer.

- AdlCopy. A command line tool that you can use to copy data from Azure Data Storage Blobs to Azure Data Lake Store, or between two Azure Data Lake Store accounts. You can use it as a standalone tool, or using an Azure Data Lake Analytics account, in order to assign the number of compute units you need to obtain predictable performances.

- DistCp. The Hadoop Distributed Copy tool needs to be installed in a Hadoop cluster, such as HDInsight, to be used. You can leverage the parallelism possibilities offered by MapReduce, finding the right number of mappers needed to perform the copy. If you need to copy data coming from an Azure Storage Blob or an Amazon AWS S3 account, this is a good option to consider.

- Sqoop. Like with DistCp, a Hadoop cluster is required here. Scoop is a tool that you should consider in case the source of data is a relational database, such as Azure SQL Database or MySQL.

- Azure Import/Export service. In case you have a huge amount of data to transfer from on-premises to the cloud, you can use the Azure Import/Export service, preparing a set of hard drives with the content that you want to move to the cloud.

Note   The Azure Feature Pack for SSIS is available for SQL Server 2012, SQL Server 2014, SQL Server 2014 and SQL Server 2017. You can download it here: `https://docs.microsoft.com/it-it/sql/integration-services/azure-feature-pack-for-integration-services-ssis`; you can download AdlCopy here: `https://www.microsoft.com/en-us/download/details.aspx?id=50358`; you can download Apache Sqoop here: `http://www.apache.org/dyn/closer.lua/sqoop/`;

Ingress/Process/Egress

The image below provides a recap of the possibilities we have to work with Azure Data Lake in terms of:

- **Ingress** data using a bulk or a service designed for event ingestion

- **Process** data using Azure Data Lake Analytics, Azure HDInsight, or any other application able to work with ADLS file system

- **Egress** information using tools capable of working with ADLS

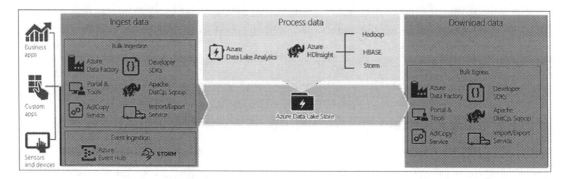

Figure 5-10. *Some of possibilities to work with Azure Data Lake Store to ingest, process, and download data*

Copy Data to Azure Data Lake using AdlCopy

AdlCopy is a command-line tool specifically designed and optimized to work with Azure Data Lake Store. Its use is simple, you basically need to have the information to access the source and the destination and that's it. In the example below, we are moving the content of an Azure Blob Storage container to a folder in Azure Data Lake Store.

```
adlcopy /source https://dataplat.blob.core.windows.net/adlcopy/ /dest
swebhdfs://book.azuredatalakestore.net/adlcopy/ /sourcekey [storage
account key]
```

```
C:\Users\francescodiaz\Documents\AdlCopy>adlcopy /source https://dataplat.blob.core.windows.net/adlcopy/ /dest swebhdfs:
//book.azuredatalakestore.net/adlcopy/ /sourcekey ██████████████████████████
█████████████
The source and destination accounts are not in the same Azure region.
Please refer to https://azure.microsoft.com/en-us/pricing/details/bandwidth for bandwidth charges that will be applicabl
e.
Do you wish to continue (Y/N)
y
Initializing Copy.
Files from 1 to 18. Copy Started.
100% data copied.
Copy Completed. 18 files copied.

C:\Users\francescodiaz\Documents\AdlCopy>_
```

Figure 5-11. *You will get prompted to insert your Azure credentials, needed to access the Azure Data Lake account*

In the example above, we used the standalone option available with AdlCopy, that doesn't require you to rely on additional services to function. In case you need to obtain predictable performances, running parallel copies, then you could use an Azure Data Lake Analytics account. The syntax doesn't change, only you need to add the two options below, to specify the ADLA service and the number of ADLA units you want to utilize for the copy.

- /Account. The name of the Azure Data Lake Analytics account.

- /Units. The number of Azure Data Lake Analytics units you want to use.

Authenticate and Copy Data to Azure Data Lake Store using SSIS

As you know, SQL Server Integration Services is one of the most powerful tools available for ETL workloads. The Azure Feature Pack for SSIS adds the ability to work with Azure services like Azure Blob Storage and Azure Data Lake Store; you don't need to learn a different visual tool to design ETL workflows that include Azure storage engines, as everything is added to SQL Server Data Tools. Installing the Azure Feature Pack for SSIS, you will get the following:

1. The SSIS Connection Manager adds the connection provider to connect to Azure Data Lake Store.

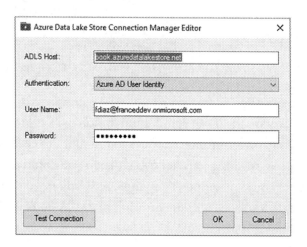

2. The SSIS Toolbox adds the data flow components to use Azure Data Lake Store as a source or as a destination in your **.dtsx** packages.

3. The canvas to design the SSIS Data Flow task can be used to integrate Azure Data Lake Store in your workflows. In the example below, we are transferring the rows of a **.csv** blob file stored in an Azure Storage Blob container to a new file that will be created in a folder in an Azure Data Lake Store account.

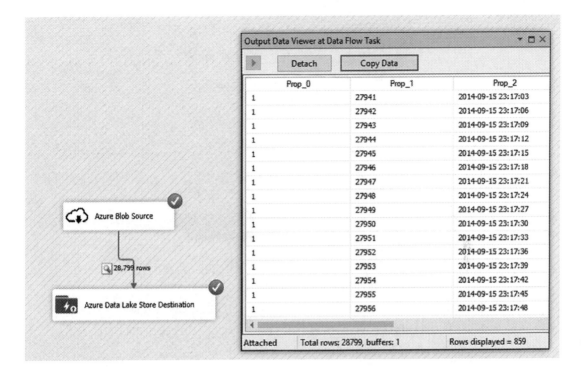

It is important to spend a few words on the authentication method that you need to use against Azure Data Lake Store. ADLS uses Azure Active Directory (AAD) as the authentication method for applications, and you have two options to authenticate, and both of them release an OAuth 2.0 token to authenticated clients:

- End-user authentication. In this case, you use the credentials of an AAD user to do an interactive connection to ADLS, and the application runs using the user's context credentials. When we created a new connection to ADLS in step 1, we used the user **fdiaz@franceddev.onmicrosoft.com** to connect. This user had been created in Azure Active Directory first, and then we also had authorized it to connect to Azure Data Lake Store, giving it the role of **Contributor** for the service. We also received the prompt request below to authorize SSIS to access the ADLS account.

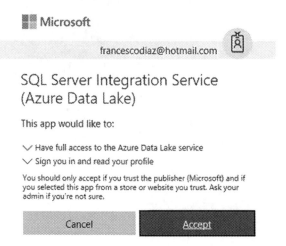

- Service-to-service authentication. In this case you register an Azure Active Directory application first, and then you use a secret key to authenticate with Azure Data Lake Store, so the authentication process is not interactive. We will quickly describe this approach in the next paragraph, using a few .NET snippets.

Authenticate Against ADLS using .NET

We will use this small section to describe how to use the service-to-service authentication method to connect to ADLS using Azure Active Directory with OAuth 2.0. To demonstrate it, we use a .NET console application. You need to perform three steps:

1. Register a new application in Azure Active Directory and generate a secret key that will be used by the application. To do that, go to the **App Registration** section in the Azure Active Directory dashboard in the Azure Portal, then click the **New application registration** button to add a new application registration.

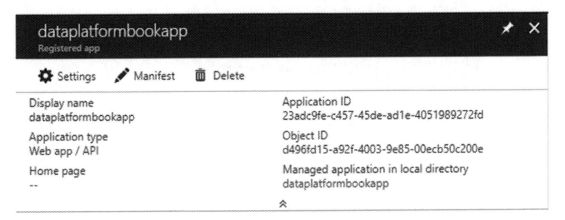

Figure 5-12. *The application created in Azure Active Directory. Properties of the application will be used in the client application. To see a tutorial on how to create an Azure Active Directory Application, visit this page:* `https://docs.microsoft.com/en-us/azure/azure-resource-manager/resource-group-create-service-principal-portal`

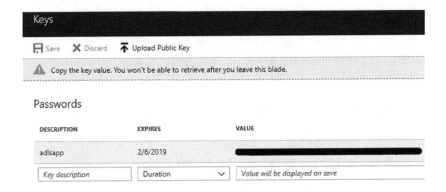

2. Authorize the application to access ADLS folders. The application is an Active Directory object; therefore you can use it to give the authorization to ADLS resources, like the file system folders.

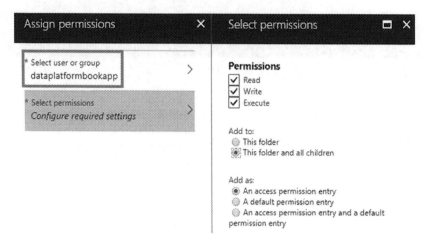

Figure 5-13. *When you assign permissions to ADLS folders, conceptually you can see the application as a user. In our case we assigned the permissions to the root folder and we have authorized it to also access the subfolders. The screenshot is taken from the Data Explorer tool, available in the ADLS dashboard in the Azure Portal*

3. In Visual Studio, download and add references to the nuget packages below:

    a. **Microsoft.Azure.Management.DataLake.Store** (we used version 2.2)

    b. **Microsoft.Rest.ClientRuntime.Azure.Authentication** (v2.3.2)

    c. **Microsoft.Azure.DataLake.Store** (v1.0.5)

4. Use a code snippet like the following to connect to Azure Data Lake Store and perform activities on the storage; in the example below we create a folder and a file.

```
using System;
using System.IO;
using System.Linq;
using System.Text;
using System.Threading;
using System.Collections.Generic;

using Microsoft.Rest;
using Microsoft.Rest.Azure.Authentication;
```

```csharp
using Microsoft.Azure.Management.DataLake.Store;
using Microsoft.Azure.Management.DataLake.Store.Models;
using Microsoft.Azure.DataLake.Store;
using Microsoft.IdentityModel.Clients.ActiveDirectory;

namespace service2service
{
    class Program
    {
        private static void Main(string[] args)
        {
            //define variables
            System.Uri adltoken = new System.Uri
            (@"https://datalake.azure.net/");
            string aadtenant = "azure active directory ID";
            string applicationid = "23adc9fe-c457-45de-ad1e-4051989272fd";
            string appsecretkey = "app secret key";
            string adlsstoreaccount = "book.azuredatalakestore.net";
            string foldername = "/chapter06";
            string fileName = "/desc.txt";

            //create client service credentials
            SynchronizationContext.SetSynchronizationContext
            (new SynchronizationContext());
            var serviceSettings = ActiveDirectoryServiceSettings.Azure;
            serviceSettings.TokenAudience = adltoken;
            var adlCreds = ApplicationTokenProvider.
            LoginSilentAsync(aadtenant, applicationid, appsecretkey,
            serviceSettings).GetAwaiter().GetResult();

            //connects to adls account and creates a folder and a file
            AdlsClient client = AdlsClient.CreateClient(adlsstoreaccount,
            adlCreds);

            client.CreateDirectory(foldername);
            using (var streamWriter = new StreamWriter(client.CreateFile
            (foldername + fileName, IfExists.Fail)))
```

```
            {
                    streamWriter.WriteLine("data lake store test");
            }
        }
    }
}
```

Copy data to Azure Data Lake using Azure Data Factory v2 (Preview)

Note   While writing this chapter, Microsoft released a Public Preview of Azure Data Factory v2. As it contains significant changes compared to the previous version, we decided to add a very short introduction to the service in chapter 04, and add some extra information here to describe how to use it to copy data to Azure Data Lake Store.

The purpose of this section is to perform a copy of the blob files stored on an Azure Storage account container, **https://dataplatformbook.blob.core.windows.net/adfv2**, to Azure Data Lake Store, using Azure Data Factory v2. We will use a Boolean parameter, **isnotstage**, to determine if the copy should go to a folder, **adl://book.azuredatalakestore.net/adfv2**, or another, **adl://book.azuredatalakestore.net/adfv2stage**, in ADLS, depending on its value. In this simple activity we can use many of the things introduced in ADFv2 (please review the end of the previous chapter if needed); we will utilize the new designer, an Integration Runtime, a parameter, a control flow activity, a trigger, and the monitoring tool. Some of the activities are done using the new designer, which you can launch from the Azure Portal.

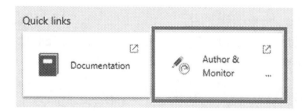

Step1. We need to create linked servers and datasets, needed to access services and map source and destinations. This part is very similar to v1, with the addition of the Integration Runtime that is the compute service that is needed to execute data movement activities or a dispatch to an external service. ADFv2, during creation, creates a default Integration Runtime; we have added another one, WestEuropeIR, only to explain that is possible to assign the compute engine to a specific Azure Region, in our case West Europe. This is important if you have several services to orchestrate that are located in different regions, and you want to have IRs close to data sources to reduce latency.

Name	Actions	Type ⇵	Status	Region
defaultIntegrationRuntime		Azure	🟢 Running	Auto Resolve
WestEuropeIR		Azure	🟢 Running	West Europe

Figure 5-14. *You can have several Integration Runtimes, to perform computation in different regions. This screenshot is taken from the designer, under the Connections tab*

Linked Servers and Datasets are very similar to v1, and they can be authored using the web tool; behind that you still have JSON, and below you can see the script to create the five objects that we need here:

- **adlsbook**. The Linked Service that can access Azure Data Lake Store. We need to use a service-to-service authentication with Azure Active Directory, so we used the same method used in the .NET SDK paragraph before, providing the application ID and the secret key during the connection configuration. **adlsbook** is connected to **WestEuropeIR** Integration Runtime.

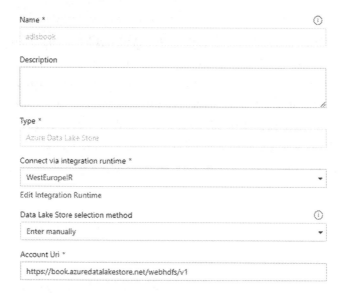

- **sourcestorageblob**. The Linked Service that connects to Azure Storage. **sourcestorageblob** is also connected to **WestEuropeIR**.

- **sourcefile**. A Dataset linked to **sourcestorageblob** that accesses the container **adfv2**.

- **destfileadls**. A Dataset linked to **adlsbook** that accesses the folder **adfv2**. A binary copy is specified therefore schema and column mappings will not be used.

Azure Data Lake Store
destfileadls

- **destfileadlsstage**. A Dataset linked to **adlsbook** that accesses the
  adfv2stage folder.

Below you can find two JSON snippets; one for the Linked Service and one for the
Dataset, both are related to Azure Data Lake Store.

ADLS Linked Service

```
{
    "name": "adlsbook",
    "properties": {
        "type": "AzureDataLakeStore",
        "typeProperties": {
            "dataLakeStoreUri": "https://book.azuredatalakestore.net/
            webhdfs/v1",
            "servicePrincipalId": "72cebb04-04be-43ee-9fed-dae67ad658de",
            "servicePrincipalKey": {
                "type": "SecureString",
                "value": "**********"
            },
            "tenant": "[tenant]",
            "subscriptionId": "[subscription id]",
            "resourceGroupName": "rg_dataplatform_book"
        },
        "connectVia": {
            "referenceName": "WestEuropeIR",
            "type": "IntegrationRuntimeReference"
        }
    }
}
```

ADLS dataset

```
{
    "name": "destfileadls",
    "properties": {
        "linkedServiceName": {
            "referenceName": "adlsbook",
            "type": "LinkedServiceReference"
```

```
        },
        "type": "AzureDataLakeStoreFile",
        "typeProperties": {
            "fileName": "",
            "folderPath": "adfv2"
        }
    }
}
```

Step2. Now that we have defined the Linked Server and the Dataset, we need to define a pipeline and the activities needed for the implementation. The script below contains three activities; one of them is **IfCondition** activity, used to read a parameter and, based on a True/False condition, define the list of the activities that will be executed when == true, and the activities to run when == false. Look at the code below first, and then we will look at the designer. As you can see in the script, the copy activities are nested in the IfCondition activity.

```
{
    "name": "copyToADLS",
    "properties": {
        "activities": [
            {
                "name": "checkStage",
                "type": "IfCondition",
                "dependsOn": [],
                "policy": {
                    "timeout": "7.00:00:00",
                    "retry": 0,
                    "retryIntervalInSeconds": 30
                },
                "typeProperties": {
                    "expression": {
                        "value": "@bool(pipeline().parameters.isnotstage)",
                        "type": "Expression"
                    },
```

```
"ifTrueActivities": [
    {
        "type": "Copy",
        "typeProperties": {
            "source": {
                "type": "BlobSource",
                "recursive": true
            },
            "sink": {
                "type": "AzureDataLakeStoreSink",
                "copyBehavior": "PreserveHierarchy"
            },
            "enableStaging": false,
            "cloudDataMovementUnits": 0
        },
        "inputs": [
            {
                "referenceName": "sourcefile",
                "parameters": {},
                "type": "DatasetReference"
            }
        ],
        "outputs": [
            {
                "referenceName": "destfileadls",
                "parameters": {},
                "type": "DatasetReference"
            }
        ],
        "policy": {
            "timeout": "7.00:00:00",
            "retry": 0,
            "retryIntervalInSeconds": 30
        },
```

```
                                "name": "AdlsCopy",
                                "dependsOn": []
                    }
                ],
                "ifFalseActivities": [
                    {
                        "type": "Copy",
                        "typeProperties": {
                            "source": {
                                "type": "BlobSource",
                                "recursive": true
                            },
                            "sink": {
                                "type": "AzureDataLakeStoreSink",
                                "copyBehavior": "PreserveHierarchy"
                            },
                            "enableStaging": false,
                            "cloudDataMovementUnits": 0
                        },
                        "inputs": [
                            {
                                "referenceName": "sourcefile",
                                "parameters": {},
                                "type": "DatasetReference"
                            }
                        ],
                        "outputs": [
                            {
                                "referenceName": "destfileadlsstage",
                                "parameters": {},
                                "type": "DatasetReference"
                            }
                        ],
                        "policy": {
                            "timeout": "7.00:00:00",
                            "retry": 0,
```

```
                            "retryIntervalInSeconds": 30
                        },
                        "name": "AdlsCopyStage",
                        "dependsOn": []
                    }
                ]
            }
        }
    ],
    "parameters": {
        "isnotstage": {
            "type": "Bool",
            "defaultValue": true,
            "identity": "isnotstage"
        }
    }
}
}
```

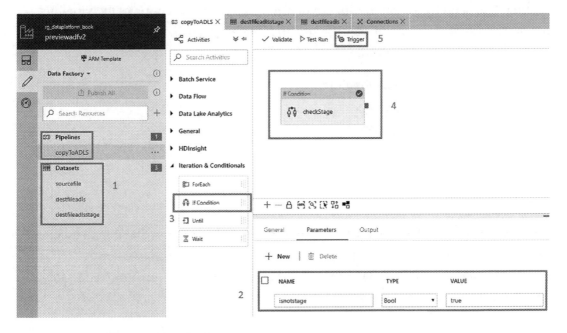

Figure 5-15. *The ADFv2 designer*

The image above represents the ADFv2 designer, where you can see:

1. The objects created, such as the Datasets and the Pipeline

2. The Pipeline variables section, in our case the **isnotstage** Boolean parameter

3. The toolbox, where we picked the IfCondition control flow activity

4. As you can see from the canvas, only the IfCondition activity is displayed, as the two copy activities are nested, therefore you can see them only using the JSON editor.

5. You can trigger the execution on-demand or schedule it

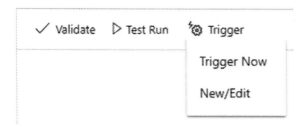

Step3. Execution and monitoring. When you trigger the execution of the Pipeline, you get prompted to insert the value for the parameter that will define which activity will be executed inside the IfCondition.

Pipeline Run

Parameters

NAME	TYPE	VALUE
isnotstage	Bool	true

You can monitor the execution using the Pipeline Monitor tool that helps you to understand how the workflow is progressing. In the example below, we performed two runs setting the parameter to **true** first, and then to **false**, therefore both folders in ADLS have received the files coming from Azure Storage.

Pipeline Name ▽	Actions	Run Start ⇵	Duration	Triggered By	Status	Parameters	Error	RunID
copyToADLS	⛃ ▷	02/08/2018, 9:42:45 PM	00:00:24	Manual trigger	✔ Succeeded	⬚		fb0aa255-9f85-449a-ad4b-ecf16055da55
copyToADLS	⛃ ▷	02/08/2018, 9:41:28 PM	00:00:26	Manual trigger	✔ Succeeded	⬚		b1b6d681-cb2e-4885-a145-2b9892c24f99

Considerations on Azure Data Lake Store Performance

Before moving to the next section, where we will speak about Azure Data Lake Analytics, we highlight a few performance guidelines that might help you to design a proper solution that includes Azure Data Lake Store as part of it.

ADLS is designed to automatically adopt its performance to workloads, and Microsoft support is also there in case you need to increase some service limits for a specific need. Its throughput is automatically tuned based on needs, but throughput is of course not only related to ADSL, but also other factors may be part of the discussion, such as the systems handling data at source.

- Connectivity. If you are running workloads on-premises that need to move data to Azure, the performance of the network connection is essential. You can connect to ADLS without a VPN connection, but in case you are designing a hybrid workload that might include data present also on Azure region, a VPN might be required. In that case, consider using a VPN Gateway that provides high performances, such as the **VpnGw1**, that could potentially achieve up to 650 Mbps. Of course, in case of a VPN IPSec tunnel, performance is also dependent on the on-premises gateway and the internet connection itself. To overcome this possible limitation, you could consider a private connection to Azure, using Azure ExpressRoute to achieve up to 10 Gbps. If you need to transfer a huge amount of data, consider also using the Azure Import/Export service, sending your physical hard drives to an Azure datacenter location in order to avoid network data transfer time. If your workloads are already on Azure, consider having data and ADLS in the same Azure Region if possible, to avoid intra-datacenter data movement that increases latency.

- Throughput allowed by the service that needs to move data to ADLS. As an example, if you are moving data from an Azure Virtual Machine, you need to take in to consideration the throughput limits of the virtual machine itself, as we have described in Chapter 2 of this book.

- Parallel copies of data. If you are using a tool capable of implementing parallelization, use it to increase the amount of data that you are able to move. For example, in the Azure Data Factory chapter we described how to execute multiple copies in parallel.

- Do not consider ADLS as a host of data when you need to work mainly with very small files, and the access is interactive. ADLS is a preferred choice for batch processing and try to avoid small files when possible. Structuring the file system in a way that is easy for the batch processing engines like HDInsight is also important for performances, as it reduces the jobs needed to organize files in a way that is easier to manage.

Note 1   To learn more about Azure VPN Gateways and Azure ExpressRoute, you can visit the following links: `https://docs.microsoft.com/en-us/azure/vpn-gateway/vpn-gateway-about-vpngateways`, `https://docs.microsoft.com/en-us/azure/expressroute/expressroute-faqs`

Note 2   In Azure Data Lake Store, you pay for the storage occupied and for the Read and Write transaction operations performed on data. Consider that, using Azure services, you also pay for the outbound data transfers; if you are moving, as an example, data from an Azure Storage Account to an Azure Data Lake Store, and the two services reside on different datacenters, the traffic that will come from Azure Storage will be paid. That's why it is also important to consider having, when possible, the services in the same Azure Region, to avoid incurring extra costs. Inbound traffic is instead free.

To get more information on Azure Data Lake Store pricing, you can visit this page: `https://azure.microsoft.com/en-us/pricing/details/data-lake-store/`. To get more information on Bandwidth pricing, you can visit this page: `https://azure.microsoft.com/en-us/pricing/details/bandwidth/`.

Azure Data Lake Analytics

This section starts the second part of the chapter; we will focus on the analytics engines available in Azure Data Lake, mainly on Azure Data Lake Analytics (ADLA), as it is the newest and has some features that make it suitable for cloud big data scenarios.

ADLA is a distributed analytics service, on-demand, built on Apache YARN, and that relies on Azure Data Lake Store to function. Its compute system handles analytics jobs that are designed to scale based on the compute required to perform tasks, and it uses a language called U-SQL that mixes the simplicity of a query language like SQL with the power of programming languages like C#.

Comparing ADLA to a standard Hadoop installation, in ADLA you don't need to care about how the cluster configuration will have to be, in terms of compute power, number of nodes, etc. It is a pure PaaS service, able to execute jobs on-demand, scaling based on the compute power required. As in other similar PaaS services available in the Azure platform, ADLA follows the concept of the focus-on-design, instead of dedicating too much time to administer the availability of the system. The developer productivity is strongly improved because of the new U-SQL language, a SQL-like language where functions and expressions can be written using the power of a language like C#.

Key Concepts

Here is a summary of the key features and concepts that ADLA offers:

- A PaaS service, with near zero effort to setup and administer the service. You can literally create a new ADLA service in seconds.

- A pay-per-use model, where the on-demand compute units will be only used when the jobs is launched against ADLA

- Built with Azure Active Directory support to manage users that need to access the service

- A powerful development language, U-SQL, with a simple learning curve, being based on SQL-like syntax, and with the possibility to be combined with C# coding

- Extensible to offer custom code and modules to cover specific workloads, such as cognitive services

- Able to execute scripts written in R and Python

- Able to access external sources, such as Azure SQL Database, Azure Storage, etc.

- Proficient authoring system, thanks to the integration with the Azure Portal and the tools available for Visual Studio and Visual Studio Code

Built on Apache YARN

Resources in ADLA are managed using Apache Hadoop YARN (Yet Another Resource Negotiator) under the hoods; YARN is a cluster management technology, responsible for the data processing activities. It is sometimes called MapReduce v2, as it brought the compute part on HDFS storage to the next level, separating the data layer from the compute layer a bit more, and enabling the ability to develop new data processing engines, like ADLA, able to work with HDFS storage, and managed using a generic resource manager service, which YARN is.

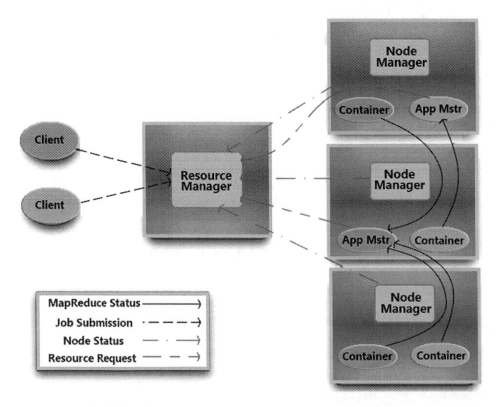

Figure 5-16. *A high level overview of how YARN manages resouces*

YARN main components are:

- Resource Manager. It manages all the resources available in the cluster, and its job is to schedule the correct utilization of all the cluster resources, based on policies that you can plug to define how the allocation rules of resources will work.

- Node Manager. It is responsible to manage the resources in a specific node of the cluster. Each node in the cluster runs a Node Manager that receives directions from the Resource Manager, and provides a health status for it.

- Application Master. An instance of a library that can specialize the work that needs to be executed in the containers. It talks with the Resource Manager to negotiate resources and works with the Node Manager (one or more) for the execution and monitoring. Thanks to this component, YARN can run different frameworks, such as Azure Data Lake Analytics.

- Container. It is the compute unit, responsible for executing tasks.

In Figure 5-17 below, you can see a recap of the four steps involved in the negotiation of resources:

Figure 5-17. *The 4 steps of the negotiation of resources*

Note   For more detail on Apache YARN, you can read the official documentation here: http://hadoop.apache.org/docs/current/hadoop-yarn/ hadoop-yarn-site/YARN.html

---

Tools for Managing ADLA and Authoring U-SQL Scripts

Now that we presented the key concepts of ADLA and did a quick introduction to Apache YARN, we are ready to start talking about managing and authoring, listing the tools that we can use to accomplish this. ADLA has a wide range of options to choose from, both for Microsoft and non-Microsoft operating systems; the table below offers a recap of the options available today:

Tool	Purpose	Platform
Azure Portal	Manage and authoring	cross
Azure CLI	Manage	cross
Azure PowerShell	Manage	Windows
.NET SDK	Manage	Windows
Python SDK	Manage	cross
Java SDK	Manage	cross
Node.js SDK	Manage	cross
Azure Data Lake Tools for Visual Studio Code	Authoring	cross
Azure Data Lake Tools for Visual Studio	Authoring	Windows

Figure 5-18. *The list of tools available to manage jobs and author scripts with Azure Data Lake Analytics*

Note   Links to download tools for Visual Studio Code and Visual Studio Code extensions for ADLA - search "Azure Data Lake Tools for VSCode" in the Marketplace; Visual Studio tools for ADLA - `https://marketplace.visualstudio.com/items?itemName=ADLTools.AzureDataLakeandStreamAnalyticsTools;`

Working with ADLA using the Azure Portal

We will start creating an account using the Azure Portal, action represented in Figure 5-19 below.

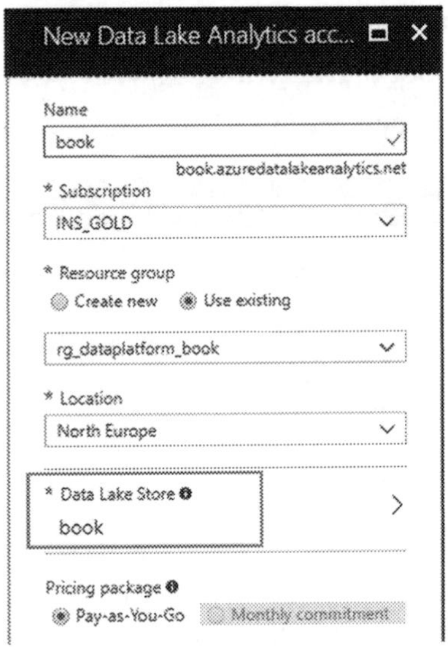

Figure 5-19. *Azure Data Lake Analytics account creation*

The options in Figure 5-19 are the only ones you need to define during the ADLA account creation in the Azure Portal. Like ADLS, ADLA requires a unique Fully Qualified Domain Name (FQDN) as it is a service exposed on the web that uses the **.azuredatalakeanalytics.net** suffix. Another option that you need to select is the Azure Data Lake Store account (red square) that will be used by ADLA to store the U-SQL catalogue.

The Azure Portal dashboard experience for ADLA contains several options that are helpful to configure the behavior of the service. Below you can find a description of some of them:

- Firewall. Like in other Azure PaaS services, including ADLS, you can enable a firewall and create rules to allow access only to authorized IP ranges

- Data sources. You can add additional data sources to ADLA, and they can be both Azure Data Lake Store accounts and Azure Storage accounts

- Pricing Tier. You can decide to use a classical pay-as-you-go model, or commit to a number of Analytics Units (AU) per month and get a discount on the cost of each AU

- Add Users. You can add authorized users to access the service. ADLA comes with four Roles you can choose from; we recommend assigning the **Data Lake Analytics Developer** role to users responsible for U-SQL script authoring. You can also choose the type of permissions to assign to catalogs, files, and folders

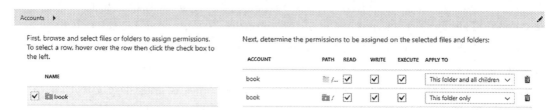

- Data Explorer. Same tool as ADLS, here you can also explore the content of the other data sources you have added, and the treeview includes the ADLA database objects too

- U-SQL job authoring editor. From here you can write and submit a U-SQL job to ADLA and decide the number of AUs that you want to use for the job. An estimation of costs, per-minute based, will be also displayed.

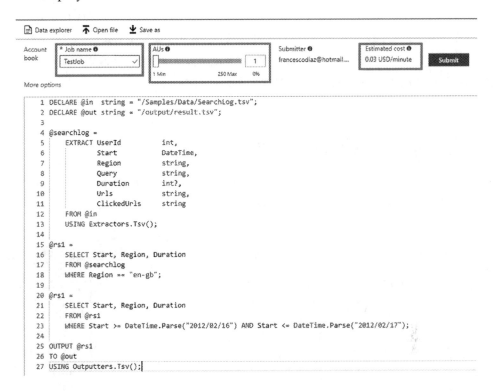

- Job management. Gives a view of the jobs run history in ADLA, including execution details on each one.

STATUS	JOB NAME	AUS	TYPE	DURATION	AUTHOR	SUBMITTED
Succeeded	Ambulance-2-2-LoadingTables	2 (0.8%)	U-SQL	1min 59s	francescodiaz@hotmail.com	2/11/2018, 4:29:01 PM
Succeeded	Ambulance-2-2-LoadingTables	1 (0.4%)	U-SQL	1min 44s	francescodiaz@hotmail.com	2/11/2018, 4:26:34 PM
Succeeded	Ambulance-2-2-LoadingTables	4 (1.6%)	U-SQL	1min 17s	francescodiaz@hotmail.com	2/11/2018, 4:24:06 PM
Succeeded	Ambulance-2-2-LoadingTables	6 (2.4%)	U-SQL	1min 18s	francescodiaz@hotmail.com	2/11/2018, 4:21:31 PM
Succeeded	Ambulance-2-2-LoadingTables	4 (1.6%)	U-SQL	1min 47s	francescodiaz@hotmail.com	2/11/2018, 4:16:36 PM

Azure Data Lake Analytics Units (AU) give the developer the ability to submit a job to multiple compute units to achieve better scaling and performances. Each AU is the equivalent of 2 CPU cores and 6 GB of RAM and, if you think about how YARN works, they can be considered as the containers that you have in YARN. Choosing the right number of AUs for a job is one of the most important aspects for both performance and costs. We will revisit this topic with more details when we describe how ADLA executes jobs, later in the chapter.

Azure Data Lake Tools for Visual Studio

Before starting to explore U-SQL, let's spend some time describe what Visual Studio offers to developers, as we will use it in this chapter.

Figure 5-20. *Azure Data Lake tools for Visual Studio*

1. Data Lake Tools options. Setup ADLA tools is integrated with the Visual Studio toolbar

2. Code behind is supported, so you can write your C# code in the **.cs** file

3. This is quite important, as you can author your scripts offline, without deploying them to ADLA all the time. In case you need to deploy them to the ADLA account, you can choose the account and the database you want to use. Pay attention to the number

of AU units you use, do not use many if they are not needed. Remember that you pay for them! The maximum number of AUs per ADLA account is 250, but in case you need more you can open a ticket to Microsoft support to increase it.

ADLA Account	Database	Schema	AU ⓘ		
book	master	dbo	5 /250	More Options	Submit

Note   Authoring scripts offline with the emulator is a good feature offered by the ADLA tools, as it avoids spending time (and money) in testing your scripts against a live ADLA account, even when it is not necessary. For more detail on how to do local authoring, you can visit this document that explains how to configure Visual Studio for that: `https://docs.microsoft.com/en-us/azure/data-lake-analytics/data-lake-analytics-data-lake-tools-local-run`

U-SQL Language

Now let's describe what U-SQL is and how we can start using it. As we discussed in the introduction of this chapter, Azure Data Lake, including Azure Data Lake Analytics, is based on Microsoft internal projects created to manage their big data workloads. In particular, U-SQL is SCOPE's son, and it combines SQL syntax with C# type, expressions, etc. Is it Transact-SQL? No, it isn't, but if you are familiar with T-SQL or ANSI SQL, you will feel at home here. Do you already know how to code with C#? Then it is even simpler to understand. But U-SQL is executed as a batch script, as it is designed for big data workloads, so don't expect interactivity like you could have with T-SQL and a relational database; you will design a script, the script will be passed to the execution engine that will distribute it across one or more execution units in batch mode, and then you will receive results.

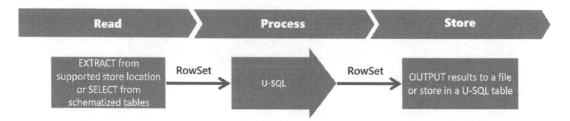

Figure 5-21. *The general execution pattern of ADLA, that follows a Read/Process/Store model*

In Figure 5-21, we put the general execution pattern used by ADLA, which from a logical point of view works with a flow where you read data from a source, a rowset, process it, and store the results, another rowset, at destination. Source and destination can be the Azure Data Lake Store, or another data source supported by Azure Data Lake Analytics.

U-SQL Query Anatomy

To understand how U-SQL works, we will use the samples available within the service dashboard in the Azure Portal and as templates when you create a new ADLA project in Visual Studio.

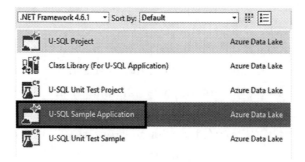

Figure 5-22. *The ADLA project templates in Visual Studio*

Let's have a look at a U-SQL query:

```
ADLA Account      Database        Schema        AU ❶
book          ▼   master      ▼   dbo       ▼   2   /250  More Options    Submit
 1  DECLARE @in  string = "/Samples/Data/SearchLog.tsv";
    DECLARE @out string = "/output/result.tsv";

2a  @searchlog =
        EXTRACT UserId          int,
                Start           DateTime,
                Region          string,
                Query           string,       3
                Duration        int?,
                Urls            string,
                ClickedUrls     string
        FROM @in
        USING Extractors.Tsv();    5a

2b  @rs1 =
        SELECT Start, Region, Duration
        FROM @searchlog
        WHERE Region == "en-gb";

    @rs1 =
        SELECT Start, Region, Duration
        FROM @rs1
        WHERE Start >= DateTime.Parse("2012/02/16") AND Start <= DateTime.Parse("2012/02/17");
                                        4
    OUTPUT @rs1
    TO @out
    USING Outputters.Tsv();    5b
```

Figure 5-23. *U-SQL query anatomy*

1. All U-SQL keyworks must be in UPPERCASE. As you can have a mix of SQL and C# in the same editor, do not forget this to avoid exceptions (as and AS is a typical example in c#/SQL)

2. 2a and 2b. The ROWSETS are used by U-SQL to pass data from one statement to another

3. The types are the same as in C#. When you find a question mark "?", like in the **Duration** variable, it means that the type is nullable

4. Expression language inside statements is C#

5. Extractors and Outputters are used by U-SQL to generate a rowset from a file (Extractor) and to transform a rowset into a file. U-SQL has three built-in extractors and three built-in outputters to work with txt files (**Extractors.Text()**), csv files (**Extractors.Csv()**), and tsv files (**Extractors.Tsv()**).

Note   An important point to highlight here is that a U-SQL script is not executed in a sequential order, as it may seem at a first look. In the script above, the variable @searchlog is not receiving the resultset of the statement, U-SQL is instead assigning the statement to the variable. Same is for @rs1. U-SQL will compose a bigger statement and it will optimize and execute it. This is called expression tree and a U-SQL script could have many execution trees that could be executed in parallel. To learn more about how a U-SQL script is executed, you can read this document: `https://msdn.microsoft.com/en-us/azure/data-lake-analytics/u-sql/u-sql-scripts`

User Defined Objects

Extractors and Outputters can be extended to add user defined objects (UDO). You can generate UDOs for the following six categories:

- Extractors. To EXTRACT (keyword) data from custom structured files

- Outputters. To OUTPUT (keyword) data to custom structured files

- Processors. To PROCESS (keyword) data to reduce the number of columns or create new columns

- Appliers. To be used with CROSS APPLY and OUTER APPLY keywords to invoke a C# function for each row coming from the outer table

- Combiners. To COMBINE (keyword) rows from left and right rowsets

- Reducers. To REDUCE (keyword) the number of rows

Create Database Objects in ADLA

Every U-SQL script will run in the default context of the **master** database and the **dbo** schema. You can create your own database and additional schemas, and change the default execution context using the **USE** statement. It sounds familiar ☺

We could, for example, create a view on the **SearchLog.tsv** file that we used above, to avoid schematizing data in each statement.

```
CREATE DATABASE IF NOT EXISTS booksamples;
USE booksamples;
DROP VIEW IF EXISTS SearchlogView;
CREATE VIEW SearchlogView AS EXTRACT
    UserId int,
    Start DateTime,
    Region string,
    Query string,
    Duration int?,
    Urls string,
    ClickedUrls string
FROM "/Samples/Data/SearchLog.tsv" USING Extractors.Tsv();

@rs = SELECT * FROM SearchlogView;
OUTPUT @rs TO "/output/result.tsv" USING Outputters.Tsv();
```

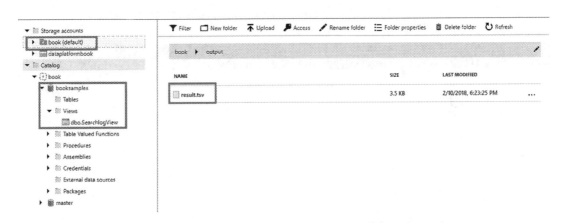

Figure 5-24. *A view from the Data Explorer of the database and the view we have created, and the result.tsv file that has been stored in Azure Data Lake Store*

If you want to optimize how data are stored, you can create a table, with the same concepts that you can find in SQL Server, such as indexes and partitions. The code below stores the data coming from **SearchLog.tsv** in a table, partitioning data using a HASH distribution scheme on the **UserId** column.

```
USE booksamples;

DROP TABLE IF EXISTS tSearchLog;
CREATE TABLE tSearchLog
(
    UserId int,
    Start DateTime,
    Region string,
    Query string,
    Duration int?,
    Urls string,
    ClickedUrls string,
INDEX sl_idx CLUSTERED (UserId ASC)
)
DISTRIBUTED BY HASH(UserId);

INSERT INTO tSearchLog SELECT * FROM booksamples.dbo.SearchlogView;
```

Figure 5-25. *The table tSearchLog in the booksamples database*

Note   To learn more on how to create tables in U-SQL, visit this document:
https://msdn.microsoft.com/en-us/azure/data-lake-analytics/
u-sql/create-table-u-sql-creating-a-table-with-schema?f=255&M
SPPError=-2147217396

Federated Queries

ADLA offers the ability to federate queries with external data sources, like what SQL Server (2016 or above) does with external tables, using the PolyBase engine to query external sources, for example an HDFS file system.

Working with federated queries adds a design scenario where you can use ADLA as a hub keeping data at source; at the time of writing, the supported sources are Azure SQL Database (**AZURESQLDB**), Azure SQL Datawarehouse (**AZURESQLDW**), SQL Server 2012 or above(**SQLSERVER**).

Accessing external data requires that the source opens the firewall ports to allow ADLA to get data. In the case of Azure SQL Database and Azure SQL Datawarehouse, it is sufficient to allow communication to Azure Services in the firewall configuration.

Allow access to Azure services

ON	OFF

In the case of SQL Server, you need to configure the firewall to allow the IP ranges related to the Azure Region where ADLA resides:

Region	IP Ranges
North Europe	104.44.91.64/27
West Europe	104.44.93.192/27
US Central	104.44.91.160/27, 40.90.144.0/27
US East 2	104.44.91.96/27, 40.90.144.64/26

To create a federated query, you need to first create a credential object to store the credentials needed to access the remote database. Then you need a data source connection and, in case you also want to schematize data, you can optionally create an external table. The **CREATE CREDENTIAL** U-SQL command has been deprecated; therefore you need to use the **New-AzureRmDataLakeAnalyticsCatalogCredential** cmdlet to do that, like in the example below that sets credential access to an Azure SQL Server Database.

```
New-AzureRmDataLakeAnalyticsCatalogCredential -Account "[ADLA accountname]"
-DatabaseName "[ADLA dbname]" -CredentialName "sqldbcred" -Credential (Get
Credential) -DatabaseHost "[AZURESQLDB].database.windows.net" -Port 1433
```

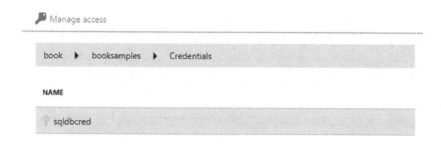

```
USE DATABASE booksamples;

CREATE DATA SOURCE IF NOT EXISTS azuresqldbsource
FROM AZURESQLDB
WITH
(
    PROVIDER_STRING = "Database=book;Trusted_Connection=False;Encrypt=True",
    CREDENTIAL = sqldbcred,
    REMOTABLE_TYPES = (bool, byte, sbyte, short, ushort, int, uint, long,
    ulong, decimal, float, double, string, DateTime)
);

@rs = SELECT * FROM EXTERNAL azuresqldbsource EXECUTE @"SELECT FirstName,
LastName FROM dbo.tUsers";

OUTPUT @rs TO "/output/getdatafromsql.csv" USING Outputters.Csv();
```

Figure 5-26. *The result of the script in the Azure Portal editor for U-SQL*

The script below can be used to create and query an external SQL Database table.

```
USE booksamples;

// CREATES THE EXTERNAL TABLE
CREATE EXTERNAL TABLE IF NOT EXISTS dbo.tUsersExternal
(
    id int,
    FirstName string,
    LastName string
)
FROM azuresqldbsource LOCATION "[dbo].[tUsers]";

// QUERY THE EXTERNAL TABLE
@rs =
    SELECT *
    FROM dbo.tUsersExternal;

OUTPUT @rs
TO "/Output/tUsersExternal.csv"
USING Outputters.Csv();
```

Using an external table can be a good choice to simplify query syntax and maintenance of scripts. As an example, a schema change on the original source would require a change only on the external table instead of modifying all the external queries.

The script below, **which is not related to federated queries,** can also be helpful if you want to access data sources that are Azure Storage Accounts or Azure Data Lake Store Accounts. Before using the script, you first need to create a Data Source, like we did before in the chapter when we described the options available in the Azure Portal to create additional data sources. The code below accesses the **inputfile.txt**, located in **input** container in the **dataplatformbook** storage account, then stores it in the Azure Data Lake Store default account used by ADLA.

```
USE booksamples;

DECLARE @in string = "wasb://input@dataplatformbook/inputfile.txt";
DECLARE @out string = "/output/output.txt";
```

```
@rs= EXTRACT stringtext string FROM @in USING Extractors.Text();

OUTPUT @rs TO @out USING Outputters.Text();
```

To summarize this section, we can use ADLA to access external data available in the following sources and destinations:

SOURCE	READ FROM	WRITE TO
Azure SQL Database	YES	NO
Azure SQL Datawarehouse	YES	NO
SQL Server in a VM	YES	NO
Azure Storage blob	YES	YES
Azure Data Lake Store	YES	YES

Use Code-Behind and Assemblies

ADLA tools for Visual Studio help to separate the U-SQL part from C# supporting code-behind. In the script below you can see first a U-SQL script, and then a simple function written in C# that is invoked inline in the U-SQL script. Submitting the script to ADLA takes care of both portions of code to make it work.

U-SQL

```
USE booksamples;

DROP TABLE IF EXISTS dbo.tUsers;
CREATE TABLE dbo.tUsers
(
    id int,
    FirstName string,
    LastName string,
    INDEX clx_id
    CLUSTERED(id)
    DISTRIBUTED BY
    HASH(id)
);
```

```
INSERT dbo.tUsers
VALUES
(
    1,
    "Roberto",
    "Freato"
),
(
    2,
    "Francesco",
    "Diaz"
)
;

USE booksamples;

@rs =
    SELECT [id],FirstName,LastName,
            USQLSampleApplication1.myFunctions.fnFullNames(FirstName,
LastName) AS FullName
    FROM book.booksamples.dbo.tUsers;

OUTPUT @rs
TO "/output/csharpfunction1.tsv"
USING Outputters.Tsv();
```

   C#

```
using Microsoft.Analytics.Interfaces;
using Microsoft.Analytics.Types.Sql;
using System;
using System.Collections.Generic;
using System.IO;
using System.Linq;
using System.Text;

namespace USQLSampleApplication1
{
    public class myFunctions
    {
```

```
    public static string fnFullNames(string firstName, string lastName)
    {
        return lastName + ", " + firstName;
    }
  }
}
```

The ability to make your code more elegant and reusable is achievable by transforming your C# code in assemblies (**CREATE ASSEMBLY** in U-SQL), uploading them to ADLA catalogue, and creating a reference (**REFERENCE ASSEMBLY** in U-SQL) in your scripts, when needed. To do that, you can use the Class Library for U-SQL project template in Visual Studio, like in the image below.

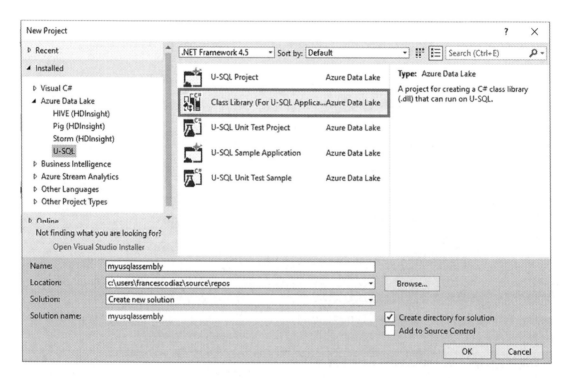

Figure 5-27. *ADLA tools for VS have a template to create assemblies for ADLA*

All you need to do is copy and paste the C# code that you used as code-behind before, and then build the solution to generate the assembly **.dll** file. Then you need to register the assembly in the data lake account of choice, like we did in the image below. As you can see from the Data Explorer, the assembly name is visible in the **Assemblies** node. The same result can be achieved using the **CREATE ASSEMBLY** U-SQL command.

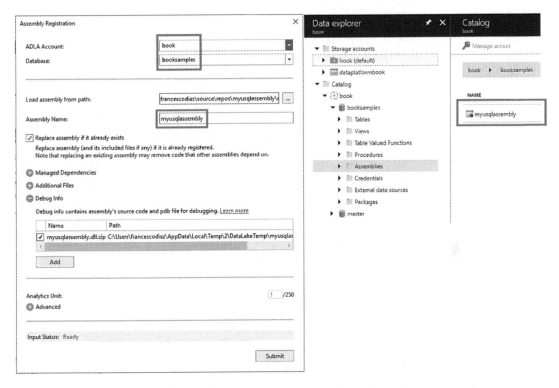

Figure 5-28. *The assembly registration process, done using Visual Studio*

Now you just need to use REFERENCE ASSEMBLY in your script to call the user defined object.

```
USE booksamples;
REFERENCE ASSEMBLY myusqlassembly;
USING myusqlassembly;

@rs =
    SELECT [id],FirstName,LastName,
            myFunctions.fnFullNames(FirstName, LastName) AS FullName
    FROM booksamples.dbo.tUsers;

OUTPUT @rs
TO "/output/csharpassembly1.tsv"
USING Outputters.Tsv();
```

U-SQL Extensions for R and Python

A clarification on R and Python extensions for U-SQL, you may find documents that describe the integration of R and Python in U-SQL. It is a different level of integration than C#, that is built-in in the language and it is part of it. Python and R are extensions, therefore their level of integration is granted thanks to the **REFERENCE ASSEMBLY** (**ExtR** for R and **ExtPython** for Python) statement. With the extensions you can enable the execution of R and Python scripts inside a U-SQL script using a reducer (**Extension. Python.Reducer** for Python and **Extension.R.Reducer** in the case of R). Microsoft published additional extensions, for example to work with Cognitive recognition services libraries for faces, emotions, OCR, etc. All of them are a good option to extend the capabilities of the language and keep the design logic in the same place.

Note   To learn more about how to use Python and R with U-SQL, you can read this document: `https://docs.microsoft.com/en-us/azure/data-lake-analytics/data-lake-analytics-u-sql-develop-with-python-r-csharp-in-vscode`

Considerations on U-SQL Jobs and Analytics Units

So, what happens when you execute a U-SQL job? We have seen that you can use one or more Analytics Units (AU) to improve performances. We also have seen that the cost model is based on AUs; therefore it is also important from this point of view.

The U-SQL compiler creates an execution plan, and the plan is divided in tasks, each of them is called a vertex. Each U-SQL job has one or more vertices.

When you run a job, the AUs are assigned to vertices for the execution. When the vertex is finished the AU is free to work with another vertex, until all the vertices are finished. Having more AUs available helps to run vertices in parallel. AUs are released when the job is finished.

As an example, if you have a job that needs ten vertices but only have one AU, vertices will be executed one at the time. Increasing the number of AUs might increase execution time. We used the verb might because this also depends on how much the execution of vertices can be run in parallel.

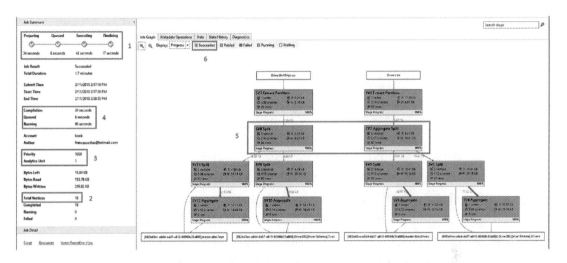

Figure 5-29. *The Job View tool available both with Visual Studio and within the Azure Portal*

In Figure 5-29 you can see the Job View tool that is displayed every time you launch a U-SQL job. In this case this simple job copies data from two files in Azure Data Lake Store to two tables in an Azure Data Lake Analytics database. The left pane displays the properties of the job that has been executed. In particular:

1. A summary of the time spent in the four phases of a job: Preparing (the script is compiled), Queued (job enters a queue, and if there are enough AUs to start it, AUs are allocated for the execution), Executing (code execution), Finalizing (finalize outputs)

2. The total amount of vertices included in this job, 18 in this case

3. The number of Analytics Units, 1, and the priority assigned to this job.

385

4. The time spent in Compilation (equivalent to Preparing time), queued, and Running (the sum of Executing plus Finalizing time)

Compilation	34 seconds
Queued	6 seconds
Running	60 seconds

4

If you look at the right pane, you can see a graph that represents the job. You have 12 green rectangles (green means that the execution is succeeded, rectangle number 6). The green rectangles indicate the Stages in which the job has been divided, and they are organized in an execution sequence, which means that vertices in later stages may depend on vertices in a previous stage. Each stage can have one or more vertices, and they are grouped because they are doing the same operation on different parts of the same data.

It is important to understand how many AUs you need to execute a job. The rectangle number 5, after a couple of tests, is the area that takes the most time Executing.

5

That rectangle includes two stages, SV8 Split and SV2 Aggregate Split, for a total of four vertices. In the run that you can see in the figure, we used one Analytics Unit, and the time spent in the Executing phase has been 42 seconds (rectangle 1). Doing a couple of runs and increasing the number of AUs up to 18 (the total amount of vertices in the job), we noticed that, the most of the time was spent in rectangle number 5, having four vertices was the right amount of vertices to use for this job, as we achieved an Executing time of 23 seconds (Figure 5-30), very similar to the result obtained adding more than four AUs. Time for Preparing, Queued, Finalizing was instead independent of the number of AUs, in this specific job.

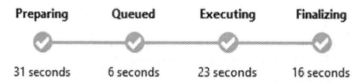

Figure 5-30. *The output of a job run with 4 AUs, where the Executing time has been reduced to 23 seconds*

Talking about job priority, rectangle number 2, this is also important for execution. The queue that contains jobs is ordered by job priority and, if a job is at the top of it, it will start running, if there are AUs available. Consider that all running jobs, including those with low priority, will not be terminated to give priority to a job that is waiting in the queue; running jobs must finish to release AUs.

Now, the job above is really a simple one, and you could have hundreds of vertices and stages to take care of in a more complex job to manage; so, is there any guidance or help for the developer on how to find the right amount of AUs required for a specific job? Luckily, you have some help, from the tools first. The diagnostic section in Visual Studio gives advice on the possible issues found during execution, like an excessive amount of AUs allocated and unused. Based on the execution profile information (do not forget to load the profile using the button highlighted below), you can get details on how the job performed.

Figure 5-31. *The diagnostics section gives access to the AU usage dashboards*

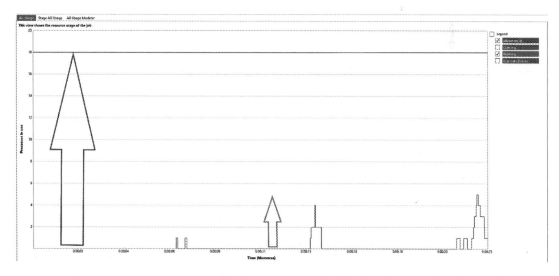

Figure 5-32. *The image represents the number of allocated AUs for this specific job (blue arrow, in this example 18 AUs), and the actual number of AUs used during the execution time (peak represented by the red arrow). Consider that you pay for the number of AUs allocated, even if unused, while you are using the resources under the red line, therefore this tuning phase is very important for every U-SQL script, to avoid unnecessary costs.*

You also have an AU usage modeller that suggests, based on the data loaded in the profile, the number of AUs that you could use to run the job.

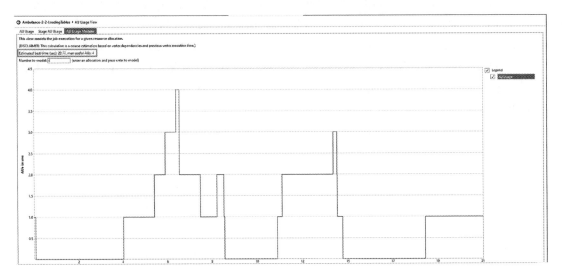

Figure 5-33. *The AU Usage Modeler dashboard*

Note 1   The details of the U-SQL language and a developer's guide are explained in the following reference documents:

U-SQL Language Reference: `https://msdn.microsoft.com/en-us/azure/data-lake-analytics/u-sql/u-sql-language-reference`

U-SQL Programmability guide: `https://docs.microsoft.com/en-us/azure/data-lake-analytics/data-lake-analytics-u-sql-programmability-guide`

Note 2   We recommend reading this document, for developers and administrators that helps to understand how to manage costs in Azure Data Lake Analytics: `https://blogs.msdn.microsoft.com/azuredatalake/2018/01/08/how-to-save-money-and-control-costs-with-azure-data-lake-analytics/`

Job Submission Policies

Another important aspect to consider is the ability to limit the maximum amount of AUs that a specific user or group can use for a job. This is of course important to avoid unexpected costs and to avoid finishing the AUs available to run other jobs. To achieve this, you can create a job submission policy, and you can use the Azure Portal to perform this task, going to the `Properties` section and clicking the `Add policy` button under the `Job submission limits`.

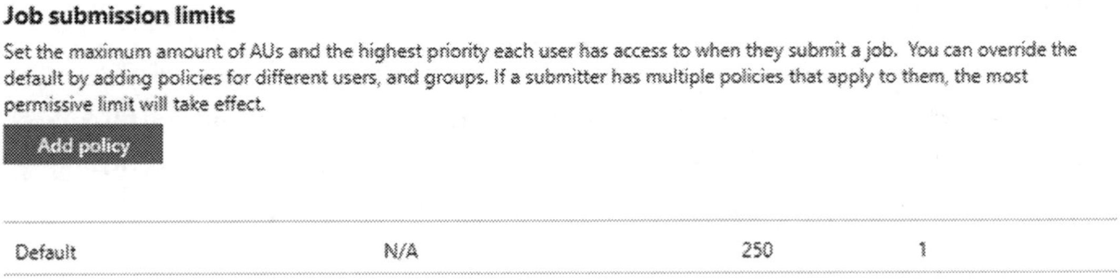

Job submission limits

Set the maximum amount of AUs and the highest priority each user has access to when they submit a job. You can override the default by adding policies for different users, and groups. If a submitter has multiple policies that apply to them, the most permissive limit will take effect.

| Add policy |

| Default | N/A | 250 | 1 |

Figure 5-34. *The Job submission area in the properties section of the ADLA dashboard. A Default policy is created together with the account creation*

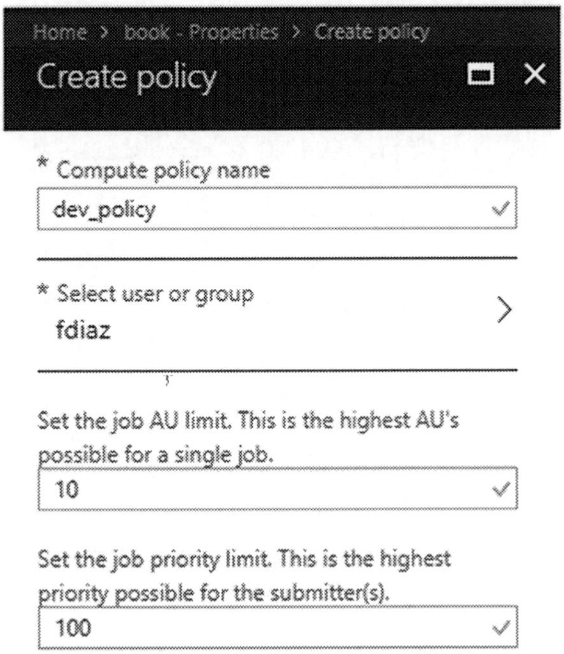

389

NAME	DISPLAY NAME	AU LIMIT	PRIORITY	
Default	N/A	250	1	
dev_policy	fdiaz	10	100	...

***Figure 5-35.** We created a policy for the user fdiaz, that limits, for a job, the utilization of maximum 10 AUs and the maximum priority that this user can assign to a job, 100 in this specific case. A higher number means a lower priority*

Job Monitoring

You can monitor the execution of Jobs using the Azure Portal. You can use `Job management` section to see the full list of jobs executed by the account, and you also have the ability to use the `Job insights` section, which adds the ability to group recurring jobs and, in the case of jobs scheduled using Azure Data Factory, pipeline jobs.

Filter My jobs New job Refresh Go to job

TOTAL: 78

STATUS	JOB NAME	AUS	TYPE	DURATION	AUTHOR	SUBMITTED	
Succeeded	Ambulance-2-2-LoadingTables	10 (4.0%)	U-SQL	1min 43s	francescodiaz@hotmail.com	4/12/2018, 11:08:17 AM	Compare
Succeeded	New job	1 (0.4%)	U-SQL	1min 9s	francescodiaz@hotmail.com	4/12/2018, 11:07:14 AM	Compare
Succeeded	Ambulance-2-2-LoadingTables	10 (4.0%)	U-SQL	1min 38s	francescodiaz@hotmail.com	4/11/2018, 3:43:30 PM	Compare
Succeeded	Ambulance-2-2-LoadingTables	6 (2.4%)	U-SQL	2min 12s	francescodiaz@hotmail.com	4/11/2018, 3:38:47 PM	Compare
Succeeded	Ambulance-2-2-LoadingTables	4 (1.6%)	U-SQL	1min 33s	francescodiaz@hotmail.com	4/11/2018, 3:35:10 PM	Compare
Succeeded	New job	2 (0.8%)	U-SQL	56s	francescodiaz@hotmail.com	4/11/2018, 3:26:04 PM	Compare
Succeeded	New job	1 (0.4%)	U-SQL	52s	francescodiaz@hotmail.com	4/10/2018, 4:51:14 PM	Compare
Succeeded	Ambulance-2-2-LoadingTables	4 (1.6%)	U-SQL	1min 20s	francescodiaz@hotmail.com	4/10/2018, 4:39:09 PM	Compare
Succeeded	Ambulance-2-2-LoadingTables	2 (0.8%)	U-SQL	1min 34s	francescodiaz@hotmail.com	4/10/2018, 4:37:01 PM	Compare
Succeeded	Ambulance-2-1-CreateObjects	1 (0.4%)	U-SQL	29s	francescodiaz@hotmail.com	4/10/2018, 4:35:38 PM	Compare
Failed	Ambulance-2-1-CreateObjects	1 (0.4%)	U-SQL	9s	francescodiaz@hotmail.com	4/10/2018, 4:32:19 PM	Compare

***Figure 5-36.** Job management section in the Azure Portal. You can also compare the execution of jobs, using the Compare option (red rectangle)*

	Ambulance-2-2-LoadingTables	Switch comparison	Ambulance-2-2-LoadingTables
Status:	Succeeded	No change	Succeeded
AUs	10	-6	4
Vertices	18	0	18
Preparing	32s	-0s	31s
Queued	0s	0s	0s
Running	1min 5s	-14s	51s
Duration	1min 38s	-14s	1min 23s
Submitter	francescodiaz@hotmail.com	No change	francescodiaz@hotmail.com
Submitted	4/12/2018, 11:08:17 AM	-19hr 32min 6s	4/11/2018, 3:36:10 PM
AU-hours	59s	-14s	44s
Input size	196 KB	0 bytes	196 KB
Output size	360 KB	0 bytes	360 KB
Runtime version	release_20180117_adl_778615	Different	release_20180117_adl_753515
	Remove from comparison	Clear comparison	Remove from comparison

Figure 5-37. *The comparison between two ADLA jobs*

Note   To learn more about job policies and job monitoring, you can read this document: `https://docs.microsoft.com/en-us/azure/data-lake-analytics/data-lake-analytics-manage-use-portal`

Azure HDInsight

Before closing the chapter, we want to quickly mention Azure HDInsight, that is not covered in this book, and that completes the Azure Data Lake offering. HDInsight offers the possibility to run Hadoop clusters running on Linux (Windows is not supported anymore), but managed by Azure. You basically need to choose:

- Cluster type (**Hadoop** - processing engine, supporting Hive, Pig, etc; **HBase** - NoSQL; **Storm** - real-time streaming, **Spark** - in-memory analytics, **R Server** - R engine, **Kafka** - messaging system, **Interactive Query** - In-memory engine)

- Storage (Azure Storage or Azure Data Lake Store)

- Number of nodes in the cluster

Evaluate HDInsight instead of Azure Data Lake Analytics in case you want:

- Have more customization options than Azure Data Lake Analytics, which is a pure PaaS service, where most of the customization options are automatically managed. HDInsight is a managed service instead, so you can have access to cluster nodes, if needed.

- If the team, or your customer, are already using and are familiar with open source tools included in the services exposed, like Hive, Pig, etc.

Summary

In this chapter we covered Azure Data Lake Store and Azure Data Lake Analytics, two PaaS services dedicated to big data workloads.

ADLS is a HDFS storage that offers the ability to scale to petabytes of data. You can use it to store any type of data and of any size (e.g. ingest telemetry data, logs, IoT data, archive of information, to extend a data warehouse architecture, etc.)

ADLA is a distributed job engine, based on Apache YARN, able to do analytics on big data stores, such as ADLS. It offers a powerful language called U-SQL, that combines SQL with C#, and it is extensible to offer flexibility to developers. You can use it to analyze data on big data stores, to run massive job processing activities that may also include external sources, such as a relational database.

In the next chapter, the last of the book, we will focus on how to manage and analyze streams of events using Azure services.

## CHAPTER 6

Working with In-Transit Data and Analytics

Working with Data is not only related to Data at rest. While it's a typical building block of any complex system, a RDBMS represents a classic data store for data at-rest. Often, the relational DB is the final point where the data goes to be safely persisted and to be re-used later. However, it is very common to let the data pass through many intermediate actors, which define integrations between parties and which are involved in specific business-related workflows.

Therefore, before data is considered at-rest, it is obviously in-transit, with a wide variety of options around this. There are transient data stores, persistent ones, and messaging solutions with the specific purpose of managing the real-time data ingestion. At the same time, when data is ingested, it is very likely to desire to have a quick look at it, even before it reaches the final destination into a persistent and, maybe relational, data store. This quick look is also known as real-time analytics, a method of collecting and organizing data while it's arriving.

This is probably the first touch point with big data we all had in the last few years. Even before talking massively about big data, we were collecting a huge amount of information from on-the-field devices or from the navigation on our web applications' users. One of the first consumer-available high-end ingestion tools has been Google Analytics and, forgive us if you do not agree with this definition, but its big data. It is, because for every website on the entire Internet that implements the tag of GA, Google Analytics will collect a huge amount of de-normalized data. Collected data is not only a page view, it can be a mouse move, a click, a custom event, and everything we want to track and analyze later. In 2015, when IoT started to be a buzzword, someone already developed its own IoT backend solution using Google Analytics!

© Francesco Diaz, Roberto Freato 2018
F. Diaz and R. Freato, *Cloud Data Design, Orchestration, and Management Using Microsoft Azure*,
https://doi.org/10.1007/978-1-4842-3615-4_6

But this is not a chapter about GA; we mentioned it just because it represented one of the first globally available ingestion services. It can be forced, but it has not been designed to be general purpose, it has a strong focus on web analytics and behavioral tracking, for both page insight and advertising purposes.

In the rest of this chapter, we will discover how we can deal with data in-transit, with basic and advanced messaging solutions, designed to be both persistent and transient. We are looking into ingestion and real-time manipulation of data, to build aggregates not only at the end of the process but while the data was being generated. Finally, we take a look at Azure AppInsights that was probably the initial response to Google's GA, which now a series of powerful features that integrate analytics with application telemetry.

Understanding the Need for Messaging

By oversimplifying, we can split the two goals of messaging into two greater areas:

- Decoupling/integrating components/systems: the messaging layer stands between two different components of the same architecture to better separate the concerns or, between two different parties, to integrate them safely.

- Implement event-driven architectures: the messaging layer is the primary layer where the business information goes and the entire system is based on the state changes arriving in the messages.

For the sake of simplicity, we are discussing just the first scenario, where messages are used to make connections between parties and where they have the primary purpose of storing information for a temporary, limited, period of time.

There are primarily two methods of interconnecting systems: synchronous and asynchronous. In the first, a component A wants to communicate with someone at the other side B and make a direct request to it, which will reply properly. In the second, the component A puts a message on an intermediate queue and when B is ready to read it, it reads and processes the message.

Please note some aspects:

- In the first case, we are not required, on the side of B, to immediately process the request. We can also return an ACK (acknowledgement) and perform the operation later. However, the client A will know this contract exactly, both for the calling parameters and the behavior of the response.

- In the second case, A can even ignore all of what is under the hood on the receiving side. From its point of view, there is only a queue where messages are sent or, conversely, a queue to read responses from remote systems.

We are not digging too much into the pros/cons of the two methods, since it is not in the scope of the book. The only point to focus on is that messaging enables asynchronous systems easily. In this case we would like to achieve synchronous communication with messaging, while it's still possible, it is harder to implement.

Let's suppose we have system A sending emails to a queue. Then, system B reads the queue and sends the actual email through SMTP. We want to notify A with the delivery receipt. With a synchronous system, it's far easier: A asks B to send and B holds A while it completes the operation. But with messages things are different:

- A sends a message X to the queue

- B processes the message X, sends the email to the destination and collects the ACK

- Then B sends a message to another queue, indicating a correlation between the message X received from A and the reply

- A, which is waiting for notifications on the second queue, receives the message and correlates it with the previous message send.

Returning to the first case, we are now analyzing the simpler fire-and-forget case, when the caller sends a message to a queue and it does not require/handle any callback from the remote system.

For the advanced reader, you probably know in Azure there is another queue technology inside the Storage Account. They are called just Azure queues or Storage queues and they are lightweight queues with missing features, compared to the Service Bus ones. We do not cover them here but there is a comprehensive reading about this here: `https://docs.microsoft.com/en-us/azure/service-bus-messaging/service-bus-azure-and-service-bus-queues-compared-contrasted`

Use Cases of Uni-Directional Messaging

There are a lot of scenarios when unidirectional messaging provides benefits. Here are some examples:

- A content management system collects the images from a third-party and sends to a queue to request to resize images as soon as possible (Figure 6-1):

  - The processing component can scale independently based on the actual resizing load and it can perform the job independently.

Figure 6-1. *The simplest scenario where a producer enqueues images for further resizing in a different component*

- An e-commerce platform collects catalogue information from vendors and sends updates to a queue to let consumers update data stores (Figure 6-2).

  - The processing component can introduce any logic while processing updates, while the producer isn't aware of the complex technical details of the operations.

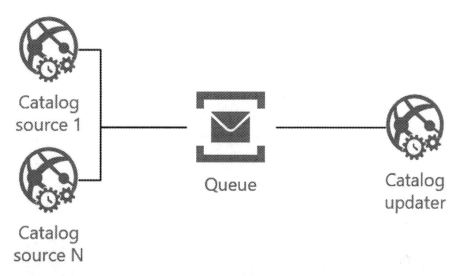

Figure 6-2. *Multiple sources of catalog updates go to the queue to be processed by a single updater process*

- An e-commerce platform collects the order from a navigating user and sends it to a notification queue (also referred as "topic" further) to notify several parties (order management systems, user notification systems, CRMs) (Figure 6-3)

    - Multiple endpoints can be notified for a single action collected on the producer side and they can perform various operations in reply to an event.

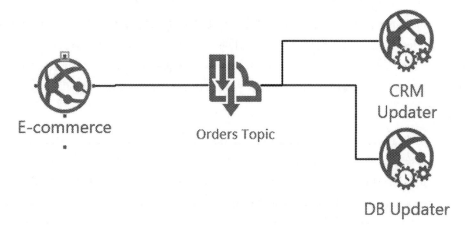

Figure 6-3. *An e-commerce system sends orders to a topic, which notifies all the proper actors simultaneously*

- Several etherogeneous components of a company send emails through messages into a queue to decouple the actual mailing logic from the applications (Figure 6-4).

  - A change to the service provider sending emails or to the workflow involved can be managed on a single consumer component instead of maintaining all the applications using the mailing feature.

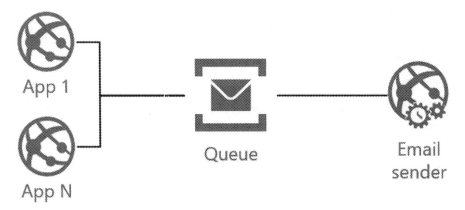

Figure 6-4. *Multiple applications will send their email messages to a queue to let a single process take them to make the actual communication with the email provider*

DESIGN EVENT-DRIVEN APPLICATIONS

The other relevant aspect involved while talking about queues are event-driven architectures. With event-driven architectures, we are preventing changing the way of thinking of our application as a combined set of components talking each other by a chain of events. We are not discussing the benefits of this kind of approach, which are many, but the focus on messaging.

In an EDA, messages are events which produce a change of in state. The state changes itself can transit within the message or not: in the latter case, the most common, this is due to the fact that messages should be used to notify only the sink (the receiving party). It is always considered a best practice, while talking about messaging, to use messages to deliver lightweight content, maybe referring some other attachment somewhere else to be fetched independently.

Using Service Bus

Azure Service Bus has been one of the first services available in the Azure Platform from its birth. It enables messaging solutions at-scale and connectivity between etherogeneous systems. From the service topology perspective, these are the basic concepts we should know:

- A service namespace is an "instance" of Service Bus, which is a logical collection of sub-services

- Each service namespace supports many instances of those sub-services:

  - Queues: FIFO queues

  - Topics: Pub/Sub queues

  - Relays: internet-faced relays which let us expose private services to the public

As an example, we can have even a single Service Bus namespace for an entire company, since we can handle multiple queues, topics, and relays in it. Of course, namespace allocation often falls into the infrastructure area, so we can have multiple namespaces to isolate domains, to provide better scalability and to refine security policies.

The Service Bus namespace comes in three flavors (Figure 6-5):

- Basic: it's the cheapest option with no topic support

- Standard: it has an included amount of brokered messages plus topics support

- Premium: despite the previous options, Premium runs with dedicated capacity (Basic and Standard are shared resources). It can scale up to 4 scale/messaging units and it has a fixed price despite the number of messages processed.

There are some other technical differences (most of them on the underlying infrastructure) between the Premium and non-Premium tiers, but they are not as relevant for the scope of the book.

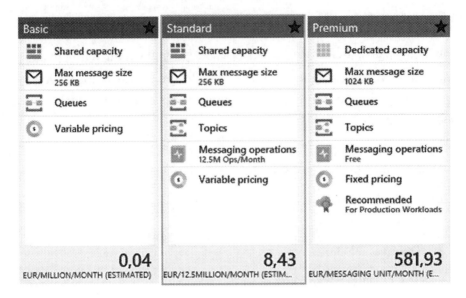

Figure 6-5. *These are the three tiers of Service Bus currently supported*

In the next pages we will investigate Queues and Topic, which is often called the Brokered Messaging feature of Service Bus. The unit of data, the message, is actually also known as Brokered Message.

Enqueuing some Messages

As .NET developers, we are writing a few lines of C# code to enque some messages in a Service Bus queue. With the supported SDK, we can connect to Service Bus to send/receive messages and perform administrative operations on the queues/topics themselves.

However, as a general-purpose suggestion, we recommend creating entities (queues/topics) via dedicated procedures, except for those cases where temporary queues are needed. The following snippet, given an existing pre-created queue, enqueues a message with some properties:

```
var connectionsString= "[connstr]";
var queueName = "helloworld";
var queueClient = QueueClient
    .CreateFromConnectionString(connectionsString,queueName);
```

```
for (int i = 0; i < 10; i++)
{
    var msg = new BrokeredMessage($"Hello from the iteration {i}");
    msg.Properties["Sender"] = "Rob's laptop";
    msg.Properties["Index"] = i;
    queueClient.Send(msg);
}
```

Here are some basic explanations:

- Connection string is the composition of those three segments:

    - Endpoint address: the endpoint URL which inherits the namespace name of the services bus.

    - Shared Access Key name: the namespace and its inner entities (queues/topics) may manage authorization with access keys, everyone consisting in the couple KeyName/KeyValue. The RootManageSharedAccessKey is the default key created at the top level, with maximum permissions on the entire Service Bus instance.

    - Shared Access Key secret: the secret(s) key(s). They are actually two to provide rotation support.

- Queue name is the name of the queue we assume is already created on the bus

- QueueClient is a class holding the logic to send/receive messages on a Service Bus queue. In this case, we are using it for sending purposes.

- BrokeredMessage is the class holding the appropriate structures to wrap and serialize the message content (in the case above it is just a string, but it can be an arbitrary object, with some limitations).

    - We also used the Properties dictionary to hold some metadata, which are technically "headers" of the message. These headers will have a primary function in the Publish/Subscribe approach while using topics.

At the other side of the system, we may have the receiver application, which can be very similar to the one above:

```
var queueClient = QueueClient
    .CreateFromConnectionString(connectionsString, queueName,ReceiveMode.
    PeekLock);

while (true)
{
    var msg = queueClient.Receive();
    if (msg != null)
    {
        var content = msg.GetBody<string>();
        Console.WriteLine($"Receiving from {msg.Properties["Sender"]}:
        {content}");
        msg.Complete();
    }
}
```

The differences here are the following:

- As the third parameter of the QueueClient factory method, we specify the ReceiveMode. ReceiveMode can be ReceiveAndDelete or PeekLock. In the first case, a message is taken from the receiver and immediately deleted from the queue. In the second, the message is taken and put into invisibility for a given timeout; a timeout that would be enough for the processing logic to process it and "complete" to remove it eventually form the queue.

- The Receive method receives the message and returns a wrapper object which is a BrokeredMessage instance. GetBody deserializes the content using the default DataContractSerializer approach.

- The Complete() method tells the Service Bus to remove the message from the queue, in order to avoid it being reprocessed in case of timeout expiration.

This two receive modes are the core concept of the majority of queue systems. To ensure reliability, we must choose PeekLock, since the consumer process may fail between receiving the message and actually completing the processing. This has a drawback, since the consumer process cannot complete in time, resulting in a message put again into a queue. To avoid this, we need to design at best the timeouts of the message to set a trade-off between reliability and efficiency. At the other side, where reliability is not the primary requirement, ReceiveAndDelete guarantees a performance improvement on the queue, which will not need any more than the explicit call to the Complete() method to permanently remove the message.

Using Service Bus Explorer

One of the best and most recognized tools to work with Service Bus is the open-sourced management tool written by Paolo Salvatori, the Service Bus Explorer (Figure 6-6).

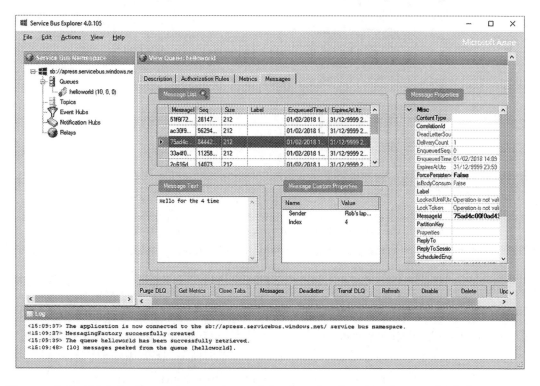

Figure 6-6. *This is the main window of the Service Bus Explorer, which lets us create queues and other artifacts, as well as reading messages, setup advanced properties and more*

With Service Bus Explorer we can administer a Service Bus namespace and its resources, by creating queues, reading messages in both the ReceiveAndDelete and PeekLock modes, inspect them through a pre-configured inspector and many other features, which make SBE a must-have.

Using Topics to Notify Parties and Route Messages

Topics is the name of the queues related to Publish/Subscribe messaging, where the messaging pattern is more considered to be for many-to-many notifications.

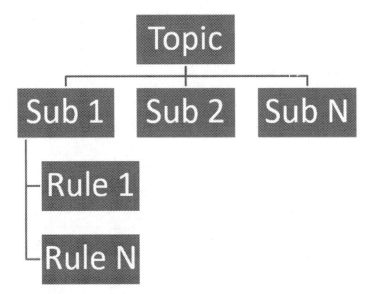

Figure 6-7. *This is the topology of a Topic. We can have multiple subscriptions and, for each of them, a set of rules to route only the appropriate messages on it.*

A Topic is a high-level collector of incoming messages and, from the perspective of the producer, can be seen as a simple queue. However, we can define one or more subscriptions under it (Figure 6-7), which behave like a queue. Each subscription, in fact, can be accessed by multiple consumers to process individual messages.

The killing feature, like in any other Pub/Sub mechanisms, is the capability to define routing rules for incoming messages, based on the headers/properties of the messages themselves. For example, if we flag our messages with a property "ClientID" and we create the "ClientID=4" rule on a subscription, that subscription will receive only the messages matching this rule.

This powerful mechanism provides a solid foundation for a set of needs we all have in distributed system development. We can implement a huge variety of notification systems by using Pub/Sub queues.

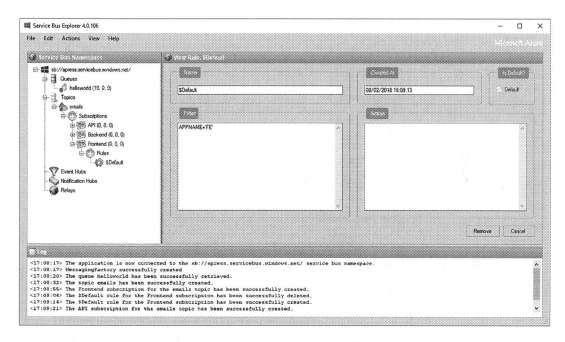

Figure 6-8. *We see the "emails" topic having three subscriptions with three different routing rules*

In the figure above (Figure 6-8), for example, we see how a Topic collecting emails can be configured. The single topic "emails" in the collector of the incoming messages. Every message sent to that topic flows directly to every subscription which has compatible rules. A rule telling 1=1 is the default rule accepting every message on the topic, as for a catch-all subscription. In the case above, we split messages by application tiers and, for the sake of simplicity, we assumed just three areas: API, Backend, and Frontend. The Frontend subscription's rule is "APPNAME='FE'", which means that incoming messages with the corresponding header (APPNAME) set to "FE" will flow directly into this subscription. Messages with this value not set or set with other values, will not go into this subscription.

A subscription can be interpreted like an individual Queue. We can attach one or more consumers to a subscription, like we do with a Queue, to scale independently of the implement reliability. The subscription behaves like a queue, it has timeout and locks, the receive modes as we mentioned eelier.

From the development point of view, the actual code to use a Topic is pretty straightforward:

```
var topicName = "emails";
var queueClient = TopicClient
    .CreateFromConnectionString(connectionsString, topicName);

for (int i = 0; i < 10; i++)
{
    var payload = new
    {
        MailFrom = "no-reply@...",
        MailTo = "idontknow@...",
        Body = $"My important email {i}"
    };
    var msg = new BrokeredMessage(payload);
    msg.Properties["APPNAME"] = "FE";
    queueClient.Send(msg);
}
```

However, this code will not work, since the payload object is an anonymous object, which cannot be serialized with the default DataContractSerializer. We have two choices:

- Implement a transfer object which is serializable with DataContract and DataMember attributes

- Pre-serialize the object with JSON and pass the resulting string as the BrokeredMessage payload

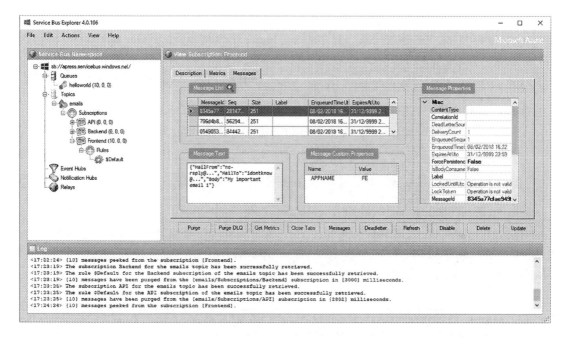

Figure 6-9. *We now have 10 messages in the Frontend subscription and none in others*

As we see in the figure above (Figure 6-9), we sent 10 messages in the topic "emails" but just one subscription, the ones with compatible rules, have received the messages. This is a powerful mechanism to notify eterogeneous systems, to decouple components and to perform message routing without any knowledge on the sender side (except for the message header attributes).

Now, we made a simple example, but the recommendation is to use message headers/properties to decorate messages with some parameters which are not useful just at the time of writing, but with some in-advance thinking to create rules on them in the future. For instance, if we are collecting an order aggregate from an e-commerce platform, we may want to proceed as follows:

- Extract from the order aggregate some high-value information like:

    - Customer ID

    - Order ID

    - Amount

- Put those values in headers too

- Serialize the entire payload and send it to the topic

Then, we can create some subscriptions to handle some scenarios, for example:

- A subscription with "huge amounts rule" (over $1000 for instance) to notify anti-fraud checks and trigger enhanced monitoring

- A subscription for customers with IDs between X and Y, to perform partitioning based on IDs, if it makes sense.

We can even create a subscription at runtime for a specific need. Assume we want to debug a specific order, without looking for it inside a subscription with thousands of other messages. We can create a specific subscription with the most restrictive rule to filter just the messages we expect to receive and it's done.

DUPLICATE DETECTION: A GAME CHANGER FOR MESSAGING SOLUTIONS

Each Service Bus Queue or Topic can be configured for duplicate detection. In practice, the engine behind the duplicate detection mechanism provides us with a method to avoid duplicates to be forwarded to the queue and, then, be read from the consumers. In the queue/topic, we specify how long the duplicate detection window is: a longer value means more resources consumed and poorer performance, a shorter value means we can miss some duplicates if they arrive outside the timeframe.

The Service Bus will use the MessageId property of the BrokeredMessage to perform the detection. That value is automatically generated while accepting the message, except if it has been provided explicitly by the sender. In that case, the sender can generate the MessageId according to the duplicate detection strategy (for example by hashing the content of the message) to guarantee two messages with the same payloads are considered equal for the Service Bus).

This has been a game changer for many scenarios, to guarantee the at-most-once logic in conjunction with the at-least-once logic provided by the PeekLock receive mode.

Using Event Hubs

Some years ago we experimented with the birth of the IoT movement for the masses. "Ingestion" was the buzzword for a while (it is already) and everyone was looking for a good ingestion technology to handle hundreds/thousands/millions of messages per second.

The reality has been different, but the market offered some alternatives. Azure already had Service Bus, which was great but the underlying SQL Server infrastructure to handle Queues and Topics cannot scale to those numbers. So, it was decided to create a spin-off product, Event Hubs, which can be considered a lightweight version of a Service Bus (partitioned) queue. In fact, if we strip off a Queue from its advanced features, like Sessions, Duplicate Detection, PeekLock, Timeouts, and more, we can obtain a queue which is much more performant, at the cost of losing some advanced features.

Event Hubs can be seen as lightweight queues, with some huge differences:

- An Event Hub instance IS partitioned by design and this partitioning is not transparent to senders and receivers (which require the sender/receiver awareness).

- An Event Hub does not offer the message deletion. Thus, if we successfully read a message, we must ensure by ourselves to not read it anymore. We must take the count.

- An Event Hub does not have advanced features, like Duplicate Detection, message forwarding, Deadlettering, and many more. If we are implementing a messaging solution which needs them, Event Hub is not an option.

So, why should we use Event Hubs? In our opinion, the response is only one: performance. If we need to scale out for a million messages, Event Hub can handle this and ingest a huge amount of messages. The challenge is to implement a reliable system on top of it, to fill the gap of missing features.

The experienced reader may think "why Event Hubs and not IoT Hubs here?" The answer is simple. Event Hubs is related to messaging, while IoT Hubs, despite it not being a secret that it has been recommended by Microsoft for most scenarios, is a composition of services designed for IoT primarily. While IoT Hubs has some components based on Event Hubs, we think it's better to understand Event Hubs for any messaging scenarios, instead of a newer service that is more specific.

The Reliability Problem

The first gap to fill is reliability or processing. In Event Hubs we do not ask for a Message (to then delete it). Instead, we are reading a sort of stream, where the next message is an advance of a specific offset in that stream. This takes us to the next big question: "how can I manage failures?" If message three (among ten messages) is broken, how can we mark that message to process it again later? We cannot.

At the opposite, we read a message and we are ready to get the next one, but the consumer process crashed. How can the resumed process know from which message in the stream it should start? It cannot.

So, the reliability of systems built on Event Hubs have to be defined on top of Event Hub itself, with strategies at infrastructure level, by using stronger algorithms and other Azure technologies.

Let's think about a solution to the problems above, with the following process:

- A process which has to read from the Event Hub starts

- It reads from a persistent, external data source the starting offset

- It starts to read messages and, for each one:

  - In case of failure, it sends the failing message to somewhere else (a Queue or another Event Hub)

  - In both cases, it moves to the next message and saves a new offset in the external storage.

This workflow should parallelize for every partition of the Event Hub itself, since partitioning is not transparent and a partition equals, more or less, a dedicated connection to read. Also, this simple workflow can help to solve the issues encountered, but adds a layer of complexity to the overall process. We notice the following:

- The "external, persistent" data source may be a bottleneck if, for every single message on a million-message queue, we hit it for a progress save.

- The "somewhere else" location for the failing messages must be handled properly. In case of another Event Hub, we must guarantee we are not just moving the problem away. In case of a Service Bus Queue, we must also deal with a separate process to consume the failed messages.

A good trade-off between reliability and performance is probably in the middle, with some arrangements in constraints definition.

The Concurrency Problem

As mentioned in the previous paragraph, as Event Hubs consumers, we must deal with multiple individual connections, one-per-partition. This leads very quickly to a concurrency problem: what happens in cases of multiple readers? Since Event Hubs is potentially fed with millions of messages per second, it is very likely the reader would scale in size and number of instance as the throughput increases.

In case there is an individual reader, we said there are multiple individual connections (one per partition) from it to the Event Hub. Each partition is a separate stream with elements. With the limits above, how can we setup a resilient job which reads from the Event Hub and can scale independently?

We must keep track of the complexities related to this scenario:

- There is an Event Hub with four partitions.

- A process on a single machine starts and opens four connections, one per partition.

  - The program workflow is the one mentioned earlier, with external persistence for offset management and failure redirection.

- The same process is started on another server to scale out.

  - Since there is no logic to mutually assign partitions complementarily, the process will connect to the whole set of partitions and it will duplicate the reading logic.

A resilient reader should be implemented to handle scaling from the first day, in this style:

- The initial process looks up somewhere if there are other instances running.

- If not, it connects to the whole set of partitions.

- The second instance, performing the check, will notice an instance already running and tries to get access to a portion of the partitions.

- The optimal solution should be an equal distribution of partitions between instances.

This logic can be achieved with another component on top of the previous ones, a sort of distributed lock mechanism which in Microsoft Azure, can be offered indirectly by the Blob Lease API in the Storage Account.

Since an Event Hub partition is not strictly a Queue, we cannot read-and-delete the messages. This makes it impossible for multiple consumers to efficiently read the same partition, as there are no simple ways to split the work. We must be aware of this, because this limits the number of maximum concurrent consumers reading from an Event Hub to the number of actual partitions. This is not a technical limitation: instead, it's a practical one.

Some Code and the EventProcessor Library

From the sender perspective, we can be unaware of the partitioning that is happening on the Event Hub. In fact, we can just say "send" with no worries about explicitly connecting to a specific partition (but we will learn it better if we are aware of it).

The code following sends random weather information to an Event Hub:

```
var client =EventHubClient.CreateFromConnectionString(connStr);
var cities = new string[]
{ "Milan", "London", "New York", "Mumbai", "Florence", "San Francisco" };
var weathers = new string[]
{ "Good", "Rainy", "Foggy", "Sunny", "Cold", "Hot", "Warm" };
var startDate = DateTime.Today;

for (int i = 0; i < 1000; i++)
{
    foreach (var city in cities)
    {
        var ev = new
        {
            City = city,
            Weather = weathers.Random(),
            When = startDate.AddDays(i)
        };
        client.SendAsync(
            new EventData(
                Encoding.UTF8.GetBytes(
                    JsonConvert.SerializeObject(ev))))
                    .GetAwaiter().GetResult();
    }
}
```

Suppose now we are attaching a reader to the Hub and suppose this reader reads only a single partition. It would be interesting to make some sort of real time analytics on the incoming data, perhaps based on the City provided. For example, we can group all the information of a single city together.

So, it is considered "good" to group all the events which are relevant to each other in the same partition. In the case above, we can partition for City and, for the simplicity of the randomization algorithm, we can assume a good distribution between partitions.

With the code above, we are sending the event without indicating the actual partition, but we can fix it as follows:

```
client.SendAsync(
    new EventData(
        Encoding.UTF8.GetBytes(
            JsonConvert.SerializeObject(ev))),ev.City)
            .GetAwaiter().GetResult();
```

The "ev.City" is passed as the PartitionKey item to the sender. PartitionKey is a value where a hash is calculated on to assign one of the N partitions available in the Hub. Assigning explicitly a PartitionKey is like having control of the way items are assigned. In the case above, since the hash for the same city will be the same on subsequent iterations, we are de-facto grouping events for the same city in the same partition.

We also definitely "can" send to a specific partition explicitly (by indicating the partition number), but it is better to use this transparent way, by indicating a preference using a Partition Key.

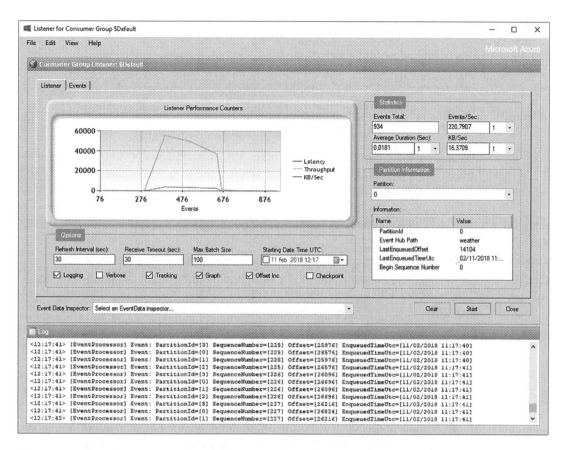

Figure 6-10. *Service Bus Explorer is reading the events generated by the previous application from the Hub. As we may notice, it is cyclying four partitions (from 0 to 3).*

Despite the sending process seeming to be very simple and straightforward, the reading counterpart can be tricky (Figure 6-10). As we discussed earlier, we must take into consideration several aspects to guarantee reliability and support for concurrency.

With the library we used for the sample above (NuGet - Microsoft.Azure.EventHubs), we can also implement retrieving logic, but at a very low level, dealing directly with partitions. A good library already written and maintained by Microsoft, that does all of the work for us, in order to be compliant with the issues above, is the Event Processor Host library (NuGet - Microsoft.Azure.EventHubs.Processor).

The library implements the following key concepts:

- Connecting to the whole set of partitions transparently

- In case other processes are making the same, using a remote Storage Account to mutually synchronize the partition assignments

- Using the same storage account, keeping track of the reading progress by saving the offset

To use that library, the key contract to implement is the IEventProcessor interface:

```
public class WeatherProcessor : IEventProcessor
    {
        ...

        public async Task ProcessEventsAsync(PartitionContext context,
            IEnumerable<EventData> messages)
        {
            foreach (var msg in messages)
            {
                dynamic ev =
                    JsonConvert.DeserializeObject(
                        Encoding.UTF8.GetString(msg.Body.ToArray()));
                //Process
                Console.WriteLine($"Receiving {ev.Weather} from {ev.
                City}");
            }
            await context.CheckpointAsync();
        }

    }
```

The EventProcessorHost will trigger this function where there are available messages. We don't know the number of messages and it depends on the runtime. Additionally, through the PartitionContext object, we can call the Checkpoint function to save the progress of the elaboration.

Keep in mind that this is a high-level library built on top of Event Hubs and Azure Storage. There's no concept of Checkpoint in Event Hubs themselves, and its usage is to be watched to avoid unwanted bottlenecks.

Final Thoughts on Event Hubs

The next lines may appear opinionated so please take them as purely our point of view. During the last years, we used a lot Event Hubs in production with the whole options to read/write on it. In case we need a reliable message store without loss, not a single message, with Event Hub it is harder to achieve. The open issues are:

- In cases where we checkpoint every message processed, we are limiting the actual power of Event Hubs, at the maximum operation speed of the storage account used for checkpoints

- In cases where we checkpoint a set of messages, we cannot deal with individual failed messages

- In cases where the code or the coordination runtime between multiple instances is not 100% safe, we can read streams concurrently by multiple messages. This should be avoided, however, in cases of robust and well-proven consumers

We can use Event Hub as the ingestor, which safely persists every message that arrived. But at the consumer side, we can also setup some pass-through logic to flood another data store, which has more reliability features, like a Queue. The reader may think a Queue after an Event Hub may represent a bottleneck, and it is, definitely. But we can also write an intelligent event consumer that does this work reliably.

We finally think that Event Hubs is very powerful if used in conjunction with a robust consumer, either a custom application or a managed service. The most important managed service that can be placed after an Event Hub, in Azure, is the Stream Analytics Job, which is the next topic discussed.

Understanding Real-Time Analytics

The current hype around the term real-time in conjunction with Analytics can be explained by the growing trend to move the moment in time aggregate data is built on raw (punctual) data closer. In the last few decades, we developed data-driven solutions which generated streams of information that went to RDBMS, to be ETLized (Extract-Transform-Load) in second time (very often, during the night).

This process is, in the majority of cases, very resource-intensive and expensive, both for maintenance and for computation. In addition, the aggregate data will become available after a considerable timespan (typically a day) which is a loss in terms of competitive gain for the "clients" of analytical data (which are, usually, the executives).

Forgive the over-simplification, but the momentum around Analytics is very interesting, in our opinion. We are moving from standard ETL solutions, which are performed "offline", where the data is at rest, to real-time solutions, where the aggregations are made while the data is in transit. This has two concurrent goals:

- Be more competitive, by having summarized data earlier

- Be leaner, by reducing the dependencies from the normalized database as the primary source of information

Of course, there are not just good points. Some critical issues are around the corner:

- ETL aggregations often start from a normalized database and, through various complex projections (using multiple JOINs to merge data from several tables), produce the output

  - In cases of real-time processing, ALL the information must transit in a single event, since there isn't (or shouldn't be) a continuous lookup into other data stores

- With ETL as a decoupled process, analytics can be done with complete unawareness of the other components of the system

  - In case of real-time processing, the event producer must be aware AND produce the appropriate aggregate during its generation

- With the traditional transformation process, we can ingest little non-redundant messages of few fields; the ETL will enrich the data appropriately.

  - In cases of real-time processing, each event should be enriched with the full set of useful (but redundant) information.

Last, but not least, the real-time processing engine must be designed to be resilient, robust, and, more importantly, powerful, in terms of computational power needed to build aggregates in real-time, especially with wide windows of aggregation.

In Azure, the best option for managed service that does this work is Stream Analytics, which is discussed in the next section.

Understanding Stream Analytics

Stream Analytics relies on the concept of processing data while it is in transit. If you have, for example, a dataset of customers like the following:

OrderID	CustomerID	CustomerName	Amount	Items	AcquiredOn
OID2145	CID5500	Mario Rossi	49,00 €	7	05/05/1938 18:03
OID8339	CID9766	John Doe	120,00 €	12	16/02/2011 08:16
OID1001	CID6800	Jane Doe	175,00 €	25	11/11/1919 19:29
OID9475	CID5500	Mario Rossi	24,00 €	4	04/01/2008 06:54
OID1870	CID9766	John Doe	486,00 €	54	12/12/2000 08:54
OID3324	CID3066	Francesco Diaz	210,00 €	21	19/02/1904 05:36
OID2096	CID9496	Roberto Freato	104,00 €	13	22/08/1934 11:47
OID2744	CID9496	Roberto Freato	80,00 €	10	16/10/1927 20:30

It's pretty straightforward to understand what the following query does:

```
SELECT CustomerID,AVG(Amount)
FROM Customers
GROUP BY CustomerID
```

In an ordinary SQL engine, this query takes the dataset, scans the rows and calculates the aggregate values. Now suppose we can write the same query in a real-time processing technology like Stream Analytics (and we can, since the query language is a SQL-like dialect): how will it work?

With in-transit data, we don't have the dataset yet at the time of query execution. Instead, data arrives "row" by "row" or event-by-event. Writing such a query is an abstraction to let us imagine we are grouping data as we did in SQL, but what happens under the hood is completely different.

In a given time T0, the first event arrived to Stream Analytics. While evaluating the query above, we can think "how can it group results if there is just one?" With in-transit data, aggregate functions hide a wait buffer of a given time, useful to perform aggregate calculations. This is why the previous query is incomplete for Stream Analytics, because there's no indication of what time should be considered for the window. Remember, with data in-transit, there's no concept of the "entire dataset", since it would probably be an indefinite wait to the end of a never-ending stream.

As mentioned above, we can also enrich data while it's in transit, by using the concept of "Reference Data" of Stream Analytics. In practice, we can define a Blob source from where ASA will fetch the most-updated blob with some data in JSON. That data then becomes usable from within the Analytics query, with a JOIN clause. This method is very practical and useful to provide a set of data which is less-frequently modified to attach to live stream at runtime.

Let's look at another one:

```
SELECT System.TimeStamp AS SamplingYear, CustomerID, AVG (Amount)
FROM Customers TIMESTAMP BY AcquiredOn
GROUP BY CustomerID, TumblingWindow(year,3)
```

This is an almost-correct SQL-like query for Stream Analytics:

- We define the input source and we set the field containing the temporal information (TIMESTAMP BY clause)

- We group by the CustomerID with an additional built-in function that evaluates the aggregate on a timespan basis

- We project the sampling reference end time (System.TimeStamp) to enrich the result

However, let's think for a moment: is Stream Analytics really taking events (maybe millions) in a buffer for an entire year? Fortunately, it is not. The maximum size of a window is currently seven days, expressed as TumblingWindow(d,7).

Finally, we need to forward those results to a sink, which may be chosen from a good variety of managed Azure services. To redirect the results to a sink, we can modify the query as follows:

```
SELECT System.TimeStamp AS SamplingYear, CustomerID, AVG (Amount)
INTO AvgAmounts
FROM Customers TIMESTAMP BY AcquiredOn
GROUP BY CustomerID, TumblingWindow(d,7)
```

Given that Customers is defined as the input, AvgAmounts has been defined as the output and the INTO clause makes the rest (Figure 6-11).

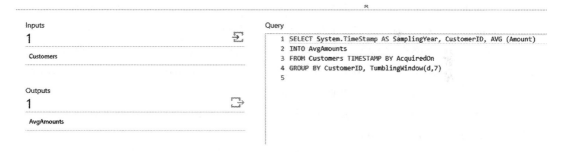

Figure 6-11. *We see a Stream Analytics Job with an input, an output, and the query*

A "sink" is an output port for the Stream Analytics query. We can define a sink going into the following series of Azure services:

- Azure Data Lake Store

- SQL Database

- Blob Storage

- Event Hub

- Power BI

- Table Storage

- Service Bus Queues

- Service Bus Topics

- Azure Cosmos DB

- Azure Functions

This enables scenarios where we filter, aggregate, project, and route incoming events into several different (and even multiple) outputs.

This is just an introduction to Stream Analytics, since we do not go deep into technical details or service features. Also, there are a lot of interesting built-in functions to inspect real-time data and where there is not integrated language; we can integrate it using JavaScript custom functions.

Understanding AppInsights

Beginning this chapter we wrote about web analytics, we quoted Google Analytics as a powerful tool to get insight from Web Application's users. We also introduced AppInsights, as a great Microsoft alternative to Google Analytics, for both Web Analytics and application telemetry. In these last few lines of the book, we try to summarize how to approach to AppInsights to get the most out of it.

Let's start by assuming AppInsights is big data. This is not relevant by the statement itself, but helps to define some boundaries:

- We can call the AppInsights API an indefinite number of times, storing tons of information generated by our side

- Every single message has to be sent de-normalized. So, if we are tracking a Page View, we need to include every relevant details to do further analysis and pivots on that

- Every application, for every Azure user, can send to AppInsights information on every method calls (at a cost, either in terms of money and application performance), and the AppInsights engine will accept them gracefully

Think about AppInsights as a sink for the emotions of our applications. We can track everything, from the users behavior on the web page, to exceptions on the server-side, to custom events where we define variables that we are going to use later to perform analysis.

```
var client = new TelemetryClient();
var properties = new Dictionary<string, string>();
var metrics = new Dictionary<string, double>();
properties["Username"] = user.Username;
properties["Gender"] = user.Gender;
properties["ZipCode"] = user.ZipCode;
metrics["TimeToRegister"] = (user.RegisteredAt-user.LandedTime).
TotalSeconds;
client.TrackEvent("userRegistered", properties, metrics);
```

The code above shows how to perform explicit event tracking through AppInsights, while the basic tracking is offered automatically via configuration and minor initialization code. In the code above, we are tracking a website registration as a lead/conversion, measuring the time between the landing and the registration itself. Username, Gender, and ZipCode are custom properties on which we will make pivots later, while TimeToRegister is a metric (a numeric value) useful to calculate aggregates on.

We can also configure a factory to create TelemetryClient instances:

```
public TelemetryClient Client
{
    get
    {
        if (Debugger.IsAttached)
        {
            TelemetryConfiguration.Active.TelemetryChannel.DeveloperMode =
            true;
        }
        TelemetryConfiguration.Active.InstrumentationKey = key;
        return new TelemetryClient(TelemetryConfiguration.Active);
    }
}
```

In this case we are telling the library to force it to speed up the pipeline to the data if we are debugging, to see results as soon as possible.

To see results, we can use the AppInsights Analytics portal as in the screenshot below:

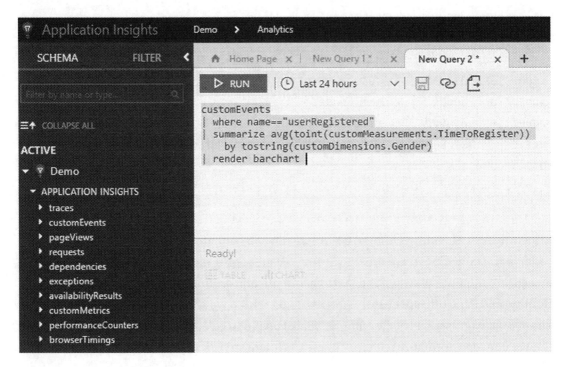

Figure 6-12. *We wrote a query using the Log Analytics query language*

The query above (Figure 6-12) will render a bar chart with the average registration time for every gender of user registered to the application, in the last 24 hours (by default) or within a timeframe of choice.

This query can also be placed inside an API call (Figure 6-13), to use AppInsights Analytics as a server-to-server service, without user interaction:

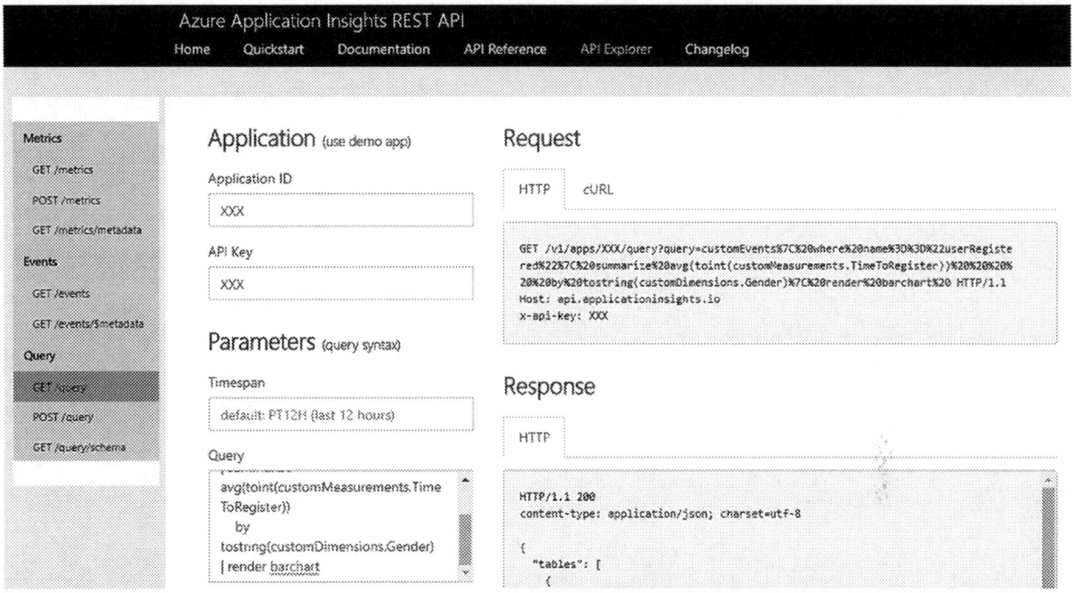

Figure 6-13. *The API portal for AppInsights Analytics*

Summary

In this chapter, we learned how data can be in-transit and which options are available. Messaging, through Service Bus and Event Hubs, is great for many scenarios where we need to decouple systems and where the complexity can be handled by loose integration. We closed the book with an introduction to real-time analytics with powerful services like Stream Analytics and AppInsights to let the reader take action on those powerful technologies. Thanks for reading!

Index

A

F. Diaz and R. Freato, *Cloud Data Design, Orchestration, and Management Using Microsoft Azure*,
https://doi.org/10.1007/978-1-4842-3615-4